STATE CRIME

Governments, Violence and Corruption

Penny Green and Tony Ward

Pluto Press

LONDON • STERLING, VIRGINIA

First published 2004 by
Pluto Press
345 Archway Road, London N6 5AA
and 22883 Quicksilver Drive, Sterling, VA 20166–2012, USA

www.plutobooks.com

British Library Cataloguing in Publication Data
A catalogue record for this book is available from the British Library

ISBN   0 7453 1785 5 hardback
ISBN   0 7453 1784 7 paperback

Library of Congress Cataloging in Publication Data applied for

10   9   8   7   6   5   4   3   2   1

Designed and produced for Pluto Press by
Chase Publishing Services, Fortescue, Sidmouth, EX10 9QG, England
Typeset from disk by Stanford DTP Services, Northampton, England
Printed and bound in the European Union by
Antony Rowe Ltd, Chippenham and Eastbourne, England

Contents

For Grace

Preface

This is a book about <u>crimes committed by, or with the complicity of,</u> <u>governments and government agents</u>. That is to say, it is a book about <u>most</u> <u>of the serious crime, and the most serious of crimes, in the modern world.</u> Given the paucity of relevant material within criminology, this has often seemed a daunting project, and the phrase about rushing in where angels fear to tread has occurred to us more than once. Much of this terrain, however, proved to have been well trodden by scholars from other disciplines, without whose work this journey would indeed have been impossible. We would also like to acknowledge the pioneering work within criminology of Greg Barak, Stan Cohen, David Friedrichs, Paddy Hillyard, Herman and Julia Schwendinger, Phil Scraton, and Joe Sim; and Ron Kramer and his colleagues whose work we discuss in Chapter 3.

There are other more immediate debts to be acknowledged. An important part of the research was funded by the Economic and Social Research Council (grant no. R000223401) and the University of Westminster. The Law Schools at both Westminster and De Montfort Universities provided periods of study leave and congenial environments in which to work. We also feel indebted to the much-maligned architect of the British Library, Colin St John Wilson, for creating such a tranquil and scholarly space in which to work and meet.

We doubt whether this book could have been written without the internet resources provided by, among others, Transparency International, Amnesty International, Human Rights Watch, the Institute for War and Peace Reporting, and the World Rainforest Movement.

To our indomitable research assistants and friends, Christina Curry and Nina Silove, we owe an enormous debt of gratitude. Christina's research on all things Turkish, and Nina's on state corporate crime and genocide, made a tremendous contribution to our work. Christina also ably assisted in compiling the bibliography. Lizzy Stanley, Jude McCulloch, Phil Scraton, Deb Coles and Paddy Hillyard provided helpful comments on particular chapters, while Joe Sim, Dave Whyte, Steve Tombs, Maggie Sumner and Tim Hillier provided useful information along the way. Graduate students of State Crime at Westminster have provided fertile ground for testing many of our ideas.

Yücel Sayman and Hacer Gündoğdu in Istanbul and Clare and Lily Leon in Ireland provided the warmest hospitality over the years. For insights into the political clientelism that is a feature of both countries, we are indebted to Peter Sweetman, Frank O'Connor, Valerie Hanley and David Healy in Ireland and to so many people in Turkey that it is difficult to know where to start, but especially to the extraordinary efforts of Ayten İnanç and, once again, the wonderful Yücel Sayman and Hacer Gündoğdu. Scientists at the Kandilli Observatory and Earthquake Research Institute in Istanbul were especially gracious in their help on the Marmara earthquake. Staff at CIDE in Mexico City provided informative conversations and use of their excellent library.

Many of our friends deserve special thanks. Belinda Webster and Abdesaddek El Fari provided Grace with an adventure playground when her mother 'needed her brain taken out'. Susan Aykut, Andrea Beckmann, Malcolm Blair, Andy Boon, Dee Coombes, Clare Fermont, John Foot, Paul Foot, Helen Graham, Elham Kashefi, Melanie McFadyean, Zubeida Malik, Andrew Pitts, Joanna Rollo, Mick and Joan Ryan and Helen Taylor all helped, both by talking about some of the ideas in the book and by *not* talking about them.

And finally Bill Spence, for enormous tolerance and endless support.

1
Defining the State as Criminal

What are states without justice but robber bands enlarged?
(St Augustine, *The City of God* [c. 427CE])

Modern states kill and plunder on a scale that no 'robber band' could hope to emulate. Any attempt to quantify their crimes is inevitably subject to enormous margins of error, but by adding up mid-range estimates R. J. Rummel (1994) calculated that from 1900 to 1987 over 169 million people were murdered by governments. Rummel's figure excludes deaths in wars (about 35 million, an unknown proportion of which resulted from war crimes), judicial executions (other than those resulting from 'show trials') and killings of armed opponents or criminals. Government officials also make a major contribution to property crime. According to a major international victimisation survey (Zvekic 1998), being asked for a bribe is the second commonest form of criminal victimisation (after consumer fraud) outside the industrialised world. But such petty corruption pales into insignificance beside the 'grand corruption' of political elites. The late Nigerian dictator Sani Abacha is accused of stealing $4 billion (£2.75 billion) from his country. This is considerably more than the annual amount stolen and damaged in all residential and commercial burglaries in England and Wales (£2.3 billion, according to Brand and Price 2000: 56).

Apart from sheer scale, the other obvious difference between 'robber bands' and 'states without justice' is that states claim the power to determine what is 'just', who is a robber and who is a tax-collector. How, then, can we speak of 'state crime'? If states define what is criminal, a state can only be criminal on those rare occasions when it denounces itself for breaking its own laws. Perhaps this is why, despite some notable individual contributions, criminology as a discipline has never regarded state crime as an integral part of its subject-matter.

In our previous work on state crime (Green and Ward 2000) we pointed to two features of contemporary states that help to resolve this problem. First, as scholars of international relations have recognised, there are certain norms of conduct in international society, many of them embodied in legal rules, that states cannot violate with complete impunity. Feeble as the sanctions applied to murderous and predatory states often appear, the pressures of domestic and international opinion, economic sanctions and boycotts, etc., are not negligible (Risse et al. 1999). There is therefore a sociological basis for saying that states, or state agencies, engage in deviant behaviour, as well as practice that violates legal norms. Secondly, we argued that some of these norms – those that define universal human rights – reflect, however imperfectly, principles of justice that criminologists ought to support. We do not believe that criminology can be neutral between human rights violators and their victims. These arguments led us to formulate a definition of state crime as *state organisational deviance involving the violation of human rights.*

The main purpose of this introductory chapter is to explain the three concepts involved in that definition: the concept of a *state*, the concept of *organisational deviance*, and the concept of *human rights*.

THE STATE

Augustine's reference to 'robber bands' was remarkably prescient. Tilly (1985) argues that modern nation-states often resemble protection rackets, in that they demand payment for protection against threats that are either imaginary or are the consequences of their own activities:

> Since governments themselves commonly simulate, stimulate or even fabricate threats of external war and since the repressive and extractive activities of governments often constitute the largest current threats to the livelihoods of their own citizens, many governments operate in essentially the same way as racketeers. There is, of course, a difference: Racketeers, by the conventional definition, operate without the sanction of governments. (Tilly 1985: 171)

Tilly argues that modern nation-states are best understood as the creations of 'coercive and self-seeking entrepreneurs', but that over a long historical period from the sixteenth century to the twentieth the most successful states have been those that 'developed a durable interest in promoting the accumulation of capital' (1985: 170) and accepted certain restrictions on their power as the price of organising their populations efficiently. On the other hand, many Third World states have not found such accommodations necessary to sustain their military power, thanks to the military legacies they received from their former colonial masters, the support of US and Soviet-led blocs during the Cold War, and the international market in arms (see also Tilly 1992). But all states, from the most autocratic to the most liberal, share one crucial characteristic: they claim an entitlement to do things which if anyone else did them would constitute violence and extortion – Weber's 'monopoly of the legitimate use of force'. That is the aspect of statehood on which we focus in this book.

When we discuss 'the state', therefore, we shall be using the term in the traditional Marxist sense to refer to a 'public power' comprising personnel organised and equipped for the use of force, 'material adjuncts, prisons and institutions of coercion of all kinds' and agencies which levy taxes (Engels 1968: 577).[1] Such 'public powers' also include those political entities (for example, the FARC – Revolutionary Armed Forces of Colombia) which deploy organised force, control substantial territories and levy formal or informal taxes but are not accepted members of the international society of states. We shall refer to such entities as 'proto-states'.

Despite the arguments of some theorists (for example, Giddens 1985) to the contrary, the use and threat of physical violence remains central to state power in liberal democracies. Cover's remarks on American criminal trials bring this out vividly:

> If convicted the defendant customarily walks – escorted – to prolonged confinement, usually without significant disturbance to the civil appearance of the event. It is, of course, grotesque to assume that the civil facade is 'voluntary' ... There are societies in which contrition and shame control defendants' behaviour to a greater extent than does violence ... But I think it is unquestionably the case in the United States that most prisoners walk into prison because they know they will be dragged or beaten into prison if they do not walk. (Cover 1986: 1607)

Where Augustine points to 'justice' as what distinguishes state coercion from the naked violence of 'robber bands', sociologists and political scientists since Weber more often speak of *legitimacy*. Legitimacy is a complex notion, which we have analysed in some detail elsewhere.[2] Without rehearsing the arguments again here, we can say that a state is legitimate to the extent that (1) it acts in accordance with the rules that it sets for itself and its citizenry, and (2) those rules are seen to be justified by shared beliefs. Gramsci (1971) showed how capitalist states secure legitimacy through a process of hegemony. Hegemony is essentially the process by which those beliefs that support the status quo are instilled in the population at large, so that they appear as matters of consensus and 'common sense'. To most citizens of states which enjoy a measure of legitimacy it appears a matter of 'common sense' that force is employed to uphold 'law and order' and to defend the country. Hegemony 'refers to an order in which a common social-moral language is spoken, in which one concept of reality is dominant, informing with its spirit all modes of thought and behaviour' (Femia 1981: 24). If the hegemonic process is successful, the specific interests of the dominant class will appear as universal interests: thus the subordinate classes see their own interests embedded in those of the ruling elite.

The most important insight that we take from Gramsci is his emphasis on the role of civil society in disseminating this common moral language. Adamson explains Gramsci's use of the term as referring to 'the space between large-scale bureaucratic structures of state and economy on the one hand and the private sphere of family, friendship, personality and intimacy on the other' (Adamson 1987/8: 320). This space is occupied in particular by organisations such as pressure groups, voluntary associations, religious bodies, the mass media and academic institutions, to the extent that they enjoy real independence from the state. Such associations 'generate opinions and goals with which they seek not only to influence public opinions and policies within existing structures and rules, but sometimes also to alter the structures and rules themselves' (Adamson 1987/8: 320–1). If civil society plays a crucial role in legitimising the state in those societies where hegemonic rule prevails, it can also play a crucial role in defining state actions as illegitimate where they violate legal rules or shared moral beliefs. Civil society, in other words, can label state actions as deviant.

ORGANISATIONAL DEVIANCE

Deviance is a term which is widely used but seldom defined. On the face of it the simplest definition of deviance is behaviour which infringes a social rule. The scope and interpretation of social rules, however, is often uncertain and contested. As Becker (1963) famously argued, deviance results from the *application* of a rule to an act: it is not an inherent quality of an act, but inheres in the relation between an act and a social audience. Here, then, is our own attempt at a definition: an act is deviant where there is a social audience that (1) accepts a certain rule as a standard of behaviour, (2) interprets the act (or similar acts of which it is aware) as violating the rule, and (3) is disposed to apply significant sanctions – that is significant from the point of view of the actor – to such violations. The matrix of an actor, a rule, an audience and a potentially significant sanction is what defines the essential subject matter of criminology (a word we use as a shorthand for 'the study of deviance and social control').

In many but not all violations of human rights all these elements are present. The relevant actors are state agencies. The relevant rules are rules of international law, domestic law and social morality, as interpreted by audiences that include domestic and transnational civil society (see below), international organisations, other states and other agencies within the offending state itself. The relevant sanctions include legal punishments, censure or rebellion by the state's own population, damage to the state's domestic and international reputation, and diplomatic, economic and military sanctions from other states.

State crime is one category of *organisational* deviance, along with corporate crime, organised crime, and the neglected area of crime by charities, churches and other non-profit bodies. It is now well established in criminology that organisations, as well as individuals, can be deviant actors (Kauzlarich and Kramer 1998 provide a useful overview of this issue). Organisations have a socially (and often legally) recognised identity which persists over time (even if the membership of the organisation changes). Organisations make decisions and implement them, set goals and pursue them, follow rules and break them. They can be subjected to formal and informal sanctions. They have reputations and can be subjected to 'shaming' (Braithwaite 1989; Risse et al. 1999). The central concepts of criminology, such as deviance, motivation, opportunity structures, control and labelling, can be applied to organisations just as well as to individuals.

Clearly the state does not always or even in the majority of cases act as a unitary force. The state comprises an ensemble of institutions which do not necessarily share a single set of interests and goals (Jessop 1982). The same will often be true of large-scale institutional structures within the state. For example, Punch (1985: 16–17) makes the point that it 'lacks subtlety' to look for organisational deviance *only* at the level of a police force as a whole. Sometimes whole forces will be deviant but the evidence suggests, at least in western Europe, that more often particular sub-units will adopt deviant goals (see Chapter 5).

Nevertheless, there are instances where the entire coercive apparatus of the state acts in a coordinated way (even if this conceals internal conflicts). Consider for example the strategy of terror pursued by the Argentinean Junta (Chapter 7), or the policing of the 1984/5 miners' strike in Britain. In the latter case, numerous ostensibly autonomous police forces, the prisons, the courts, the security services and the military[3] were centrally coordinated in a strategy that was both deviant (in the sense that it violated widely held perceptions of the proper role of the police) and violated human rights on a wide scale (see Callinicos and Simons 1985; Fine and Millar 1985; Green 1990). What both these examples illustrate is that, in times of economic and political crisis, the capitalist state does pursue an overarching goal of defending the existing order.

It is by identifying the *operative goals* of an organisation or sub-unit that we can distinguish between individual and organisational deviance, or to use Friedrichs' (1995) terminology, between 'political white-collar crime' and state crime. The former is carried out for direct personal benefit, the latter in accordance with the operative goals of a formal organisation (Schrager and Short 1977: 412). The operative goals of an organisation are those that its members actually work together to achieve, which may or may not reflect the goals the organisation publicly proclaims (Punch 2003).

It is important to bear in mind that the organisational goal served by an act need not be the same as the individual motive of the actor. For example, a soldier in war may commit rape purely for reasons of personal gratification but still contribute to organisational goals such as demoralising the enemy or promoting 'ethnic cleansing' (see Chapter 9). The organisational goal may be of little importance to the soldier himself, but may be an important reason for his comrades and superiors to turn a blind eye to his action. If, on the other hand, the soldier is promptly court-martialled, we may infer either that he acted *contrary* to an important organisational goal (perhaps the army's goal of presenting itself as the liberator of the local population), or that the organisation is riven by conflict over its goals or the means of pursuing them. The organisation's reaction (or lack of it) to individual deviance will generally be the clearest – even if not a totally reliable[4] – indication of the deviant act's perceived compatibility with organisational goals. In the course of this book we will be exploring in some depth the intersection between state organisational goals and individual motivation.

The most sophisticated attempt to conceptualise state crime as a form of organisational deviance is found in the work of Ronald Kramer and his colleagues (we examine this body of work, so far as it relates to state-corporate crime, in Chapter 3). In *Crimes of the American Nuclear State*, Kauzlarich and Kramer (1998) identify the need to integrate structural, organisational and social psychological factors and it is this integration which forms the analytical framework of our own investigation. Building on Merton's anomie theory as extended to organisational crime by Passas (1990), they argue that:

> Criminal behaviour at the organisational level results from a coincidence of pressure for goal attainment, availability and perceived attractiveness of illegitimate means, and an absence or weakness of social control mechanisms. (1998: 148)

Kauzlarich and Kramer emphasise the goal-driven, instrumentally rational nature of organisational deviance. Their 'integrated framework' is a useful starting-point for the analysis of state crime although, as they themselves acknowledge (1998: 148–50), goals, means and control mechanisms are so interdependent that any attempt to separate them out can be somewhat artificial (see Chapter 7 on state terror).

HUMAN RIGHTS

There are many forms of state organisational deviance that it would be inappropriate to label as 'crimes'. These include breaches of international economic regulations, for example, US steel tariffs, which are more analogous to domestic civil disputes; and deviations from rules which are themselves repressive: for example, the non-compliance of Danish state agencies with Nazi diktats to such an extent that the whole Danish police force faced deportation (Arendt 1965). One reason for incorporating a human rights standard into our definition of state crime is to exclude cases such as these. Another reason for employing a normative standard is that without it we could end up with an account that was literally Machiavellian – one in which the various forms of political violence and deception were assessed purely in terms of their effectiveness.

The obvious normative standards to adopt might appear to be those of domestic and international law, a position taken by many leading scholars of state and organisational crime including Schrager and Short (1977) and Kauzlarich and Kramer (1998). These standards have the advantage of being almost universally accepted. No state that we know of openly repudiates the Universal Declaration of Human Rights, and the great majority of internationally recognised states have ratified the International Covenants on Civil and Political Rights and on Economic, Social and Cultural Rights.[5] We agree, however, with Julia and Herman Schwendinger (1975) that the definition of crime should not be dependent on arcane legal arguments about the meaning of what are often highly ambiguous and unsatisfactory laws (see for example Chapter 9 on the laws of war). We prefer, like the Schwendingers, to rely on what we take to be the fundamental premises underlying human rights law. In simple terms these premises can be stated as follows.[6]

Human beings have certain needs that are fundamental in the sense that without them they cannot be effective purposive agents, able to pursue their chosen goals and participate in society. These include, at the most basic level, needs for freedom from physical restraint and debilitating pain, and for food, clothing and shelter. They also include, for human beings living in modern political societies, needs such as education and the opportunity to participate in cultural life and the political process (Doyal and Gough 1991). When we say that a person has not merely a *need* for some good but a *right* to it, 'we mean', in J. S. Mill's classic formulation, 'that he has a valid claim on society to protect him in the possession of it, either by the force of law, or by that of education and opinion' (quoted by Peffer 1990: 326). When we call a right a 'human right' we mean that everyone has such a morally valid claim simply by virtue of being human, or (what is almost, but not quite, the same thing)[7] of being a 'prospective purposive agent' (Gewirth 1978).

Since this is not a treatise on moral or political philosophy, we shall not embark on a discussion of the moral validity of human rights. Since much of our analysis is influenced by Marx[8] we shall, however, briefly explain why we do not see a contradiction between Marxism and advocacy of human rights (for full discussion of this issue see Campbell 1983; Peffer 1990).

In his early essay 'On *The Jewish Question*', Marx had some scathing things to say about 'the rights of man', referring to the narrow, formal conception of 'liberty, equality, security and property' contained in the French *Declaration of the Rights of Man and of the Citizen* and other late eighteenth-century texts. Marx expressly excluded the 'rights of the citizen' from his critique, and it is equally inapplicable to the broad conception of civil, political, economic, social and cultural rights set out in the Universal Declaration of Human Rights. In a later work, *Critique of the Gotha Programme*, Marx famously wrote that 'the narrow horizon of bourgeois right' could be transcended, but only in the 'higher phase of communist society' (1968: 320) – one in which there would be no place for a state and, obviously, no state crime. More relevant for us is Marx's observation that 'Right can never be higher than the economic structure of society and its cultural development conditioned thereby' (1968: 320). This is true in at least two senses.[9] First, people in a feudal or slave-owning society could not meaningfully claim human rights *within that society*, because the society could not protect such rights without negating its very basis as a society. Secondly, while a certain formal equality of rights is necessary to a capitalist society, such societies are not structured so as to meet the basic human needs of all their citizens. This is most obviously true of the less developed capitalist societies: see for example the case studies in Chapter 3. Even advanced democracies like the US and the UK, with their massive inequalities and high levels of social exclusion, cannot credibly claim to extend to all their citizens the 'equal worth of political liberty' as defined by Rawls (1971) or the full panoply of rights envisaged by Gewirth (1982). That is a flaw of advanced capitalist societies (although some, for example, Sweden, have notably better records than others: Doyal and Gough 1991), not of the concept of human rights.

We are not arguing that every denial of human freedom and well-being in capitalist states is a crime. That would be to equate 'crime' with the much broader concept of 'social harm', and would call for a kind of analysis that goes far beyond criminology (see Ward, forthcoming, 2004). State agencies face real pressure from domestic and/or international society to conform with some, but not all, human rights norms. What we seek to explain is why, despite those pressures, they violate those norms. It is also important, however, to recognise the inconsistent and inequitable manner in which such pressure is applied.

There is an enormous gap between the normative ideal of human rights – or the often admirable phraseology of the Universal Declaration – and the selective and hypocritical promotion of such rights by powerful states and transnational institutions such as the World Bank and International Monetary Fund. The role that human rights play in the strategies of such states and institutions can in our view best be understood in terms of the concept of *global hegemony.*

Cox (1993) has extended Gramsci's analysis of hegemony to international relations, arguing for a 'hegemonic concept of world order … founded upon not only the regulation of inter-state conflict but also upon a globally conceived civil society'. This global civil society is the product of 'a mode of production of global extent which brings about links among social classes of the countries encompassed by it' (Cox 1993: 61). International organisations play a central role in conveying global hegemony. As Cox argues:

International institutions embody rules which facilitate the expansion of the dominant economic and social forces … the rules governing world monetary and trade relations are particularly significant. They are framed primarily to promote economic expansion. (1993: 62)

World or global hegemony is expressed 'in universal norms, institutions and mechanisms which lay down general rules of behaviour for states and for those forces of civil society that act across national boundaries – rules which support the dominant mode of production' (Cox 1993: 62). These include the human rights norms which are accepted by virtually all the juridically recognised states in the world as well as the economic norms enforced by the World Bank, the International Monetary Fund (IMF) and the World Trade Organisation (WTO).

Human rights have been particularly salient in international politics since the mid-1970s. Although French atrocities in Algeria raised the importance of torture as an international issue in the 1950s and 1960s (Peters 1996), the 1970s were an important turning point for several reasons, of which we will mention only a few. The Pinochet coup in Chile, and the success of local dissidents and exiles in mobilising international support around the theme of human rights, was a key stimulus to the growth of 'transnational advocacy networks' (Ropp and Sikkink 1999). Oppositional movements in the US and other western countries had adopted civil rights as a rallying point. But this was also a time when the United

States was in need of a new political strategy in the light of economic crisis and its defeat in Vietnam. As Dezalay and Garth observe:

> The discourse in favour of human rights – limited generally to 'political and civil rights' – offered a substitute ideology [to that of 'endless economic expansion'] that had the virtue of breaking away from the hard laws of the economy. It was not inconsistent with a new emphasis on the needs of business. (2001: 131)

And in the Cold War climate it was a convenient stick with which to beat the Soviet Union.

The role of human rights is highly ambiguous. They have on the one hand provided a powerful weapon in the armoury of what Chomsky (1999a) calls the 'new military humanism' – that is, the paradoxical notion that human rights are best protected by bombing or invading recalcitrant nations (see Chapter 12). On the other hand they have provided oppositional groups in many repressive states with an international network of campaigning support and a common discourse. We shall return to this point in Chapter 11. Here it is sufficient to say that in using the language of 'state crime' we are certainly not advocating an extension of global processes of policing and punishment. Bodies such as the International Criminal Court may come to play a useful role in some respects, but that role is likely to be a limited and largely symbolic one – as is (at best) the role of domestic criminal justice systems in respect of 'conventional' crime. We do not have the space to explore this issue in any depth, nor to discuss alternatives to criminal justice such as truth commissions; the interested reader should consult the extensive literature on the subject.[10]

In the chapters that follow we explore the dynamics of some of the more salient forms of state crime, from corruption (Chapter 2) to genocide (Chapter 10). We shall try to avoid the marked bias of the existing criminological literature on state crime towards exposés of wrongdoing in advanced democracies, without veering too far in the other direction and suggesting that poor or authoritarian states have a monopoly over such crime. We shall draw in a somewhat eclectic fashion on a wide range of disciplines and theoretical perspectives. Perhaps the greatest surprise to emerge from our research is how much has been written about state crime (without usually naming it as such), and how little most criminologists know about it.

2
Corruption as State Crime

Don't steal! The government does not like competition.
(Guatemalan poster, quoted in *Red Pepper*, April 2003, p. 15)

Political and administrative corruption often takes the form of 'political white-collar crime', committed by individuals against the state. The widely used definition of corruption as 'the abuse of public office for private gain' is appropriate to this kind of individual deviance. Other corrupt acts, however, are either committed in pursuit of the organisational goals of state agencies, or are tolerated for organisational reasons. It is that kind of corruption that we class as state crime.

What distinguishes corruption from other forms of official deviance is that it involves some form of clandestine exchange (Mény 1996). This may take the form of simple bribery, of an exchange of 'favours' between state and non-state actors, or of embezzlement which is tolerated as an informal 'perk' of an official position. More loosely, the term can be applied to illicit transactions by officials which result in some kind of improper reward (for example, the Westminster City Council case discussed below). In the policing literature, discussed in Chapter 5, the term 'corruption' is sometimes used of *any* abuse of an officer's position. As an illicit form of social exchange, corruption is closely connected with (and not always easily distinguished from) other types of informal exchange engaged in by political actors. In particular, it is closely associated with the phenomena of *clientelism* and *patrimonialism*. One reason for beginning our study of state crime with a discussion of corruption is to introduce these concepts which, we shall suggest, are crucial to understanding not only corruption, but state crime in general. First, however, we need to get a sense of how big a problem corruption is, and to what extent it is truly a form of state crime.

QUANTIFYING CORRUPTION

Like other kinds of white-collar crime, corruption mainly victimises people indirectly and without their knowledge. It is therefore difficult to quantify in any meaningful way, although many researchers have tried. Some 'petty' corruption, as opposed to the 'grand' corruption practised by senior officials, does involve measurable direct victimisation. From a survey of 15,000 Mexican households Transparencia Mexicana (2001) calculates that 214 million bribes are demanded by officials each year; bribes consumed an average of 6.9 per cent of the income of those households that reported paying them, and 13.9 per cent for those with incomes at or below minimum-wage level. The second and third sweeps (1992–94 and 1996–97) of the International Crime Victimisation Survey asked respondents whether they had been asked for a bribe in the past year. The results revealed that 'on average, bribery is – second to consumer fraud – the most diffused form of victimisation of citizens in all but the industrialised world'. One-year prevalence rates in the third sweep were 17.6 per cent in the developing world, 12.8 per cent in ex-communist 'countries in transition' but only 1.0 per cent in the industrialised world (Zvekic 1998: 48). The low figure for industrialised countries indicates not that corruption is an insignificant problem, but that it rarely takes the form of extortion from individuals. A survey by World Bank researchers (Hellman et al. 2000) asked executives in ex-communist states whether various forms of corruption had 'a significant impact' on their business (a phrase which could cover being either an offender or a victim). This revealed, for example, that 44 per cent of firms in Azerbaijan reported being significantly affected by corrupt decisions in the criminal courts.

Most quantitative research on corruption, of which there is now a great deal (see Lambsdorff 1999; Andvig et al. 2000, for reviews), relies on indices of *perceived* corruption, based mainly on surveys of business people. The use of such data raises numerous methodological problems. Perhaps the most serious for our purpose is that the questions asked do not distinguish between petty corruption by individual officials (which is likely to be relatively visible) and 'grand' corruption at high levels of government, which respondents may be either ignorant of or complicit in (Johnston 2002). Apart from the difficulty of measuring corruption, there is also great difficulty in measuring the subtle social and cultural factors with which it may be associated (Kang 2002). For example, Sung (2002) proposes a simple and elegant theoretical model which, among other factors, very plausibly highlights 'particularism' as an important incentive for corruption and the strength of civil society as an important factor militating against it. To test his model, he uses male suicide rates as an inverse indicator of particularism, and the density of internet hosts as an indicator of the strength of civil society. The connection of these indicators to what they purport to measure appears tenuous at best.

CORRUPT ORGANISATIONS

Corruption can be regarded as a form of *organisational* deviance where (a) it is engaged in as a means to an organisational goal, or (b) the condonation or tacit encouragement of corruption serves organisational goals, or (c) the pursuit of profit through corruption itself becomes an organisational goal.

(a) Corruption as Means

As deLeon argues in his study of corruption in the US, officials, or businesses dealing with government, may view corruption as 'an alternative, informal, maybe unfortunate means toward ... salutary ends' (1993: 211). The Iran–Contra affair (the sale of arms to the Iranian regime to fund right-wing rebels in Nicaragua) is the best-known of deLeon's examples. Similarly, the Milošević regime in Serbia used corruption and drug trading as a source of money for paramilitaries (as well as for Milošević and his family, reputed to have stashed away some $10 billion: *File on 4*, 27 March 2001; IWPR 2002). The Indonesian armed forces are believed to raise at least half of their operational costs from illegal activities, including oil and drug smuggling and the protection of illegal logging, which is also an important source of income for the police (ICG 2001a, 2001b).

A striking 'success story' in the use of corruption to serve governmental goals was South Korea in its period of military rule from 1961 to 1987. Moran (1998: 170) writes that after Park Chung Hee's coup in 1961, corruption was 'nationalised' and businesses paid 'large sums with no guarantee of assistance but rather to keep on the right side of the state'. Some of the money was channelled into the Red Cross, anti-communist groups, or sports clubs as well as helping to maintain the elite's power base. The state provided favoured businesses with development loans and allowed them to evade tax, but businesses had to perform well enough to pay the expected kickbacks (10–20 per cent of the loan) to political funds. Corruption raised huge political revenues for the ruling party, enabled the ruling elite to enrich themselves on a grand scale, and also fostered capitalist development, albeit with a dangerous tendency towards overcapacity and indebtedness (Kang 2002). Kang argues that this relatively favourable outcome was possible because corruption, 'although endemic, was constrained by the collusion of a powerful business class and a coherent state' (2002: 150).

In China, corrupt practices often serve local organisational goals at the expense of national ones. Provincial officials, eager to attract enterprises to their areas, will help them to evade national taxes and regulations in exchange for local benefits such as building roads and bridges (Smart 1999). 'Working for the people' often means, in practice, working for one's particular province, county or work unit (Kwong 1997). Lü (2000) has documented numerous forms of illegal or unauthorised revenue-raising activities which serve to enrich state agencies as organisations (rather than particular officials) at the expense of consumers, local residents and the central government.

Another common form of official deviance in China and other command economies (see for example Solnick 1998) is the manipulation of resources and information with the goal of *appearing* to meet goals set from above. The results can be catastrophic, as in the famine which accompanied China's 'great leap forward' (see Chapter 4). Pressures to massage performance figures still persist despite economic reforms. In 1997, for example, a rural official anxious for his district to qualify as a 'township with a strong economy' boosted reported per capita income by persuading farmers that it would be good for their health to sell their blood. Drives to meet government-imposed targets are often funded by levies imposed, legally or illegally, on peasants (Lü 2000: 170–74).

The growing obsession with quantitative targets in western bureaucracies can encourage similar forms of deviance, such as the manipulation of hospital waiting-lists in the UK (National Audit Office 2001). Target-setting has combined with an increasingly 'entrepreneurial' culture to encourage a number of instances of fraud in publicly funded (but now technically charitable) further education colleges (Denham 2002).

One of the commonest forms of organisational corruption in western democracies occurs where the 'dominant coalition' of a state agency (Sherman 1978) – the individuals with the effective power to determine organisational goals – use the agency's resources to further the interests of their political party by illegitimate means. For example, public works contracts may be given in exchange for contributions to party funds: 'It has been claimed that French democracy is funded by four major public works companies' (Wolfreys 2000: 132). French, Spanish, Italian and Greek politicians have defended corruption for the benefit of political parties as 'essential for the smooth working of democracy' (Mény 1996: 311). These politicians prefer their acts to be interpreted as what we could call state crimes rather than as personal corruption, portraying themselves as honourable individuals compelled to violate legal norms in the service of high public goals (Guidoni 2000). Comparative studies suggest that this type of corruption is most likely to flourish in states with high levels of electoral expenditure and 'politicised' bureaucracies that readily adopt party interests as organisational goals (Etzioni-Halevy 2002; Heidenheimer 2002; Pujas and Rhodes 2002).

Another kind of abuse of power for party political ends occurred in the City of Westminster, where senior Conservative councillors used the sale of council houses to increase the proportion of owner-occupiers (who were presumed to be likely to vote Conservative) in particular electoral wards. After protracted litigation the House of Lords ruled that the council's policy 'was a deliberate, blatant and dishonest misuse of public power: not for financial gain but for electoral advantage. In that sense it was corrupt' (*Porter* v. *Magill* 2002: para. 48). Strictly speaking there was no corrupt *exchange* in this case, although the labelling of the policy as 'homes for votes' implied that there was (Cowan 2003).

(b) Tolerated Corruption

In the second type of organisational corruption, those who directly engage in corrupt activities are not motivated by the pursuit of organisational goals, but their behaviour is condoned or tolerated by other officials who are so motivated. The most obvious and widespread example of this type of state crime occurs where public officials are paid such low wages that corruption is a necessity for economic survival (see for example Szeftel 1998; Tanzi 1998; Harrison 1999). This not only saves the organisation money but also provides a tool for controlling subordinate officials who know that their superiors' condonation of their activities can be withdrawn at any time (Coolidge and Rose-Ackerman 1997; Vásquez-Léon 1999).

The state's attitudes to corruption as a supplement to income may be highly ambiguous. In Miller et al.'s survey of 'street-level' officials in four post-communist European countries, less than half thought their government regarded bribe taking as 'a corrupt practice that it must liquidate', over a third thought the government considered it 'unfortunate but unavoidable until it could pay officials better salaries' and a fifth thought it was accepted by their government as 'an informal way of charging for state services and paying officials' (2001: 243).

A government that does not positively condone corruption may accept it as an undesired but known or foreseen consequence of its policies. As Gong puts it in is study of corruption in China, 'The actor may be simply indifferent to that consequence though he or she has sensed it. Or the actor may be prepared to accept that consequence for the sake of other, higher, goals' (Gong 1994: 30). The Chinese regime's policy of encouraging capitalist enterprise while maintaining an authoritarian, notionally communist, political system has been pursued by allowing a degree of autonomy to local cadres and enterprise managers which creates numerous opportunities and incentives for individual and organisational corruption (Gaylord and Levine 1987; Smart 1999; Lü 2000). The Chinese government's response to corruption is analogous to western governments' response to street crime: it applies harsh but ineffective 'law and order' measures (including executions of high-ranking officials), but refuses to modify the economic policies that give rise to the problem. While the regime clearly bears a large measure of indirect responsibility for the extent of corruption, claims that it condones corruption are debatable (Lü 2000). Organisational corruption in China seems, rather, to be a prime example of crime or deviance by state *agencies*, *against* the interests of the state as a whole. At the same time, corruption may have positive effects on the stability of the regime, since it gives officials a stake in preserving the status quo (Solnick 1998).

(c) Corruption as an Organisational Goal

In the third type of organisational corruption, illicit gain becomes in itself a goal of a state agency, and the pursuit of profit determines the agency's decisions. Where whole states operate in this way, aiming to maximise the personal profits of a small number of individuals in the same way that a commercial undertaking aims to maximise profits for its shareholders, they are commonly referred to as 'kleptocracies'. Kleptocrats cannot pocket everything for themselves: some people must be allowed a share of the spoils in exchange for their support. To run a state as an *efficient* profit-maximising business – what Rose-Ackerman (1999) calls a 'strong kleptocracy' – is a difficult if not impossible task, because it would require subordinate officials to act 'honestly' in pursuit of the kleptocrat's dishonest goals. Weak and inefficient though they generally are, kleptocracies can be extremely profitable. President Marcos of the Philippines may have had as much as $12 billion in gold stashed in Swiss warehouses – twice the reserves then held by the Bank of England – and President Mobuto of Zaire and his associates are estimated to have smuggled $8–9 billion out of his impoverished country (Holsti 1996: 114). President Suharto of Indonesia and his family are alleged to have stolen some $45 billion, but his trial for stealing $570 million of the money was abandoned on grounds of ill-health (BBC News, 15 March 2001). The family of the late President Abacha of Nigeria reneged on a settlement by which they would repay £650 million ($1 billion) to the government, allowing them to keep £100 million of his plunder (*Financial Times*, 24 September 2002).

Corruption can determine organisational goals by shaping the rules or policies which state agencies implement. Hellman et al. (2000) use the term 'state capture' to refer to bribery which, rather than purchasing discre-tionary administrative decisions such as the award of a particular contract, induces legislators or judges to alter the legal 'rules of the game'. They conducted a quasi-self-report study in which business people were asked how 'firms like yours' behave (on the, perhaps questionable, assumption that the answers would reveal the respondents' own behaviour). The results indicate that among the former communist states the highest rates of state capture occurred in countries like Azerbaijan, Moldova, Russia and Ukraine which had undergone a limited degree of liberalisation. Belarus and Uzbekistan, with authoritarian regimes and little privatisation, had lower rates of state capture, as did the most liberal states such as Poland and the Czech Republic.

In a report on corruption in Macedonia, the International Crisis Group coins the term 'total state capture' to refer to 'the fusion of private or party-owned or associated firms with elements of the state structure' (ICG 2002b: 8). For example, customs officials coerced importers and exporters into using a favoured freight forwarding firm, by obstructing any goods transported by rival carriers. In effect the customs agency and the firm were two arms of a single corrupt operation. The report also points to close involvement of the state in illicit trafficking of tobacco and firearms. (A subsequent change of government was followed by the arrest of several former ministers on corruption charges: Gjorgjevic 2003.)

At least two apparent examples of state capture can be observed in the Republic of Ireland, where they are being exhaustively investigated by a tribunal chaired by Mr Justice Flood. One concerns the rezoning of land (that is, changing the type of use for which it was reserved) by Dublin County Council from the 1980s to the early 1990s. A 'core group' of councillors steered rezoning motions through the council in return for substantial bribes (Cullen 2002: 84). 'According to reliable sources', reports the leading writer on Dublin planning, 'almost every major rezoning decision adopted by the council during the early 1990s was contaminated by corruption' (McDonald 2000: 223).

A key member of the 'core group', Ray Burke, was found by the Flood Tribunal (2002) to have received corrupt payments dating back to 1973. Burke later held posts in the Irish cabinet. In 1989, as Minister of Communications, he issued a directive forcing the state broadcasting corporation, RTÉ, to reduce drastically the fee it would charge a new private radio station, Century Radio, to use its transmission facilities. Flood found that Burke made this decision not 'in the public interest but … to serve the private interests of the promoters of Century Radio' from whom he received shortly afterwards a 'bribe' of IR£35,000 (2002, paras 6.48, 7.44). In 1990, at the request of Century's promoters (whose business was going badly), Burke rushed through legislation to cap RTÉ's advertising revenue, giving Century a bigger share of the market (Cullen 2002: 191–6; Flood 2002). By 'capturing' a single key politician, Century was able to rewrite the 'rules of the game' in its relationship to RTÉ.

The corrupt use of administrative discretion is often a form of individual deviance *against* the state. 'Rent-seeking' – the use of administrative powers as a source of profit – may, however, become institutionalised as an organisational goal, where agencies set out to maximise their opportunities for lucrative discretionary decision making (della Porta and Vannucci 1999), or where bureaucratic procedures proliferate for no other purpose than to extract 'grease money' to speed the process up (Kaufmann and Wei 1999). Coolidge and Rose-Ackerman's (1997) case study of Somalia shows the latter process running wild, leading eventually to the complete disintegration of the state.

CORRUPTION, HUMAN RIGHTS AND DEMOCRACY

In most but not all cases, corrupt practices directly or indirectly entail violations of human rights.

Indirect violations of human rights come about because corruption diverts resources from the poor in a way which deprives them of necessities such as food, clean water, education and health care (Cockroft 1998). Corruption facilitates illegal despoliation of the environment, harming those who rely on the environment for a living (see, for example, ICG 2001b; Chapters 3 and 4 below). Rights are turned into commodities made available on the basis of ability to pay (Ruggiero 1994). For example, a survey in Uganda found that the parents of one in ten children had to pay for primary education, which is supposedly free (UN 2000b). A Russian study estimates that 12 million people a year are denied necessary health care because they cannot afford to bribe their doctors.[1] The corrupt redistribution of resources usually favours the rich at the expense of the poor. Japan, according to Bouissou (1997), is an exception, where corruption favours residents in poorer, rural constituencies at the expense of urban voters.

Political corruption directly violates the *right to political participation* (Steiner and Alston 2000). Human rights secure the conditions which human beings require in order to act as purposive agents with any chance of success (Gewirth 1978). One important form of agency in political societies is that of contributing to the political process. In a democratic society, corruption violates principles of equality and transparency that are (ostensibly) at the heart of the democratic process (della Porta and Pizzorno 1996; Heywood 1997). For example, even though many Dublin councillors who voted for a major shopping centre development lost their seats as a result, the developers were still able to buy enough votes to have the decision confirmed (Cullen 2002). As Ruggiero (1994) argues, corruption makes political decisions fundamentally unpredictable and thus leads to a 'political de-skilling' of the population; it undermines the conditions for any effective political agency. As the International Crisis Group illustrates in its report on Macedonia, the result is 'massive cynicism' which only reinforces the invulnerability of the corrupt elite. 'Go ahead', a corrupt minister is alleged to have said when threatened with exposure, 'there is no "public opinion" here' (ICG 2002b: 14).

Even in the absence of corruption, ostensibly democratic states usually fall far short of democratic ideals of equality and transparency. Indeed Scott (1972) argues that one of the benefits of democracy is to provide legitimate, non-corrupt channels for the political influence of the wealthy. In Ireland, for example, a 'golden circle' of wealthy individuals and corporations enjoys immense political influence and, before legal reforms in 1995 and 1997, transparency about such matters as the sources of party funds was conspicuous by its absence. This has led some Irish political commentators to raise very pertinent questions about the distinction between the 'normal' political influence of the wealthy and what is labelled as corruption (Browne 2000; O'Toole 2000).

The distinction is a fine one, but the case of the donations received by the former Irish prime minister Charles Haughey illustrates how it can be drawn. In the 1960s a group of businessmen called Taca gave more or less open financial support to Fianna Fáil.[2] The group was disbanded because it 'acquired a reputation for influencing ministerial decisions' (Collins and O Raghallaigh 1997: 159). Although Taca's apparent influence damaged the government's legitimacy, it was an influence which the electorate could judge for itself and for which it could (and possibly did) punish Fianna Fáil at the polls (Rose-Ackerman 1999: 133; Keena 2003: 40–46). When some of the same individuals turned to privately subsidising Haughey's extravagant lifestyle, they crossed the ethical line between 'normal' ruling-class behaviour and what ought to be labelled corrupt. Even on the most charitable interpretation of their conduct – that they were motivated by genuine support for Haughey's policies and leadership qualities, and expected no individual reward – they were concealing from the electorate a situation which would have given rise to a reasonable *belief* that Haughey was under their influence. They deprived the electorate of the ability to make an informed choice whether to place its trust in Haughey. That, we would argue (following Thompson 1995: 124–5), was *in itself* a form of corruption. But the same argument applies to many other secret donations (notably those received by the other major party, Fine Gael) which were perfectly legal at the time (Crowley 2000).

All these arguments presuppose a democratic constitution. In non-democratic systems some forms of corruption may be harmless or positively beneficial (Klitgaard 1988). Soviet enterprises, for example, commonly employed *tolkachi* ('pushers') whose job was to use informal channels to circumvent bureaucratic restrictions and obtain necessary supplies. According to Ledeneva, such deviant activities not only made the economy less inefficient but 'could reduce the feeling of individuals that they were alienated and dominated by forces beyond themselves' (1998: 86). Corruption may also be a means of evading human rights abuses. A Chinese official who sells false sterilisation certificates (Lü 2000: 198) surely does less harm than one who dutifully coerces women into being sterilised.

LABELLING AND DENIAL

The ethical issue of defining what *ought* to be considered corrupt is distinct from, but closely connected with, the sociological question of which social exchanges are 'normal' in a given society, and which are deviant. In both cases the transparency or concealment of the conduct concerned is of central importance. Deviant behaviour is not only that which other people so label, but that which the actors conceal because of their anticipation of how a social audience would label it if it became known. In the Westminster City Council case, for example, it was the 'history of pretence, obfuscation and prevarication which surrounded the policy' that convinced the Law Lords that the councillors knew they were doing something unlawful (*Porter* v. *Magill* 2002: para. 39). Some forms of exchange that are quite commonplace in a given society may nevertheless be deviant in the sense that the actors know they must be concealed (Elster 1989: 271). Philp (1997), for example, makes this point about some of the conduct recorded in the famous diary of the seventeenth-century official Samuel Pepys. This may explain why, even though anecdotal evidence suggests that the existence of widespread corruption in Italian (Colazingari and Rose-Ackerman 1998), Irish (Collins and O'Shea 2000) and South Korean politics was 'common knowledge' (Kang 2002: 1), the public disclosure of particular incidents can still provoke an 'active sense of outrage' (Gardiner and Lyman 1978).

The distinction between transparent and clandestine exchanges is complicated by the fact that certain forms of exchange depend upon the participants refusing to acknowledge 'the truth of their exchanges' to one another or even to themselves (Bourdieu 1977: 6). The common phrase, 'I owe you a favour' captures this ambiguity: to call something 'a favour' implies that it is gratuitous, yet to do someone a favour is often a means of creating or repaying a debt. Ledeneva (1998) argues that the 'misrecognition' of the exchange relationship is an important common element between informal exchanges of favours (*blat*) and corruption. The same applies to the influence of political donors in western democracies. As a leading fundraiser for the US Democratic Party put it:

'I don't mind donors bringing up that they have a problem with government. But don't ever try to create the impression with me, or ever say it, if you say it it's over, that your money has bought you something. There's a real delicate line here.' (quoted by Calavita et al. 1997: 103)

A striking feature of some accounts of corruption (for example, Ledeneva 1998) is that the parties will cloak their transactions in euphemisms even when they are obviously negotiating a bribe.[3] For example, a key witness at the Flood Tribunal investigating corruption on Dublin County Council was Frank Dunlop, who described himself as a 'broker' between property developers and councillors. He testified that one councillor, in the course of a conversation about a particular planning application,

> indicated the difficulties of fighting an election … Costwise. I indicated to him that if I could be of assistance to him I would … I gave him a thousand pounds.
> **Q:** Yes. He hadn't nominated any particular sum?
> **A:** No. (*Irish Times*, 20 April 2000)

This is a classic 'technique of neutralisation': to enable himself to break the rule, the councillor redescribes it in acceptable terms (doing a favour/accepting a political contribution). For the exchange to work he must, as Bourdieu (1977) argues, be aware that he is making it, while at the same time refusing to recognise it.

CLIENTELISM AND PATRIMONIALISM

The term 'clientelism' refers to a pattern of social exchange between patrons, normally the holders of political administrative offices, and clients, who may be private citizens, businesses or more junior officials. The patron exercises power or influence in favour of the client, who reciprocates by offering electoral support, political donations or personal gifts. Clientelism can flourish alongside modern, bureaucratic government. Law and bureaucracy provide the framework within which patrons can offer to advance their clients' interests by exercising discretion (or influencing its exercise) or by 'bending' the rules.

Patrimonialism, on the other hand, is the antithesis of bureaucratic government; it is the form clientelism takes where a rational-legal bureaucracy does not exist. Patrimonial authority, which Weber (1968) describes as characteristic of pre-industrial societies, is exercised not through impersonal rules but through personal ties between rulers and their subordinates. Official duties are defined not by rules but by personal loyalties. There is no clear distinction between the private wealth and interests of the ruler and the wealth and interests of the nation. Much behaviour that would be corrupt in a rational-legal bureaucracy would be perfectly acceptable in a patrimonial state.

Even if Weber's concept of patrimonialism accurately describes the reality of the way power is exercised in many less developed countries, such states nowadays almost invariably adopt the outward form of bureaucracies governed by impersonal rules. The combination of rational-legal form and patrimonial substance is often referred to as *neo-patrimonialism* (see Theobald 1999; Médard 2002). When neo-patrimonial elites treat their country's resources as their own and distribute them in accordance with criteria of political loyalty, kinship, etc., they are violating both their own laws and the norms upheld by important audiences such as foreign donors and the World Bank, even if, according to some commentators, such behaviour is expected and accepted by many of their own people (see, for example, Bayart et al. 1999; Chabal and Dalloz 1999).

We can say, then, that clientelism introduces elements of personalism into a predominantly rational-legal system of government, whereas neo-patrimonialism *is* a system of government, operating behind a rational-legal façade. The distinction is not clear-cut. For example, de Souza Martins (1996: 195), describes the 'politics of favour' as 'the base and foundation of the Brazilian state', but adds that such politics are 'disguised behind the appearances and external trappings of a modern, contractual system … [P]atrimonial rule does not set itself up … as the rival of rational-legal rule … it feeds off it and contaminates it.' Is this a description of a neo-patrimonial system 'disguised behind' a rational-legal façade, or a rational-legal system 'contaminated' by clientelism?

As Roniger (1994: 9) argues, at the 'level of principles, the logic of civil society and democracy run counter to the logic of clientelism'. Civil society is made up of associations independent of the state that articulate purportedly collective interests or universal principles. Clientelism is based upon individuals, in a relationship of dependence on, or interdependence with, state officials, pursuing overtly particular interests. If civil society plays a key role in the definition and censure of deviant behaviour by state agencies, then we can expect clientelism, which erodes civil society and democratic processes, to be inherently criminogenic. *A fortiori*, neo-patrimonial states, in which patron–client relationships pervade the entire political system, can be expected to be prone not only to corruption but to all varieties of state crime.

An important collection of essays edited by della Porta and Mény (1997) highlights the link between clientelism and corruption in the liberal democracies of western Europe and Japan. The editors conclude that although clientelism and corruption are analytically distinct, the two tend to occur together because they share an emphasis on exchange relationships, 'instrumental friendship' and networking skills (see also della Porta and Vannucci 1999). A former Dublin County Councillor (of the Green Party) gave us a similar explanation of why some of his political opponents had been open to bribery in relation to planning decisions (David Healy, interview, 4 October 2000). Clientelism, he said, was very important in Irish local politics. Councillors had little real power (except the power to 'rezone' land for development) but claimed credit for 'pull' when decisions went in their clients' favour (Higgins 1982, gives a similar account of the 'illusion of influence'). Such practices, though not in themselves corrupt, encouraged councillors to see politics as being all about 'favours', and this made it easier for them to accept bribes as part of 'the way things are done'.

In their study of the major corruption scandal that broke the grip of the Christian Democrats and their coalition partners over Italian politics, della Porta and Vannucci (1999) describe clientelism, corruption and mal-administration as forming two interlocking 'vicious circles'. Clientelism increases the costs of politics, as politicians compete to buy votes, which increases the demand for corrupt payments, which in turn further fuels clientelistic competition (South Korea in the 1990s affords a particularly striking example of this phenomenon: Kang 2002). The more corrupt a state agency is, the more unpredictable its decisions become, and the more citizens seeking a decision from the agency turn to 'brokers' (such as Mr Dunlop in Ireland) who know how to 'get things done'. The brokers know which politicians are bribable and at what price. The more it becomes apparent that bribery is unavoidable if one wants anything done, the lower the 'moral costs' (guilt and fear of exposure) that citizens and officials attach to corrupt exchanges. Della Porta and Vannucci's study adds sociological depth to the several economic models that predict vicious (or virtuous) circles of corrupt (or honest) behaviour, producing an equilibrium (stable state) at either a high or low level of corruption (Rose-Ackerman 1999; Andvig et al. 2000).

In states with a reasonably free and effective civil society, and a reasonably independent judiciary,[4] the highly corrupt equilibrium is a fragile one (Bufacchi and Burgess 1998). Corruption breeds resentment among those who, for one reason or another, feel they have got a poor deal (Ruggiero 1996a). As events both in Italy and Ireland (Cullen 2002) illustrate, a single 'defector' who chooses to confess to the press or judicial authorities can set off a 'chain reaction' in which extensive networks of corruption are exposed to public view. The threat of violence, such as was provided in the South of Italy by the Mafia and Camorra, can be a useful deterrent to such defections (Bufacchi and Burgess 1998; della Porta and Vannucci 1999).

Della Porta and Mény (1997) describe clientelism as a system of generalised exchange guaranteed by gratitude, in contrast to corruption which is based on specific exchanges guaranteed by the expectation of a 'replay' – politicians or administrators who keep their word can expect further bribes in future. We doubt whether the distinction can be so neatly drawn. Some 'generalised exchanges' are widely seen as corrupt. For example Charles Haughey was generally seen to have been disgraced by his acceptance of his wealthy friends' largesse, even though no one has yet produced a 'smoking gun' linking the gifts to any specific political decision. John Poulson, the architect who plied British politicians and civil servants with gifts and consultancy fees in the 1960s and 1970s, was convicted of corruption although he did not pay specific bribes for specific decisions (Doig 1984). Rather he was acquiring a kind of intangible asset, akin to an option in a financial market (Cartier-Bresson 1997). It was for placing himself under a heavy obligation to the millionaire Ben Dunne, not for doing Dunne any specific service, that Charles Haughey was censured by a tribunal of inquiry (McCracken 1997).

The boundary between corruption and clientelism is marked not so much by the nature of the exchange as by the (actual or anticipated) reaction of a social audience. For example, a World Bank study of corruption notes that:

In the UK, according to newspaper reports, one in three of the ruling Labor [sic] Party's biggest donors in the last general election has gained a peerage, a ministerial position or advisory role on policy after donating millions of pounds to the party's election war chest. (Ofosu-Amaah et al. 1999: 26, citing the Sunday Times, 30 August 1998)

To an outside observer this may well look like corruption, but in British political culture such transactions, though considered vaguely 'sleazy', are seldom labelled as corrupt. It seems, as Theobald (1990) suggests, that the generally honest conduct of day-to-day administration in Britain makes it possible to tolerate flagrantly clientelistic, or even patrimonial, relations between the political and business elites.[5]

While the case of Ireland illustrates the link between clientelism and corruption, it also shows that the damage done by clientelism can be relatively localised (Collins and O'Shea 2000). Although there is some political patronage over the civil service, Ireland has largely maintained the insulation of the bureaucracy from politics that it inherited from Britain (Dunphy 1995; Coakley 1999). In this respect it is less susceptible to systemic corruption than Italy and other southern European countries with which it shares a political culture marked by clientelism or 'brokerage' (Collins and O Raghallaigh 1997; Gallagher and Komito 1999; Pujas and Rhodes 2002). As in Italy though on a smaller scale, politicians reared in a culture of 'crony capitalism',[6] 'favours' and 'networking' (Bax 1976) have proved susceptible to corruption; this has been exacerbated (as in Japan) by an electoral system in which politicians of the same party compete for seats in multi-member constituencies. Ireland does not stand out as a particularly 'criminal' state, though in Transparency International's 'Corruption Perceptions Index' it is singled out as showing a '[n]oteworthy ... downward trend', and now ranks only just above Botswana – reputedly the least corrupt African country – France, Portugal and Italy (Transparency International 2002). In recent years the corrupt activities of certain ministers and councillors have received extensive press coverage and have been the subject of a series of exhaustive judicial inquiries, without (so far) provoking the kind of vicious political backlash against the judiciary that has occurred in Italy. Moreover, there seems little evidence that the cronyism and corruption affecting certain sectors of the economy (notably construction, communications and beef: O'Toole 1995) has had any marked effect, either for better or worse, on the 'Celtic tiger's' rate of economic growth.

In developing countries, clientelism or patrimonialism is typically much more pervasive and, together with corruption, clearly does affect economic growth. The importance of clientelism reflects the paucity of alternative sources of legitimacy:

> Third world states are invariably riven by deep internal cleavages centred upon ethnic, religious, linguistic or regional divisions which are overlaid by extremes of wealth and poverty. Under such conditions it is extremely difficult if not impossible for an overall consensus, in the sense of basic agreement on rules of the political game, to emerge. An atmosphere of acute distrust prevails; politics becomes a ruthless zero-sum contest in which contending parties strive not simply to stay on top but to eliminate their opponents altogether ... Under such circumstances it is easy to appreciate the immense significance that will be attached to building up and maintaining the cohesion of clientele networks. (Theobald 1990: 93–4)

It is also easy to appreciate that clientelism, corruption and violence will tend to occur together. What is not so clear is whether clientelism serves as an alternative to violence (Clapham 1982), or increases it. In very broad terms, it is possible to discern two contrasting patterns of clientelistic politics in less developed countries. In one, elegantly analysed in Khan's (1999) study of South and South-East Asia, the state buys off opposition to capitalist development by extracting money from the emerging capitalist class in exchange for subsidies, credits, irrigation, etc., and uses some of the proceeds to buy off opposition to the unjust allocation of resources by a mixture of corruption and (legal) patronage. At least in some of these states, corruption does seem to be an alternative to violence. For example, the neo-patrimonial regime of Ferdinand Marcos in the Phillipines was infamously corrupt but not, as dictatorships go, particularly violent (violence was more a feature of local than of national politics). As the system of patronage crumbled, violence increased (Kang 2002).

The second pattern occurs in states where a powerful class of indigenous capitalists does not emerge, because the economy is based largely on the extraction of natural resources for the benefit of foreign-owned businesses. In such a society, the state's capacity to garner a share of income from natural resources, or to attract overseas aid, provides one of the few ways for an indigenous bourgeoisie to accumulate wealth (Schatzberg 1988; Theobald 1990; Szeftel 1998). A class that depends upon its control of the state to expropriate resources for itself is incapable of articulating a hegemonic conception of the 'public interest'. Only by a patrimonial distribution of resources can it create a particularistic form of hegemony, an apparent identity of interest between the rulers and particular factions among the ruled (Bayart 1993). The elite nevertheless has to pay lip service to the globally hegemonic ideas of 'good governance' promoted, in particular, by the World Bank (Riley 1998; Doig and Theobald 2000; Kaufmann et al. 2000).

There are two variants on this form of neo-patrimonial rule. In some instances, an astute use of patronage and sensitivity to local conditions may endow the ruling clique with a certain degree of legitimacy and stability. Côte d'Ivoire under the long rule (1960–93) of Félix Houphouet-Boigny is perhaps the clearest example (Bayart 1993). The other variant is one which more resembles Weber's 'sultanist' type of authority than patrimonialism, in that nakedly material ties between rulers and subordinates, rather than traditional or charismatic authority, provide the basis for loyalty.[7] The state is almost entirely predatory; it does little to benefit any ruling class external to itself, let alone the population at large. While the ruler or ruling clique may well pose rhetorically as the embodiment or 'father' of the nation (for example, Schatzberg 1988: 81), the state's power to control those outside a shrinking circle of beneficiaries depends primarily on violence. Nugent's (1995) study of Ghana in the 1970s and 1980s illustrates the slide from a semi-legitimate form of patrimonialism – it was accepted that the 'big men' of politics would enrich themselves to a certain extent – to a naked military kleptocracy that was violently overthrown in 1982.

The political logic of clientelism and patrimonialism is central to understanding many forms of state crime. For example, we shall argue in Chapter 12 that Iraq under Saddam Hussein fits a pattern similar to that just described. The genocide in Rwanda, discussed in Chapter 10, can at least partly be explained by a 'crisis of clientelism' (Hintjens 1999: 261), triggered by falling coffee prices and the World Bank's Structural Adjustment Programme (Newbury 1998), which led to an increasing concentration of power in the shadowy and corrupt 'Akazu' network centred on the family of the President's wife (de Waal 2000; International Panel 2000). Both these cases illustrate the same essential point. The more a neo-patrimonial regime is starved of resources, the more it is likely to abandon such services as it provides its citizens, concentrate its patronage on a small network of supporters, and rely on violence to control the rest of the population (or give up trying to control parts of its territory at all: Reno 1999). Thus, trying to make corrupt and inefficient states retrench through 'structural adjustment' and economic liberalisation stands a good chance of making corruption and misgovernment worse:

> ... austerity measures, meant to correct bad policies, [tend] to constrain political uses of state resources. Rulers are forced to seek new ways to keep intra-elite coalitions together so as to ensure the regime's stability and survival. These new strategies frequently breach the boundaries between public and private that reforms are designed to reinforce ... The irony of structural adjustment and its assumptions of state-society dichotomies is that they strengthen the very patrimonial features of African governance that the policies are meant to address. (Reno 1999: 11–12)

It may also, as Reno shows, push states in the direction of fragmentation and civil war. Real reform in developing countries depends on genuine, and reasonably equitable, economic development. How this can be accomplished is beyond the scope of this book.

3
State-Corporate Crime

> We present illustrative examples of illegal land seizure, false imprison-
> ment, forced labour, summary expulsion, enforced resignation,
> intimidation, rape, violence, arson, torture, and murder enacted upon poor
> and vulnerable communities at the alleged behest of shrimp farming
> concerns, often with the apparent complicity of corrupt officials.
>
> (Environmental Justice Foundation 2003: 4)

States, the perpetrators of the most serious and widespread crimes, do not
always work alone. Very frequently, deviant state actions intersect with the
criminal actions of corporations to produce massive human rights and
environmental violations. State-corporate crime is thus a significant form
of high-level criminality, involving a coincidence of interest and enterprise
between two powerful entities typically viewed by criminologists as
separate. Over the past decade, a small group of criminologists have
converged to develop a methodology to examine this intersection between
state crime and corporate crime. This scholarship extends previous criminological inquiry into corporate crime, and contributes to emerging state
crime theory by identifying the central role of the state in initiating or facilitating major forms of corporate deviance (Kramer 1992; Matthews and
Kauzlarich 2000).

State-corporate crime has been defined by Kramer and Michalowski as

> ... illegal or socially injurious actions that result from a mutually
> reinforcing interaction between (1) policies and/or practices in pursuit
> of goals of one or more institutions of political government and (2)
> polices and/or practices in pursuit of the goals of one or more institutions
> of economic production and distribution. (quoted in Matthews and
> Kauzlarich 2000: 282)

If we substitute 'deviant actions or omissions that cause human rights
violations' for 'illegal or socially injurious actions', this definition is
consistent with our generic definition of state crime.

The study of state-corporate crime involves an examination of the intersection of state and corporate actions on three levels of analysis: individual, institutional and structural or societal (Matthews and Kauzlarich 2000; Kramer 1992). On each of these levels, scholars have drawn on existing approaches which Kramer sums up as follows:

> The first is differential association theory as developed by Sutherland ... The second perspective is based on organizational theory and argues either that organizations are inherently criminogenic due to performance emphasis on goals ..., or that organizations commit crime due to defective operating procedures. The third perspective locates the criminogenic forces in the wider political, economic structure of the society. (Kramer 1992: 215–16)

State-corporate crime scholars have endeavoured to bring these levels together in a 'powerful integrated theoretical model [which] ... would unite the three levels of social experience that constitute the dialectical totality of human life' (Kramer 1992: 216). They have identified three 'catalysts for action' to explain the occurrence of state-corporate crime: (1) organisational motivation or goals, (2) opportunity, and (3) social control (Matthews and Kauzlarich 2000). Organisational crime is said to result from 'a coincidence of pressure for goal attainment, availability and perceived attractiveness of illegitimate means, and an absence or weakness of social control mechanisms' (Matthews and Kauzlarich 2000: 293).

In the context of state-corporate crime, the goal of either direct capital accumulation (by the state, the corporation or individual actors within either entity) or the promotion of capital accumulation (by the state for the corporation or individuals within the corporation) is frequently a 'highly criminogenic force'. Where legitimate means to pursue this goal are scarce as a result of either institutional or structural factors, organisational deviance is more likely to occur. Social control acts as 'a critical element in constructing symbolic frameworks that will operate at the societal, organizational, and personal levels' (Kramer 1992: 217) to restrain deviance. Organisational deviance is likely to occur where there is a failure of social control at one or more of the three levels of analysis, combined with opportunity and motivation.

A trawl of the literature (largely non-criminological) reveals a great many cases where corporations and states have colluded in criminal enterprise for mutual benefit. Spectacular examples emerge from the literature on the Third Reich – IBM and its German subsidiary Deutsche Hollerith Maschinen Gesellschaft (Dehmag) provided the technology, for significant profits, which enabled the Nazi regime to trace Jews, run the railroad network and to organise concentration camp labour (Black 2001); I. G. Farben provided the Nazis with the deadly Zyklon B gas used to gas millions of Jews, as well as owning and operating 'an enormous industrial establishment' for the exploitation of slave labour at Auschwitz (Borkin 1978). More recent case studies include the explosion of the Space Shuttle *Challenger* in 1986 as a consequence of the joint agendas of a government agency, NASA (National Aeronautics and Space Administration), and Morton Thiokol Inc. (Kramer 1992); the production of nuclear weapons (Kauzlarich and Kramer 1998), and the crash of ValuJet Flight 592 as a result of the 'mutually reinforcing interaction' between the American Federal Aviation Administration (FAA) and private corporations (Sabre Tech and ValuJet) (Matthews and Kauzlarich 2000).

In order to explore the theoretical and empirical parameters of state-corporate crime this chapter focuses on three industries in which the dynamics of cooperative and organised deviant actions by states and corporations have resulted in human rights violations: the Latin American shrimp industry, the Nigerian oil industry, and the US and British arms trade.

In Latin America, since the early 1980s, there has been a rapid boom in the shrimp aquaculture industry primarily in Honduras, Guatemala, Ecuador and Mexico. Multinational aquaculture corporations have developed large-scale semi-intensive shrimp farms along coastal wetlands and mangroves, displacing local communities from the communally held land from which they have long derived their sustenance. The shrimp corporations have aggressively policed the farms, brutally repressing protests by the local communities, resulting in the murder and torture of several fishermen. The state has facilitated the actions of the corporations in three ways: (1) by granting virtually free land concessions to shrimp farm operators, (2) by failing to enforce environmental laws protecting mangrove areas, and (3) by terrorising fishing communities through employing repressive policing tactics, while affording absolute immunity to shrimp farm operators whose private security forces commit atrocities against local people. The actions of shrimp corporations in Latin America and the role of the state in facilitating these actions have, with the notable exceptions of a handful of authors, received almost no attention in academic literature or from human rights organisations, despite continuing human rights violations and a growing worldwide campaign against the shrimp industry.

In contrast, the Nigerian oil industry, which in many ways parallels the shrimp industry, has received considerable attention. As with the shrimp farms in Latin America, Nigerian oil installations have displaced local communities, caused massive environmental devastation, and have been ruthlessly policed by both the private security employed by oil corporations, and by the Nigerian state.

The arms trade illustrates examples of state-corporate crime where states and corporations have colluded covertly to breach embargoes on repressive states, or trade in weapons or equipment which have devastating consequences for the civilian populations upon whom the arms are employed.

THE ROLE OF THE STATE

Matthews and Kauzlarich (2000: 283) have identified two forms of state-corporate crime, state-initiated and state-facilitated:

> ... the former occurs when corporations, employed by the government, engage in organizational deviance at the direction of, or with the tacit approval of, the government. State-initiated state corporate crime includes cases such as the space shuttle *Challenger* explosion and the environmental and human injury caused by nuclear weapons production. In both of these instances, a government agency (NASA in the *Challenger* case and the Department of Energy in the nuclear weapons case) actively pursued a shared goal with a private corporation (Morton Thiokol and Rockwell International, respectively).

State-facilitated crime by contrast is defined by Kramer and Michalowski as the failure of governmental regulatory agencies 'to restrain deviant business activities, because of direct collusion between business and government, or because they adhere to shared goals whose attainment would be hampered by aggressive regulation' (1990: 6). It is this type of crime that is chiefly in evidence in the case of the Latin American shrimp industry.

The first way in which the state facilitates crimes by shrimp companies is by land concessions. In Honduras, such concessions 'have effectively turned ... common property resources into private property' (Dewalt et al. 1996: 1196). During the 1980s, the Honduran government

> ... began granting rights over state-owned coastal land to investors, thereby supplanting the previous claims of traditional, communal users. Renewable concessions are leased to individuals or corporations for 25 years at the ridiculously low cost of about US $4–5 per year ... Despite the low cost of leases, their lack of political power to influence the award of concessions (along with the high costs of farm construction and maintenance, lack of technical assistance, insufficient credit opportunities, and high interest rates) has impeded entry of small producers, agrarian reform cooperatives, and poor coastal communities into the industry. (Varela et al. 2001)

Several commentators have reported that the nature of the land concessions reflects a clear bias towards large corporations to the detriment of the local communities (Stonich 1991; Dewalt et al. 1996).

According to Varela, these land concessions represent violations of the Honduran constitution, which provides that only Hondurans, or 'societies created by Honduran people', may own land in coastal and border areas, whereas the major aquaculture companies are largely American- (or in one case Ecuadorian-) owned (Varela 2001: 159).

State facilitation in the form of land concessions is also found in other Latin American countries. In Ecuador, for example, successive governments have granted favourable land concessions to shrimp aquaculture corporations. In August 2000, the government introduced a law to convert the existing concessions into outright ownership of the land, but the Ecuadorian Constitutional Court declared 22 articles of the law unconstitutional (World Rainforest Movement 2001b).

In addition to flouting land ownership laws to benefit the expansion of the shrimp industry, states have consistently failed to enforce environmental regulations against the industry. According to the environment group Accion Ecologia, by 1985 the Ecuadorian government had recognised the increasing environmental damage to mangroves:

> Since the trees stood on intertidal zones, traditionally considered public land by governments around the world, the ecosystem could be protected by decree. Ecuador issued laws forbidding the shrimp farmers from clearing any more trees without a government concession. But these efforts were paper-thin ... [F]rom 1987 to 1991, almost 85 more square miles of mangroves vanished to make room for shrimp ponds, despite appeals from village environment groups to the government. (Nixon 1996)

In Honduras a Decree issued in 1997 imposed an eight-month moratorium on the installation or expansion of shrimp farms in the Gulf of Fonseca. During this period, environmental impact studies were to be carried out to assess measures necessary for the conservation of mangrove forests and coastal wetlands. According to Nuila (1998), however, at the end of the moratorium not one such study had been carried out. Illegal shrimp farms constructed on wetland sites protected by the Honduran government under the Ramsar Convention[1] are allowed to function with impunity, despite repeated calls from local communities and environmental groups for the government to act to prevent illegal farm construction (Varela 2001).

Beyond the destruction of mangroves, serious environmental consequences flow from the development of shrimp farms while they are in operation (World Rainforest Movement 2001d). Despite this environmental devastation, states have consistently failed to enforce environmental regulations against existing shrimp farms. For example, in Honduras, Varela (2001: 160) reports that 'more than 16,000 hectares of shrimp farms discharge their polluting wastes directly to estuaries without any treatment', in blatant contravention of Honduran law.

In many countries in Latin America, the state has also been implicated in the brutal repression of local communities protesting against the lack of access to coastal wetlands as a result of land concessions to the shrimp industry. The state has both been directly involved in this repression, through the use of violent policing tactics, leading to the deaths of members of local communities, and has allowed absolute immunity for shrimp farm operators whose private surveillance units have been involved in the torture and/or murder of community members (Dewalt et al. 1996; Gonzalez 2001; Varela et al. 2001; World Rainforest Movement 2001d, 2001e, 2001g). For example:

On the evening of October 4, 1997, two fishermen, Israel Ortiz Avila, thirty years old, and Marin Zeledonio Alvarado, twenty-eight years old, were fishing in the Todo Mundo estuary, adjacent to CRISUR shrimp, which is established within the Las Iguanas wildlife refuge. According to a witness, the two men were trapped, tied up, and tortured by shrimp guards. In the early morning hours of the next day, the two men's bodies were deposited by the owner of the shrimp farm at the entrance to Guipo, the town where the men lived. They had been shot at gunpoint. Immediately after the incident, before any investigation had taken place, the National Aquaculture Association of Honduras (ANDAH) defended the killings, implying that the fisherman were thieves. Ortiz's widow pleaded, 'if they were thieves, why were they killed? Why were their bodies dumped here in our town, rather than left at the scene for an investigation?' (Varela et al. 2001)

Between 1992 and 1998, eleven people active in the regional fishermen's alliance CODDEFFAGOLF were reportedly murdered (by gun shot or machete) as a result of the conflict between CODDEFFAGOLF and the Honduran shrimp industry. No prosecutions have ensued.

This corporate immunity is in stark contrast to the treatment of local community members accused of stealing shrimp from farms, who have received penalties of more than five years in jail (Varela et al. 2001).

In Nigeria, the role of the state differs slightly as it is directly involved in formal joint ventures with the oil mining corporations, while in Latin America, only individual government officials and not the government *per se* have ownership interests in shrimp farm operations (Meltzoff and LiPuma 1996; Stonich and Bailey 2000). The state-owned Nigerian National Petroleum Corporation (NNPC) owns 55 or 60 per cent of the joint ventures carried out by European and US corporations (Human Rights Watch 1999d). Given this degree of state involvement, the case of the Nigerian oil industry might more accurately be described as a case of state-initiated crime.

The actions of the Nigerian state follow a similar pattern of favourable land grants, lax environmental regulation (Human Rights Watch 1999d, Ch. IX), and repressive tactics against local populations. In Nigeria, however, the state is more often immediately involved in protecting the interests of the oil corporations by violently repressing local dissent. Whereas in Latin America, in general, the state provides immunity to private security forces who in turn employ violent tactics, in Nigeria the atrocities are committed either by the state security forces themselves, or by the 'private' security forces who are trained by the Nigerian state, and remain integrated with state security forces:

> All the oil companies in Nigeria hire 'supernumerary police', sometimes known as 'spy police', to protect their installations. These police are recruited and trained by the Nigerian police force, but paid for by the oil companies, at rates well above those paid by the Nigerian government. They remain accountable to Nigerian police command structures ... Shell stated to Human Rights Watch that 186 armed members of the regular Nigerian police force, employed by the Nigerian government rather than Shell, were deployed to SPDC [Shell Petroleum Development Corporation Nigeria] facilities, including several dog handlers. Both sets of police officially report to the commissioner of police and operate according to the procedures and practices of the Nigerian police, though SPDC decided where they are to be deployed. (Human Rights Watch 1999d: Ch. VII)

In addition, in several of the oil-rich states of Nigeria, the Nigerian government has established special units and restructured existing security forces to protect oil industry interests.

Agencies of criminal justice have been specifically employed by the state to eliminate leaders of protest movements against the oil industry. In a celebrated case in 1994, Ken Saro-Wiwa and eight other members of MOSOP (Movement for the Survival of the Ogoni People) were arrested in connection with the murder of four traditional leaders in Ogoni. The charges were widely understood to be false – a pretext for eliminating the troublesome leadership of MOSOP. Despite widespread international protest condemning the charges, Saro-Wiwa and his compatriots were hanged by the military government of Sani Abacha on 10 November 1995, 'after a trial before a tribunal which blatantly violated international standards of due process and produced no credible evidence that he or the others were involved in the killings for which they were convicted' (Human Rights Watch 1999d: Ch. I).

States play varied roles in committing crimes in association with corporations in the trade of arms: condoning, promoting or ignoring arms transfers to embargoed states; failing to institute appropriate measures to regulate the arms trade; financing the purchase of arms through export credit; subsidising the manufacture and promoting the trade of torture equipment.

The US and Britain, in conjunction with weapons companies such as British Aerospace (now BAe Systems) and Lockheed Martin, played a central role in arming the Indonesian occupation of East Timor. According to Jackson (2001: 45), the US 'supplied over 90 per cent of the weapons used by the Indonesian military in the invasion'. In 1977, hearings conducted by the House International Relations Committee revealed that

> ... several major US weapons systems [were] sold to Jakarta during this period – including sixteen Rockwell OV-10 'Bronco' counter-insurgency aircraft, three Lockheed Martin C-130 transport aircraft and thirty-six Cadillac-Gage V-150 'Commando' armored cars ... (Berrigan 2001)

The Bronco aircraft were financed with the aid of an official US government foreign military sales credit (Taylor 1991: 84).

The British state and British companies similarly played a significant role in arming the brutal occupation. John Pilger reports that

> ... in 1977, with the East Timorese cut off from the world and fighting for their existence, David Owen, foreign secretary in the Callaghan Labour government, approved the sale of the first Hawk fighter-bombers to Indonesian dictatorship. Owen said that the reports of killings in East Timor had been 'exaggerated' and that the 'most reliable' figure was 10,000, and anyway, 'the scale of the fighting had been reduced.' As Owen concluded the deal, a letter written by a Portuguese priest hiding in East Timor reached Lisbon. '*The invaders,*' he wrote, '*have intensified their attacks from land, sea, and air. The bombers do not stop all day. Hundreds die every day.*' (Pilger 1999)

Again, in 1996, despite public concerns that any arms sent to Indonesia would be used for internal repression, the Conservative government awarded BAe 'another morally dubious trade agreement' which involved a large shipment of arms, including 16 Hawk fighter aircraft, to be sent to Jakarta (Corporate Watch 2002).

The Matrix Churchill/'Supergun' scandal revealed Britain's role in arming Saddam Hussein's dictatorship in Iraq. Norton-Taylor explains that

> ... Iraqi businessmen approved by the Baghdad regime ... set up TDG, which in 1987 bought Matrix Churchill, the Coventry machine tool company, whose computer-controlled lathes were suitable for making shell and missile cases and parts for Iraq's nuclear programme. Shortly after the cease-fire in the Iran–Iraq war was declared in August 1988, British ministers secretly relaxed the guidelines on exports to the combatants. (Norton-Taylor et al. 1996: 14)

This 'relaxation' allowed the state to approve the export of equipment needed to develop the 'Supergun', a weapon with a proposed range of up to 1,000 miles.

The British state and British companies have also been implicated in breaching the arms embargo on Sierra Leone by facilitating the activities of British-based company, Sandline International. Human Rights Watch reports that the

> ... embargo on Sierra Leone, imposed in October 1997, was lifted in June after the deposed government of President Ahmad Tejan Kabbah was restored to power by the forces of ECOMOG, the Economic Community of West African States Cease-fire Monitoring Group, assisted by ... Sandline International. The involvement of Sandline stirred controversy, as its sale of arms and ammunition to President Kabbah, with the seeming approval of the U.K. government, appeared to constitute a violation of the embargo, which the U.K. had been instrumental in bringing about. (Human Rights Watch 1999a)

The British government, in the interests of promoting British exports to Saudi Arabia, has also concealed corruption in the arms industry. According to Norton-Taylor, the 'unprecedented' £20 billion Al-Yamamah arms deal between Britain and Saudi Arabia provides a very clear illustration of the extent to which governments have been prepared to go in order to support the British arms industry. In the course of this deal hundreds of millions of pounds were paid out in secret commissions, commissions which the Thatcher Conservative government always vigorously denied. Roger Freeman, Defence Procurement Minister at the time, told the House of Commons in October 1994: 'The transaction between Her Majesty's

Government and Saudi Arabia was on a government to government basis in which no commissions were paid and no agents or any middlemen were involved' (cited in Norton-Taylor and Pallister 1999). A National Audit Office report on the Al-Yamamah deal, which included references to alleged 'kickbacks' paid by British companies, 'was suppressed by the Commons Public Accounts Committee on the grounds that its publication would upset the Saudis and thus put British jobs at risk' (Norton-Taylor et al. 1996: 15).

While at pains to distance themselves publicly from 'terror regimes', both the United States and Britain have been directly involved in the trade of torture equipment to these very regimes. Details of this involvement are elaborated in Chapter 8.

STATE-CORPORATE ACTIONS AND HUMAN RIGHTS VIOLATIONS

The role of the state in initiating or facilitating corporate crime could be perceived as a human rights violation in and of itself. Varela (2001) argues that the 'systematic institutionalized failure to apply a nation's laws justly' – as in the case of Honduras – 'is a violation of the human rights of its people' (Varela 2001: 161). In general, however, it is the actions of the shrimp corporations which have had more direct human rights consequences.

Industrial shrimp aquaculture requires shallow ponds situated on the margins of estuaries between five and twenty hectares in size. In order to accommodate the expansion of the industry, corporations have clear-cut mangroves to make way for the construction of these ponds (Dewalt et al. 1996; Earth Summit Watch 1997). According to a 1995 study, shrimp farms have consumed 178,071 hectares, or 53 per cent, of the mangrove forests in Ecuador's coastal ecosystem (Earth Summit Watch 1997).

Honduras has also experienced environmental devastation as a result of the activities of the shrimp industry. Varela provides figures which illustrate the rapid increase in mangrove destruction as a result of the construction of shrimp ponds, which covered 80 hectares in 1973 and 16,000 hectares in 1998 (Varela 2001: 15; see also Rodriguez 2001).

Once a land concession is granted, investors treat the holdings as their private property, despite the fact that concessions only confer use rights. As a result, access to coastal wetlands, traditionally used by local communities for fishing, has been closed off with fences, mezquite (a thorny plant) and barbed wire (Varela et al. 2001). Armed guards, employed by the shrimp corporations to patrol the shrimp ponds, have been implicated in the murder and torture of members of local communities protesting against the expansion of the shrimp industry. In Champerico, Guatemala, in 2001, a demonstration outside a shrimp farm 'ended with serious confrontations, during which Pernardo Chiyoc died and seven people received bullet wounds from security guards and other Camarsa employees' (World Rainforest Movement 2001e).

More than a million people directly rely on the resources of the Gulf of Fonseca for their survival. These 'coastal wetlands made up of mangrove forests, lagoons, and estuaries contain a wide array of biological resources that satisfies the need for food, income, shelter and economic well-being' (Varela 2001: 156). The effects of loss of access to this area are devastating. Martinez-Alier quotes an Ecuadorian woman explaining the consequences of the expansion of the shrimp industry:

> ... if the mangroves disappear, a whole people disappears, we all disappear ... I do not know what will happen to us if the mangroves disappear, we shall eat garbage in the outskirts of the city of Esmeraldas or in Guayaquil, we shall become prostitutes, I do not know what will happen to us if the mangroves disappear ... We think, if the *camaroneros* [owners of the shrimp farms] who are not the rightful owners nevertheless now prevent us and the *carboneros* [charcoal makers] from getting through the lands they have taken ... shouting and shooting at us, what will happen next, when the government gives them the lands, will they put up big 'Private Property' signs, will they even kill us with the blessing of the President? (cited in Martinez-Alier 2003)

In Nigeria, there has been a similar pattern of forced displacement, environmental devastation and serious human rights abuses committed by the security forces – both state and 'private' – in the interests of the oil industry.

The 'Parabe Platform' incident provides an instructive corporate example of state collusion in the commission of serious human rights abuses:

> In May 1998, two youths were killed on Chevron's Parabe Platform, off Ondo State, by members of the security forces *transported to the Platform by Chevron* to remove two hundred protesters who had closed down production. The protesters had demanded compensation for environmental damage caused by canals cut for Chevron which opened local waterways to the sea. (Human Rights Watch 1999d: Ch. I, our emphasis)

The security forces were transported to the platform in three helicopters, and shot at the protesters, killing two, even before the helicopters had landed.

Bola Oyimbo, a leader of the anti-Chevron protests arrested and tortured by Nigerian authorities, claims that while in custody he was told by a soldier involved in the platform incident that Chevron paid the Nigerian state. He reported, 'When they brought us to the naval base, the Chevron representative handed them their money and actually there was a row between them ... [because] that was not the amount they had agreed on' (Knight 2000).

The Parabe incident is not an isolated occurrence, nor is it the most severe instance of state-corporate repression in Nigeria. In 1990, state action against a protest occurring outside Shell facilities in Rivers State resulted in the murder of 80 unarmed protesters, and the destruction of 495 houses by the police (Human Rights Watch 1999d: Ch. VII). In 1998,

> ... following a major Mobil oil spill in January ... up to three hundred people who demanded compensation were reportedly detained; in July, further protests over damage done by the spill and delays in compensation payments led to disturbances in which eleven people were reportedly shot dead by police. (Human Rights Watch 1999d: Ch. VII)

In 1998 and early 1999, a military crackdown in Bayelsa and Delta States led to the deaths of up to one hundred people. In a separate incident in 1999, around one hundred soldiers attacked two communities using a helicopter and boats commandeered from a facility operated by Chevron. The attack followed an alleged confrontation that took place at a nearby Chevron drilling rig. It is estimated that fifty people may have died in this incident, which some of the villagers believe 'was aimed to clear away the village and allow the pipeline to continue along the most convenient line for Chevron' (Human Rights Watch 1999d, Ch. I).

In addition to the gross human rights violations committed by the security forces, the rights of the communities of the oil-producing regions are violated as a result of the environmental damage caused by oil-mining operations, which has caused deaths, severe illness and economic hardship for many Nigerian communities. Following the major Texaco spill of 1980, for example, it was reported that 180 people died in one community alone as a result of the consequent contamination of water supplies. According to Human Rights Watch, even 'a relatively minor oil spill' can wipe out a family's food supply and livelihood for a year (1999d: Ch. V).

East Timor provides one of the many examples of the connection between state-corporate collusion to export weapons, and the human rights violations resulting from their use. In the 1970s, US Bronco and Skyhawk aircraft were deployed in an offensive which 'involved saturation bombing ahead of advances of ground forces, the use of defoliants to deny cover to Fretilin forces, and the use of chemicals to kill crops and livestock' (Phythian 2000b: 165). In April 1978, the British government first sold BAe Hawk aircraft to Indonesia, which were then used frequently in East Timor. The East Timorese leader Jose Ramos-Horta declared:

'I want to make it clear that Hawk ground attack/"trainer" aircraft fitted with missiles have been used in East Timor regularly since 1983 ... The cease-fire was unilaterally broken by the Indonesians who thought that they could wipe out the resistance with the new aircraft they acquired.' (quoted by Phythian 2000b: 165)

The Indonesian occupation of East Timor, armed and secured for 25 years by Britain and the United States, resulted in the deaths of 200,000 East Timorese, representing a quarter to a third of the overall population (Jardine 1995). Chomsky argues that this represents 'perhaps the greatest death toll relative to population since the Holocaust' (Chomsky 1994: 7).[2] This is one of many examples of the massive human rights violations committed using US and British weapons, including the murder of some 300,000 members of the Kurdish population by the Turkish government using BAe military equipment exported by Britain (Human Rights Watch 1994b).

DEVIANCE

Does the behaviour of the states and corporations involved in our three case studies amount to 'deviance', in the sense defined in Chapter 1? We would argue that it does, for the following reasons. First, all three case studies have involved the breach of multiple institutionalised rules. In Latin America and Nigeria, the relevant state-corporate actions were manifestly illegal, in breach of environmental and human rights laws (Martinez-Alier 2003; Varela 2001; Human Rights Watch 1999c). In the US and British arms trade, the deviant state-corporate actions range along a continuum, with clear illegality at one end, and breach of a more nebulous ethical rule at the other, with what Ruggiero (1996b: 11) describes as 'grey' arms transfers in between.

According to Ruggiero, the arms trade descends into illegality in a number of respects:

The illegality may reside in the quality and quantity of arms produced, which are subject to international restrictions and regulations. Frequently, inspectors in charge of monitoring these aspects of the arms industry are part of an international elite which is closely associated with manufacturers and may, therefore, be exposed to corruption. The illegality may reside in the false claim regarding the country for which the arms are destined. Finally, illegal practices may be adopted by financial institutions through which payments for illegal sales are processed. These institutions conceal the identity of purchasers and sellers along with the sums involved. (Ruggiero 1996b: 9–10)

At the other end of the spectrum are those arms transfers that are not illegal *per se*, but breach the moral rules to which governments profess to subscribe. For example, the continuing British arms exports to Indonesia breach the 'ethical foreign policy' institutionalised by the Labour government. Shortly after coming to power the then Foreign Secretary, Robin Cook, promised that 'Britain will refuse to supply the equipment and weapons with which regimes deny the demands of their peoples for human rights' and reaffirmed 'Labour's policy commitment that we will not supply equipment or weapons that might be used for internal repression' (Cook 1997). To breach a solemn and public promise is clearly a deviant act (even for a politician). Even before 1997, British governments had some notional commitment to human rights, which was inconsistent with complicity in genocide.

In between outright illegality and the 'legal' breach of ethical rules are those deviant actions which 'are neither entirely legal nor entirely illegal' (Karp 1996: 12). The controversial export of dual-use machine tools by the UK company Matrix Churchill to Iraq in 1988–89 can be argued to fit within this hinterland of dubious legality. Ruggiero describes this hinterland as a 'grey market' representing 'policy in flux, as exporting and importing countries experiment with new diplomatic links' (Ruggiero 1996b: 12). The advantages for deviant trade with countries operating under embargoes is obvious, but the clandestine nature of the 'grey' limits the volume and nature of the trade. The Matrix Churchill affair was certainly an example of covert government action. The Scott Inquiry into the affair uncovered 'a pervasive culture of secrecy on the part of the Government and a deep-seated unwillingness to reveal what it knew to either the public or Parliament' (Norton-Taylor et al. 1996: 64). In this instance, government ministers relied on public interest immunities to prevent investigation into the government's encouragement of the export of war supplies to Iraq. Another technique of concealing deviant acts is the use of commercial confidentiality, which is frequently cited by government officials as an excuse for secrecy (Campaign Against the Arms Trade 1991).

The covert nature of British and American arms exports to embargoed regimes provides a further reason to regard them as deviant. Both governments have at various points in recent history adopted elaborate measures to conceal or deny their involvement in supporting violent regimes. In relation to East Timor, Pilger reports:

> In December 1975, after US Secretary of State Henry Kissinger returned from Jakarta, having given Suharto the green light to invade East Timor, he called his staff together and discussed *how a congressional ban on arms to Indonesia could be circumvented*. 'Can't we just construe a

communist government [in East Timor] as self-defence?' he asked. Told this would not work, Kissinger gave orders that he wanted arms shipments *secretly* 'started again in January' ... Robin Cook continued to lay claim to the title of Britain's most discredited politician with his statement that for two years no government 'has done more for East Timor' and 'arms sales have all but vanished'. As he spoke, three Hawk fighters were approved for their onward journey from Bangkok to Jakarta. (Pilger 1999, our emphasis)

Becoming 'Britain's most discredited politician' was, we presume, a significant sanction from Cook's point of view.

The actions of all three industries examined have been labelled as deviant by both national and international civil society organisations, which have attempted to institute sanctions against the relevant states and corporations ranging from public shaming and consumer boycotts to direct action and sabotage of corporate installations. A resistance movement founded in 1988 by poor people living on the Gulf of Fonseca coast has received support from a global network, including 'the public, press, and international organizations of environmental and social activists' (Varela et al. 2001: 30). Similar grassroots movements exist in Mexico and Ecuador (World Rainforest Movement 2001c; 2001i). The establishment of the Mangrove Action Project represents a significant advancement of the movement against the shrimp industry, linking 400 organisations and 300 individuals in more than 60 countries (Stonich and Bailey 2000). Similar organisations have emerged in Nigeria, receiving worldwide support in condemning the actions of the Nigerian oil industry (Sierra Club n.d.). Numerous national and international civil society organisations have condemned US and British arms transfers to regimes that employ the arms to violate the human rights of citizens, including Campaign Against the Arms Trade, Amnesty International and Human Rights Watch, as well as pressure groups that focus on individual countries, such as the East Timor Action Network (ETAN).

THE ROLE OF INDIVIDUALS

It is clear that close personal connections between state and corporate actors motivate and facilitate many instances of state-corporate deviance. In Latin America, the shrimp farms charged with directly committing the most serious human rights abuses against the local communities employ poorly paid workers who are brought in from other regions where they would be unlikely to find employment. Thus, shrimp farm employees generally have no attachment to the local community living in the vicinity of the shrimp farm, and are not required to act against their own communities (Cissna 1997).

In some instances it is difficult to distinguish between the state and the corporation in identifying the individual government officials who are implicated in the crimes of the shrimp industry:

> [In] Honduras, Ecuador, and elsewhere, a duality of interests often pervades the shrimp industry – government officials mandated to oversee the industry also are shrimp farmers, processors and exporters, with personal political and economic interests. (Stonich and Bailey 2000: 23–36)

Further, corruption is endemic among the relevant government officials, and government agents depend on industry kickbacks as a source of income or use their position to secure their own business in the shrimp industry (Meltzoff and LiPuma 1996: 366). Accion Ecologia in a submission to the Shrimp Tribunal in 1996 reported:

> Shrimp farmers often avoid the official zoning rules for shrimp ponds by bribing government officials, often at rates of up to $100 a hectare, and/or including a government official or public servant in their business venture who will smooth the political process of obtaining permits for the construction of shrimp ponds.[3]

In Ecuador, according to Meltzoff and LiPuma, obtaining the 'free' concession can itself be a costly and time-consuming process requiring a set of authorisations from a range of government agencies. The applicant's social position or rank is highly influential in determining the success of the application. In normal circumstances, and depending on personal connections, approval takes between one and three years:

> ... the key to quick approval can be a series of unofficial payments given to members of the various government agencies. These payments vary depending on the size of the concession sought, time coordinates, and the applicant's negotiating skills. Total unofficial payments (i.e., cash, gifts, tips, and services) of US$10,000 are by no means unusual for a 100-hectare concession ... For government officials seeking concessions, the government end of the process is quicker and less costly. This is especially true for ranking members of those ministries that oversee natural resources, almost all of whom have become shrimp pond owners. (Meltzoff and LiPuma 1996: 366)

A similar pattern of individual investment and corruption in the oil industry is evident in Nigeria (Human Rights Watch 1999c, 1999d).

The close individual connections between state actors and players within weapons corporations provide some explanation for the occurrence of state-corporate crime in this arena. For example, the corporation implicated in selling weapons to Iran and supplying the Nicaraguan Contras in the Iran–Contra affair, GeoMiliTech Consultations Corporation (GMT), was established and presided over by Barbara F. Studley who for many years previously had worked as a political lobbyist, chiefly for the Pentagon. The executive vice-president, two vice-presidents, the secretary-treasurer and the four consultants that constituted the remainder of GMT all had strong links to the US or Israeli states, or both. Block describes GeoMiliTech as 'a half-way house for spies, both official and self-selected, situated on a magical highway running between Tel Aviv and Washington, Lisbon and Tehran' (Block 1997: 66). Similarly, the identification of the individuals in control of TDG, owner of Matrix Churchill, is instructive in understanding how the company came to commit the 'grey' criminal acts it did. According to the Campaign Against the Arms Trade, TDG was bought by the Al Arabi trading company of Baghdad in 1987. The company's Iraqi directors claim to have no connection with the Iraqi regime but three of them, Fadel Jawad Kadhum, Dr Safa Habod and Hana Jon, were claimed to be senior officials in the Nassr State Enterprise for Mechanical Industries, an adjunct of Iraq's Ministry of Industry and Military Planning (Campaign Against the Arms Trade 1991).

INSTITUTIONAL FRAMEWORKS FOR STATE-CORPORATE CRIME

The 'duality of interests' in the Latin American shrimp industry does not only operate on an individual level, it determines the organisational goals of the regulatory institutions. Melzoff argues that a 'defining feature' of Ecuadorian mariculture is the duality of interests maintained by both government appointees and elected officials:

> They are shrimp producers and exporters, and simultaneously members of the regulatory agencies … Under these conditions, there is every reason to suppose that planning and regulatory members will (1) seek to advance their own institutional and personal aims; (2) translate these aims into policy objectives; (3) measure any proposed policy on the basis of how it serves their priorities; and (4) support a national policy on the same basis. (Meltzoff and LiPuma 1996: 366–7)

Similarly, in Nigeria corruption among government officials is so endemic as to be accurately described as institutionalised. Further, brutal and repressive policing tactics are institutionalised among the state security services out of which the special task forces (described above) for the oil-producing areas have been created (Human Rights Watch 1999d: Ch. 1).

An institutional feature of the British government's control over the export of arms is a lack of Parliamentary power and oversight. The Import, Export and Customs Powers (Defence) Act of 1938 delineates the power of government to control the export of arms and other related equipment and authorises the Department of Trade and Industry (DTI) to order 'such provisions as it thinks expedient' in the regulation of trade. As a consequence, Phythian argues, 'Parliament has had no input into the decisions on the imposition, duration or lifting of arms embargoes' (Phythian 2000a: 48). The DTI is said to form an 'axis' with the Ministry of Defence (MoD) who together 'battle for the defence industry' against the Foreign Office (MacAskill 2000). Lack of Parliamentary scrutiny no doubt allows a tighter confluence of interests to be brought into play when making export decisions, by narrowing the circle of potential opponents and restricting the flow of information.

British government agencies also display a performance emphasis on the goal of maintaining the reputation of the British arms industry as a reliable provider of weapons among arms-buying countries (MacAskill 2000). This performance emphasis propels government officials to continue deviant acts under pressure from the arms industry, even where such acts might be contrary to immediate economic or foreign policy interests.

POLITICAL ECONOMY

The broader political-economic framework mediates the relationship between states and corporation, and thus influences both the individual circumstances of those implicated in perpetrating state-corporate crime, as well as the development of institutional frameworks.

Central to many examples of state facilitation and state instigation of corporate crime in the developing world is debt. As David Barnhizer has suggested, 'the debt service obligation almost compels governments to look the other way when foreign and domestic investors offer some hope of increasing economic development and hard currency earnings from foreign trade' (2001: 146–7).

The shrimp industry in Latin America was promoted by overseas development agencies such as USAID and international institutions such as the World Bank and the Asian Development Bank from the early 1980s, in response to what were perceived as deteriorating social and economic conditions, namely the Sandinista revolution in Nicaragua, civil wars in El Salvador and Guatemala, and the militarisation of Honduras. In 1994, the 'Caribbean Basin Initiative' was implemented, with the goal of establishing 'regional stability through economic growth stimulated by domestic and foreign investment. Agricultural diversification through the promotion of a new set of "non-traditional" exports was the foundation of this scheme.' Shrimp aquaculture has been crucial to the realisation of this scheme (Stonich 1991: 729).

As such, shrimp aquaculture has been financed by international and national agencies including the US Agency for International Development (USAID), the European Commission (EC) and the Canadian International Development Agency (CIDA). The World Bank financed the initial farms in Guatemala (Gonzalez 2001) and continues to finance farms in Latin America, amounting to loans of $82 million (Rodriquez 2001). In 1999, 'the International Finance Corporation (IFC) – private sector branch of the World Bank – granted a $US 6 million loan to SBMF [San Bernardo Marine Farms], where U.S. investors hold majority shares' (World Rainforest Movement: 2001h).

Susan George (1992: 3) argues that the 'export-led growth model, on which the [International Monetary] Fund and the World Bank insist, is a purely extractive one involving more the "mining" than the management – much less the conservation – of resources'. Both George and Varela associate this model with the accumulation of wealth for the elite to the detriment of the poor. Varela (2001: 157) argues that

> ... international financial organizations, international aid agencies that seek to stimulate economic development, and organizations concerned with the issues of food security tend to work with the national elites of developing countries to enrich them. They also tend to support the production of cheap food for export and the generation of high incomes for investors from the developed countries.

Similarly, George (1992: 3) explains that export-oriented growth

> ... encourages not only industrial-scale agriculture but also the granting of huge timber licenses and mining concessions, geared to short-term profit ... Such concentration of wealth and advantage in few hands leads directly to disregard for the environment, as it leads to poverty and marginalization for the majority.

States accept the export model as it is presented as the only possible means of generating foreign exchange to finance debt. Like the states of Latin

America, Nigeria has attempted to service its debt through exports, 90 per cent of which are provided by the oil industry, which also provides 80 per cent of foreign revenue (Human Rights Watch 1999a: Ch. I). The IFC and other agencies have supported this process through financing the oil industry, and continue to do so (see, for example, Sustainable Energy and Ecology Network 2001).

The US and British arms trade, rather than being at the mercy of the global political economy, plays a significant role in setting the political and economic agenda. This will be discussed in greater detail, under 'Motivation', below.

MOTIVATION

The first 'catalyst for action' in Kramer's explanatory framework 'is the emphasis on goal attainment' (Kramer 1992: 217). In Latin America, pressure for goal attainment derives very directly from the political economy: state institutions are strongly motivated to increase exports in order to obtain foreign exchange to finance debt. In both Nigeria and Latin America, the desire to generate foreign exchange at an institutional level coincides with the desire of individual government officials and corporate elites to extract a personal profit from the shrimp or oil industry.

There is some debate in the academic literature regarding the motivations of states in facilitating or initiating the crimes of corporations in the arms trade. As Phythian has argued, it is difficult to find a rational explanation for Britain's high-profile involvement in the arms trade. Defence economists see weapons exports as relatively unprofitable and justify the trade in terms of military security; political analysts on the other hand are generally sceptical of security justifications and point to the economic advantages. The dominant official justification for Britain's more problematic arms sales relationships has been the number of jobs reliant on the industry. This justification (and any other economic rationale proffered, such as absorbing some of the costs for domestic weapons production) is underpinned by

... Britain's desire to afford and maintain an independent defence capacity sufficient for the country to continue to play a global role which allows for the pursuit of British interests, the assumption of a leading role in various defence groupings, and the basis to justify Britain's continued occupancy of one of the five permanent seats on the UN Security Council. (Phythian 2000b: 32)

As Norton-Taylor and Gow (2000) put it, arms sales are perceived as helping Britain to 'punch above its weight'.

Ruggiero attributes the centrality of arms production to its simultaneous role as both 'an instrument of economic development for the manufacturing countries and an instrument of foreign policy for their governments' (1996b: 14). This is clearly evident with regard to, for example, arms transfers to Indonesia. The stated goal of the United States government was to maintain control of the region to promote US investment, while the British government declared that 'seen from here it is in Britain's interests that Indonesia should absorb the territory as soon and as unobtrusively as possible' (Barbedo de Magalhaes 1992: 14). Phythian argues, however, that with the demise of the Cold War there has been a significant de-politicisation of the arms trade. Profit considerations have now largely replaced foreign policy as the motivation driving the illicit trade in armaments (2000c: 1). Gabelnick and Rich (2000) concur with this assessment in evaluating US arms exports.

The catalytic motivations of corporations in the arms trade support Matthews and Kauzlarich's assessment that the goal of capital accumulation is frequently a 'highly criminogenic force' (2000). For example, arming the Iraqi regime was a highly lucrative venture for British corporations such as Matrix Churchill, who became dependent on the capital accumulated through exports to Iraq. According to the Campaign Against the Arms Trade (1991), 'Matrix Churchill ... was able to return a profit of 2.4 million pounds in the 1988/9 financial year instead of making the loss it had done for the previous ten years.'

OPPORTUNITY STRUCTURE

As we have seen, both individuals with a 'duality of interest' and governments concerned to pay off debt are strongly motivated to expand shrimp aquaculture in Latin America. This, in turn, further requires the construction of shrimp ponds on appropriate land. The legitimate means to do this are scarce.

Shrimp farming can be developed on mangroves, salt flats and agricultural land. However, to be profitable, shrimp ponds ideally need to be located below the high-water mark (Meltzoff and LiPuma 1996: 362). Once the most readily available, suitable land had been used, the shrimp-farming companies were impelled to maximise their potential profit by clear-cutting mangroves to construct shrimp ponds. This illegitimate means of meeting the goal of capital accumulation was rendered a favourable alternative to legitimate means through corruption, lax government environmental regulation and free government concessions (Earth Summit Watch 1997).

Restrictions on legitimate means for governments and corporations to achieve their organisational goals have been a key factor behind the illegal arms trade. As Phythian notes:

> [The] demand for arms through illicit channels at a state level is a consequence of the application of either embargoes or restrictions on the flow of certain categories of equipment to target states ... Embargoes are the life-blood of the illicit arms trade. (2000c: 2, 20)

With legitimate means blocked, these states and the conflicting factions within them are propelled into the illicit arms market to purchase weapons.

LACK OF CONTROL

In his study of the *Challenger* Space Shuttle disaster Ronald Kramer concluded that a lack of control and enforcement mechanisms leads to the 'erosion of norms supporting the use of legitimate means to accomplish organizational goals' (Kramer 1992: 237). The corollary of this process is the promotion of what Matthews and Kauzlarich have termed the 'normalization of deviance' (2000: 294). The failure of the state to appropriately regulate corporate actions is an outstanding feature of the three case studies examined.

Immunity for criminal acts committed by corporations is, as discussed above, pervasive in the Latin American shrimp industry. This is even admitted by government officials, such as the Undersecretary for Fisheries for the Government of Ecuador, who stated that there 'has not been a correct process in following these complaints about illegal activity ... Many of these complaints have "rested in peace", after they have been received, that is true' (Icaza 1997).

The government agencies charged with overseeing the shrimp industry have confused and overlapping jurisdictions. According to Stonich:

> The lack of unclouded demarcations of agency responsibilities has led to dissension and confrontation. Concessions are often granted without taking into consideration environmental suitability, the competence of the applicant, or even whether the current request overlaps with previous concessions. (1991: 742)

More insidiously, as we have already shown, control structures that do exist are frequently influenced by the shrimp industry itself. The Camara, a private industry group in Ecuador, funds the Fundacion Natura, which receives and investigates complaints of illegal shrimp industry activity (Earth Summit Watch 1997).

Compounding these regulatory and enforcement failures are singularly inadequate environmental assessment procedures. In Mexico, for example, the National Ecology Institute (INE) approves or rejects construction based on an environmental impact assessment which is normally prepared by consultants contracted by those proposing the shrimp-farm construction. As such the process is open to corruption (Cruz-Torres 2000). In addition, further evidence suggests that environmental impact statements operate to a standard format incapable of acknowledging geographical particularities central to determining appropriate sites.

Similarly in Nigeria, environmental control mechanisms are rarely enforced against the oil industry, and the government agencies charged with regulation lack clear mandates, allowing government officials to avoid taking responsibility for controlling deviant corporate activity. As one study concluded:

> Most state and local government institutions involved in environmental resource management lack funding, trained staff, technical expertise, adequate information, analytical capability and other pre-requisites for implementing comprehensive policies and programmes. In the case of the oil industry, overlapping mandates and jurisdiction between [two agencies] frequently contribute to counterproductive competition. (Human Rights Watch 1999d: Ch. V)

The Nigerian government 'effectively entrusts the ... companies themselves to provide the facts on such matters as land claims and valuation, environmental impact assessments, agreed terms of compensation for property and labour, assessment of sabotage, and damage claims' and appears to exercise little effective scrutiny over such assessments (ibid., Ch. 9).

Both the US and British government agencies charged with controlling the arms trade operate according to a widely divergent set of conflicting interests. According to Phythian, Britain's Department of Trade and Industry is charged with export control yet, 'its raison d'etre is export promotion, resulting in a conflict of loyalties, the resolution of which, recent history suggests, tends to favour exports over constraint' (2000c: 53). Gabelnick and Rich describe a parallel situation in the US where the conflict of interest is even more pronounced and the Pentagon has effectively become 'an advocate for U.S companies interested in exporting arms' (2000: 38).

As in the Nigerian oil industry, government agencies overseeing export applications from weapons corporations in Britain and the US appear to produce extremely high rates of corporate export application approval, suggesting a disturbing lack of adequate control. Pilger reports that in Britain 'Fewer than one percent of applications were turned down between August 1997 and August 1998' (1999).

A particular feature of the British failure to institute appropriate control mechanisms is the failure to control arms exports by corporations in Crown dependencies, allowing British corporations to export arms at will, despite embargoes. This occurred in 1994, when Mil-Tec Corporation Ltd, a 'British company registered in the Isle of Man, ... whose directors operated from the Channel Island of Sark', exported over US$5.5 million worth of arms to the genocidal Hutu regime in Rwanda (Phythian 2000b: 22).

CONCLUSION

The close parallels between the three seemingly disparate case studies in this chapter indicate that the approach developed by state-corporate crime scholars is a significant advance towards developing 'a powerful integrated theoretical model' (Kramer 1992: 216), and can easily be synthesised with our own framework for analysing state crime. At each level of analysis, potentially criminogenic factors can be identified, many of which overlap across time and conditions. Similarly, the catalysts for deviant state-corporate behaviour are remarkably comparable across the three case studies. In particular, the specific factors associated with lack of control, such as conflicts of interest and undue industry influence within those government bodies charged with overseeing the industry, are evident in all three case studies.

Together, states and corporations are responsible for the vast majority of the human rights violations inflicted on citizens throughout the world. The corporations that inflict human rights atrocities against citizens may be afforded immunity by the states in which they operate. By identifying their behaviour as criminal, and locating the deviant role of the state in supporting this behaviour, the potential arises for civil society to impose informal sanctions (at the very least) on those agencies that are criminally responsible for so much human suffering and environmental degradation.

4
Natural Disaster as State Crime[1]

This earthquake is a declaration of bankruptcy for the Turkish political administrative structure. The Turkish political and administrative systems must be investigated from the ground up.

(Erkan Mumcu, Cabinet Minister, August 1999)[2]

Now is not the time for bringing infrastructural problems to the agenda. Now is not the time for blame.

(Suleyman Demirel, Turkish president, 20 August 1999)[3]

Constructing 'natural' disasters as state crime requires, at first glance, a considerable leap of the imagination. Earthquakes, tsunamis, volcanoes, cyclones, hurricanes and floods are elemental: they are so clearly the manifestations of geophysical activity that it seems beyond the bounds of reason to suggest that they and their consequences could be labelled as state crime. But the consequences and sometimes the precipitants of these geophysical 'extremes' are necessarily the products of social interactions with the environment.

The idea of state responsibility for natural disasters is not entirely new. The work of a small group of radical ecologists and geographers identifies state structures as the root cause of what the United Nations now euphemistically describe as 'complex emergencies'. But we are suggesting that in a great many natural disasters the state is in fact directly culpable through a series of criminal actions and negligent practices. We are arguing that a less distant relationship between underlying structural causes and natural disasters exists in many catastrophic floods, famines, earthquakes, cyclones, and so on.

Without the presence of nearby human settlements, the impact of disasters would largely be limited to an ecological disruption. It is the presence of human life and organisation and their interaction with the physical world which introduces the concept of 'vulnerability to calamity'. As Coburn and Spence observe, 'earthquakes themselves are only natural energy releases. An earthquake will not be a disaster unless it strikes a populated area' (1992: 1).

Natural disasters are, however, distinguished from the rest of human–environment relations: they are unscheduled, disorganised – a rupture in the fabric of productive and orderly human–habitat relations (Hewitt 1983).

The dominant understanding and conventional representation of disaster embodies a sharp distinction between the geophysical event and the calamity that ensues.

In the preface to his book on natural hazards or 'calamities' geographer Keith Hewitt has argued that 'a narrow focus upon "the hazard" as an occasion of natural extremes, and upon the loss, crisis relief and rehabilitation in disasters can mislead us as to the decisive human ingredients of natural hazards' (1983: viii). It is these 'decisive human ingredients of natural hazards' with which this chapter is concerned.

The chapter will first explore definitions of natural disasters, their scale and form and then consider their relevance to the discipline of criminology. In order to understand 'natural disasters' within a state crime framework the issues of population vulnerability, human rights, ecology, political economy and state formation will all be examined. Two case studies are employed to highlight the relationship between states and natural disasters: famine (because there is an enormous extant literature within the social sciences which already suggests famine as a consequence of state crime), and earthquake – specifically the 1999 Kocaeli earthquake in the Marmara region of Turkey which has been the research focus for one of the authors for the past two years.

Kai Erikson's (1979) study of a West Virginian mining community's response to a devastating flood is the only natural disaster study we are aware of, which has captured the interest of criminology. This marvellous ethnography of a community's response to the impact of disaster does not, however, address the questions which primarily concern us in this volume.

The role of states in natural disasters has not immediately lent itself to criminological analysis. This may be a product of the relatively parochial nature of the discipline and its emphasis on domestic questions of criminal justice. However, a review of the disasters literature causally suggests a catalogue of state crimes. In order to pursue this line of analysis we must first isolate the social, political and economic factors that conspire to play such a crucial role in the manifestation of natural disasters.

DEFINITION

Natural disasters are to be distinguished from those disasters that are the product of direct human intervention, that is, disasters where geophysical extremes do not form part of the catastrophe equation (for example, the Union Carbide chemical leak in Bhopal, India; the nuclear disaster in Chernobyl; the Southall, Clapham and Paddington rail disasters in the UK; the Hillsborough football stadium crush; the Piper Alpha oil rig fires and so on). Though these disasters are undoubtedly the result of human intervention, determining the nature of that intervention and ultimately of responsibility has been a site of contestation to which critical criminology has made a major contribution (Carson 1970; Cassels 1993; Mokhiber and Weissman 1999; Scraton 1999).

The kind of natural disasters which we are concerned with here, as criminologists, are those for which responsibility (in terms of deaths, injuries – 'life-safety' – and destruction of the built environment) can be traced, in some significant degree, to the state but which at face value are more easily attributed to natural causes.

Relief operations following 'natural disasters' have played a crucial role, not only in responding to disaster but also in shaping and constructing a particular view of disasters which has come to define them in the public consciousness. Understanding begins with the event itself and ends with the rescue operation and the humanitarian aid and relief which it tends to elicit. The precipitating context is lost beneath rubble, ash, water, mud or lava.

The role of states in fashioning disaster is underplayed as the state's role in response and relief becomes a more significant standard against which a government may be measured (so criticism was directed at the Turkish state and military for not responding quickly to the earthquake emergency rather than to their role in creating the conditions of the disaster).

Disasters are thus often effectively de-politicised, understood and represented in terms of geophysical extremes and reconstructed as essentially relief operations. But as Alex de Waal makes clear in his important work on famine (1997), relief is merely a footnote or endnote to a disaster. The dominance of relief impresses more urgently, we believe, the need for a political criminology of natural disasters which confronts issues of culpability, blame, responsibility and regulation. Staying with de Waal's metaphor, the decisive stage for the scholar of state crime must be not the endnote but the preface, that is, that set of political and organisational conditions which give rise to policies and practices which jeopardise the security and safety of citizens and in so doing increases population vulnerability to natural disaster.

Quantification, until quite recently, characterised the definition of disaster. The League of Red Cross Societies, for example, defined disaster as satisfying at least one of the following criteria:

a) at least $1 million in damage,
b) at least 100 dead persons,
c) at least 100 injured persons.

The United Nations classifies disasters on a five-point scale around four types:

a) sudden elemental, prompted by climatic and geophysical forces;
b) the foreseeable, such as famine and epidemic;
c) the deliberate, as with the case of war and civil turmoil;
d) the accidental, resulting from technological mishap.

Some disasters may embody a combination of these types. What we find most interesting is the role not simply of human intervention but of state intervention in precipitating or fostering the first two of these categories.

More sociological definitions have focused on normality and disruption. Cisin and Clark defined disaster as an event (or a series of events) which seriously disrupts normal activities (1962: 263) while Hewitt and Burton (1971) link their definition very much to the continuity between disaster events and everyday life and define disaster as an *extension* of everyday life, an interaction between 'the physical event itself and the state of human society'. Susman et al. (1983) introduced an important political component to the definition when they focused on the notion of vulnerable groups, defining disaster in relation to its victims: 'without people there can be no disaster. And poor people are generally more vulnerable than rich ones. Disaster is therefore defined as the interface between an extreme physical event and a vulnerable human population' (1983: 264). This notion of vulnerability is crucial to our approach to understanding disasters as a form of state crime and plays a central analytical role in the examination of responsibility and culpability.

NATURAL DISASTERS AS STATE CRIMES

Given the working definition underpinning this book, natural disasters constitute state crime when, in addition to violating human rights, those violations result from a form of organisational deviance.

There is little dispute when we examine the victims of earthquakes, famines, cyclones, floods, fires or volcanoes, that basic human needs – on a mass scale in the case of major catastrophe – have been violated. These kinds of catastrophic events result in deprivations of basic human needs: needs for life, for shelter, food, sanitation and so on. But can *rights* be violated by geophysical or climatic extremes? It seems clear that a natural event cannot in itself violate rights, because rights imply correlative duties. A volcano breaches no duty when it erupts. Only voluntary agency in some form can violate rights. The form of agency that concerns us here is organisational deviance.

The types of organisational state deviance which emerge from the literature on natural disasters may be summarised as follows:

- systemic corruption, of the kinds analysed in Chapter 2;
- state-corporate crime, that is, the collusion of governments in illegal and dangerous acts by private corporations;
- the collusion of governments in illegal acts by members of the governing elite itself, for example, illegal deforestation leading to floods, landslides, etc.;
- war crimes as a cause of famine;
- negligence, that is, the gross failure of state agencies to pursue effectively their publicly proclaimed goals, or to follow generally accepted professional standards, for example, in civil engineering. Examples include wilfully ignoring scientific warnings, failing to develop national systems of quality assurance or regulation in industries like construction, failing to install early warning systems (in areas prone to cyclones, hurricanes, etc.) and encouraging or forcing land settlements in hazardous zones;
- post-disaster cover-ups and concealment of evidence, indicating governments' fear of censure if the true consequences of their acts and omissions became known.

Examples of all these forms of organisational deviance will be discussed in the course of this chapter.

SCALE OF THE PHENOMENON – COUNTING DISASTERS

There are clearly major methodological issues when we attempt to calculate the extent and scale of 'natural' disasters. The human and economic costs of natural disasters have increased 'exponentially' in recent decades. According to the United Nations International Strategy For Disaster Reduction (UNISDR) the past 40 years have witnessed a ten-fold increase in economic losses resulting from natural disasters (UN 2002: 1). Data collected and analysed by the reinsurance giant Munich Re suggests that the number of what it classifies as 'great' disasters (that is, disasters which result in deaths and losses so high as to require external assistance) has increased dramatically in the past 50 years, from 20 during the 1950s to 86 during the 1990s. Munich Re also provide evidence which demonstrates that the overall number of natural disasters has also increased – from an average of 650 per year during the 1990s to 850 in 2000 (Munich Re 2001). Yet while there is a continuing debate over climatic change and its impact on hydrometeorological extremes there is no scientific evidence to suggest that geophysical extremes such as earthquakes or volcanic eruptions have increased in either frequency or intensity. What this suggests is that the rising trend in reported disasters is less a product of an increasing number of natural catastrophic events than a product of increasing population vulnerability.

The 1976 Guatemalan earthquake was perhaps the defining moment in focusing attention on the urban and rural poor's vulnerability to natural disaster and exploitation: 22,000 people were killed, almost all from the impoverished rural highlands and dangerous squatter settlements of Guatemala City. The middle classes remained virtually untouched. Such was the 'bias' of this earthquake that it became widely known as a 'class-quake' (Blaikie et al. 1994).

VULNERABILITY

Despite widespread global wealth and the unprecedentedly high real income per head in the world, millions of people die prematurely and abruptly from intermittent famines – and a great many millions more die every year from endemic undernourishment and deprivation. The Bread for the World Institute's report on hunger (2001) revealed that throughout the 1990s 841 million people suffered chronic undernutrition in the developing world while 200 million people were vulnerable to the risk of famine:

> Starvation is the characteristic of some people not *having* enough food to eat. It is not the characteristic of there not *being* enough food to eat. While the latter can be a cause of the former, it is but one of many possible causes. (Sen 1981: 1, original emphasis)

While Sen's contribution to the study of famine has been enormous, his focus on individual entitlements and some of the immediate causes of famine has left the larger structural questions relating to 'entitlement' unanswered. What remains for a fully theorised understanding of famine production is what Watts has described as 'a political economy of entitlement creation and destruction' (2001: 130).

Famine, the literature is clear, is about social dislocation and breakdown, political corruption and abuse, war crimes, the suppression of truth, economic deprivation, policy shifts in relation to food entitlements, restrictions on movement and communication and health crises (Sen 1981; Becker 1996; de Waal 1997; Watts 2001; Davis 2001).

While drought may be a 'trigger', famine can occur without the presence of any 'natural' environmental change or 'trigger'. It takes only a limited development of the theory to locate the primary causes of famine within a state crime analysis and not, as is commonly assumed, in drought.

In his seminal work on the political economy of famine in Africa, Alex de Waal (1997) attributes famine to massively unequal relations of power, the abuse of a range of fundamental human rights such as the right to food, civil and political rights, abuse of the laws of war, and so on. We shall argue that these violations of human rights have been, to a significant extent, the product of organisational deviance by or on behalf of states and state agencies, or what Michael Watts has described as one of the 'crimes of capitalism … the manufacture of hunger and starvation' (2001: 138).

War – through the disruption of food production and distribution, deliberate crop destruction, the commandeering of food for invading armies, blockades of food and populations, the restriction of movement, etc. – is a major cause of famine (Blaikie et al. 1994; de Waal 1997). In an analysis of the 1983–85 Ethiopian famine, de Waal argues that it was in fact a war crime. Concentrating on Tigray and Northern Wollo, he demonstrates that while drought and harvest failure did contribute to the exceptionally severe famine suffered in these regions, the cause of the famine was primarily caused by a counter-insurgency campaign directed at the Tigrayan People's Liberation Front by the Ethiopian army and airforce, and that 'the zone of severe famine coincided with the war zone' (de Waal 1997). The counter-insurgency campaign created famine in a number of very direct ways: military offensives in surplus-producing areas, the bombing of markets in rebel-held territory, trade and individual movement restrictions, forced population relocations and the hijacking and plundering of relief operations. De Waal quotes the acting Foreign Minister at the time, Tibebu Bekele, as publicly revealing that, 'food is a major element in our strategy against the secessionists' (1997: 117).

The increase in deaths, injury, displacement and economic damage that we have seen as a result of natural disasters is a direct consequence of the rise in population vulnerability. According to the World Bank around 97 per cent of natural disaster-related deaths take place in the developing world (World Bank 2000–01: 170). Similarly, in terms of economic loss as a proportion of Gross National Product, developing countries suffer damage far in excess of developed countries (UNDP 2001).

While the UN interprets the increased vulnerability of people who live in the developing world as 'induced by current and human determined paths of development', the reality is that it is states, international organisations such as the World Bank and IMF, and multinational corporations which play the primary role in determining these paths.

There are three fundamental conditions which enhance a population's vulnerability to natural disasters: poverty, corruption and political authoritarianism. These three conditions, often – though not always – combined, emerge throughout the literature on disasters as causally integral to large-scale catastrophe and without question locate natural disasters within the subject frame of criminology.

Poverty

Poverty dramatically increases vulnerability to disaster and without arguing that poverty creation is itself a state crime (although it is tempting) we do want to underscore its centrality in the victimisation of those at risk of natural disaster.

Globalisation has contributed to the vulnerability of those in the poorest and most marginalised countries in the world.

While there has been an unprecedented growth of global finance capital flows (which nevertheless has left the poorest countries on the margins of international finance and reliant on aid flows), the growing networks of trade have not spread evenly across the globe. Instead, there has been a process of regionalisation centred on the core zones of North America, western Europe and South-East Asia; and marginalisation in most of Africa and much of South and Central Asia and Latin America (Ellwood 2001: 33; Harman 1996: 7; Held et al. 1999: 177–82; Hirst and Thompson 1996).

This pattern is replicated in relation to foreign direct investment, which in the developing world has tended to be in countries with a relatively skilled and well-paid workforce.[4] Most of Africa and the poorer parts of the Third World have been bypassed.[5]

As a result, social inequality has increased, and is made worse by recession and the debt crisis. By 1999, Third World debt had reached nearly $3,000 billion, representing approximately $400 per person in the developing world, where average income is less than $1 per day (Ellwood 2001: 48). Between 1960 and 1997, the ratio of the income of the richest fifth of the world's population to that of the poorest fifth increased from 30:1 to 74:1 (Human Development Report 1999: 3).

Mike Davis argues convincingly that linkage to the world economy has made the peasantry of the developing world much more vulnerable to the ravages of flood and drought (2001: 15). This argument can be extended to other natural disasters such as earthquakes, cyclones and landslides. For example, the impact of US banana companies in collusion with regional governments has significantly increased the vulnerability of the poor in Central America. Extensive deforestation of fertile valleys and the development of roads and railways to facilitate banana production and export forced local peasants to cheaper land, often on hill and mountainsides. In order to grow their staple crop of maize, these peasants were forced to clear forests leading to severe soil erosion and ultimately to flooding and landslides in the event of hurricanes and cyclones to which the region is prone.

It is not coincidental that many of the world's most impoverished people live in the most hazardous of environments. In Bogota over 60 per cent of the population live on steep slopes subject to landslide induced by heavy rains and earthquake. In Manila, many of the 35 per cent of the population living in squatter settlements are forced into areas subject to coastal flooding. Many of Asia's most destitute live in slums on hazardous flood plains and a quarter of Kenya's population live in that country's drought-prone 'marginal' lands.

Wealth is a major protection against natural disaster. According to Munich Re's definition of disaster (which importantly does not include famine), almost 561,000 people were killed in natural disasters between 1985 and 1999. Only 4 per cent of those killed were from fully industrialised countries. The remaining 96 per cent of victims lived primarily in Asia (77 per cent), and in South and Central America (14 per cent). These figures become even more skewed when drought and famine are factored in. The Red Cross provides powerful evidence to show that drought and famine accounted for 42 per cent of disaster-related deaths between the years 1991 and 2000 (Red Cross 1999).

Early warning and detection systems, and the implementation of disaster prevention strategies mean that single great catastrophes which may claim the lives of hundreds of thousands of people are infrequent occurrences (Abramovitz 2001). At the same time, however, there has been no equivalent decline in economic loss arising out of disaster, rather, 'economic losses'[6] during the 1990s were more than three times the figure in the 1980s, almost nine times that in the 1960s and more than 15 times that in the 1950s (ibid.). Economic losses have a far more devastating impact on poorer countries where, often uninsured, losses comprise a proportionately much larger share of the national economy. While the most economically advanced countries sustained 57.3 per cent of recorded economic losses, this represents only 2.5 per cent of their GDP. For the poorest countries, which endured 24.4 per cent of the total economic loss for disasters, this meant a huge 13.4 per cent of their GDP.

Moreover, evidence from the *World Disaster Report* reveals that the number of those *affected* by disaster has risen to around 211 million people annually (Red Cross 1999). Again, Asia has been hardest hit with 90 per cent of its total population affected by natural catastrophe.

There is a very clear correlation, then, between poverty and population vulnerability. In developing nations where dependency has been encouraged (often through the transition from subsistence production to cash cropping for multinational corporations), then the ultimate cause of environmental disaster may well be traceable to imbalances between rich and poor countries.

Corruption

According to the *World Disaster Report*, 'Corruption and vested interests in and around government play a large role in many of the long-term precursors to disaster' (Red Cross 1999).

The literature on natural disasters is littered with examples of political corruption and official links with organised crime. In Indonesia the devastating forest fires which swept vast swathes of the country in 1997 and 1998 were started by timber and palm oil plantation owners who deliberately and illegally cleared land with fire to develop their plantations. Almost 10 million hectares were ravaged by the fires and around 20 million people were exposed to harmful smoke-borne pollutants for months. In a scathing indictment of the Suharto regime Barber and Schweithelm (2000) point directly to state criminality as responsible for this 'unprecedented human and ecological disaster':

> The fires of 1997–1998 were the direct and inevitable outcome of forest and land-use policies and practices unleashed by the Suharto regime and perpetuated by a corrupt culture of 'crony capitalism' that elevated personal profit over public interest, the environment or the rule of law. Top Suharto regime officials and their business cronies treated Indonesia's forests as their personal property for more than 30 years, liquidating valuable timber through reckless and destructive logging practices, clear-cutting forests for palm oil and pulp plantations, and running roughshod over the interests of the millions of forest-dependent peoples living in traditional communities throughout the archipelago. (2000: vi)

As we argued in Chapter 2, systemic political and administrative corruption usually results in violations of human rights. One way in which it does so is by aggravating and precipitating natural disasters. Systemic corruption tends to occur in societies where 'normal' political life is characterised by clientelism, patrimonialism and informal exchange relationships.

In the case of the Turkish earthquake, our research (Green et al. 2002) found that clientelistic practices systematically undermined the possibility of compliance with and enforcement of existing (and wholly satisfactory) building standards and regulations, and that the magnitude of the disaster was a function of systematic corrupt practices by state actors in both urban planning and development, local and national government and the construction industry.

On 17 August 1999, at 3.02 a.m., the heavily industrialised Marmara region of Turkey, just south-east of Istanbul, experienced an earthquake of moment magnitude 7.4. The earthquake resulted from a rupture – approximately 125 km long – along the North Anatolian Fault Zone (NAFZ),[7] and killed between 35,000 and 50,000 people.[8] Most were killed when concrete apartment blocks collapsed on their sleeping inhabitants. Official estimates of housing loss are 285,211 residences and 42,902 businesses.[9] A further estimated 200,000 people were made homeless, and losses to Turkish industry were estimated to be around US$3.5 billion.[10]

Turkey lies over one of the most seismically active regions in the world. Ninety-five per cent of Turkey's surface area is at first or second-degree risk of earthquakes, an area which is home to 98 per cent of its industry, and 92 per cent of its population. According to Andrew Coburn, 'On average a damaging earthquake occurs somewhere in Turkey once every nine months' (1995: 66). The probability of a large earthquake occurring in or near Istanbul (in the Yalova, Izmit, Princes' Islands, or central Marmara regions) in the next 30 years is now estimated to be 62 per cent (Parsons et al. 2000).[11]

Rapid industrialisation and the attendant jobs it created along the fault zone attracted millions of migrants fleeing repression and poverty in southeastern Turkey and led to significant housing shortages in the region. Much of the demand for housing new immigrant workers was met by the construction of *illegal* three to six-storey reinforced concrete buildings with hollow clay tile infill walls.[12] Thousands of these buildings were to collapse. The buildings most likely to collapse or to be damaged were buildings of four storeys or higher.[13] Another distinguishing feature of collapsed buildings was that proportionally, the newest of the buildings were the most likely to collapse, indicating deterioration in quality across time.[14]

An extensive review of the findings of international engineering research teams established that the scale of destruction could be attributed to a lack of adequate engineering, a lack of industry inspection and quality assurance and a lack of discipline on the part of the state authorities. The very heavy damage suffered in Adapazari, Izmit, Yalova and other areas could be attributed to soil profiles:[15] loose silt and sand layers, soft organic clay layers which turn to liquid in earthquake conditions; the weakening effects of the removal of walls in many buildings; the poor-quality cement used; inadequate reinforcing members and the proximity of building structures to the Izmit Bay shore (EEFIT 1999; MCEER 1999; EERI 1999).

In the immediate aftermath of this earthquake responsibility for the disaster was placed on individual building developers and contractors who allegedly cut corners, used poor-quality building materials, failed to employ soil and other safety checks and ignored earthquake-proofing regulations. The government and mainstream nationalist media were central in the attribution of this blame. But there is little evidence to support this as a central explanation of causality. Rather Green and colleagues (Abbas Al Hussaini and Christina Curry) found that a combination of political, legal and human rights abuse was the most significant factor contributing to the destruction of the region.

Following the 1980 military coup d'état in Turkey the government of Turgut Özal introduced the liberalisation and globalisation of the Turkish economy. As part of this process public lands were made increasingly available for privatisation. Hundreds of restrictive rules and regulations were repealed and Turkish entrepreneurs were encouraged to ignore those that remained. Many such capital-poor entrepreneurs established construction companies relying on the help of friends in local politics to win contracts.

Enterprising firms and individuals were effectively encouraged to build on undeveloped public land. These illegal housing developments would then acquire legitimacy on the eve of elections when the passing of construction amnesties could be virtually guaranteed. Vast unlicensed housing developments were then legitimately sold to individuals or companies.

It is estimated that 65 per cent of housing in Istanbul, a city of 12 million people, is *kaçak* (unlicensed).[16] Illegal building and illegal housing have flourished as a direct result of state policy and practice and, given that at least 60 per cent of land in Turkey is state-owned and the majority of illegal housing has been built on state land, responsibility for the consequences arising from natural disasters in these settlements must lie with the state.

The institution of the building or construction amnesty is perhaps the most pernicious state collusion with corrupt practice – a cynical and populist device which effectively acts as the 'legitimisation of corruption'. Despite strong opposition from professional groups such as the Turkish Chamber of Architects and Engineers, Turkish politicians have regularly institutionalised both penal[17] and construction amnesties. Between 1948 and 2001 there were at least twelve construction amnesties in Turkey (*Cumhuriyet*, 17 August 2001).

The construction amnesty gives a green light to developers, contractors and owner-occupiers to continue to build and extend dwellings without regard for building design, soil suitability or earthquake regulations. Knowledge that populist government practice will continue to ignore and then 'forgive' building code violations actively conditions against compliance. Once 'legitimate', many of these buildings are sold at huge profit, the developers having avoided the extra costs necessarily involved in building safe structures. The clear message is that developers, builders and contractors need feel no compulsion to implement regulations, to utilise sound materials or to employ qualified professionals in the construction of homes and businesses.

Despite vocal protests in the wake of the earthquake, another amnesty bill was approved by the Turkish Parliament in the summer of 2001. On this occasion, however, the President of the Republic exercised his prerogative and vetoed the bill.[18]

One case study from research conducted by Green et al. (2002) in Turkey illustrates the frequently compromised and corrupt relationship between government and the construction industry. It involves the mayor of Esenyurt since 1989, Gürbüz Çapan and his family, lawyer, municipal assistant and administrative manager, along with two building contractors, hotel owners and construction company owners – all of whom are currently (and exceptionally) the subject of a range of corruption charges in Istanbul's State Security Court. Essentially – in the spirit of clientelism – over a ten-year period many of the mayor's friends and family won lucrative construction tenders; land was confiscated from individuals under the pretext of the 'Law for Prevention of Unlicensed Housing' and then sold on to developers; unlicensed construction was actively encouraged for the purpose of eliciting bribes; intimidation gangs were employed to threaten those who attempted recourse through legal means, and 'foundations' (such as the Esenyurt Public Works and Development Foundation) were established into which individuals were forced to make 'donations' should they require municipal services.

The Turkish government has also been spectacularly unwilling to distance itself from those private companies and individuals guilty of failure to comply with building and urban planning regulations, suggesting that lack of regulation favours state interests and was hence pursued as deliberate policy. A case in point is that of major construction firm Ceylan Insaat, known to be responsible for the construction of failed buildings which involved the deaths of at least 260 people. Ceylan, despite this record, was granted government contracts by the Ministry for Public Works and Housing to build permanent housing for the earthquake survivors, whilst a court case against the group 'for reasons of causing the deaths of 260 people', remained pending in the Yalova Aggravated Felony Court.[19]

Authoritarianism and Repression

A review of natural disasters, their scale and devastation, suggests a strong correlation between the authoritarian nature of a state and the degree of vulnerability of those who become victims of such disasters. This devastation is not simply the result of underdevelopment, but the weakness of civil society under repressive political arrangements. As Robert Putnam (1993) has shown, the absence of civil society correlates with an absence of or weak democratic processes. An assessment of major disasters reveals a strong correlation between the absence of a highly developed civil society – strong domestic grassroots and other non-governmental organisations – and the scale of death and destruction. Government commitment to civil and political rights has proven itself a protection against needless devastation from so-called 'natural' disasters and as de Waal demonstrates in his study of famine, 'The number, variety and resilience of liberal institutions make it more difficult for famine to recur' (1997: 11).

Caution, however, is essential because the evidence suggests that liberal democratic institutions, particularly in impoverished countries, are not in themselves enough: also required is the administrative capacity to deliver strategies of prevention, mitigation and relief; and an open public forum where information, publicity and debate is readily accessible. This has been the case in India where famine has effectively been almost eradicated, as a consequence not of wealth but of a range of factors central to civil society: a political commitment to employment for the poor; an independent press; strong civil society including a trade union movement, interest groups, a competent civil service and a recognition of the commitment to prevent famine as a 'political contract' (see Drèze 1990: 92).

Sadly, there is evidence that in parts of India this 'contract' is breaking down as a result of corruption, the caste system, bureaucracy and political indifference. In late 2002 the deaths from starvation of more than forty members of the tribal Sahariya (untouchables) community were reported in south-eastern Rajasthan. When impoverished villagers fall below the poverty line they should be issued with ration cards entitling them to purchase subsidised grain from government outlets. But as food became scarce the village head distributed the ration cards to friends and members of his own caste. At the same time government shop managers refused to sell grain to the Sahariya untouchables. Meanwhile government grain mountains (estimated at 60 million tonnes – a small proportion of which has been sent as aid to neighbouring countries like Afghanistan) lie mouldering in government warehouses while villagers like the Sahariya die from lack of food.

The absence of a strong civil society means that authoritarian states are also more likely to attempt to conceal evidence of state deviance. This was clearly apparent in the Turkish earthquake.

The official estimate of the number killed stands at 17,840 deaths, with almost 44,000 wounded and 505 permanently disabled. However, the unofficial death toll is certainly much higher – in the region of 40,000.[20] What is most striking about the media and official coverage of the earthquake is the total absence of information about the number of missing.[21] The striking discrepancy between the official and unofficial earthquake figures and the government's determined refusal to issue a missing list strongly suggests that the Turkish state reduced the number of dead in order to reduce the impact of its incompetence and the scale of its own corrupt practices.

In states where we find persistent and systematic violations of human rights, high levels of corruption, endemic torture, restrictions on freedom of expression and criminal justice abuse, we find concomitantly large-scale devastation as a result of 'natural catastrophe'.

The immigrants from Turkey's south-east who came to live in the dangerously constructed housing of Izmit Bay illustrate the direct link between repression and natural disaster. The Turkish state's 15-year war against the Kurdish minority had a dramatic impact on internal migration: millions left the devastation and repression of the south-east to seek jobs in the more secure industrialised parts of the country. It was from this pattern of forced migration that much of the demand for mass cheap housing emerged and it was this population – already victims of state repression – who became victims of a wilfully negligent state and the dangerous housing it positively encouraged which collapsed in the earthquake.[22]

There is no clearer illustration of the link between authoritarianism and disaster than the devastating 1958–61 Chinese famine, arguably the greatest disaster – and the greatest state crime – of the twentieth century. As with many other state crimes involving massive loss of life, the Chinese famine has never been officially acknowledged but according to the most reliable estimate at least 30 million people died from starvation (Becker 1996).

China witnessed a deliberate and organised conspiracy of silence about hunger and famine to conceal the crimes of the Maoist state. From 1960 the export of all domestic publications was banned, restrictions on communications were introduced so peasants who were now unable to travel or to come into contact with other travellers were denied outside knowledge. Few Chinese had access to telephones and mail was controlled and censored so that news of famine did not spread.

Starvation was forbidden as a documented cause of death on death certificates and doctors were forbidden to tell patients that they were starving (Becker 1996: 199). When Party leader Liu Shaoqui visited his home town in Hunan province, to see for himself the evidence of famine, he discovered bizarre deceits designed to keep Chairman Mao in ignorance of the famine, 'starving peasants had torn the bark off the trees to eat, so officials plastered the trees with yellow mud and straw to conceal the scars' (ibid.: 236). This famine was not about drought. Rather, as we argued in Chapter 2, it was the result of officials seeking to create the illusion of success in implementing the hopelessly unrealistic decrees of Mao's regime. The state granaries were full and grain exports rose but in many provinces people starved. Appallingly, those provinces which provided the greatest grain surplus were also the provinces where starvation killed the greatest numbers.

CONCLUSION

Authoritarian states willing to commit wide-scale human rights violations are uniformly disinterested in protecting their citizenry against the potential catastrophe of a natural disaster. Examples such as the 1958–61 Chinese famine, the Northern African famines in the Sudan, Ethiopia and Somalia in the latter half of the twentieth century, the 1976 Guatemalan earthquake and subsequent landslides and the 1999 Turkish earthquakes illuminate the direct links between gross human rights violations, corrupt practices and natural catastrophes and suggest that strategies of disaster mitigation will remain largely ineffective until the underlying structural and political dimensions of disaster-prone societies are understood and responsible states exposed and sanctioned as culpable.

The value of a political criminology of natural disasters should, we think, be evident. Until states are interrogated as specifically criminal agents, the disasters arising from floods, cyclones, famines, earthquakes, and so on will continue to be wrongly attributed to natural causes; and solutions will be sought outside the political sphere of state structures. As population vulnerability continues to increase and pressures on the environment mount, it is imperative that the direct links between political repression, corruption and poverty, and the devastating consequences of so-called natural disasters are exposed not as the inevitable products of geophysical disruption but as the direct consequence of state deviance.

5
Police Crime

'We're not here to fight fair, we're here to win.' 'If you place one of our brother officers in danger or you hurt him, you can believe that son of a bitch is gonna get an ass whipping … ' 'When an officer gets jumped, officers ask, what happened to the suspect? We're concerned whether the guy went to the hospital before going to jail.'

(US police officers quoted by Cancino 2001: 155)

Of all the subjects discussed in this book, police crime is by far the most familiar to students of criminology. The sociological literature on policing is, very largely, a literature on police deviance. Numerous British, American and Australian studies have shown that extra-legal violence, perjury and the fabrication of evidence are, in certain circumstances and against certain people, accepted parts of the 'occupational culture' of police work.[1] Police crime ranges from unlawfully arresting young working-class men, and occasionally beating them up, to maintain 'social discipline' in an English town (Choongh 1997), to the routine use of torture by police in much of the world (discussed in Chapter 8) and the 'social cleansing' murders of the street children, prostitutes and homosexuals known in Colombia as *desechables* – 'throwaway people' (Neild 2000: 227). Yet even though such behaviour not only infringes human rights but in many cases is manifestly illegal, it is only rarely referred to as 'crime'.

Police behaviour can be considered 'deviant' when it is perceived and labelled as brutal, corrupt, etc., by others – particularly the victims and their communities – or when the police themselves find it necessary to conceal or lie because they know it would incur some form of censure if it were revealed. Behaviour that meets those criteria cannot be quantified in any meaningful way. The best evidence for it comes from ethnographic studies that both observe the police behaviour and elicit the victim's or community's perception of it, as Penny Green did in her study of the 1984 miners' strike (1990). In countries with reasonably open systems of justice, court hearings and official inquiries can sometimes provide real insight into police deviance, although 'what really happened' often remains maddeningly elusive. Tony Ward was involved in research of this kind for many years through the British organisation INQUEST, and we use some of INQUEST's more recent research in this chapter.

Although many scholars have documented police violence and corruption in developing or transitional countries (see, for example, Bayley 1969; Marenin 1996; Cole 1999; Shelley 1999a; Harriott 2000; Hills 2000; Shaw 2002; Baker 2003), these studies do not furnish the kind of ethnographic data that informs the North American, British and Australian policing literature. It is on the latter body of literature that this chapter will mainly draw, along with Paul Chevigny's (1995) excellent comparative study of urban police violence in the US, Latin America and Jamaica.

As we stress throughout this book, the study of state crime (and especially state violence) needs to integrate the analysis of individual action, organisational processes and cultures, and social structure. We shall draw on the work of W. K. Muir (1977) in analysing police crime at the level of individual behaviour; on Janet Chan's (1996, 1997, 2000) work in relating individual behaviour to its organisational and cultural context; and on Steven Box's (1983, 1988) pioneering studies of police crime in relating it to its broader structural determinants. What these theories have in common is that they seek the reasons for police deviance in fundamental, and apparently universal, features of policing: the centrality of coercive force, the need to make rapid discretionary decisions, and the task of preserving the existing social order in a class society. Consequently, if these theories are sound, they should be applicable in widely different cultures, economies and political systems.

COERCION AND THE INDIVIDUAL OFFICER

Muir's Weberian perspective on the police focuses on the element of coercion which, since Bittner's (1975) seminal study, has been widely seen as the defining feature of police work.

Coercion, for Muir, takes place wherever one person threatens something another person values (a 'hostage') in order to persuade the other person to do (or refrain from) some action. Coercion, therefore, does not necessarily involve violence, and it can be used by the public against the police, as well as by the police against the public. When policing the 'respectable' public, the police can rely on the implicit threat that being arrested and/or publicly labelled as criminal will seriously damage the status, and possibly the income, of anyone who defies police authority. The explicit threat of pain, injury or death is usually a last resort. Conversely, the respectable public are more likely to threaten the police with legal action or scandal than with violence.

Three of the four 'paradoxes' that frame Muir's analysis are variations on a single point: namely that the harder it is for the police to threaten a person with some kind of non-physical harm, the greater the likelihood that they will resort to physical force. The people who are hardest to threaten with non-physical harm are the 'dispossessed' (those who have very little to lose); the 'detached' (who do not care about what they have to lose); and the 'irrational' (who do not understand the threats they face). But when the police confront people whom they perceive as falling into one of the categories (for example, the very poor, the emotionally distraught or the mentally ill), recourse to physical force is rarely the *only* option. The simplest option is often to avoid enforcing the law, especially if the dispossessed are victimising one another (see, for example, Shaw 2002). Another option, characteristic in Muir's view of good professional policing, is to redouble one's efforts to find, or create, some 'hostage' that the citizen cares about enough to be motivated to comply. One of Muir's examples is an officer policing the impoverished and frequently drunken inhabitants of 'skid row', who operated as a kind of one-man social welfare agency. Because people valued his friendship, advice and occasional small loans, they had reason to stay on the right side of him. This form of street-corner social democracy was much more effective, Muir argues, than the brutality meted out by some other officers. By provoking the men of 'skid row' to violent retaliation, they discovered the hard way that even the most powerless citizens can apply coercive sanctions to the police.

An important reason why violence going beyond necessary restraint or self-defence is an attractive option for some officers is what Muir calls the 'paradox of face': '*the nastier one's reputation, the less nasty one has to be*' (1977: 41). That is, the more formidable one's reputation for violence, the more likely it is that the mere *threat* of violence will suffice to intimidate an opponent. Someone who invests in this strategy must, however, be prepared to carry out their threats whenever their bluff is called: to 'lose face', especially in the presence of onlookers, would be disastrous. While contests over 'face' are particularly associated with confrontations between men, they are something in which women police officers also learn to engage (Hunt 1985; Westmarland 2002).

Muir's theory helps us to construct an explanation at the level of individual action for some of the well-known features of police violence.

Dispossession

Violence tends to be directed against 'persons of marginal status and credibility' (Skolnick and Fyfe 1993: 19). Being of marginal status, they may have little to lose besides their physical integrity. Some police officers come to believe that violence is the only language the poor understand

(Harriott 2000: 64). Chevigny found that *marginals* in Brazil (the term means both the socially marginal and 'outlaws') were considered to be immune to considerations of reason and morality. A former prosecutor told Chevigny that the military policeman 'believes he is allowed to kill when the person is poor, black and a thief' (quoted by Chevigny 1996: 27).

Moreover, the victims' lack of credibility and political 'clout' leaves them little capacity to threaten the police with legal action, community censure or press exposure (Chambliss 1994; Kappeler et al. 1998). In a mirror image of the police attitude to them, marginal groups may come to believe that violent resistance is the only language the police understand. Such informal sanctions can be effective: Keith (1993) records that in parts of London in the 1980s junior officers were afraid to make arrests out of fear for their personal safety. Anti-police riots, such as those in Brixton and Broadwater Farm (London) in 1981 and 1985, 'can thus be presented by participants as a simple answer to the repressive practices of the police with an equivalent moral status' (Gilroy 1987: 238). In turn, such resistance may lead police to redouble their efforts to impose order without consent (Keith 1993).

Irrationality

Excessive force is often used against those 'emboldened by drugs, alcohol, mental illness, or all three' to resist police authority (Skolnick and Fyfe 1993: 37). As Muir argues, such apparently 'irrational' opponents can be particularly threatening because they may prove oblivious to risks that would deter others. Officers must respond skilfully to avoid an escalation of violence:

> Unless … officers are sophisticated enough to identify these people quickly and deal with them appropriately – on the whole, non-confrontationally – they may find themselves backed into corners and compelled to use more force than they intended, perhaps killing or seriously injuring a suspect who might have been taken into custody. (Skolnick and Fyfe 1993: 37)

Of 20 people shot dead by English police from 1998–2001, 17 were described as having mental health problems, being intoxicated or having a history of substance abuse (Police Complaints Authority 2002). In the Australian state of Victoria, seven people with a history of mental illness were shot dead by police between 1990 and 1995 (McCulloch 2001: 107). A psychiatric service user indicates some of the reasons:

> The key thing is about [armed police squads] moving in and imposing their force, their will upon the situation. They want to control it

immediately through the threat of force or the command of their voice or something. And when that doesn't work – and why would it work with someone who is distressed, terrified or angry? That's when you've got the potential for disaster. (quoted by McCulloch 2001: 107)

The other side of the 'paradox of irrationality' is that it can sometimes be advantageous, even rational, for officers to react in ways which they themselves define as irrational. Assaults or fatal shootings can be attributed to a temporary loss of control (Chan 2000), adrenalin (Warren and James 2000), 'the natural outcome of strong, even uncontrollable emotions' or a 'combat high' (Hunt 1985: 325–6). But violence against those who resist police authority also serves instrumental purposes.

Face

It is a recurrent theme of all studies of police violence 'that defiance of the police, whether in a full-fledged car chase or simply in a refusal to move off a street corner, is very likely to provoke punishment from the police, because defiance of them is tantamount to defiance of order' (Chevigny 1995: 11). 'Street encounters between the police and the public are often resolved by someone "winning", and from the officer's point of view, it has to be the police' (Westmarland 2002: 182). The police can never be seen to 'lose' a confrontation, especially in the presence of onlookers. Several studies show that the presence either of other members of the public or other officers increases the likelihood of force or a serious complaint (Friedrich 1980; Maguire and Corbett 1991; Locke 1996; Worden 1996). In such situations officers commonly appear to prioritise 'short-term considerations of face [over] long-term considerations of professional prestige' or legitimacy (Friedrich 1980: 97).

Choongh's study (1997) of two English police stations provides a very clear example of policing based on 'face'. Arrests, he found, were used less as an investigative tool than as a sanction against lower working-class men who were considered to have been disrespectful towards the police. In the police station, suspects were taught a lesson in deference by being 'forced to accept absolute police control over their bodies' and submit to various humiliating orders (Choongh 1997: 81). The few suspects who refused to obey faced violent punishment: 'To allow a suspect "victory" in such a situation would not only defeat one of the purposes (indeed, in some cases the only purpose) of bringing him to the station, but would threaten the dominance of the police over the policed generally' (ibid.: 85).

Police violence against indigenous young people in Australia follows a broadly similar pattern of contests of public space and summary punishment in the police station (with the difference that beatings, according to Cunneen

2001, are more often aimed at extracting information). This kind of policing, which both Muir (1977: 71) and Cunneen (2001: Ch. 5) characterise as a form of terror, differs only in degree from the forms of state terror and torture discussed in Chapters 7 and 8.

Detachment and Cynicism

As Muir observes, the less one values something, the less an opponent has to gain by threatening it. Officers who adopt what Muir calls a 'cynical perspective' towards those to whom they regularly apply coercion do not need to worry about such people's disapproval. As van Maanen puts it in a classic essay, the actions of those categorised as 'assholes' (English equivalents include 'prigs', 'scrotes' and 'dross') 'are viewed by the police as stupid or senseless and their feelings as incomprehensible (if they can even be said to have feelings)' (1985: 148). The officers in Choongh's (1997) study regarded the local 'dross' as not only beneath contempt, but innately anti-police, and appeared quite unconcerned if a prisoner complained about his treatment. As in the case of indigenous youth in Australia (Cunneen 2001: 114), most victims of unlawful detention or violence saw no point in making a complaint.

INDIVIDUAL ACTION AND ORGANISATIONAL CULTURE

The main limitation of Muir's analysis lies in his reliance on differences in 'personality' to explain variations in police behaviour. Muir delineates four types of police personality which, as Reiner (2000: 102) observes, correspond to those identified by several later researchers. The type he identifies as especially likely to resort to violence is the 'enforcer': an officer who is comfortable with the use of force in pursuit of police goals and adopts a cynical perspective towards the policed. According to Worden, however, 'the few efforts to systematically test [such] hypotheses have produced little or no support' (1996: 27), because officers display little consistency between attitudes and behaviour, or between behaviour in one type of situation and another.

In place of the deceptively simple notion of 'personality', Chan (1996, 1997) borrows Pierre Bourdieu's concept of habitus. Habitus is a set of dispositions to respond in certain ways to the social situations one encounters. It is the 'feel for the game' (Bourdieu 1990: 11) that enables social actors to act *as if* they were calculating rationally, even when lack of time, information, etc., make rational calculation impossible, as they typically do in police decisions to use force (Manning 1997). Muir's officers displayed just such a 'feel for the game' (to very variable degrees) in their responses to the paradoxes of coercive power. The factors which officers would need to take into account if they were calculating rationally constitute what Chan, following Bourdieu, calls the 'field' of policing: the structure of social relations within which officers struggle to exercise power and authority, stay out of trouble with their superiors, and remain on good terms with their peers. The 'field' includes 'historical relations between certain social groups and the police, anchored in the legal powers and discretion the police are authorised to exercise and the distribution of power and material resources within the community' (Chan 1996: 115).

According to Chan, officers acquire the dispositions necessary to act successfully in the policing field largely, but not exclusively, through a body of 'organisational knowledge' learned from their peers. Chan distinguishes four types of organisational knowledge. 'Dictionary knowledge' provides schemas by which people and events can be rapidly classified. These classifications serve as cues for the application of 'directory knowledge' of how such people and events are normally dealt with. 'Recipe knowledge' comprises both the informal moral code of the police and a set of pragmatic 'recommendations and strategies': how to stay out of trouble, how to 'cover your ass' (Chan 1997: 79). 'Axiomatic knowledge' defines the operative goals and values of the organisation, which may be perceived differently by the rank-and-file and by senior management.

The police culture has certain features that appear to be both universal – at least in the relatively few jurisdictions where it has been studied (Skolnick and Fyfe 1993) – and almost self-evidently criminogenic:

> … its sense of mission; the desire for action and excitement, especially the glorification of violence; an Us/Them division of the social world with its in-group isolation and solidarity on the one hand, and racist components on the other; its authoritarian conservatism; and its suspicion and cynicism, especially towards the law and legal procedures. (Waddington 1999c: 287; see also Reiner 2000)

In fact, the values and attitudes associated with the police culture are almost exactly those of Muir's 'enforcer': a strong sense of the rectitude of using force in pursuit of the police 'mission', coupled with a deeply cynical and disrespectful attitude towards those who bear the brunt of police coercion. Yet Anglo-American researchers generally agree that the 'enforcer' represents only one among a range of policing styles (Reiner 2000: 101–3). As Chan argues (1996, 1997), individual officers have considerable leeway to resist or adapt to the culture in their own ways. The 'canteen culture' does not *require* officers to be violent and disrespectful (Waddington 1999c), but it *permits* such conduct by providing officers with a range of 'techniques of neutralisation' (Kappeller et al. 1998) and, crucially, by its norms of solidarity and silence (Worden 1996). As Muir (1977: 71) illustrates, those officers who adopt 'the enforcement response against the dispossessed' *need* to be backed up by colleagues and superiors – often by perjury and the intimidation of witnesses. Officers who strongly disapprove of a colleague's violent behaviour may nevertheless feel obliged to support and protect him (Punch 1979; Smith and Gray 1985). Those whose 'feel for the game' enables them to resolve conflicts without resort to force do not have the same need for back-up, and may not feel inclined to brag about their achievements in the station canteen.

CULTURE AND ACTION: THREE CASE STUDIES

We can illustrate the interplay of police culture and individual decision making by discussing three recent controversial deaths involving the (London) Metropolitan Police.[2] The police in these cases used 'excessive force' in three of the senses identified by Klockars (1996). In two of the cases the force used was deemed excessive in legal proceedings (the third is unresolved at the time of writing). The deaths provoked a degree of 'public scandal', and it seems clear that the police used 'more force than a highly skilled police officer would find necessary' (ibid.: 8). In all three cases the victims were categorised in ways that made the police perceive them as particularly threatening. As Holdaway argues, some such 'typifications' – simplified summaries of information about the social world – are indispensable to social interaction; but in police culture such typifications often harden into stereotypes, which 'are less complex, more rigid and virtually irrefutable' (1996: 157). Police stereotypes about ethnic minorities, such as the 'superhuman strength' that British police seem frequently to attribute to black men, are thought to contribute to the disproportionate number of black people who die at the hands of the police (INQUEST 1996; Kushnick 1999). Evidence of racial stereotyping by the Metropolitan Police led to possibly the most damaging public censure of British police deviance in recent years, when a public inquiry attributed the bungled police investigation of a racist murder to 'institutionalised racism' (Macpherson 1999; Holdaway 1999).

Ibrahima Sey

In March 1996, police were called to the home of Ibrahima Sey, a mentally ill Gambian asylum seeker, by his wife who was alarmed by his strange behaviour (INQUEST 1997). The officers succeeded in escorting him to the police station entrance without any resistance, largely thanks to a friend who was allowed to accompany him. Up to this point, the officers' approach was 'professional' in Muir's sense: they had found a way to persuade Mr Sey to comply without using force. But once they arrived at the station, although Mr Sey was pleading for his friend to stay with him, the police insisted that he could not come in. It seems that the cultural imperative to assert firm control over a 'body' in their exclusive territory of the police station (Young 1991) took precedence over any desire to avoid violence. Six or more officers then set upon Mr Sey in order to subdue him. After he had been brought to the ground and handcuffed, Mr Sey appeared to go limp. One of the officers then sprayed him with a CS spray. He was taken into the police station where he collapsed in a corridor. He was then taken into the custody suite where he was placed face down on the floor with his hands still cuffed behind his back. Some four to six officers continued to hold him down by his head, arms and legs – including two officers with their feet on his legs – for the next 15 minutes or more. It was while he was still restrained in this position that he suddenly became relaxed and, after being checked, was found not to be breathing.

The police ignored the guidelines issued by the Association of Chief Police Officers (ACPO), which stipulate that CS spray should be used only in self-defence, that 'the restraint methods used after a person has been sprayed and the physical position they are placed in [must] not adversely affect breathing ... prisoners must not be left in or transported in a prone face down position'; and that particular attention must be paid to 'those exhibiting bizarre/violent behaviour or experiencing breathing difficulties' (quoted by INQUEST 1997). They also ignored specific warnings they had been given, in the light of earlier deaths, about the dangers of restraint in the face-down position. Such disregard of approved methods of restraint is consistent with the findings of Uildriks and van Mastrigt in their research on police violence in Scotland, that the police learn from their colleagues to ignore official guidance and simply 'grab [the prisoner], the nearest part of his body ... you half choke 'm to death' (1991: 78). 'Directory knowledge' acquired by seeing and talking about how things are done in reality takes precedence over definitions of legitimate means propounded by senior officers (Hunt 1985). The coroner's jury found that Mr Sey had been unlawfully killed but no prosecution ensued. The coroner acknowledged that the verdict reflected 'growing public concern' about police methods of restraint and called for an inquiry in to the use of CS spray (Tyler and King 2000).

ACPO's response to the 'fairly persistent and predictable' breaches of their guidelines on the use of CS spray was to replace the guidelines with vague guidance, which removed any specific reference to acting in self-defence (Rappert 2002: 699–700).[3] The guidance exploits the inherent vagueness of the police mandate to use coercive force (Bittner 1975). As Rappert argues, this attempt to legitimise the use of force by dispensing with inconvenient rules ignores the perceptions of force by the communities subjected to it: 'In the context of strained relations with some members of the public, the sprays are seen as a tool for instilling fear into communities' (2002: 703).

Glenn Howard

A similar tragedy occurred the following year, when two Metropolitan Police officers were called to take Glenn Howard to a psychiatric hospital. In this case the officers' evidence at the inquest made clear how their attitude was shaped from the outset by their 'dictionary knowledge' of mentally ill people as irrational and hence, unpredictably dangerous. They testified that when they dealt with the mentally ill they were always on their guard for potential violence and that this was on their minds when they arrived outside his home. They radioed ahead that they were dealing with a mentally ill man 'in case we shout' – appealing to a shared 'directory knowledge' that backup is sometimes required in such cases. As Chan observes, officers tend to resist evidence that contradicts their initial categorisations (1997: 75). At the inquest, the officers denied any recollection that a nurse had told them that Mr Howard was *not* a violent man. A witness described Mr Howard as calm and cooperative. According to the police he was initially compliant but then tried to 'give them the slip' and a violent struggle ensued. By their own account, officers brought Mr Howard to the ground and placed him in a 'reverse bear hug' for up to four minutes, hit him with a police baton, and placed him face down with another officer crossing his legs behind his back. These actions, which again ignored Metropolitan police guidance, caused Mr Howard's death from postural asphyxia. The coroner's jury considered that the 'excessive restraint' used against Mr Howard, coupled with a subsequent lack of medical care, amounted to 'unlawful killing'. The officers were not prosecuted (INQUEST 2000a).

Harry Stanley

The Metropolitan Police's firearms unit, SO19, was called in 1999 to investigate a report that an Irishman had been seen carrying a sawn-off shotgun. In reality Harry Stanley had a Scottish accent and was carrying a table leg in a plastic bag. The equation of 'Irishman' with 'terrorist' put him in the most dangerous category of 'symbolic assailant' (Skolnick and Fyfe 1993: 97). The police shot him dead (INQUEST 2000b).

Binder and Scharf (1980) break down encounters with potentially violent suspects into four phases. After the 'phase of anticipation', where the 'officer reacts emotionally and intellectually to cues received' comes a 'phase of entry' where he or she sizes up the situation at first hand. In the

Stanley case, the 'phase of entry' consisted of officers spotting Mr Stanley, following him and observing 'that he was holding in his right hand, down by his side, a tightly-rolled blue plastic bag which contained a cylindrical object' (*Independent*, 20 June 2002). Then came the 'phase of information exchange' which consisted, according to Inspector Sharma, of his shouting: 'Armed police. Drop the gun. Armed police' (ibid.). Finally the officer decides whether to shoot (or use some other kind of force). In the Stanley case the police claim that Mr Stanley pointed the supposed gun at them, but this is contradicted by evidence that his back was towards them when he was shot. The phases between anticipation and decision may be extremely brief, sometimes based on only 'momentary cues' (Binder and Scharf 1980: 117).

In such situations the initial categorisation of the incident, with its emotional overtones, may produce a near-automatic response. Fyfe (1986) argues that this 'split-second syndrome' occurs because officers rush into action without first diagnosing the situation and planning their response. A lack of planning was apparent in the way officers approached Mr Stanley from behind, leaving themselves exposed when the supposed terrorist turned towards them. The inquest jury was clearly unimpressed by the police officer's evidence. The coroner would not allow them to find 'unlawful killing', but rather than declare the killing 'lawful' the jury returned an open verdict. That verdict was quashed by the High Court, which accepted that the coroner's conduct of the inquest had not complied with the European Convention of Human Rights.[4]

POLICING AND SOCIAL STRUCTURE

In an important study of police crime and other crimes of the powerful, the late Steven Box argued that 'micro processes' of individual motivation and police culture are important to answering the question 'why do they do it?', but it is also important to ask 'why are they allowed to do it?' The latter question, he argued, can be answered only 'by situating the police in a broader, historically informed frame', and examining their role in 'supporting and reproducing forms of domination, and suppressing, fracturing and demoralising forms of resistance' (Box 1983: 93).

What an historically informed analysis of policing in Britain and the US indicates is that its development in the nineteenth century was driven more by the elite's fear of the 'dangerous classes' than by considerations of crime prevention and social welfare (Box 1983: 111–13; Phillips 1985; Miller 1999). The discretionary powers of the police were explicitly targeted against the poorest, least 'respectable' section of the working class (Davis 1989; Gatrell 1990). As Cohen (1979) and Jefferson argue, 'a structurally-based divide [opened] up between those workers with a stake in the new urban order (the "respectables") and those without (the "roughs")' (Jefferson 1990: 24). This is the same divide between the 'respectable' and the 'dispossessed' that Muir observed at street level in an American city, and that Chevigny describes between the 'wild' and the 'cultivated' in Brazil (1995: 151). While a 'negotiated' form of order emerged in the policing of the 'respectable', the 'rough', or the dispossessed, have always borne the brunt of police coercion. In times of economic crisis and industrial conflict, the same coercive response has been extended to hitherto respectable trade unionists and working-class communities, leading to an abrupt change in their experiences of policing (Green 1990).

Box (1983, 1988) argues that police violence tends to increase with elite fears of disorder, and that the more unequal a society is the more acute the elite's fears of disorder are likely to be. The more fearful the elite becomes, the more it is likely to extend the legal repressive powers of the police, and the more it is likely to tolerate illegal violence against potentially dangerous groups. Box's argument draws on research by Jacobs and Britt (1979), comparing US states, which found that the police were most likely to use deadly force in the most unequal states, even when levels of violent crime were taken into account. Subsequent research by Sorenson et al. (1993, cited by White 2002) confirms this association.

Box's theory is also borne out by the fact that states with extremely unequal social structures, as in Latin America, are typically characterised by high levels of police – and sometimes military – violence against the poor, facilitated by elite indifference (or impunity, as the human rights NGOs call it: see, for example, Human Rights Watch 1997a). A stark example of the way marginal groups in developing or transitional economies are treated is the violence documented in many parts of the world against street children (Human Rights Watch 1999e, 2003b). Brutality, rape and murder directed at homeless young people seem generally to be met with indifference both by state officials and the middle-class public, who see them as little more than a social pest.

Box's theory requires some refinement. We need to understand the police as operating within a complex 'field' structured by their relations not just to political elites but to a range of social audiences, both in other state institutions and civil society. We also need to distinguish between the dynamics of coercion in 'strong' and 'weak' democracies. (For police crime in authoritarian states see Chapters 7 and 8.)

Strong democracies are those such as Great Britain[5] and the US where the state has an effective monopoly of violence and has historically enjoyed a high degree of legitimacy. The British case is the subject of an extensive and sophisticated literature which developed in the wake of the seminal,

Gramscian analysis by Hall et al. (1978) (see in particular Scraton 1987; Jefferson 1990). A central theme of this literature is that the governmental/judicial elite not only legally authorises some forms of coercion and turns a blind eye to others, but also seeks to construct an *authoritarian consensus* among the 'respectable' majority in support of repression of marginal and dissident groups. Scraton (1999) points to the 'dehumanisation' and 'demonisation' of such groups – epitomised by Prime Minister Thatcher's infamous labelling of striking miners as 'the enemy within' – as a common factor linking democratic and authoritarian regimes.

A further important theme in the British, US and Australian literature is the growth of 'paramilitary' policing, defined by Jefferson as 'the application of (quasi)-military training, equipment, philosophy and organisation to questions of policing (whether under centralised control or not)' (1990: 16).[6] Critics of paramilitarism argue that it does not merely 'license' police deviance as Box argues, but actively incites it. Training police squads, like the Special Operations Group in Victoria, in tactics modelled on those of elite military units, does not instil an attitude to firearms use in keeping with human rights concepts of 'minimum necessary force' (McCulloch 2001). Dangerous levels of force are used when their proportionality to law enforcement goals is highly questionable: for example, armed police bursting into American homes without warning to find drugs before they can be flushed away (Kraska and Kappeller 1997). Militaristic approaches to crowd control in Britain set up an 'amplificatory spiral' of unnecessary force and retaliation (Jefferson 1990). Moreover the training and culture of these elite units heightens the very features of the police culture that are most conducive to violence: the perception of danger, fear of outsiders, isolation, secrecy, intense group loyalty, and pleasure in 'warrior fantasies' (Jefferson 1990; Kraska and Kappeller 1997: 11; McCulloch 2001).

The current 'war against terrorism' has consolidated and intensified the trend towards paramilitary policing. History demonstrates that measures originally justified on the basis of countering terrorism are quickly absorbed and translated into everyday policing, particularly the policing of protesters, dissidents and marginal groups (Hillyard 1987; McCulloch 2003).

In strong democracies, however, the state rarely has things entirely its own way. Police coercion generates countervailing pressures within civil society. In Britain, for example, the increasing effectiveness of legal representation at inquests, and the willingness of some coroners or their juries to censure the police (Ryan 1998), the growth of civil actions against the police (Smith 1996), occasional media exposés of police malpractice, and the official censure of institutional racism all serve both to increase the incidence of publicly labelled police deviance, and to encourage some degree of restraint on the part of the police. Clear evidence of successful legal and political pressures on the police can be seen in the marked decline (at least 30 per cent and possibly more than 50 per cent)[7] in fatal police shootings in the US in the 1970s and 1980s. Walker (1993) attributes this to new police rules introduced as a result of local protest and civil litigation – and despite the growing conservatism of the US Supreme Court. Sherman (1983) argues that the intense public criticism leading to the rule changes, and consequent changes in administrative and disciplinary attitudes, were crucial factors.

What this all adds up to is that there is a complex and contradictory relationship in the advanced democracies between economic change, police coercion, and the labelling of some forms of coercion as deviant. There is no way of measuring violent police crime and establishing a simple correlation between it and inequality. These complexities should not, however, obscure the unmistakable trend, in the 20 years since *Power, Crime and Mystification* was published, in the direction Box identified: an increasingly unequal '40:30:30' society (Young 1999) in which the poor experience increasingly repressive, authoritarian and sometimes criminal forms of control.

'Weak democracies', as discussed by Chevigny (1995), are states which do not have an effective monopoly of violence. Clientelistic politics militates against any notion of equal rights or political accountability. Of the countries studied by Chevigny, Brazil and Jamaica most clearly fit this pattern, with Brazil being the more extreme case. High levels of street crime, resulting from desperate poverty, lead to vigilantism, which is tolerated by the state, with the police often acting like vigilantes themselves: 'ill-controlled violence ... thinly disguised as legally justified force, is the characteristic of policing in weak democracies' (Chevigny 1995: 224).[8] Since there appears to be no alternative means of controlling street crime, police violence meets with considerable support, or at least acquiescence, not only from the elite (Human Rights Watch 1997a) but from the 'respectable' poor (Scheper Hughes 1992; Chevigny 1995; Harriott 2000; Paes-Machado and Vilar Noronha 2002). It might appear, in these circumstances, that police violence is not really 'deviant', but a normal, socially approved activity (cf. Melville 1999: 11; Waddington 1999c). Chevigny disagrees:

[E]verywhere, and especially in countries in transition to democracy, such [violent] policies are recognised to be risky. In all the places in this study, government officials, as well as citizens who think about the issue, know that police have no legitimate power to bypass the justice system and punish summarily ... [T]hus officials, including the police, try to conceal arbitrary police violence, to assimilate it to the requirements of the law. The bunker mentality of the police is strengthened, the alienation of the police from the public is increased, and the cycle of demand for official accountability is set in motion. (1995: 144)

Even in a country such as Brazil, domestic and international civil society can generate significant pressures for conformity to human rights and legal norms. Although an opinion poll showed 41 per cent public support for a massacre of 111 unarmed but rebellious prisoners in 1992 (Chevigny 1995: 178), the reaction by Brazilian and overseas human rights groups led the São Paulo authorities to take

… significant steps to reduce the shocking rate of police homicides. In 1993, the number of civilians killed by the military police, according to official figures, fell from 1,470 to approximately 400, demonstrating how attitudes at the top could affect events on the street. (Human Rights Watch 1997a)

Since 1997 the São Paulo police have ostensibly embraced 'community policing', attempting to build legitimacy through forms of public consultation (Frühling 2000). Brazil may have better prospects for such reform than a country like Mozambique with a weak civil society and no real experience of the 'rule of law', where it appears difficult for a process of police legitimisation to get started (Baker 2003).

CORRUPTION AND VIOLENCE

One of Chevigny's most significant findings is that in 'all the places studied, the abuse of violence is perpetuated through corruption and political interference in the police' (1995: 225). At first sight this positive association between corruption and violence may seem counterintuitive, because corruption (in our sense of illicit exchange: see Chapter 2) is often an alternative to violence. Instead of coercively enforcing the law, one can take a bribe to look the other way. Instead of beating information out of a suspect, one can offer him drugs.

The relationship between corruption and violence becomes clearer when we distinguish, on the same lines as we did in Chapter 2, between different forms of corruption. Often corruption is not organisational at all but involves an individual 'bent' officer who, for example, sells information to a criminal acquaintance (the commonest form of police corruption in England according to Miller 2003). The officer who is 'bent for self' can be contrasted with those who are 'bent for the job' (Morton 1993) and use illegitimate means to pursue legitimate organisational goals. Much so-called 'noble cause corruption' does not involve corruption in the sense of illicit exchange, but the fabrication or falsification of evidence to convict people the police 'know' are guilty (Crank and Caldero 2000; Punch 2003). Some 'noble cause corruption' does involve illicit exchange: for example, covertly dropping charges or 'losing' evidence against informants (Wood 1997: 90–2), or allowing an informant who is an escaped prisoner to remain at large (Dunnighan and Norris 1999).

A third, and arguably more pernicious, type of corruption occurs where being bent *is* part of the officers' job: in other words, where one of the organisational goals of certain teams of officers, or even of the force as a whole, is to make money by illicit means (Sherman 1978; Punch 1985). One of the best-documented examples of highly organised corruption pervading an entire force was the New York Police Department (NYPD) at the time of the Knapp Commission's investigations in the 1970s (Chin 1997a). The Metropolitan Police's Obscene Publications Squad in the 1960s and early 1970s was an example of an organisationally corrupt sub-unit (Cox et al. 1977). New York in the 1990s, according to the Mollen Commission of 1994, exemplified what we characterised in Chapter 2 as organisationally tolerated corruption. Corruption was organised only at the level of small squads or informal 'crews' of officers, but among higher management there was 'a deep-seated institutional reluctance to uncover serious corruption … [A]voiding bad headlines, and tolerating corruption, became more important than ending it' (Chin 1997b: 17, 71).

The categories of being 'bent for the job' and 'bent as a job' are not mutually exclusive. As with other types of corruption, there is a spectrum of clandestine exchanges, from relations with informers that are an accepted part of detective work (Punch 1985; Hobbs 1988), to the informal 'licensing' of illicit markets (Manning and Redlinger 1977; Dixon 1999) and direct police involvement in theft and drug dealing (Chin 1997b; Wood 1997), and officers can progress from one type of exchange to another (Waddington 1999c). In perhaps the best-documented recent example of organised police corruption in England, a team within the South East Regional Crime Squad used information gained from a particular drugs dealer both to arrest her rivals and to acquire drugs to sell for profit (*Panorama* 2000; Miller 2003: 12).

Officers can make a tidy profit for themselves and, at the same time, impose a certain kind of extra-legal order. As the Mollen Commission said of New York:

While money is still the primary cause of corruption, a complex array of other motivations also spur corrupt officers: to exercise power over their environment; to vent frustration and hostility over their inability to stem the tide of crime around them; to experience excitement and thrills; to prove their mettle to other officers and gain their acceptance; and to administer their own brand of street justice because they believe the criminal justice system will administer none. Corrupt officers usually raided drug locations for profit, but sometimes also to show who was in control of the crime-ridden streets of their precincts; sometimes to feel the power and thrill of their badges and uniforms; sometimes because they believed that vigilante justice was the only way to teach a lesson or punish those who might otherwise go unpunished. (Chin 1997b: 21)

It was this type of corruption, in which predatory crime is fused with a distorted sense of 'mission', that Chevigny observed not only in New York but in the other cities he studied. Chevigny argues that corruption and violence combine in an extreme manifestation of the tendency of police in all societies to see law and order as interchangeable concepts, and to become impatient with the law administered in the courts: 'the police become the embodiment of order and ... administer justice directly in the streets and the station houses' (1995: 253). In Mexico and Brazil, Chevigny (ibid.: 142) found that bribes formed the basis of a kind of extra-legal justice not unlike that operated by eighteenth-century thief-takers in London. Victims paid the police to recover their stolen property; the police found it by torturing suspected thieves; the thieves (at least in Brazil) paid the police to ease off on torture or to drop charges once they had confessed. In Argentina, police used the proceeds of corruption to buy themselves impunity for crimes including torture, murder and kidnapping (ibid.: 197). In some respects their activities were a continuation of the pattern of state terror discussed in Chapter 7.

CONCLUSION

Because the theories we have examined in this chapter relate police crime to seemingly universal features of policing, it is a reasonable hypothesis that they will be applicable to police in a wide range of jurisdictions.

To summarise, the argument is that in encounters with the economically marginal and with those they see as 'irrational' (such as the mentally distressed, the drunk or drugged, and political 'fanatics') the police have fewer means of non-physical coercion at their disposal, and fewer incentives to refrain from physical force, than they do in dealing with 'respectable' citizens. Sometimes the use of force is necessary to accomplish legitimate police goals. But lack of skill, lack of incentives to limit the use of force, and positive incentives to use excessive force to maintain 'face', mean that such people tend to bear the brunt of illegitimate as well as legitimate violence. The more unequal a society – the more extreme the levels of dispossession, and the greater the fear it engenders among the respectable – the more this structure of incentives will tend to favour violence against the poor. Inequality, however, is only one among several factors affecting levels of violence.

The police do not respond to this structure of incentives (the 'field' of policework) by rationally calculating the costs and benefits of different tactics in each case. Rather, they acquire a 'habitus', a set of dispositions that enables them to size up situations rapidly and respond in an approximately rational manner. These dispositions are acquired largely (but not exclusively) through learning the classificatory schemes, ways of acting, informal rules and values comprising 'cop culture'. 'Cop culture' tends to endorse violent and discriminatory behaviour and protect the officers who use it. It does not mandate such behaviour, but makes it available to officers as an option.

The nature of the police culture has led some commentators, such as Reiner (2000), to conclude that only by changing this culture can police behaviour be changed. Chan (1996, 1997) argues that the culture or 'habitus' of the police can be changed if the 'field' of police work changes. As in other areas of state crime, the role of civil society – pressure groups, civil rights lawyers, the media, etc. – is vital to ensuring that marginal and dissident groups cannot be victimised with impunity. For example, an unofficial inquiry into the violent policing on the anti-globalisation protest in Genoa in 2001 highlighted the growing role of journalists and lawyers in monitoring and preventing illegal police activity (Trucco 2002). But tackling police crime is an uphill struggle because, like political corruption, it feeds upon itself. Police violence leads to violent resistance, which can lead to more violence, and also heightens police solidarity and silence, making more violence possible (Muir 1977; Skolnick and Fyfe 1993). Corruption ensnares police, and sometimes politicians, in a web of complicity which discourages reporting of any malpractice and fosters both further corruption and violence (Chevigny 1995).

Police corruption is closely associated with organised crime, and it is to the wider relationship between organised crime and the state that we now turn.

6

Organised Crime and the 'Deep State'

> But consider the definition of a racketeer as someone who creates a threat and then charges for its reduction. Governments' provision of protection, by this standard often qualifies as racketeering. To the extent that the threats against which a government protects its citizens are imaginary or are consequences of its own activities, the government has organised a protection racket.
>
> (Tilly 1985: 171)[1]

Charles Tilly has emphasised what he describes as the interdependence between the historic processes of war-making and state-making and organised crime. 'Banditry, piracy, gangland rivalry, policing and war-making all belong on the same continuum' (1985: 17) or as Gallant puts it 'bandits helped make states and states made bandits' (1999: 25). While European states, on Tilly's account, started out as 'protection rackets' in the early modern era, they have since acquired a degree of legitimacy (even if challenged) not afforded the racketeer. The examples of Burma (see below) and Liberia (see Chapter 9) represent a modern-day recapitulation of Tilly's portrayal of the quasi-criminal process of state-making.

However, states also act in concert or in parallel with conventionally understood organised crime networks and in these instances they do so covertly and without the legitimacy normally afforded them.

An economically broad definition of organised crime is 'systematic criminal activity for money or power' (Woodiwiss 2001: 3). In this sense state crime, corporate crime and anti-state political crime are all forms of organised crime. The type of organised crime that we are concerned with here is characterised by trading in illicit markets, and typically seeking to secure a monopoly of a particular product or service in a particular region (Schelling 1984). Naylor (1999: 3–6) usefully also includes the following characteristics: a penetration of the licit economy, specialisation in enterprise crimes and a reliance on violence and corruption.

Organised crime almost invariably involves some form of corrupt relationship with the police and/or other state officials. Corrupt influence over low-level enforcement decisions can extend beyond the bribery of individual officers to the 'capture' of entire police departments or city administrations (Gardiner 1970; Sherman 1978). Corruption can constitute an informal 'licensing' system for traders in illicit markets that enforcement authorities find they cannot completely suppress (Dixon 1999). In a much-cited paper, Manning and Redlinger (1977) argue that corruption in illicit markets tends to focus on enforcement agents because illicit businesses (in contrast to legitimate corporations) cannot easily lobby or influence the higher echelons of the state. In many instances, however, organised crime networks can and do negotiate and collude with political elites at national level. It is this type of high-level collusion that we focus on here.

As this chapter explores the role of states at the intersection of organised crime we are less interested in organised crime as a criminological concept (which has been usefully reviewed by, for example, Chambliss 1978; Block and Chambliss 1981; Passas 1995; Ruggerio 1996b, 2001; Woodiwiss 2001; Berdal and Serrano 2002; Levi 2002) than we are with the reliance by states on organised crime for the furtherance of state goals.

STATE-ORGANISED CRIME

William Chambliss, in his pioneering work on 'state-organised crime', has exposed a 'clear congruence' between organised crime and the political and economic structure within which it emerged (1999). His identification of political elites with serious organised crime remains a central defining feature of the subject, though one which is often overshadowed in the literature by political attempts to control transnational crime.

A central argument of this chapter is that organised crime, and especially state-organised crime, can only be properly understood in relation to the state (and the class structure) in which it emerges. For analytical purposes we distinguish strong from weak states in terms of their relationship with organised crime. As we shall argue, there is a tendency in weaker states, often characterised by clientelistic or patrimonial relations, for organised crime to fill the vacuum created by an ineffective state. In these circumstances organised crime is able to flourish and even to compete with the state in terms of specific administrative and political functions. Here, 'the absence of a monopoly over coercive, economic, and political resources may lead rulers to encourage rent-seeking and to strike various "deals" or "contracts" with other bearers of economic, political or coercive resources' (Berdal and Serrano 2002: 21). Examples from Liberia, Turkey, Italy, Russia, Burma and Colombia will illustrate the extent of organised crime penetration into the affairs of state under patrimonial or clientelist structures.

CRIMINAL ORGANISATIONS

In 1978, Chambliss challenged the dominant view of organised crime in America as an ethnically integrated implant of malevolent 'outsiders'. Rather, he introduced the political elite into the equation, arguing that organised crime was better characterised by loose affiliations[2] of 'businessmen, politicians, union leaders and law enforcement officials who cooperate to coordinate the production and distribution of illegal goods and services' (1978: 151). This characterisation holds good in all those states where serious crime is organised.

The extensive literature on the Sicilian Mafia, the Colombian drugs cartels, the Chinese Triads, the Russian and Turkish Mafiya and the Japanese Yakuza suggests that there are three characteristics which define criminal organisations of this type: first they are businesses, often adopting many of the practices of legitimate corporations while dealing in illicit commodities and services; secondly they are secret societies which operate covertly; and finally, in certain geographical contexts they are also shadow or proto-states (Bequai 1979; Gambetta 1993; Fiorentini and Peltzman 1995; Scaperdas and Syropoulos 1995; Clawson and Rensselaer 1998). For the purposes of this chapter we are most interested in the business and shadow-state roles of organised crime and their interconnections with the functions and goals of states.

Business

For Gambetta, the mafia is 'a specific economic enterprise, an industry which promotes, and sells private protection' (1993: 1). It deals in both legal and illegal markets and the commodities or services provided are by nature or delivery illegal.

Block has also alluded to the ideological underpinnings of organised crime which embed it comfortably within the legitimate political economy. 'The power of ethnic criminal organisations', he writes, 'is always contingent upon a large population base whose patterns of social and geo-graphical mobility reflect a strong adherence to working class lifestyles and petty bourgeois capitalism' (Block 1999: 218).

It is clear, then, that the goals of organised crime are essentially those which characterise all rational actors in capitalist markets – maximisation of power and profit, and reduction of risk. As Chambliss illustrated, organised serious crime benefits from the developments in the political economy in the same way as legitimate business (1978: 153).

Lupsha argues, however, that criminal organisations have a particular advantage over legitimate corporations because of their vast resources and readiness to resort to the criminal strategies of corruption and intimidation (1996: 16).

There are many organisational similarities between state-corporate crime and state-organised crime. Much of the time organised crime pursues the same primary goals as legitimate corporations: both are the products of free market capitalism, both seek to maximise profit margins and reduce financial risk.

As with the study of state-corporate crime, state-organised crime involves an examination of the intersection between state and organised crime actions on three levels of analysis: individual, institutional and structural or societal (Kramer 1992; Matthews and Kauzlarich 2000). Organisational crime is said to result from 'a coincidence of pressure for goal attainment, availability and perceived attractiveness of illegitimate means, and an absence or weakness of social control mechanisms' (Matthews and Kauzlarich 2000: 293). As with state-corporate crime, the goal of either direct capital accumulation (by the state or organised crime) or the promotion of capital accumulation (by the state *for* organised crime) is frequently a 'highly criminogenic force'. Where legitimate means to pursue this goal are scarce as a result of either institutional or structural factors, organisational deviance is more likely to occur. Organisational deviance is likely to occur where there is a failure of social control and where trust between civil society and the state has broken down.

Shadow State

According to Arlacchi (1988: 38) there has been a long-standing acknowledgement of the authority of the mafia by the Italian state and much of the work on the mafia explores the state's inability to retain the monopoly over the use of force in southern Italy. Gambetta argues that while states and mafia do both deal in violence it is *protection* which is the ultimate commodity, with violence more a resource to facilitate the production of 'protection':

> In both legal and illegal markets those who enlist Mafiosi to sort out their disputes to retrieve stolen property, or to protect their cartels from free riders and competitors do not perceive that protection as bogus … this practice differs from extortion proper, where the payment aims only to avoid costs directly threatened by the 'protectors'. (Gambetta 1993: 3)

Additionally, in certain circumstances the organisational interests of both organised crime and states converge. Gambetta argues that in regions within Sicily where the mafia is efficiently organised, 'problems of law and order and public hazards are kept under control' (1993: 3); thus Sicily claims a relatively low drug overdose rate attributed to the quality control offered by the mafia (1993: 4). Further the mafia cooperate with the agents of law enforcement when they wish to eliminate 'unorganised' criminals or certain rivals. Similarly the ultimate demise of the Medellin cartel was achieved with the collaboration of the Cali cartel (Gambetta 1993: 133) so that the war against drugs has itself required collusion with powerful sections of organised crime.

There are numerous examples of politicians – from a range of political parties – who have formed criminal alliances with the mafia 'in order to exploit the ability of the latter to act as guarantors of complex sales of votes and illicit interparty arrangements' (Gambetta 1993: 4; see also Chapter 2 above). Allegiances forged between politicians and mafiosi mean that these politicians are highly unlikely to invoke state opposition to the mafia.

Interestingly there is also a current of belief within certain criminal justice agencies that the mafia operates a parallel legal system which complements the work of police and other agents of social control. Arlacchi cites the Attorney General of the *Corte de Cassazione* (Court of Cassation):

> The mafia has been said to despise the police and the judiciary. This is inaccurate. The mafia has always respected the judiciary – the law – and bowed to its verdicts; nor has it obstructed the judges' work. In hunting bandits and outlaws it even sided with law enforcers …
>
> Today, Don Calogero Vizzini's successor is making his reputation, and in time he will succeed to his predecessor's authoritative position in the counsels of the secret conclave. May his labours increase the respect in which the laws of the state are held, and may they be for the social betterment of all. (Arlacchi 1988: 40–41)

Arlacchi goes on to argue that until the 1970s the central state, by making mafiosi their proxies in local civil and judicial administration, actually achieved a high degree of political integration of local political culture into the national political system: 'through the Mafiosi, a good many elements of local political life participated in the national political system' (1988: 41).

Drug cartels and their illicit activities have served to finance a number of repressive Latin American states including Bolivia during 1980–81 under Luis Garcia Meza and the regime of General Manuel Noriega from the mid to late 1980s in Panama (Farer 1999). Equally, according to Fiorentini and Peltzman, organised crime frequently substitutes itself for government, 'employing the typical tools which characterise public intervention in the economy, from levying taxes to restricting entry in different markets, from regulating the quality of goods and services to the coercive provision of public goods' (1995: 12). They go on to argue that organised crime is best understood in terms of its competitive relationship with the state and other criminal organisations for a monopoly over the use of force in a particular territory.

The relative success of organised crime in this arena in Colombia, Bolivia, Peru, Italy and Russia is, to a considerable extent, a function of the lack of political legitimacy that governments in these states command and the weakness of civil society. This is explored further below.

ORGANISED CRIME IN PERSPECTIVE

According to Clawson and Rensselaer, cocaine represents approximately 7 per cent of the GDP of Colombia, Bolivia and Peru. While this may represent some $10 billion in earnings for the Andean countries (of which Colombia receives the lion's share – 80 per cent) it is 'not the heartbeat that sustains the body economic' (1998: 33). Clawson and Rensselaer's 'conservative' estimate of the global size of the cocaine market is between $47 billion and $74 billion (1998: 7).

In Russia the picture is more shocking (Handelman 1995; Rawlinson 1997; Voronin 1997). In 1995 the shadow economy was estimated to represent 25 per cent of the country's gross national product with over 8,000 criminal organisations actively engaged with corrupt state officials 'to create not so much a new market economy but actually a new criminal state' (Voronin 1997: 53).

CLIENTELISM AND PATRIMONIALISM

As with corruption, organised crime is most prevalent in societies characterised by clientelism and patrimonialism. Such societies tend to be characterised by enormous disparities between a rich minority elite and an impoverished majority. The extent and penetration of organised crime is also associated with degrees of poverty and inequality (Taylor 2002). Arlacchi has shown there is a traditional link between clientelism and organised crime in the liberal democracies of western Europe and Japan:

> One very important index of the existence of a clientelistic relationship of the diffuse kind is that favours are not limited to any particular sphere of the beneficiary's needs and interests. Favours asked may concern grave violations of the penal code, or insignificant problems of everyday life. (Arlacchi 1988: 43)

As we discussed in Chapter 2, the more corrupt a state agency is, the more unreliable and apparently random its decisions become. In these circumstances individuals seeking a decision or outcome from a particular state agency are propelled toward 'brokers' who can mediate between the individual and the agency in order to secure a result. Brokers know which politicians may be bribed and the cost of such a service.

If, as Gambetta so cogently argues, the main market for organised crime services is in those illegal transactions where there is a trust deficit, then it is the production and sale of guarantees which distinguishes a mafioso from a patron. Patrons or brokers supply privileged information that enables their clients to 'connect ... to higher authorities' (1993: 18). This information includes

> ... introductions, recommendations, advice about competition for public contracts, the names of key people to approach; they back new legislation or applications for jobs and benefits; they translate client demands into appropriate language, simplify rules, and identify means of avoiding sanctions and obtaining favors. (Gambetta 1993: 18)

What they are unable to provide is protection: guarantees or safeguards against bad promises, commodities, rights, crime, competitors, and so on. The provision of information, unlike the provision of protection, does not require the resource of violence. The existence of patron–client relations in the political fabric thus creates a demand for the commodity of protection dealt in by organised crime.

The Medellin cartel promoted the development of paramilitary groups to protect their rural investments and developed some links with army personnel. The paramilitaries have been responsible for gross human rights violations against left-wing guerrilla organisations and their peasant supporters in Colombia's hinterlands (Clawson and Rensselaer 1998: 176). The Cali cartel, meanwhile, developed better intelligence capabilities against the Medellin cartel than the police itself and established alliances with the police and politicians (Thoumi 1999: 133–4): 'The conflicts between the cartels and their links with different parts of the government resulted in widespread divisions and widespread distrust among government offices fighting the war on drugs' (ibid.: 134).

In 1989 the Colombian state faced a crisis of legitimation. In the midst of a carnival of violence orchestrated by the Medellin cartel against any public officials who threatened the illicit drug trade – politicians, cabinet ministers, judges, police officers, presidential candidates[3] – the authority of the state had been effectively subsumed by the power of drug lords and guerrilla organisations. The illicit economy had grown very quickly. The state had not only lost its monopoly over the use of force but the undemocratic, elitist and clientelist political system was unable to confront the political and social crisis that resulted (Thoumi 1999: 131).

Lupsha (1996) suggests a three-stage evolutionary paradigm to explain the development of organised crime in relation to the state:[4] a *predatory stage* in which gangs employing violence attempt to gain territorial control and a monopoly over the use of force, all the while, however, being subject to the forces of law and order; a *parasitical stage* in which state prohibitions, war, conflict, UN sanctions, etc., create the conditions for criminal organisations to flourish and to connect with corrupt sections of the political elite; and finally a *symbiotic stage* in which 'organised crime has become a part of the state; a state within a state' (Lupsha 1996: 30–32). At its most extreme we have those predatory states sometimes described as kleptocracies (Bayart et al. 1999) or 'captured states', such as Nigeria under Sani Abacha, Zaire under Mobuto, Liberia under Charles Taylor or the former Yugoslavia under Slobodan Milošević. In these states the pursuit of political power and authority is integral to private gain. Without relatively strong and efficient civil administrations markets may become a means by which political authority is exercised. Direct intervention in markets by ruling elites enriches and empowers. Accumulation, via theft of resources, is thus transformed into political power. States like Burma may also usefully be described as 'kleptocracies' or economies of plunder (Bayart et al. 1999), where a kleptocratic state holds as its primary goal the maximisation of political rent (H. I. Grossman 1995: 147). As Reno has shown, organised crime – illicit production, drug and diamond smuggling and protection rackets – has become central to 'the building of political authority' in a range of African countries (1999: ix).

In these conditions it becomes impossible to distinguish state officials from organised criminals, given that the goals of the state and their means of attainment have merged with those of organised crime. Voronin describes a classic kleptocracy in which gangsterism is now indistinguishable from government in Russia. He reports Ministry of Internal Affairs data which suggest that over 40,000 businesses (including 1,500 state enterprises, 4,000 share-holding societies and 550 banks) in Russia are under the control of organised crime; he presents a picture of the almost total insertion of organised crime into the machinery of government. The same government data suggest that organised crime currently controls around 40 per cent of Russia's GDP (Voronin 1997: 53).

Kleptocratic or predatory states like Taylor's Liberia are not only criminal organisations in themselves, they also provide a welcome haven to an extensive range of organised criminals including mercenaries, arms and drug traffickers. Close relations with Charles Taylor ensured lucrative profits for those involved in organised crime as the case of international illegal arms dealer Leonid Minin reveals. Minin (a Ukrainian-born Israeli) not only supplied Taylor's brutal regime with arms (breaking internationally imposed weapons sanctions against Liberia) but also profited from Taylor's connections with the Sierra Leonian diamond trade (Silverstein 2002).

STRONG STATES

Mindful of Dick Hobbs' warning (2001: 549) that too great a focus on international organised crime encourages us to locate it as a foreign rather than local phenomenon, we are concerned here to demonstrate the significance of powerful states in the maintenance and fostering of organised crime. In strong states such as the United States, organised crime offers much less in the way of governance or shadow statehood. Rather than as a competitor or a threat to state power, organised crime in America has coexisted and to a certain extent complemented the legitimate structures of power and authority (Woodiwiss 2001). In these circumstances the state has employed organised crime for quite particular ends – as in the covert funding of right-wing guerrilla organisations in Latin America. The American state, often through its intelligence services, has periodically employed the assistance of organised crime (for example, right-wing narco-guerrillas such as the Contras) for covert political ends in South-East Asia and Latin America – most notably to crush left-wing political movements seen as threatening to US commercial interests. CIA involvement with organised drug smugglers has been documented in Nicaragua, Vietnam, Colombia, Afghanistan and Pakistan (Scott and Marshall 1991; Chambliss 1999).

American naval intelligence agencies collaborated with organised crime during the Second World War to guard the New York docks against sabotage. Following the war, the CIA supported organised violent Corsican gangs to harass (and sometimes murder) militant trade unionists and to break waterfront strikes (Woodiwiss 2001: 364). Similarly, the CIA has periodically employed the services of hired killers/organised crime to carry out political assassinations (Chambliss 1999: 146).

These are cases where the state or agencies of the state call upon the organisational skills of an illicit organisation to secure a particular state goal through covert means. Why do strong states rely on and collude with the services of organised crime? The overriding goal of the American state is to ensure and protect the conditions most favourable for the maintenance of capitalist relations of production. In certain circumstances the skills and operational resources of organised crime make it the best means to fulfil those goals. As Naylor remarks, it is not surprising that intelligence services and organised crime have a history of communion. Covert action defines both their spheres of activity and they share the same conservative political goals of defending capital and free market relations. Naylor suggests that engagement in mutual operations is a rational and logical development (Naylor 1995: 57).

Until legislation in the 1970s which forced disclosure of campaign funding sources, American political parties, particularly the Democratic Party, relied heavily on the financial contributions from organised crime (Chambliss 1978: 182).

THE 'TRANSNATIONAL' DIVERSION

In recent years the notion of organised crime has been to a significant degree supplanted by the more globally resonant 'transnational crime' or 'transnational organised crime'. This nomenclature seems less an indication of qualitative changes in the practice of international organised crime than a response to international policing and control strategies that have become increasingly global in scope. The widespread adoption of 'transnational' as the preferred prefix for international organised crime also appears to reflect the more general American and European anxieties associated with 'otherness' – terrorism, asylum seekers, etc. – and the demise of the Soviet Union. As Block suggests, there is a perception of increasing vulnerability expressed in the conceptualisation that transnational organised crime represents a threat to social and political life even in some of the world's most stable and prosperous nations.

The evidence from Tilly (1985), Gallant (1999), Friman and Andreas (1999), Block (1999), Chambliss (1999) and others demonstrates that a cross-border, 'transnational' component has always been a feature of certain forms of organised crime. That component has, however, changed with the developments in transportation, communication, the size and structure of illicit organisations, financial and trade liberalisation, deregulation and law enforcement facilitated by increased globalisation. In turn this has created the conditions for the expansion of organised crime internationally (Berdal and Serrano 2002; Taylor 2002; Lupsha 1996). Arlacchi has also argued that the global expansion in illegal markets has had a qualitative impact on the nature of organised crime, creating both 'an acceleration of the process by which the criminal elite identifies with the forces of accumulation and the market' and a situation of vertical integration in which organised crime has become increasingly linked to 'common' or 'street' crime (1988: 218–22). While this is true it also reveals the centrality of organised crime's relationship to the nation-state.

Central to our argument is the fact that organised crime, while frequently participating in illicit international markets, is by virtue of its covert nature, its familial, tribal, clan or cult relationships, its reliance on localised and personalised political networks, its territorial character and most fundamentally its relationship to the nation-state, at heart a local phenomenon. Gambetta illustrates this point by likening the protection industry to mining, that is, heavily dependent on the local environment for raw materials and resources:

> [I]nformation gathering and advertising, for instance, exploit independent networks of kinship, friendship and ethnicity ... Even the apparent exception of the U.S. mafia is misleading. Mafia families were not exported to America but emerged spontaneously, as it were, when the supply of and demand for protection met ... (Gambetta 1993: 251)

As Block points out: 'It is unexceptional to find organised criminals, no matter where, with strong ties to local, regional and national politicians cornering state generated capital' (1999: 218). These ties have acted, as Friman (1999) illustrates in the case of the Japanese Yakuza, to prevent access to local markets by transnational or other international criminal networks. The Yakuza, Friman argues, are so firmly integrated into the relatively closed social and political fabric of Japanese life that the penetration of outside organised crime is extremely difficult.

Berdal and Serrano (2002: 16) distinguish what they see as competing paradigms (transnational and local) in the causal explanation of organised crime. The 'transnational school' (including Nadelman 1993; Ruggiero 1996b; Naylor 1995, 1999; Andreas 1999), primarily concerned with the study of illicit markets and trafficking, theorises organised crime as a consequence of state prohibitionist strategies. The 'local' school (Schelling 1984; Gambetta 1993) by contrast, argues that organised crime is relatively distinct from illicit markets and much more a product of local social, political and economic conditions which result in a deficit of trust in certain transactions; it is this deficit which produces a demand for protection. These 'schools', however, need not be mutually exclusive. Both paradigms, significantly, are predicated on a relationship between criminal organisation and the nation-state.

CRIMINAL ORGANISATIONS AND
THEIR RELATIONSHIP WITH THE STATE

As we have argued, it is the relationship with the state that *defines* the parameters and power of organised crime such as that evidenced by the Sicilian mafia and the Latin American drug cartels.

The penetration of organised crime into the inner workings of Latin American drug-producing states is particularly extreme. An investigation by the Colombian Prosecutor General's office which began in 1984 and reported in 1996 found that some twenty Members of Congress had ties to drug traffickers; the former Minister of Defence Fernando Botero was imprisoned accused of soliciting cartel funds as a campaign manager in the 1994 election; four senators and a former ambassador to the UN were arrested for 'illegal enrichment'. Testimony from former Cali cartel accountant Guillermo Pallomari implicated an additional 35 mayors, 80 Congress members and 30 senators – 35 per cent of the Colombian Congress. Pallomari claimed that in excess of $7 million had been transferred from the cartel to these politicians between the end of 1991 and mid-1994 (Clawson and Rensselaer 1998: 171).

Effectively the drug trafficking, or 'narco elites', of Latin America have in the past been politically indistinguishable from traditional, 'legitimate' economic elites. They have acted, and continue to act, as political lobbyists influencing legislation and government policies that relate to the illicit drugs trade, and funding political campaigns, building political parties. As Farer (1999) demonstrates, narco-executives are frequently the principal source of election funding in some Latin American regions. During the 1980s drug barons also made considerable efforts to seek political office. Through the vehicle of his own political organisation, *Civismo en Marcha* (Good Citizenship on the March), Pablo Escobar was elected to the Colombian Congress in June 1992 as an alternate deputy[5] (Clawson and Rensselaer 1998: 48; Thoumi 1999: 13).

Herschel Grossman suggests that criminal organisations such as the mafia represent real competition to states in terms of the allocation of resources and the distribution of income. Moreover he argues that the existence of criminal organisations is beneficial to the public because in terms of his economic analysis competition between the mafia and the state *increases* the provision of public services and the net income of the representative producer: 'As long as the state remains viable, the existence of the mafia reduces the income only of members of the ruling class or political establishment whose main source of income is political rent extracted by the state' (H. I. Grossman 1995: 154). Only when the activities of criminal organisations become so disruptive as to threaten the viability of the state do the interests of representative producers become vulnerable; an organised crime monopoly over the provision of public services would not be in their interests, according to Grossman, but competition between state and mafia limits the ability of the incumbent ruling elite to extract political rent (1995: 155). These organisations compete with the state in other, non-fiscal ways:

> Drug trafficking has also exercised a wide impact on political and administrative systems in Colombia and other Latin American countries.

Cocaine money finances extensive protection and intelligence networks, including accomplices, informants in key national institutions such as the military, the various police forces, the court system, the government bureaucracy, the legislature, the church, the news media, the national telephone system, and (in Colombia) the national fingerprint registry. (Clawson and Rensselaer 1998: 169)

This degree of penetrative power exercised by the cartels created a situation in which Colombian state officials up until the mid-1990s preferred to negotiate with Cali cartel leaders rather than criminalise them (ibid.: 61):

In modern narcotics enterprises, criminal authority tends to grow at the expense of legitimate state authority. Narcocorruption, of course, diminishes the legitimacy of governing institutions. Yet traffickers not only buy government officials, politicians and electoral outcomes, they also increasingly displace the state in the performance of key social and political functions. (ibid.: 175)

In countries such as Colombia, Bolivia and Mexico the cartels, in an effort to cement regional political legitimacy, have injected vast sums of money into the poorest regional sectors in the form of development projects and public works, money and gifts, social welfare, housing, sports complexes, counter-insurgency and maintenance of law and order (Clawson and Rensselaer 1998; Thoumi 1999). Following the 1995 Kobe earthquake in Japan, the Yakuza filled the gap created by the state's inability to respond quickly. They were able to provide food, water and other provisions through organised and extensive networks (Shelley 1999b: 35–6). Guerrilla organisations like the Colombian FARC and ELN demand land reform, respect for human rights, protection against paramilitarism, reduction in poverty and a reduced spending on the military. During the mid-1990s, these organisations collected taxes from each of the phases of the illicit drug trade – cultivation, processing and transport (Shelley 1999b). Through the threat and exercise of excessive force, corruption and social largesse, the cartels have seriously contributed to a de-legitimation of the institutions of government. Jose Toft, Drug Enforcement Agency representative in Colombia, said in 1994:

I cannot think of a single political or judicial institution that has not been penetrated by the narco traffickers – I know that people don't like to hear the term 'narco-democracy' but the truth is it's very real and it's here. (cited by Clawson and Rensselaer 1998: 172)

The enormous power and resources of the drugs cartels have allowed them to hijack many functions of government. Friman (1999) argues that the Japanese state – because of accommodations to organised crime – facilitated the rise of extensive drug distribution networks, organised and controlled by domestic crime syndicates.

The Sicilian mafia and the Medellin and Cali cartels were also notorious for attempting to directly influence the electoral process. Ernesto Samper's election as Colombian president in 1994 was predicated upon a $6 million donation from the leadership of the Cali cartel (Rensselaer 1999: 7).

Some criminal organisations (mafias, drugs cartels, gangs, and so on) become, in essence, *de facto* states with their own territories, laws and private armies, extracting rents from the local population as well as providing public services (Bequai 1979: Scaperdas and Syropoulos 1995).

The extraordinary reign of Burma's drug lord, Khun Sa, is a powerful illustration. Khun Sa controlled over 50 per cent of the world's heroin supply between the early 1980s and 1995, marshalled an army of some 20,000 men – the Shan United Army – and controlled significant swathes of territory along the Thai–Burmese border for more than a decade. McCoy accounts for this phenomenon in terms of a parallel with early modern banditry:

> As states expand, they often leave peripheries that are, like Khun Sa's native Shan State, poorly integrated into a central apparatus still struggling to take form. In these mountain and maritime fringes, weak state control can provide an opening for men of prowess – pirates, bandits, warlords or ethnic chiefs – to mediate between the center and its margins. (McCoy 1999: 130)

When organised crime becomes too powerful weak states sometimes attempt to co-opt the essence of this power in order to bolster their own organisational goals. In an effort to consolidate and extend its fragile power base, the Burmese military regime (State Law and Order Council – SLORC) finally challenged Khun Sa's army in 1996. First, in order to fund the assault, SLORC aggressively took control of the opium trade along the Thai border; then, having defeated the drug lord, it transformed Khun Sa from rival warlord into a key economic asset, exploiting his international Chinese connections and his vast economic assets to foster Burmese economic development (McCoy 1999: 160).

We would now like to turn to a Turkish case study which encapsulates many of the themes this chapter has raised.

SUSURLUK: DEEP STATE AND ORGANISED CRIME IN TURKEY

A car crash on a remote Turkish highway has torn the veil from a cosy brotherhood of gangsters, warlords and nationalists apparently acting with impunity as part of the state's fight against Kurdish and leftist dissent. (Lyons 1996)

On 3 November 1996, near Susurluk in central Turkey a truck crashed into an armoured Mercedes, killing three of the four occupants. The occupants were Abdullah Çatlı (an ultra-right-wing gang leader, wanted for at least seven political killings, and a convicted narcotics smuggler wanted by Interpol), Sedat Bucak (who survived the crash – a member of parliament for Tansu Çiller's True Path Party and a tribal warlord/clan leader with his own heavily armed 10,000-strong private militia); Hüseyin Kocadağ (a Deputy Chief of Police for Istanbul who had at one time commanded Turkish anti-guerrilla forces in the conflict against the PKK), and Gonca Üs (Abdullah Çatlı's girlfriend and a former beauty queen). Accompanying them in another car were police special agents Ayhan Çarkin, Ercan Ersoy and Oğuz Yorulmaz.

Former Prime Minister Tansu Çiller[6] – forced to resign in 1995 over 'domestic security issues' – attended Abdullah Çatlı's funeral, where she declared: 'Anyone who fires bullets for the State … is an honourable person.'[7] Susurluk exposed much about the murky relationships which exist between Turkey's political elite, its state functionaries, the intelligence services and organised crime – a relationship feared and condemned by Turkish people as *Derin Devlet*, the 'Deep State'.

Some 15 or so years after the Turkish state had eradicated its illicit opium production, Turkey re-entered the narcotics trade as a major transit route from Afghanistan to the markets of western Europe. This resurgence was closely linked to the onset of a bitter war between the Turkish state and Kurdish insurgents (the Kurdish Workers Party or PKK) in south-east Turkey (see Chapter 8). In these conditions of conflict, smuggling easily evaded a Turkish state preoccupied with razing Kurdish villages and terrorising their inhabitants. Opium smuggling also served to fund the activities of the PKK, central as they were in controlling activities at the borders.

Emerging revelations about the Susurluk affair and Turkey's 'deep state' led to a parliamentary commission of inquiry that was widely reported. Journalists alleged that a secret force, nicknamed the 'contra-guerrillas', was out of control, using official sanction to conduct a 'shadow' war against Kurdish nationalists in the south-east. They were also alleged to have official sanction to smuggle heroin, trade in arms, launder political contributions, and pursue mafia and personal vendettas. This force was made up from members of ultra-nationalist groups such as Ulkucu Ocaklari (who regularly transgressed the margins of legality) and members of police 'Special Teams' (that is, Turkish Commando Units) (Robins 2002). By February 1997, the population of Turkey had taken to the streets in 'Clean Hands' marches and protests, and the military – ever the custodians of Turkish public order – took action to depose the government, launching a lawsuit to close down the prime minister's party and pressuring coalition partners to resign.

In 1992, Turkey's supreme decision-making and military authority, the National Security Council, adopted a counter-insurgency strategy which involved pre-emptive strikes and the branding of all PKK supporters as terrorists. The security forces entered into a phase of 'low-intensity conflict' which 'took the war to the PKK': remote villages thought to be harbouring or supporting guerrillas were evacuated and razed, guerrilla strongholds in urban areas were attacked, death squads were organised and local populations were terrorised. A Security Council document was reported to have documented a list of people who could be relied upon to take part in death squads aimed at killing 'terrorists'. The list included gangsters such as Abdullah Çatlı, as well as members of police 'Special Teams'. Tansu Çiller was cited in the media at the time as saying 'We will dry up the sources of support for the PKK.' At that time, the major sources of funding for the PKK were drugs, extortion and international support. Seven alleged drug traffickers, accused of funding the PKK, were murdered. At the same time various offices of the pro-Kurdish newspaper *Özgür Ülke* were firebombed. The bombers were arrested and immediately released.

In December 1996, subject to intense public pressure, Prime Minister Erbakan opened a parliamentary inquiry. The evidence presented to the Commission demonstrates a deep, integrated and mutually reinforcing relationship between the Turkish state and organised crime. Some of the more revealing findings are documented below:[8]

- Abdullah Çatlı, a man wanted for nearly two decades for narcotics offences and seven political killings, and wanted by Interpol since his escape from a Swiss prison in 1990, was carrying false papers at the time of his death identifying him as a 'police expert'. He also had papers testifying that he was 'Mehmet Ozbay', a gun license signed by Interior Minister Mehmet Agar, a green passport (only available to senior civil servants, former and current ministers), and documents which stated that he was a secret agent.[9]

- A top intelligence official acknowledged at the Commission that Turkey's intelligence agency had used Çatlı for 'operations carried out in foreign countries'.[10]
- Turkish officials had reportedly used criminals such as Çatlı to battle leftist extremists and terrorists allied with Armenian separatists in the 1970s and 1980s (in at least eleven operations on Armenian group ASALA between 1982 and 1984), and more recently to support the conflict against the PKK.[11]
- Sedat Bucak (the MP who survived the crash) was a member of Tansu Çiller's True Path Party and is the leader of a clan that was receiving millions of dollars from the government to provide paramilitary village guards to fight the PKK.[12] Allegations were also aired that he was extorting money from gambling houses in Ankara.[13]
- The three police in the second car, Ayhan Çarkin, Ercan Ersoy and Oğuz Yorulmaz were detained after 'casino king' Ömer Lütfü Topal (one of the seven alleged drug traffickers mentioned above) was murdered. During the interrogation Çarkin reportedly said they had been involved in a series of assassinations, including Topal's.[14] Taped evidence of their confession exists.[15]
- Ayhan Çarkin, one of the three 'special team' members, admitted that he had taken time off without permission on the day of the Topal murder. He said, 'Many political figures offered us a lot of money to ensure that we fled and did not face the judiciary. I will disclose their names if needed when things reach the trial stage.'[16]
- Istanbul's former police chief Kemal Yazıcıoğlu said that immediately after he detained the three special team members, Sedat Bucak called from Ankara four times, asking why the three were detained. The three men were mysteriously released after confessing 'on orders from Ankara'.[17] They were then immediately assigned to Sedat Bucak as personal guards.[18] One of the three special team members suspected of having killed Topal said during the interrogation that Abdullah Çatlı ordered the murder and that Çatlı had received his orders from Sedat Bucak; Bucak had received his directions from Interior Minister Mehmet Agar, who in turn, received orders from Özer Çiller (Tansu Çiller's husband).[19] The week after the crash, Agar resigned.
- Ibrahim Şahin, the former head of the Security General Directorate's Special Operations Department, had testified before the Parliamentary Commission that he did not know Abdullah Çatlı. Following his testimony, however, three mainstream newspapers published a photograph of the pair dancing arm-in-arm at a circumcision party in 1995.[20]

- Şahin, head of the Special Operations Department responsible for the special teams, was asked, 'Could the state have made a decision to kill people such as Behcet Canturk and others claimed to have been aiding the PKK?' Şahin replied, 'We do not have the power to make such a decision. But it is pleasing that people such as Behcet Canturk and Savaş Buldan have died.'[21]
- The assassins of the Söylemez brothers (a narcotics gang in rival operation with Abdullah Çatlı) stayed in the home of MP Sedat Bucak after the murders.[22]
- Uğur Mumcu was a journalist investigating alleged 'right-wing gangs' within the state when he was murdered in 1993. Mehmet Agar, the interior minister, visited his widow, who challenged him about police mishandling of the case. Mehmet Agar reportedly admitted the investigation was being blocked, and said that there was nothing he could do.[23]
- The opposition leader Mesut Yılmaz presented the photocopies of three documents to the Parliamentary Commission: (1) a document signed by former interior minister Mehmet Agar which was issued to Yaşar Öz, a narcotics dealer who was close to Abdullah Çatlı; (2) an Interpol document inquiring why the fax number of the office of the private secretary of the Turkish Prime Minister was found on a Canadian narcotics smuggler; (3) the official green passports issued to Yaşar Öz and Tarik Umit, the alleged National Intelligence Organisation (MIT) informer who has been missing amid claims that he has been abducted by the Çatlı team. Agar had apparently also issued falsified documents to Haluk Kırcı, a prime suspect in a number of political killings, identifying him as a police expert. According to Yılmaz, some forty such documents had been issued to underworld figures.[24]
- Abdullah Çatlı was paid from a prime ministerial 'slush fund' to organise ultra-right-wing youth to confront a Greek motorcycle demonstration crossing the line into Northern Cyprus on 11 August 1996. He was reportedly in Northern Cyprus shortly before this date.[25]

The report recommended that 35 people have criminal investigations opened against them, including Sedat Bucak; Halil Tug, the deputy director general of security; Ibrahim Şahin, the former acting director of the Special Operations Department, and Istanbul's former police chief and deputy chief.[26]

Despite the public controversy, however, little has been done about the Susurluk report's recommendations. The report recommended that former interior minister Mehmet Agar's parliamentary immunity be lifted and a criminal investigation opened into his activities; this was not done. Instead Agar was elected leader of the True Path Party in December 2002. On 8 December 1997, investigating Judge Akman Akyurek was killed in an automobile accident; an MIT agent investigating the case also died in an automobile accident with his wife and child in August 1997. On 12 February 2001, after a four-year investigation, 14 people tried over the Susurluk affair were convicted. Most of them had already been released from prison, in 1998. Korkut Eken (a former MIT official) and Ibrahim Şahin (the former deputy director of security) were given the most severe sentences, of six years' jail each.

Susurluk reveals a natural communion between states and organised crime when the political stakes are high enough. The emasculation of the PKK and an end to Kurdish separatist demands were the overriding goals for Turkey's Kemalist regime and the intimate relations between Turkey's intelligence services, key members of mafiya organisations, ultra-right-wing nationalists, senior police commanders and members of the government provided a powerful and sinister mechanism by which to undertake a 'shadow' war against the Kurds – one in which even the woefully limited rules of engagement officially promulgated could be contemptuously by-passed or flouted. While internationally appealing to European favour, the Turkish state in collusion with the darkest forces of organised crime thus conducted a parallel, subterranean criminal campaign of terror in the south-east.

CONCLUSION

In summary then, organised crime can only be understood in relation to the nation-state. It is this relationship which ultimately defines its power, character and persistence. Organised crime is, as we have shown, a precursor, a competitor, and sometimes an ally of the nation-state. In the conditions of weak or predatory states – in which patrimonialism characterises the economy – the state itself has been shown to be organised for criminal goals of kleptocratic accumulation. The use of terror by states and their criminal confederates is further explored in the next chapter.

7
State Terror and Terrorism

terrorism
A system of terror.
   1. Government by intimidation as directed and carried out by the party in power in France during the Revolution of 1789–94 ...
   2. *gen.* A policy intended to strike with terror those against whom it is adopted; the employment of methods of intimidation; the fact of terrorizing or condition of being terrorized.

(Oxford English Dictionary Online)

It should be apparent from the preceding description of the 'shadow war' in Turkey that there is a degree of symmetry between the actions of the PKK and those of the state and its allies. If we are going to apply the language of 'terrorism' at all to such situations, then the label must be applicable to both sides. To use it only of the insurgents would be to collude in the hypocrisy of the Turkish state and numerous others.[1]

We can distinguish three forms of state or state-sponsored violence in the Susurluk case study:

1. 'Classic' terrorism, that is, the clandestine use of violence against civilian targets for purposes of intimidation, or to create a climate of fear, in pursuit of political goals, for example, the firebombing of newspaper offices.
2. State terror, in which civilian targets such as Kurdish villages are attacked for purposes of intimidation, but the perpetrators are not considered 'terrorists' because they are uniformed servants of the state.
3. Assassinations or extra-judicial executions, which are not strictly speaking terrorist acts if the main objective is to eliminate a specific opponent rather than to intimidate others. In practice, however, the same murder often serves both purposes, particularly where it is carried out by a clandestine death squad linked with the state.

In this chapter we shall use the term 'terror' to refer to all three phenomena, and 'terrorism' (more restrictively than the dictionary definition warrants) to refer only to the first.

Terror is, as we shall see in Chapter 9, an increasingly prevalent means of warfare. As we shall see in this chapter and the next, state terror in the shape of massacres, 'disappearances', torture and the like is also a mode of governance used by many modern states.

In a sense, of course, all states rule partly by fear. Violence and the threat of violence always lurk beneath the 'civil façade' (Cover 1986) of even the most law-abiding state. But as E. V. Walter argues in his classic analysis of state terror:

> The fear of punishment is different from the fear generated in the terror process. There is a great deal of difference between the individual who can calculate, 'I fear that if I take this course of action, it will lead to violent punishment', and the turbulent, irrational fear, scarcely permitting thought, stirred up in the reality of unpredictable violence. (Walter 1969: 25–6)

Many gradations are possible between Walter's ideal-type of the state of terror, in which '[i]nnocence is irrelevant', and the contrasting ideal-type of the rule of law. Law courts can be instruments of terror, as in Stalin's USSR and Idi Amin's Uganda. Amin's military tribunals, which tried both political and non-political offences with minimal regard to due process, have been described as 'the "open face" of state terrorism' (Kannyo 2000: 162).

In modern states, terror is an illegitimate and largely clandestine activity. As Walter (1969) illustrates in his account of the rule of the Zulu King Shaka in the early nineteenth century, societies have existed where terror was an open and legitimate method of governance. Killings were carried out according to a simple rule – that the King could order the death of anyone with or without a stated reason – and that rule was justified by a shared belief in the omnipotence of the King. Shaka and his successors were cruel despots but it makes little sense to call their actions *criminal*. In modern states, however,

> witness to torture and systematic brutality is not acceptable to the wider public. The secret society, terror operating behind the state, is fundamental to totalitarian regimes. It is this very concealment that is new ... Modern democratic experiences render unacceptable behaviour which Shaka could employ openly, namely the public execution of the ostensibly innocent. (O'Kane 1996: 195)

Even when acts of terror, such as massacres and the destruction of homes, are performed by uniformed agents of the state, efforts are usually made to conceal them from the outside world. Modern state terror is a form of deviant behaviour, which breaks widely accepted norms (usually including the state's own laws) and which must therefore be concealed or denied.

STATES, TERRORISM AND COUNTER-TERRORISM

States instigate or participate in terrorism (in the narrow sense) in a variety of ways. State personnel may themselves carry out terrorist acts while concealing (or at least not openly acknowledging) their official roles; or they may instigate or condone actions by non-state agencies that enjoy varying degrees of autonomy. The relationships between the Colombian armed forces and right-wing paramilitaries, for example, range from the armed forces actually setting up a particular group, through soldiers 'moon-lighting' as paramilitaries, to the Army simply allowing paramilitaries to operate unhindered (Human Rights Watch 2000e, 2001c). States may use or sponsor terrorism against sections of their own population (including émigrés),[2] or against the population of other states, whose regimes they either oppose or support.

A different relationship between terrorism and the state can be seen in the case of Al-Qaeda, the network almost certainly responsible for the September 11 attacks in the US. The intricate story of Al-Qaeda's origins in the 1980s, its links with Pakistan, Saudi Arabia, the US and the international drugs trade, has been chronicled by John Cooley (2000). The CIA's willingness to work with various elements of organised crime, including drug traffickers and terrorists, in pursuit of its goal of defeating the USSR parallels its activities in Latin America which we discussed in Chapter 6.

Al-Qaeda remains deeply involved in organised crime, including drug, diamond and arms smuggling, as a means of funding its political goals (Cooley 2000; Global Witness 2003a). According to Fred Halliday, Al-Qaeda 'has arisen and been sustained in countries with very weak states', particularly Afghanistan and northern Yemen (2002: 41). Al-Qaeda's capacity for organised violence and ability to levy informal taxes mirrors that of many weak states, but unlike them it does not have a territorial base; its exercise of violence is global.

The September 11 attacks have in turn been used to justify state terror. Without actually using the term 'state terror', Human Rights Watch (2003c) reports several examples. The US has established a $64 million operation to support the Georgian government's anti-terrorist campaigns. Those campaigns have involved at least one extra-judicial execution and four 'dis-appearances', a form of state terror discussed below. In the name of anti-terrorism the US has resumed its aid to the Indonesian military, which was cut in response to its reign of terror in East Timor in 1999, without any guarantee of reform. Russia has increasingly used anti-terrorist rhetoric to justify its use of state terror – massacres, indiscriminate bombing, torture and 'disappearances' – in Chechnya, and has met an increasingly uncritical response from Europe[3] and the US. In Uzbekistan, which has invoked counter-terrorism to justify the detention and torture of followers of independent Islam, Human Rights Watch has documented over a hundred cases of torture, including five people who were tortured to death (2003c: 24).

STATE TERROR AS RATIONAL ACTION

As we saw in Chapters 1 and 3, a useful framework for analysing state crime is one based on three types of 'catalysts for action': motivation, opportunity structures and social control (Kauzlarich and Kramer 1998: 248). An underlying assumption of this framework is that organisations tend to be dominated by instrumental rationality, adopting what they perceive as efficient means to achieve organisational goals. According to Nordlinger (1977), this kind of goal-oriented rationality is particularly characteristic of military institutions and regimes: a point chillingly illustrated in Jennifer Schirmer's (1998) remarkable study of the Guatemalan military. Certainly official discourse about state terror in the shape of US Army training manuals and the like is strongly characterised by instrumental and utilitarian reasoning (McClintock 1992).

Motivation

Gurr (1986) postulates that states are more likely to use terror against internal 'challengers' (1) the greater the threat the challengers pose; (2) the more support the challengers have; (3) if they use terror themselves, and (4) if they are socially marginal rather than having links to the elite. All these factors presumably increase the pressure on the agencies of repression to defeat the challengers; factors (3) and (4) are also likely to reduce informal social controls that inhibit the use of violence.

A strong commitment to ideological goals is another important motivational factor. The Libyan regime of Colonel Ghadafi, for example, has until recently displayed an unusually strong adherence to its ideological commitments, pursuing them even when it appeared to have nothing to gain pragmatically: for example, by supplying arms to the Provisional IRA (Arnold 1996). An alignment to one side or the other during the Cold War was one of the factors most strongly associated with the use of terror (Gurr 1986; Wolpin 1986), as both superpowers tended to encourage their satellite regimes to pursue victory by virtually any means. American military doctrine, widely and uncritically adopted in Latin America, 'tended to make a virtue of terror, in so far as it was anti-Communist, counter-insurgent terror' (McClintock 1985: 41).

Opportunity Structures

Opportunity structures are defined by the relative availability, and attractiveness, of legitimate and illegitimate means for an institution to achieve its goals. Brockett (1991) argues that the use of repression by states is determined *inter alia* by the resources available for repression and the resources available to resolve conflict by other means. For example, Honduras in the 1980s faced a rebel threat of comparable severity to those in Guatemala and El Salvador, but although it employed a CIA-trained death squad to 'disappear' and torture suspected guerrillas (National Commissioner 1994), it did not engage in the wholesale murder and destruction practised by its neighbours (see McClintock 1985; Schirmer 1998). Brockett argues that because Honduras had a weak army, less coercive and exploitative rural class relations than Guatemala or El Salvador, and sufficient land available to concede some of the peasant movement's demands, it did not perceive the guerrilla threat as warranting such an extreme response. Similarly, Jonas (1991) attributes the exceptional brutality of Guatemalan repression from the 1960s to the 1980s, in which an estimated 200,000 people were killed (CEH 1999), to the attitudes of the ruling elite following the US-backed overthrow of a progressive elected government in 1954. The elite was unwilling to contemplate concessions to peasants or to the working class, and unable to formulate any political project that would achieve broad support. Thus violent repression, for which (thanks to the US) it was well equipped, appeared the only available means to achieve its goals.

Gurr (1986) argues that weak states are relatively likely to resort to violent means of control. By weak states he means those that have limited capacities to maintain order, or respond to the demands of their citizens, by legitimate means. Welsh (2002) finds that East Asian states that are weak in this sense (and lacking in professionalism and accountability) tend to have high levels of state violence and/or vigilantism.

Gurr (1986) further argues that when violent means have been used successfully on one occasion they will tend to appear more attractive on future occasions. Regimes that have come to power through violence are likely to see violence as an appropriate means to retain power. States often learn techniques of repression from examples in their own history, or from other states. For example, French methods in Algeria appear to have influenced both Argentine and Guatemalan state terror (Hey 1995: 144).

Social Control

The pervasive fear induced by state terror can itself be a very effective means of social control, including control over the agents of terror themselves. For example, one of the main objectives of the most intensive phase of massacres (1982–83) in Guatemala was to coerce peasants into joining 'civil patrols' and terrorising other peasants. At one stage a quarter of the adult population was recruited into such patrols (Jonas 1991: 150). Civil patrols were often forced to carry out killings in their own or neigh-bouring villages – or be killed themselves (Schirmer 1998: 91). As Linda Green (1999) has documented, the effect on the cohesion of rural communities was devastating. Professional soldiers, too, were victims as well as perpetrators of terror. Military training was a brutal, desensitising process (REMHI 1999: 127–32). The professional torturers and killers of G2 (army intelligence) were told: 'When you are no longer serviceable to this section, your own *compañeros* will be the ones who are going to kill you' (Schirmer 1998: 293).

In situations of all-pervasive terror, when the state 'feeds upon itself' (Arendt 1995), Becker's (1963) maxim that deviance is what other people so label acquires a terrible new meaning. What an actor takes to be conformity can always be retrospectively defined as deviance. For example, some of the most zealous leaders of the Stalinist terror were bewildered at being made scapegoats for the chaos it produced, forgetting 'that right and wrong ... were what the party defined them to be at a given ritual moment' (Getty and Naumov 2000: 503).

Forms of social control that may help *restrain* state terror include moral norms proscribing violence and cruelty, national and international law, domestic and transnational civil society, and pressures from other states. Moral inhibitions against murder will be discussed in more depth in Chapter 10. Suffice it to say that their effectiveness is diminished by forms of social stratification and ethnic division that impede the development of empathy between oppressors and their victims (Gurr 1986; Brockett 1991; Falla 1994). Some officers of the law, especially in democratic states such as Colombia (Human Rights Watch 2001c) and the UK (Taylor 1987), make determined efforts to investigate and curtail state terror. On the other hand, the appearance of constitutional legality can be an effective mask for terror (Schirmer 1997, 1998; Uyangoda 1996).

Gurr (1986) argues that democracies are relatively unlikely to resort to terror, and Rummel (1994) documents their relatively low rates of mass killing. The records of Spain and the UK (see below) are consistent with Gurr's argument that democracies use terrorism only on a relatively small scale. Other states, however, have democratic constitutions and high levels of state terror: notably Guatemala from 1986 to 1993 (Schirmer 1998), Colombia (Giraldo 1996), India,[4] Sri Lanka,[5] Russia, Israel (both during the war of independence and the recent *intifada:* Bloom 2001; Human Rights Watch 2002c) and Zimbabwe (Human Rights Watch 2002b). These are democracies that lack legitimacy from the standpoint of large parts of their population (as does the UK in Northern Ireland), or which as in Chechnya and Palestine (and arguably Northern Ireland)[6] use terror in the role of a colonial or occupying power. With the exception of Zimbabwe, they have acted in response to armed resistance and terrorism by their enemies. It may be the hegemonic rule characteristic of the wealthier democracies, rather than democracy *per se,* that either inhibits terror or reduces the need for it.

Regimes of terror often operate in states where civil society is historically weak. Argentina, for example, had very few non-governmental organisations other than the Catholic Church, which was virtually an arm of the state (Marchak 1999: 321). Chile, on the other hand, had an authentic tradition of democratic politics and provided one of the earliest and most important examples of the 'boomerang effect', whereby domestic civil rights activists are able to transmit information to transnational networks which can use it effectively to damage the state's international standing (Ropp and Sikkink 1999).

PARADOXES OF IRRATIONALITY

The analysis so far has presented states as goal-directed organisations responding more or less rationally to the threats, opportunities and pressures they encounter. Such a model captures many important features of state terror but, as has been argued particularly in the anthropological literature (for example, Taussig 2002), there are other important features of terror that it overlooks.

First, some states pursue goals that are wildly unrealistic. Where terror is used to promote unrealistic goals (or inappropriate means, such as the pseudo-scientific farming techniques of Mao's 'Great Leap Forward': Becker 1996), it may prevent officials from assessing prospects of success realistically or from reporting failures or the reasons for them. Where failures are acknowledged they can only be blamed on sabotage, which must be countered by greater use of terror. Rather than being a rational means of pursuing goals, such terror makes rational decision making impossible. The 'Great Leap Forward' and Cambodia under the Khmer Rouge are extreme examples of this form of self-destructive, 'substantively irrational' state terror (O'Kane 1996).[7]

Secondly, it can be argued that terror is not necessarily an *instrumentally* rational response to threat, but rather is a response that is *symbolically* appropriate or achieves expressive purposes (Zulaika and Douglass 1996) – much as judicial punishment is very largely a symbolic and expressive, rather than instrumentally rational, response to officially defined crime (Garland 1990). For example, Mahmood (2000) interprets state and anti-state violence in Punjab and Indian-ruled Kashmir in terms of a dialectic of humiliation, revenge and renewed humiliation. Actions such as the destruction of the Sikh Golden Temple in Amritsar in 1984, although 'applauded by the people of India generally', were 'nothing less than disastrous' in their impact on the militants, since by offering the profoundest possible insult to their religion they give a further impulse to acts of spiritually inspired martyrdom (Mahmood 2000: 81–2). It is not entirely clear from Mahmood's account whether such actions should be seen as 'forms of performance or ritual' (2000: 82) or as instrumentally motivated, but misjudged, attempts 'to destroy the fulcrum of a possible mass resistance' (2000: 77). Grossman's (2000) account suggests that, between 1990 and 1993, India's use of death squads, enforced disappearances and other terrorist techniques constituted a highly effective form of counter-insurgency against Sikh militants.

Thirdly, regimes may react rationally to their *perceptions* of threat, but those perceptions may be grossly distorted. This is the central thesis of Pion-Berlin's (1989) important study of the Argentinian repression of 1976–82. This period of terror, in which an estimated 25,000 or 30,000 people[8] were 'disappeared', tortured, and in most cases killed, is the subject of a large and varied scholarly literature, and merits discussion at some length. According to Pion-Berlin:

> Ideologies that are conceptually flawed, anachronistic, or simply incompatible with contemporary realities are sure to 'map' the political terrain incorrectly and thus generate serious misperceptions. The more firmly perceptions are embedded in doctrine, the more glaringly discordant they become with the external world. Exaggerated or implausible accounts of national conditions are then fully internalized, and mistaken options (such as the excessive use of force against complacent populations) seem imperative. (1989: 101)

At the same time, Pion-Berlin shows clearly that the military and the political right in Argentina had experienced a 'learning curve of repression' (1989: 90) since 1955, as successive governments found that relatively moderate levels of repression were insufficient to reverse the gains made by organised labour under the earlier Perónist regime. *Some* escalation of repressive violence was, therefore, instrumentally rational, even if the level of terror unleashed by the military junta was not.

The manifestly excessive level of repression, as in the infamous 'night of the pencils' when schoolchildren were tortured and murdered for demanding subsidised bus fares (Feitlowitz 1998: 179), has led some commentators to argue that in 'concentrating on the instrumental aspects of the repression ... researchers have not paid sufficient attention to the psychological and expressive aspects of the terror system' (Suárez-Orozco 1992: 238). While he recognises a high level of rationality and planning in the implementation of the terror, Suárez-Orozco argues that the Junta was following an irrational 'paranoid script' that placed Argentina at the 'epicentre of a global attack on the Western way of life' (1992: 238) and defined all forms of dissent as the instruments of godless subversives. Similarly, Graziano argues that the Junta embraced Cold War national security ideologies 'with a medieval religiosity, burdening these political interpretations with otherworldly obligations' (1992: 26). The leftist guerrillas, having already been effectively defeated at the time of the 1976 military coup, were 'a largely imaginary enemy whose resistance was necessary ... for the repressors' (Graziano 1992: 29). So necessary, in fact, that there is strong though not conclusive evidence that the Junta itself controlled the key guerrilla leaders and instigated their terrorist actions (Andersen 1993; Marchak 1999).

One of Muir's (1977) paradoxes of coercive power, which we discussed in Chapter 6, is that it can be rational to be irrational:

It may be necessary to become sincerely irrational and to believe what is otherwise illogical, so that one's adversaries come to believe that one has the will to do things that are senseless in terms of economic efficiency, civilized decency, and human awareness. (1977: 43)[9]

Similarly, it can be rational for an organisation to have some of its members (and possibly even its leaders: see Walter 1969: 8–9) hold and act upon irrational beliefs. Their irrationality may make the use of terror all the more effective.

The Argentine regime's 'paranoid' reaction to any manifestation of dissent appears to have been very effective in silencing anyone who might have been tempted to 'make waves' (Suárez-Orozco 1992: 234). One reason why arbitrary terror is effective lies in a further paradox. In order to respond to terror with a degree of rationality, its potential victims need to discover some form of order or rule that will render the future at least minimally predictable (Malamud Goti 1998). This drives them to accept that the random violence of the state must, after all, reflect a hidden rationality. 'They must have done something' was a common reaction to disappearances in Argentina, one that rendered the repression somewhat less terrifying, but made the bystanders complicit in the terror (Graziano 1992: 78; Suárez-Orozco 1992: 244). Feldman (1991: 106–9) reports a similar response to harassment by the security forces in Northern Ireland, which was perceived as marking the person concerned as a potential murder victim.

Closely related to Muir's paradox of irrationality is what we may call the 'paradox of paranoia'. If regimes contemplating terror calculate the effects of their actions in cost-benefit terms, it may be organisationally rational to adopt a 'paranoid' overestimate of the threat their opponents pose. The reason is that the 'costs' to be factored into the cost-benefit equation include 'moral costs' such as the adverse reactions of domestic and international audiences, and the psychic distress experienced by perpetrators (Duvall and Stohl 1986). Van Creveld (1991) argues that such costs – in particular, the disintegration of military morale – are likely to be disastrous where great violence is unleashed against a much weaker enemy. But if the enemy can be defined, however unrealistically, as an immensely powerful threat to the existence of the nation, then the moral costs of terror will be much reduced, since people who believe they are fighting for survival often feel free to disregard the conventions of war (van Creveld 1991: 145). A 'paranoid' exaggeration of the potential benefits of terror can thus produce a real reduction in its costs, and thereby enable certain real benefits (such as crushing trade union resistance to monetarist economic policies in Argentina) to be achieved.

In the light of these paradoxes, it would be misleading to draw too sharp a contrast between explanations of terror as instrumentally rational behaviour on the one hand and as irrational or expressive behaviour on the other. Terror can be seen, rather, as an attempt to harness irrational and expressive behaviour in pursuit of rational ends, or to harness rational behaviour in pursuit of irrational ends.

In the case of Argentina, we can see that the 'learning curve of repression' provided a rational motive for the terror, and the evidence of state infiltration of the guerrilla leadership suggests that elements of the military cynically manufactured the enemy activity needed to justify repression. There is also ample evidence that the religious and paranoid world-view fostered by the military leadership helped to neutralise the moral unease associated with terror:

From the detention centers themselves survivors reported the repressors' initial hesitation and guilt in regard to torturing and executing teenagers, but these feelings were always allayed in the 'final solution' context ('it's better not to let those with this social restlessness grow up') or by direct resort to the underlying mythological infrastructure of the 'dirty war'. One victim was told, for example, 'You are our best young people …

valuable people, but ... this is a holy war and you want to disrupt the natural order ... you are the Antichrist ... I'm not a torturer, I'm an inquisitor.' (Graziano 1992: 31, ellipses in original)

After my first flight [with a consignment of sedated prisoners who were thrown out of the aeroplane over the sea] it was very hard for me to accept it on a personal level ... The next day I didn't feel very good and I was talking with the chaplain of the [Naval School of Mechanics, a major torture centre], who found a Christian explanation for it ... that it was a Christian death, because they didn't suffer, it wasn't traumatic, they had to be eliminated, that war was war and even the Bible provided for eliminating the weeds from the wheat field. (Adolfo Francisco Scilingo, ex-Naval Officer, in Verbitsky 1996: 30)[10]

It was a total fight in which one side was going to win and one was going to lose. We lived it as a war. And in a war – in any war, even a conventional one – in order to win, procedures that are against human rights are frequently used ... Torture is a desperate method that is used to try and win when there are no other ways of doing so. ('Colonel Lorenzo' in Marchak 1999: 272–3)

But terror and paranoia, once unleashed, are difficult to control (Taussig 2002). Roniger and Sznajder write that the relatively decentralised command structure of the Argentine armed forces 'generated a pattern of uncoordinated autonomy' which 'produced in turn a very intense and relatively undiscriminating use of violent repression', reflecting the 'specific subculture of the repressors and their latent values and orientations' rather than direct orders from above (1999: 21, 38). To the dismay of some officers, intelligence groups operated without control, and what 'started out as a fight against subversives was extended until every group in the population was threatened' ('Major Bobbio' in Marchak 1999: 308). Moreover the initial use of terror generated forms of secondary deviance:

This illegal methodology, even apart from the moral and legal problems, has the defect that when you use criminal procedures, normally you have to commit other crimes to cover up for the first one. If you kidnap them and submit them to interrogations with torture, later you have to commit other crimes to cover up those previous crimes, and many times the way to cover them up is to kill the person. In that period of euphoria, the armed forces and the police thought they were invincible. That also explains why a criminal methodology spread ... Always, when illegal procedures are used, the notion of what's criminal and what's not gets lost. Therefore, to take things that do not belong to the state, that belong to the prisoners, sometimes was thought of as a kind of war booty. ('Major Villegas' in Marchak 1999: 295, ellipsis in original)

According to Andersen (1993: 266) greed quickly became 'the primary motivation for many dirty warriors'. Soldiers and police killed each other in quarrels over loot; the deaths were attributed to guerrillas.

THE DYNAMICS OF CLANDESTINE TERRORISM

Another paradoxical aspect of state terrorism is its clandestine nature. Modern states cannot torture and murder openly, but their acts of torture and murder must be made known in order to be effective as terror (Graziano 1992; Campbell 2000). The most important methods adopted by states to achieve the desired combination of publicity and concealment are the disappearance and the death squad.

Disappearances

In international criminal law, 'enforced disappearance' is applied to acts of arrest, detention or abduction that are 'followed by a refusal to acknowledge that deprivation of freedom or give information on the fate or whereabouts' of the victim (ICC Statute, Art. 7(2)(i)). This definition correctly identifies the hallmark of a disappearance not as *secrecy*, but rather as *denial* (Graziano 1992; Cohen 2001). Typically, as in Argentina, the actual arrests or abductions are

> ... not, as the term *disappearance* might suggest, invisible affairs. Members of the armed forces in helicopters, military trucks and jeeps cordoned off the area under siege. The victim was abducted, often yelling or screaming for help, by a group of heavily armed men ... The victim would usually be thrown down on the back seat of the waiting car, and the group would drive away, recklessly, flaunting. Yet no one was supposed to see or, more specifically, admit to seeing what was going on ... The scenario became increasingly surreal as the junta disavowed the state terrorism that people saw with their own eyes ... The military blinded and silenced the population which had to accept and even participate in this production of fictions. (Taylor 1997: 98)

While the denial of disappearances is presumably intended to deceive international audiences (or to permit them to feign ignorance), its effect on the local population is to enforce complicity or acquiescence. Denial is an integral part of the technique of terror, as is the invisibility of the victim after the initial abduction. Several writers on Argentina have noted that, in contrast to the early modern spectacles of torture and death discussed by Foucault (1977), the torture and murder of the disappeared achieves its effect though the absence of direct public witness. As Graziano puts it, 'The eerie, overwhelming silence of the victims – tortured but absent – was paralleled by that of the audience, terrorized by having "witnessed" the abstract spectacle that the Junta at once staged and forbade' (1992: 73). Feitlowitz writes that even as the Junta flatly denied the existence of its 341 concentration camps, 'it exploited several of them for maximum local terror' (1998: 166). Neighbours who heard the screams and the gunshots, and saw the helicopters landing and the coffins carried out, 'lived under constant stress, as if we ourselves were also prisoners' (witness quoted by Feitlowitz 1998: 167).

Death Squads

Campbell (2000: 1–2) defines death squads as

> … clandestine and usually irregular organizations, often paramilitary in nature, which carry out extrajudicial execution and other violent acts (torture, rape, arson, bombing, etc.) against clearly defined individuals or groups of people. Murder is their primary or even their sole activity.

Death squads, Campbell notes, generally operate with the support or acquiescence of the state, or some section of the state, but they nearly always involve private as well as state interests and operate with a degree of autonomy.

The death squad phenomenon therefore lies on the borders between state and non-state violence (or state-organised crime: see Chapter 6), and between terrorist and non-terrorist murder. Rather than attacking random victims, death squads tend to target specific individuals whose elimination is seen as desirable. At the same time, death squads generally aim to create a wider effect of terror. When death squads leave the mutilated bodies of their victims on the street, as was common practice in Argentina, El Salvador and Guatemala, the terrorist purpose is obvious.

Some death squads are simply soldiers in plain clothes, but more typically they reflect a 'symbiosis between state and non-state interests' (Campbell 2000: 3), for example, between the El Salvador government and the ARENA party, which defended the interests of major landowners; or between the UDR and UDA in Northern Ireland (see below). In Brazil, death squads are part of the private security industry, staffed by off-duty police officers and hired by commercial undertakings such as supermarkets to kill people, including children, whose existence is deemed to be bad for business (Huggins 2000). As in other countries, especially in Latin America, Brazilian death squads also target people on the ground of their sexual orientation – a form of 'social cleansing' that is tolerated, though not directly instigated, by the state (Mott 1996; Ungar 2002).

As Huggins observes, death squads are a means by which 'governments can lower the political costs of their repressive goals by refocusing national and international attention away from the state and toward supposedly random, unplanned, and at least officially "unofficial" violence' (1998: 220). This can be a tempting strategy for democratic as well as for authoritarian states, as the following cases illustrate.

Death Squads in Spain

GAL (the Anti-terrorist Liberation Groups) killed 27 people in Spain between 1983 and 1987. Many victims were members of ETA, a Basque separatist group engaged in terrorism, but nine had no ETA connections (Woodworth 2001: 7). Subsequent investigations have established that GAL was a mixture of police officers and mercenaries organised and funded by government ministers and leading Socialist Party politicians. The government's involvement was first clearly revealed through the confessions of two police officers involved in a kidnapping in France in 1983. The GAL abducted a salesman called Segundo Marey whom they mistook for an ETA activist. The senior government officials directing the GAL then decided Marey should be kept in captivity in order to put pressure on the French authorities to release four Spanish police officers arrested after an earlier bungled abduction. Allegedly they also proposed that he should be killed. In an analysis of the police officers' confessions, the anthropologist Begoña Aretxaga argues that they reveal

> ... a state suffused with affect; it gets excited, exhilarated at trespassing into the fantastic space of terrorism, carried away by its own fantasy of the omnipotence attributed to the terrorist, unbounded by the rule of law, unrestrained by the parameters that define the civilized reality of parliamentary democracy. (2000: 61)

What Aretxaga calls 'mimesis' (the state imitating the terrorist) contains elements of Muir's 'paradox of irrationality': in order to convince their opponents (the French government) that they were operating outside conventional political rationality, the senior officials became genuinely irrational, behaving in a way that was not only morally outrageous but fraught with disproportionate risk for their own government.

Aretxaga's account is also reminiscent of the excitement of transgression and secrecy evoked in Katz's *Seductions of Crime* (1988). Katz himself speculates whether the incompetence of many acts of state terrorism may reflect a similar emotional dynamic to that of armed robbers who use violence less as 'a rationally self-serving act than a commitment to the transcendence of a hard will' (1988: 187, see also 321–4). The problem with this analogy is that Katz's robbers were making split-second decisions whether to shoot, whereas the decisions of state agencies to engage in terror are generally much more calculated. But given the difficulty of predicting the costs and benefits of political violence with any accuracy, the emotional seductions or repulsions of clandestine violence may sometimes be a decisive factor in the choice between terrorism and alternative political strategies.

Death Squads in Northern Ireland

Sluka (2000: 141) argues that loyalist paramilitaries in Northern Ireland fit the definition of death squads 'to a tee'. The Ulster Defence Association (UDA), which sometimes operates under the name Ulster Freedom Fighters (UFF), and other paramilitary groups emerged in the early 1970s independently of the state, but drew on a tradition of loyalist paramilitarism established in particular by the 'B' Specials, a part-time police reserve notorious for its partisanship and violence (Feldman 1991: 40–1; Taylor 1999). Allegations of collusion between paramilitaries and the state date back to 1972–73, when members of the Royal Ulster Constabulary (RUC) are said to have provided files which the UDA used as a basis for sectarian assassinations (Sinn Fein 1997). The most serious (but unproven) allegation of collusion in the 1970s is that the British intelligence service was involved in planning the 1974 bombings in Dublin and Monaghan in the Irish Republic, in which 33 people were killed (see Bell 1996; Rolston 2001).

What is undoubtedly true is that there was a substantial overlap between the membership of the UDA and the part-time Ulster Defence Regiment (UDR). In the 1970s and 1980s, UDR soldiers 'moonlighting' as paramilitaries were responsible for many terrorist crimes and more than a hundred members of the regiment were convicted of serious offences including murder, attempted murder, causing explosions and having explosive substances (Dillon 1990: 220). The UDR did not enjoy the same degree of impunity as most of the world's death squads (Warren 2000): it achieved the remarkable distinction for a state agency of having a *recorded* crime rate twice that of the general population (Tomlinson 1998). It appears to have been the UDA and the Ulster Volunteer Force who infiltrated the UDR, rather than *vice versa*, but the UDR's willingness to allow dual membership of the regiment and the UDA clearly facilitated the UDA's murderous activities (Dillon 1990; Coogan 1996). It stretches credulity to suppose that this was entirely unforeseen. Ellison and Smyth (2000: 140) argue that the

UDR 'operated a system of low-level state terror that was tolerated because it fitted into the overall goals of the security apparatus', relieving pressure on the regular Army and 'instilling fear into the nationalist population'. The UDR ceased to exist as a separate organisation in 1992, when it was merged into the Royal Irish Rifles.

The best-documented example of collusion between the state and UDA surrounds the activities of the military intelligence agent Brian Nelson, who was sentenced to ten years' imprisonment in 1992 on charges of conspiracy to murder. Nelson had been a UDA intelligence officer who became an Army informer before leaving Northern Ireland to live in Germany. In 1987 he was recruited by the Force Research Unit (FRU), a section of Army intelligence which ran agents within both loyalist and republican paramilitary groups. At their instigation he rejoined the UDA and rose to become its chief intelligence officer. The records of Nelson's meetings with his FRU handlers suggest, according to journalists who have seen them, that the FRU 'recruited Nelson for the specific purpose of ensuring that the UDA's death squads, instead of murdering Catholics indiscriminately, would target only people involved in republican terrorism' (Ware and Seed 1998).

Nelson's and the FRU's definition of 'legitimate' targets extended well beyond active members of the Provisional IRA. For example, one of the targets whose details were supplied to Nelson by the FRU was Alex Maskey, a prominent Sinn Fein councillor, who survived to become Lord Mayor of Belfast (Davies 1999; *Panorama* 2002). This was one of several operations for which the FRU allegedly arranged 'restriction orders' to ensure that RUC and Army patrols kept away from the location of an intended murder (Davies 1999: 17–18, 57). Francisco Notarantonio was murdered by a UDA death squad although had not been involved in the IRA since the 1940s. The FRU allegedly set him up as a target in order to divert the UDA's attention from an IRA member who was a key informer for the British Army (Clarke 2000; Taylor 2001).

The most controversial murder in which Nelson was involved was that of the solicitor Pat Finucane, who often represented high-profile Republican defendants. According to some sources, RUC detectives encouraged the UDA to target Finucane and two other solicitors (LCHR 2002: 44; *Panorama* 2002). In February 1989, the UDA's third attempt to kill Finucane succeeded despite information passed to the security forces by Nelson and by William Stobie, a UDA quartermaster and RUC Special Branch informer (see Moloney 1999; BIRW 2000; LCHR 2002). A former FRU member told investigators from the Lawyers Committee for Human Rights that he believed 'Special Branch made a conscious decision not to prevent the murder the third time around' (LCHR 2002: 41). An RUC detective claims to have been threatened by Special Branch to stop him arresting a UDA man who had admitted the murder (*Panorama* 2002). According to Davies (1999), the FRU provided Nelson with Finucane's home address – though he could have found it in the telephone directory. Stobie was subsequently charged for his part in the murder, acquitted, and then murdered. A report by the Metropolitan Police Commissioner (Stevens 2003) confirmed the involvement of Nelson and Stobie (described as an 'agent' of the RUC Special Branch) in the murders of Finucane and a student called Brian Lambert.

Davies (1999) portrays Nelson in 1988–89 as an agent 'out of control', who increasingly identified himself with the UDA's, rather than the Army's, values, and disregarded the distinctions drawn by his FRU handlers between 'legitimate targets' and 'ordinary decent Catholics'. Nelson emerges in this account as an example of Huggins and Haritos-Fatouros' (1998) 'lone wolf mode of masculinity': a man who, far from sheltering behind any excuse of 'only following orders', exulted in his hardness and cunning. 'Pitting your wits against those who you seek to compromise acts like a drug', he wrote in his prison journal. 'The more you experience it the more you want it, regardless of the moments of intense fear' (quoted by Geraghty 1998: 157). His desire for the respect due to his paramilitary accomplishments clashed with the professional imperative of secrecy, and he took to bragging about his work for the UDA in loyalist clubs (Davies 1999). Whatever the personal motives of Nelson and other loyalists, however, there was a coherent strategy behind their attacks on 'ordinary decent Catholics'. They were designed to show nationalist communities that the IRA could not protect them, and thereby put pressure on the IRA to abandon its campaign (Taylor 1999; Sluka 2000).

Between 1990 (when Nelson was arrested) and 1994, the loyalists stepped up their campaign of sectarian killing. Relatives for Justice (1995) list 170 sectarian or political killings by loyalists in this period and claim that in 110 of them there is evidence of some form of collusion by the security forces. In a majority of these cases the only evidence of collusion appears to be that the killers used South African weapons, which Brian Nelson played a role in procuring (though according to Taylor (1999: 188), he was 'cut out of the loop' by the UDA at an early stage). In other cases, however, the victims had been warned by the police that intelligence information about them was in the hands of loyalists (warnings which could be construed as either well-intentioned or menacing) or had been repeatedly harassed by the security forces.

Two very different explanations have been proposed for this escalation of sectarian terror. Geraghty (1998) points out that it coincided with the abandonment of the Army's tactic of allowing IRA units to proceed with their operations up to a point when they could be ambushed and killed with

the appearance of legality (see Urban 1992; Ní Aolain 2000). Incidents
such as the 1987 Loughgall ambush, in which the Army shot dead eight
armed IRA men but also killed one passer-by and seriously injured another,
and the killings of three IRA members in Gibraltar which were found to
have violated the European Convention of Human Rights (*McCann* v.
UK 1995), made the legitimacy of such tactics increasingly difficult to
defend. Geraghty, who attributes loyalist effectiveness in the 1990s to
British intelligence leaks, suggests it 'is not impossible that a precisely
tuned counter-insurgency strategy, fouled up by bad publicity, was replaced
by a Loyalist assassination offensive' (1998: 117). If this speculation is
correct, it illustrates Campbell's (2000: 13) point that pressures on states
to be seen to respect human rights may actually encourage the use of covert
death squads.

By contrast, Bruce (1994) and Urban (1996: 273) maintain that the
UDA was able to escalate its terror campaign because the security forces
lost the degree of control they had formerly exercised over its leadership.
Some of the key British agents in the UDA, including Nelson, were arrested
by the Stevens Inquiry, a team of police from outside Northern Ireland sent
to investigate intelligence leaks. When the UDA was banned in 1992, a
spokesperson said it was because the security forces had directed the
organisation for the past 16 years but 'they couldn't direct us any more'
(quoted by Coogan 1996: 335). Urban also maintains that the UDA strategy
was so successful that it led directly to the IRA's decision to call a ceasefire
in 1994. But this raises the question: if the UDA was doing such a brutally
effective job, how motivated were the security and intelligence services to
stop them? According to Davies (1999), both MI5 (the branch of the secret
service dealing with internal security) and the FRU were divided on this
issue during the period when Brian Nelson was operating. Intelligence from
Nelson was used to prevent specific loyalist killings, including the planned
assassination of Sinn Fein leader Gerry Adams, but the FRU received no
orders to bring their agent's involvement in sectarian murder to an end.
Ultimate responsibility for this acquiescence in UDA murders rests, in
Davies' view, with the Joint Intelligence Committee chaired by the then
Prime Minister, Margaret Thatcher.

CONCLUSION

This chapter has analysed state terror as a technique of coercive governance,
and state terrorism as a technique in which state terror is coupled with
denial. We have seen that both authoritarian and democratic regimes have
adopted terrorist techniques as an instrumentally rational response to
political threats, especially but not exclusively to the threat of anti-state

terrorism or armed revolt. While emphasising the rationality of state terror(ism), we have also recognised the importance of irrational or non-instrumental motives and effects of terror, and the autonomy enjoyed by many state-sponsored terrorist organisations. These factors can lead to levels of political violence far exceeding those to which purely rational decision-making would lead. When, in Chapter 10, we turn to consider genocide, we shall observe an even more lethal interplay between rational political calculation and the irrational or emotional process that such calculations may set in train.

8
Torture

It is the survivor's poem
That is the most eloquent.
The cut tongue tells it best.
(Muzaffer Orucoglu)[1]

MAPPING TORTURE

Torture is not confined to a small number of particularly brutal regimes. Amnesty International documents evidence of torture in almost half of the world's states. As one might expect, torture is more prevalent under authoritarian regimes such as Saudi Arabia, Iraq and China but it is not confined to such regimes nor to the period of dictatorships between the 1960s and 1990s. The United States, Israel and the United Kingdom, First World democracies characterised by multi-party political systems, free elections and a separation of powers, have also been clearly identified as torturing nations.[2] At the beginning of the twenty-first century, deaths as a result of torture take place in over 80 countries; torture or ill treatment of suspects by state agents occurs in over 150 countries and torture is widespread in over 70 countries (Amnesty International 2000b). While political prisoners remain the most studied of victims of torture, evidence seems to suggest that the majority of torture victims are criminal suspects from the poorest and most marginalised sections of society. The majority of torturers are police officers.

Despite the illegality of torture in most domestic jurisdictions (Israel until recently being a notable exception: see below) and its clear condemnation in international law, criminology has largely ignored the crime of torture – a product of what Fattah (1997: 67) has described as 'criminology's traditional and persistent bias'. This chapter examines torture as a behaviour which is perceived as deviant by the international community and by certain domestic audiences. We will examine the historical, political and sociological nature of torture and how acts of torture are facilitated by state agencies and how they in turn promote state organisational goals.

DEFINING TORTURE

The standard definition of torture, adopted by the United Nations General Assembly in 1984 is contained in the UN Convention Against Torture and Other Cruel, Inhuman or Degrading Treatment or Punishment and reads:

> ... any act by which severe pain or suffering, whether physical or mental, is intentionally inflicted on a person for such purposes as obtaining from him or a third person information or a confession, punishing him for an act he or a third person has committed or is suspected of having committed, or intimidating or coercing him or a third person, or for any reason based on discrimination of any kind, when such pain or suffering is inflicted by or at the instigation of or with the consent or acquiescence of a public official or other person acting in an official capacity. It does not include pain or suffering arising only from, inherent in or incidental to lawful sanctions.[3]

Stover and Nightingale, while acknowledging as integral the infliction of pain to the definition, usefully add that 'the purpose of torture is to break the will of the victim and ultimately to destroy his or her humanity' (1985: 5).

Torture is a process: a limited dialectic between torturer and prisoner and an expressive dialectic between a torturing regime and its internal enemies. It is a limited dialectic between torturer and tortured because the prisoner is unable to exercise reflexivity, is denied the possibility of agency in the torture context. This denial or, better, destruction of agency at the hands of the torturer is possible because as Scarry writes, 'intense pain is world destroying' (1985: 29).

There are three main points of contention arising out of attempts to define torture in a meaningful and specific sense: a) the degree to which all forms of state-inflicted pain (including capital punishment) might to some extent satisfy the definition of torture; b) problems with limiting the torturer's identity to that of a public official when militias and paramilitary forces have been proven perpetrators of torture; and c) the extent to which acts of terror initiated against women and children in the domestic sphere should be understood as torture.

We will deal with each of these challenges briefly. The concept of torture employed in this chapter is restricted in a number of ways. Whilst recognising the strong parallels between torture, capital punishment and other aggravated forms of state-inflicted punishment, our emphasis remains on the more narrowly defined category of torture. Capital punishment, imprisonment and other official punishments are, we believe, best understood as a separate category of state power.[4] In support of this restricted usage we would argue that a definition of torture cannot usefully encompass all forms of human pain and suffering inflicted by the state. As Edward Peters notes, there is no utility in a concept of torture founded upon a 'moral-sentimental term designating the infliction of suffering, however defined, upon anyone for any purposes – or for no purpose' (1996: 2).

The most recent challenge to the definition of torture argues that the emphasis on the agency of a public official excludes the agency of individuals in the private or domestic sphere where women, in particular, suffer enormous physical and mental cruelty and terror.[5]

This proposed expansion of the definition creates a category of harm too broad for our specific purpose of examining crimes committed by states and their agents. For us the involvement of the state as direct perpetrator (rather than its failure to protect victims from terror) must remain a central element of the definition.[6] It is therefore more appropriate to confine our examination to acts perpetrated by state officials rather than private individuals. In many cases these acts of torture are directed against women and children and take the form of sexual assaults, sexual humiliation, and the destruction of honour (see, for example, Amnesty International 2003; Human Rights Watch 2003f).

In working toward a definition appropriate to the late twentieth century, Peters stressed the importance of the public nature of torture: 'Torture began as a legal procedure and has always had as its essence its public character, whether as an incident in judicial procedure or as a practice of state officials outside the judiciary proper' (1996: 4). For our purposes this public character is central to the definition of torture.

By focusing on the public character of torture – whether in strict legal procedure or in the hands of sub-legal or paralegal agencies – we may be able to regard torture in and after the twentieth century no longer in the simplistic terms of personality disorder, ethnic or racial brutality, residual primitivism, or the secularisation of ecclesiastical theories of coercion, but as an incident of some forms of modern public life, no longer, as in the past, restricted to formal criminal legal procedure, but occurring in other areas under state authority less regulated than legal procedure, less observed, but no less essential to the state's notion of order (Peters 1996: 7).

The third point of contention relates to the incorporation of non-state terror perpetrators. The UN Convention against Torture has come under significant criticism for failing to acknowledge torture that is inflicted by non-state entities such as paramilitary organisations, terrorist groups and militias (see, for example, Suedfeld 1990; Dunèr 1998). We argue that many of the non-state entities referred to (such as the Indonesian-backed right-wing militias, responsible for appalling episodes of brutality in East Timor, and the Taliban regime before the US and its allies waged war against the people of Afghanistan) have fundamental links to repressive states and as such can be understood as extra-state functionaries, or are themselves *de facto* states holding a monopoly over the 'legitimate' use of force and levying taxes.

One of the most telling definitional features of torture, for us, is the powerful context of public terror in which it occurs (see Chapter 7). The public/state element of torture allows for its capacity as 'world destroying'. If the state perpetrates or tacitly condones the terror there can be no escape, no other world.

Amnesty International, Human Rights Watch, the International Rehabilitation Council for Torture Victims, the United Nations Human Rights Committee, the European Commission on Human Rights and other non-governmental and inter-governmental agencies have all provided a catalogue of examples of medically verified forms of torture. Peters has synthesised this harrowing mass of testimonial evidence, collected from over a hundred different countries, a fraction of which includes: beatings such as jumping on the victim's stomach; *falacca* or *falanga* which involves beating the soles of the feet with rods; *telephono* where the torturer claps flattened palms over the victim's ears rupturing the tympanic membrane in the process; the use of electricity including tying victims to a metal bed before applying a current and the use of pointed electrodes placed on the victim's genitalia; burning ('including roasting on a red hot grill'); *submarino*, the submersion of the victim's head in dirty water until the point of suffocation is almost reached; rape and forced sexual assault; suspension in mid-air with knees bent over a rod and tied tightly to wrists; deprivation of water; fake executions, the forced witnessing of the torture of the victim's family or children; being held incommunicado; sensory deprivation; the forced injection of psychotropic drugs or 'faecal matter' (Peters 1996: 169–71).

A survey by Amnesty International of its own country records between 1997 and 2000 reveals that the most common form of torture is that of beating, 'with fists, sticks, gun-butts, makeshift whips, iron pipes, baseball bats, electric flex. Victims suffer bruises, internal bleeding, broken bones, lost teeth, ruptured organs and some die' (Amnesty International 2001e: 1).

THE RE-EMERGENCE OF MODERN TORTURE

Edward Peters suggests that the revival of torture practices is intimately linked to the development of political police in the twentieth century and to the influence of a 'quasi-jurisprudence' within that other agency of state violence, the military, with its own rules, practices and punishments (1996: 114). Both came to prominence with the rise of fascism in Europe and the events following Stalin's rise to power in the years after the Russian revolution:

> Infinitely more wealthy and powerful, moved by ideologies that excited more and more of its citizens, possessed of organs and intelligence that could dispense with traditional divisions of authority, the coercive revolutionary state of the twentieth century could re-introduce torture into any or all of its procedures, for it had developed not only new powers, but a new anthropology. In place of the rights of man and citizen, there was substituted the exclusive right of the Volk or Revolution. (Peters 1996: 131)

Otto Kirchheimer eloquently describes the conditions by which torture was able to re-emerge and flourish under the Third Reich. Writing in 1941, he described the system of 'technical rationality' which the Nazis used as the basis of law as superseding

> ... any system for the preservation of individual rights ... [making] law and legal practice an instrument of ruthless domination and oppression in the interest of those who control the main economic and political levers of social power. Never has the process of alienation between law and morality gone so far as in the society which allegedly has perfected the integration of these very conceptions. (Kirchheimer 1969: 109)

The exercise of colonial power is also important, particularly in explaining the role of modern democractic states in the practice of torture. To some extent it challenges the centrality of Peters' 'new anthropology thesis'. After all, states which elevated the civil rights of the individual citizen such as France and England have both been responsible for torture in the name of the 'metropole', specifically in colonial formations. And Peters certainly acknowledges the contribution of colonialism in his theory:

> The colonial experience indeed seems to have contributed to the reappearance of torture, but not because colonial administrators and police learned such practices from the populations they governed; rather the very circumstances in which they governed populations which became increasingly restive during the twentieth century led to the abuse of authority that included torture and later became routine in places like Algeria. (Peters 1996: 138)

While many liberal democratic analysts attributed the rise of torture to the specific and anomalous political/economic formations of Nazi Germany and the Soviet Union, the emergence of evidence in the late 1950s which implicated France in the practice of torture revealed something far more widespread, insidious and confronting for the liberal democratic state. The evidence suggests that torture is most likely to occur when the following conditions prevail: economic crises, political violence, significant cultural change, societal chaos and social disorganisation, and the imposition of authoritarian rule (Staub 1989; Peters 1996; Rejali 1994).

Given these structural conditions torture is then more likely to appear in states where:

- There has been a historical devaluation of a section of the population.
- There is, in the society, a strong respect for authority.
- The culture is both monolithic and enjoys a high degree of popular identification (that is, Staub's 1989 'cultural self-concept' evidenced most strongly in countries like Nazi Germany, modern Turkey, Cambodia and Argentina in the 1970s).
- There is embodied within the dominant ideology the clear designation of an enemy, for example, Jews in Nazi Germany, 'subversives' in Argentina, Kurdish militants in Turkey. (Staub 1989: 62)

EXPLAINING TORTURE

Why do states torture? In the twenty-first century, with seemingly limitless means of coercion and strategies of social control, why is it that almost one-half of the world's countries continue to engage in the practice of torture? In a strictly functionalist sense it would appear that torture is effective, not in extracting confessions so much as in silencing opposition. The extensive literature on torture reveals a variety of theoretical approaches – from political economy and structural explanations (Chomsky and Herman 1979; Tomasevski 1998; Peters 1996; Rejali 1994) through socio-cultural/humanist analyses (Arendt 1973; Staub 1989) and Foucauldian historiography (Foucault 1977), to the extensive and often celebrated psychological approaches exploring obedience and authority (Milgram 1974; Haney et al. 1973; Huggins and Haritos-Fatouros 1998; Sottas 1998). This chapter draws primarily on the political economy, structural and social-psychological literature to explore the existence and persistence of torture in the twenty-first century. We begin, however, with a brief critique of Arendt's humanist theory.

In *The Origins of Totalitarianism*, Hannah Arendt argues that torture in modern society arises when public democratic life is overwhelmed by the force of bureaucratic structures. The bureaucracy from this perspective assumes a life force of its own. Unaccountable and difficult to regulate because of its less public and technically complex nature, bureaucratic structures are in conflict with the forces of democracy. In situations where bureaucracy overwhelms democratic structure and practice – described by Arendt as situations of 'instrumentalist rationality' – people's behaviour is no longer determined by 'the rule of law' but by the rules and restrictions imposed by the needs of the bureaucracy. Arendt argues that under these conditions people are more readily able to dispense with human dignity in the course of carrying out the requirements of the bureaucracy. The major critique of this analysis is that it posits a misleading relationship between public and administrative life. An idealised vision of 'public life' guided by the 'Rule of Law' is contrasted with everything external to this vision. And as Rejali rightly concludes, 'The notion of a rule by bureaucracy is constructed on the basis, not of observations, but of a hypothetical opposite to the rule of law' (Rejali 1994: 162).[7]

Rejali sees it as important to distinguish between different forms of bureaucracy – torture exercised by bureaucracies but often in a range of very different manners: 'In some bureaucracies, human beings relate to one another as *objects* to be manipulated ... Yet there are also bureaucracies where people are treated as subjects to be transformed, converted or healed' (1994: 162). The church and psychiatric institutions are examples – both of which have played an important historical role in the development of torture.

Drawing on the work of Jürgen Habermas, Rejali identifies three different kinds of instrumentalist rationality (that is, ways of treating people as objects):

- Treating people as a means to an end, for example, torturing for confessions (associated with rigid legal systems with severe standards of proof).
- Torturing individuals, as part of a systematic policy of deterrence, to set an example for others, for example, parading those tortured on national television so they may praise the regime's policies. Here torture does not stop with a confession because there is no information to give.
- Interacting with people as opponents to be strategically defeated, in order to create an environment too hostile for political opposition, for example, torturing political opponents. (1994: 163)

Torture may be characterised by one or other, or a combination, of these rationalities.

The declared purpose of torture is to force the enemy, the outsider, the insurgent, the criminal to talk – to reveal secrets and information which are perceived in some way to threaten the state. In this way it is argued that torture is a justifiable practice employed only to protect the lives and integrity of legitimate citizens.[8] But torture has a much more significant purpose as the testimony of torture survivors reveals – that of subduing a population by state terrorism.

For Elaine Scarry torture embodies 'the conversion of absolute pain into the fiction of absolute power' (1985: 27). It involves the infliction of pain through a dialogue of interrogation. She argues that the physical and mental pain, induced by torture, are inseparable and together work to cause the 'disintegration' of the victim's world.

Ruchama Marton describes the torture that the Israeli state uses against Palestinian 'outsiders' as a 'kind of mental superstructure of violence' by which is meant that torture has another purpose altogether from that declared by the Israeli state (Marton 1995: 4). An Israeli physician and founder member of the Israeli-Palestinian Physicians for Human Rights, Marton has both treated Palestinian victims of torture and campaigned against Israel's use of torture. From his experience, 'the victim's confession is useless. The torturer knows that the victim's words are worthless. A tormented person will tell the torturers what they want to hear – empty mute speech' (1995: 4). Of course, even a false confession can be 'useful' in obtaining a conviction. Paul Hill, falsely arrested and imprisoned for the 1974 Guildford Bombings in England, recalls:

> It does not take long to lose a life. I was arrested on Thursday morning, 28 November 1974. By Friday evening I had confessed to eight murders. The police wrote out the statements and I put my name to them. With each signature I signed away my life. The confessions were false. (Hill 1990: 57)

In the majority of situations of torture there is no revealing of secrets. In fact the real purpose of torture is silence – a silence induced by fear and terror. Torturers and their states recognise that fear is contagious. It spreads to other members of the oppressed group to both silence and politically paralyse them. It is the imposition of silence through violence, which is, in Marton's analysis, the real purpose of torture. Douglas Johnson (1998) develops this analysis further, arguing that torture is not only about silence and fear; it is also, fundamentally, about the elimination of leadership – specifically oppositional leadership – whether it be that of the PKK[9] in Turkey, Hamas in the West Bank, the FLN[10] in 1950s Algeria, Fretilin[11] in East Timor, 'subversives' in Argentina, Guatemala and Brazil, or the ANC during the years of the apartheid regime. The process of torture deprives a community of its leaders as well as spreading fear and political paralysis.

It therefore needs to be understood as part of a state strategy with well-designed political and social consequences: it is about the elimination of oppositional civil society.

Elaine Scarry, in her seminal work on torture, expands on the political purpose of torture by exploring the psychology of this process:

> In compelling confession, the torturers compel the prisoner to record and objectify the fact that intense pain is world destroying. It is for this reason that while the content of the prisoner's answer is only sometimes useful to the regime, the form of the answer, the fact of his answering, is always crucial. (Scarry 1985: 29)

The 'fact of his answering' is crucial because, as Chomsky and Herman make clear, torture is a 'mode of governance'. It is not an aberrant strategy or punishment employed by individual rogue agents, rather torture needs to be understood as part of a process of control through terror. Only states have the physical resources and the monopoly of violence required for systematic terror of this kind. As Herman writes, torture is thus characterised by, 'standard operating procedures in multiple detention centres, applicable to hundreds of detainees and used with the approval and intent of the highest authorities' (1982: 113–14).

One of the most telling illustrations of such a terror network was found in 1978, in Cambodia, after Vietnam's routing of the Khmer Rouge. At Tuol Sleng, the torture complex employed by Pol Pot's forces, human rights researchers found torture manuals, torturers' biographies, very thorough prison records, detailed accounts of interrogations, confessions and medical examinations and elaborate diagnostic flow charts apparently detailing the interrelationship of enemy networks derived from forced confessions (Hawk 1986: 25–31).

In Argentina at the height of the 'Dirty War' (1976–79) there existed

> ... a huge torture complex which has at its disposal the most modern and sophisticated equipment, and which requires an increasing number of staff – jailers, drivers, executioners, typists, public relations officers, doctors and others ... a network of some 340 secret torture centres and concentration camps. (Feitlowitz 1998: 8)

For the regime the network was required to destroy the 'hidden enemy', to rid the world of subversive forces (that is, intellectuals, writers, trade unionists, psychologists, journalists) and to impose a world of military order (see Chapter 7). According to one of Feitlowitz's respondents, a lawyer who had been imprisoned for two years in an Argentine concentration camp,

'The only way to identify this occult enemy is through information obtained through torture. "And for torture to be effective," they'd tell us, "it has to be limitless"'(cited in Feitlowitz 1998: 8). In East Timor, Indonesian torture manuals exhorted torturers to brutally interrogate until they received the 'required answer' (Pilger 1999). There is, however, a basic paradox implicit in torture: it involves the destruction of human beings but if death results then the torturer has failed. Torturers must have a particular discipline to keep their captives in pain and useful for political purposes. Rejali's study of torture in Iran suggests, however, that torture complexes encourage indiscipline and this creates particular problems for states that torture. He also argues that in fact, torture complexes are 'remarkably inefficient', noting the lax discipline within the Iranian complex he studied. Guards and other bureaucrats stopped doing their jobs in order to exploit opportunities for making private profits and engaging in personal pleasures (1994: 169). The Brazilian military government phased torture out of its policing strategy partly because it became necessary to rein in and bring 'those undisciplined military and police personnel under at least a degree of central government control even though there was little effort to punish them for their crimes' (Amnesty International 1973: 68).

The kinds of networks described above are sustainable only in terms of organised state resources and are frequently reinforced as Chomsky and Herman (1979) illustrate, by the global economic system (see below) – most specifically arms suppliers (see Chapter 3), training by foreign governments and a global interaction between torture networks (see also Ackroyd et al. 1980; Amnesty International 2001f). The United States Army School of the Americas (SOA),[12] for example, has played a pivotal role in the training of Latin American torturers (see below), among them Panama's General Manuel Noriega, Nicaragua's former dictator, Anastasio Somoza and the last Argentine commander of the murderous 'dirty war', General Leopoldo Galtieri. Following the public disclosure of the SOA's training manuals in 1996 the Pentagon was finally forced to admit

> ... that its students were taught torture, murder, sabotage, bribery, blackmail and extortion for the achievement of political aims; that hypnosis and truth serum were recommended for use in interrogations and that the parents of captives be arrested as an inducement for the prisoner to talk. (Feitlowitz 1998: 9)

The French also played an important role in the globalisation of torture. Up until 1975 France, drawing on its Algerian experience, advised the Argentine state in the ways and means of dealing with internal subversion. Maran cites one particular communication from France which claimed,

'Torture is the particular bane of the terrorist ... reports of results are magnificent' (1989: 49).

POLITICAL ECONOMY AND THE ROLE
OF US AND EU FOREIGN POLICY

Torture, while widespread, does not occur in all states and in those states where it does occur it takes place over discrete periods rather than remaining a permanent feature of governance and social control (albeit that these discrete periods of systematic torture may last many years). But torture is not a random consequence of political rule. It grows out of the very specific political and economic conditions described above – usually in the context of internal civil and political conflict.

The examples of Israel and Turkey make absolutely clear that the prevalence of torture within a state plays little or no inhibitory role in influencing US (and to a considerable extent) European foreign policy and aid.[13] Donor states (of which the US is the largest) wittingly fund torturing regimes under the guise of 'national security' interests. Indeed, from the late 1980s, the scope of 'national security' (and therefore the justification for torture internationally) has extended its reach to include terrorism, drug trafficking and organised crime (Tomasevski 1998).

TECHNIQUES OF NEUTRALISATION AND OTHER DECEITS

The deployment of neutralisation devices is a feature of almost all torturing states. As Sykes and Matza (1957) first noted, 'techniques of neutralisation' imply an awareness of infringing a rule that the actor, at some level, accepts as legitimate (see also Ward and Green 2000).

Stan Cohen describes the stages involved in the 'complex discourse of denial' which states engage in to deny or justify their involvement in torture and other violations of human rights. First there is outright denial followed, when the evidence of abuse is incontrovertible, by a reclassification of what has taken place (not torture but 'self-defence' or the application of 'moderate physical pressure'), and finally by admission coupled with a claim of complete justification (usually for interests of 'national security' or necessary for the prevention of terrorism) (Cohen 1993). In the case of Algeria, denial was followed by a declaration that while rare incidents of torture had taken place they were committed by the Foreign Legion and not by the French military, or that claims were exaggerated, and then that given the circumstances 'duress' not amounting to 'torture' was used. The infamous Wuillaume Report commissioned by the French government and published in 1955 abounds with euphemisms such as 'long established police practices', 'excesses' and 'methods' while the term 'torture' appears only twice in the whole report (Maran 1989).

For states which have had a prior history of democratic rule denials and justifications for torture are framed within a general acceptance of international human rights norms. The UK's history of derogation from European Court of Human Rights judgments against it was on the basis of the emergency conditions pertaining in Northern Ireland. In Turkey's 'fragile' democracy, the validity of human rights norms is generally accepted, but in practice it is, to a considerable extent, denied. Parliamentarians, judges and state officials have publicly condemned torture; a Ministry of Human Rights has been established and the Minister of Foreign Affairs described torture in Turkey in 1997 as 'an agonising disgrace'. None the less the systematic and widespread nature of torture that continues in Turkey is consistently denied by government (Green 2000).

A further, and widely employed 'technique of neutralisation' is not simply denial of the existence of torture but denial of the victim. Israel's long record of gross human rights violations against the Palestinian people is punctuated by shallow justifications, denials and 'techniques of neutralisation'. The 'prevention of terrorist attacks' is perhaps the most common of all utilitarian torture 'neutralisations'. In the 1985 trial of the former members of the Argentine Junta responsible for the atrocities committed in the 'Dirty War', General Harguindeguy (who ran his own kidnapping organisation from within the Ministry of the Interior: Feitlowitz 1998: 31), asked, 'Wouldn't it [torture] be justified if a terrorist had planted a bomb in an apartment building that would kill 200 people?' To which his prosecutor replied, 'But if you can't identify the bomber you end up torturing the residents' (Graziano 1992: 28). The Argentine Junta deployed other neutralisations but, as Feitlowitz argues, in the years of 'night and fog' the 'unprecedented and obscurant usage' of the term *desaparecido* was a means of 'denying the kidnap, torture and murder of thousands of citizens … A *desaparecido* was someone who was "absent forever", whose "destiny" it was to "vanish"' (Feitlowitz 1998: 49). And more generally the Junta relied on an ideological rhetoric, what David Pion-Berlin (1997) has called 'propagandistic responses', which identified terrorist plots, subversive connections and revolutionary activity as the enemy of Argentina (see also Chapter 7).

In Khiam Detention Centre in Israeli-occupied South Lebanon, Israeli security forces paid and trained the South Lebanon Army (SLA) in the ways of torture and then used the information extracted under torture. Following the revelations of routine and systematic torture in Khiam, the Israeli Defence Force admitted that

... there is a connection between the General Security Service (GSS) and the SLA, as far as concerns the gathering of intelligence and interrogations that are geared towards preventing terrorist attacks ... In this framework GSS personnel cooperate with members of the SLA, and even assist them by means of professional guidance and training, however they do not participate in the frontal interrogation of detainees. (Brigadier Dan Halitz, cited in Amnesty International 2001f: 46)

The 1987 Landau inquiry gave Israeli forces permission to use 'moderate physical pressure', interpreted by Shin Bet, the Israeli special services, as permitting such practices as violent shaking of prisoners, depriving them of sleep and forcing them into painful positions for long periods, and *shabach*, the placing of urine or vomit-soaked hoods over individuals' heads and blasting them with loud music. Human rights activists in Israel estimated in 1999 that these types of practices had caused the deaths of ten Palestinian prisoners. The legality of these interrogation techniques was unchallenged by the Supreme Court prior to 1999 despite the fact that Israel is a signatory to the Convention Against Torture, which states 'No exceptional circumstances whatsoever, whether a state of war or a threat of war, internal political in stability or any other public emergency, may be invoked as a justification of torture.' However, in a long-overdue ruling on 6 September 1999, nine justices of the Israeli Supreme Court unanimously ruled that such practices had no place in interrogation, declaring 'A reasonable investigation is necessarily free of torture and cruel, inhuman treatment'(*Public Committee Against Torture* v. *State of Israel* 1999).

Despite this ruling, documents provided by various human rights groups, including Amnesty International, Human Rights Watch, and the World Organisation Against Torture (OMCT) provide evidence of the practice of ongoing torture, particularly since the commencement of the intifada in September 2000:

... the GSS continued to employ interrogation techniques including beatings, sleep deprivation, prolonged periods handcuffed to chairs, placing detainees with 'collaborators' who beat, tortured, and threatened them to obtain confessions; and long periods of incommunicado detention. (Human Rights Watch 2001b; see also Amnesty International 2001b; OMCT 2001)

In May 2002, an OMCT report documented concerns that Palestinian children in Israeli prisons were being subjected to

... beating, being handcuffed and blindfolded for extended periods of time, severe lack of food or no food, no access to medical treatment, being forced to sleep outside with shortages of, or no, bedding and repeated psychological and physical abuse. If released, detainees are taken to outlying areas in the middle of the night where they are left in dangerous situations without means of getting home. (OMCT 2002)

In November 2001 Amnesty International reported that the state of Israel continued to deny, in the face of the 1999 Supreme Court ruling, that its methods of interrogation constituted torture. According to Human Rights Watch in February 2003:

An estimated 4,500 Palestinian civilians, including children, were arrested for questioning during Operation Defensive Shield, and a steady stream of arrests continued throughout the year. Reports of ill-treatment were widespread, including kicking, beating, squalid conditions, deprivation of food and drink, and even gradual reversion to the use of torture. (Human Rights Watch 2003a)

THE TORTURED

As soon as we arrived in the camp they stripped, and began torturing me. The worst torture was with the electric prod – it went on for many hours, with the prod in my vagina, anus, belly, eyes, nose, ears, all over my body. They also put a plastic bag over my head and wouldn't take it off until I was suffocating. When I was on the verge of a cardiac arrest they called in a doctor who gave me pills. Then I had convulsions, lost consciousness. So he gave me something else and that brought me round. I wanted to die but they wouldn't let me. They 'saved' me only so they could go on torturing me.

They were always saying, 'We have all the time in the world.' 'You don't exist. You're no one. If someone came looking for you (and no one has) do you think they'd ever find you here?' 'No one remembers you any more.' The impunity they had. One would go eat, another would take his place, then he would take a break, and another would replace him.

(Ana Maria Careaga, aged 16 and 3 months pregnant at the time of her disappearance and torture in Argentina, cited in Feitlowitz 1998: 51)

Every year tens of thousands of people are tortured in countries across the world. What we know about the tortured is very much a product of the research and documentation of Amnesty International and of the centres for torture victims (such as the Danish-based International Research Centre for

Torture (IRCT) and the Medical Foundation for the Treatment of Victims of Torture in London). Victims of torture are either associated with a torturing state's political opposition or they tend to come from the marginalised, criminalised and impoverished sections of society. They are also very often from already discriminated against minorities such as drug users, asylum seekers, street children and ethnic minorities (IRCT 2000; Amnesty International 2000b).

As a consequence of civil war and disorder, increasing numbers of torture survivors have come to world attention as asylum seekers. Whereas in 1976 there were officially 2.7 million refugees worldwide, that figure had leapt to around 23 million by 1997 (United Nations High Commissioner for Refugees 1997). According to psychiatrist Derrick Silove, the refugee and the tortured populations, 'overlap to a considerable extent so that it is often difficult to make clear distinctions among torture survivors, war-affected communities and combatants' (1999: 200).

According to estimates, between 30 and 60 per cent of refugees have been tortured in their homeland (Nightingale 1987, cited in Bouhoutsos 1990), thus suggesting a global figure for torture survivors of enormous proportions.

Who are the tortured? By what process of selection do individuals bypass the more transparent and predictable modes of criminal justice for a punishment of terror? The victims of torture tend to be representative of the generalised threat that torturing regimes perceive themselves to face. Torture is a form of terror designed to combat political or social 'subversion'. In Argentina under the dictatorship victims were workers, trade union leaders, intellectuals, gays and dissident members of the military – all of whom were perceived as straying from 'western, Christian traditions'. In Turkey it is the Kurdish population who threaten the indivisibility and integrity of the authoritarian Kemalist state; in Israel it is the young Palestinians of the *intifada* who challenge the crimes and barbarity of the Israeli state; in Colombia in the past ten years of civil conflict the majority of victims have been community leaders, trade unionists, church workers and human rights defenders; in China among other groups it is members of the *Falun Gong* spiritual movement, and in the United States it is those 'unlawful combatants' – Taliban prisoners who have been classified as 'terrorists'.

Testimony from the survivors of Argentina's 'Dirty War' has been invaluable in revealing how the process of the destruction of the victim's world and humanity was to take place. Through torture, starvation, a permanent threat of death and illness, victims were manipulated by torturers in what Feitlowitz calls the 'lowest human instincts' – 'envy and competition, bullying and scapegoating' (1998: 655).

The agony of torture does not, however, end with release. Medical evidence reveals that victims of torture experience a translation of the intense and acute pain of torture into a chronic pain when free. The extent of post-torture suffering is extensive and involves *somatic sequelae* (gastrointestinal disorders, rectal lesions and sphincter abnormalities, dermatological disorders, organic brain damage, cardiovascular disorders, gynaecological disorders, difficulties in walking, etc.), *psychological sequelae* (anxiety, depression, psychosis, lethargy, insomnia, nightmares, memory and concentration impairment, hallucinations, sexual problems, alcohol intolerance, etc.) and the *social consequences* of the somatic and psychological sequelae (inability to work, impairment of social personality, negative self-image, inability to relax, inability to relate positively with family members, etc.).[14] For the direct victims of torture the post-traumatic sequelae are described by Helen Bamber (1995) as a 'form of bondage through which the torturer ensures that his interventions will last over time'.

The crime of torture also creates victims well beyond the tortured person. The evidence accumulated by the torture treatment centres around the world reveals a powerful intergenerational legacy. Children of tortured parents, whether or not they themselves were tortured, are reported to suffer a range of reactive symptoms including psychological trauma, recurrent nightmares, increased states of anxiety, emotional, sleeping and eating disorders, developmental delays, problems with the regulation of aggression and an inability to develop basic trust (Bamber 1995; Bangladeshi Rehabilitation Centre for Trauma Victims 2000; Peters 1996). In this sense torture can be understood as an act of cultural transformation, moulding and shaping societies within its framework of, often arbitrary, cruelty, and creating in its wake dislocated, apathetic and fearful populations who withdraw from public life.

THE TORTURERS: PERPETRATORS

'He went to work like an executive, wearing a suit and tie. He tortured all morning, went out for lunch then tortured in the afternoon. In the evening he went home to his family.' (Santiago Mellibovsky on the murderer of his 29-year-old daughter, cited in Feitlowitz 1998: 95)

'We are a poor but decent family ... and now I see him in the dock as a torturer. I want to ask the court to examine how a boy whom everyone said was a "diamond" became a torturer. Who morally destroyed my home and my family?' (Alexander Lavranos, father of one of the Greek torture trial defendants, cited in Amnesty International 1975)

According to Amnesty International, most torturers are police officers. In Argentina during the years of the Dirty War regime concentration camp guards and torturers were recruited from the ranks of the police force and from the penal system (Feitlowitz 1998); during the repressive years of the Greek Colonels it was military policemen selected for specialised torture units; in Turkey it is the Jandarma (military police) and to a lesser extent the civilian police (HRFT 1997, 1998; Human Rights Watch 1995b) who commit acts of torture; and in Israel it is agents of the General Security Services (GSS). A study by the World Organisation Against Torture (OMCT) examined 350 perpetrators of gross violations in Colombia between 1977 and 1991. The profiles that emerged revealed that 248 of the torturers were members of the armed forces and 102 belonged to the National Police. More significantly, of the 248 soldiers *all* bar one were high-ranking officers within the military hierarchy.[15] Military and police training, based as they are on hierarchical models of authority and obedience, lend themselves to 'ordered' violence.

One of the central questions arising in the literature on torturers (and *genocidaires*: see Chapter 10) concerns the issue of causation. What induces human beings to behave with such extraordinary cruelty to other human beings? What is it that distinguishes torturers from the rest of the population? The research evidence seems clear that the willingness or, better, the ability to torture and to commit atrocity is not confined to a limited number of sadistic, mentally deranged individuals. The celebrated experiments of Stanley Milgram (1963, 1974) and Haney et al. (1973) very specifically screened out individuals predisposed to cruelty and sadism (see Chapter 10 for a discussion of this research in relation to genocide). Their results and those of Lifton in his study of Nazi physicians (1986), Staub on the *Einsatzgruppen* (1989) and Haritos-Fatouros (1988) in her study of Greek torturers reveal that 'ordinariness' in terms of personal and social backgrounds is what characterised the majority of torturers. Janice Gibson in her review of factors contributing to the creation of torturers concludes: 'individual personality and background information about individuals, by themselves, cannot distinguish individuals who will commit torture or other cruel acts from those who will not' (1990: 79). And Stanley Milgram wrote following his disturbing studies into obedience and authority: 'This is perhaps the most fundamental lesson of our study: ordinary people simply doing their jobs, without any particular hostility on their part, can become agents in a terrible destructive process' (1974: 6).

What conditions, then, turn an ordinary man or woman into a torturer?

Robert Lifton explains it thus: some institutions are 'atrocity-producing … so structured … that the average person entering … will commit or become associated with atrocities' (1986: 425).

While 'ordinariness' is the overwhelming character of would-be torturers, 'Perpetrators both select themselves for their role and are selected by those in authority' (Staub 1989: 56). The research illustrates that ideological persuasion is an important feature of this 'ordinariness'. Those who demonstrate a strong obedience to authority, and are either fiercely anti-communist or attracted to fascist ideology are more likely to be pre-selected as torturers (Haritos-Fatouros 1988; Gibson 1990; Lifton 1986; Staub 1989).

Training represents an important part of the acculturation of torturers although there is evidence outside the controlled experiments of Milgram and Haney et al. which indicates that training is not a necessary condition of torturers (see Conroy 2000). Gibson and Haritos-Fatouros (1986), Haritos-Fatouros (1988), Gibson (1990) and Conroy (2000) have all documented the brutalising and humiliating training that many torturers have received and argue that this form of initiation assures the success of the training. In addition, torturers are trained to dehumanise 'enemies of the state' and they themselves are encouraged to see themselves as superior and elite members of the regime. According to psychologist Janice Gibson, evidence from Greece, Brazil and Argentina, suggests

> ... that the formal lessons are designed to make the act of torture efficient by utilising new scientific information about the body and its nervous system, but also to reduce the strain of committing torture by providing prospective torturers with social modelling and systematic desensitisation to acts of violence. (Gibson 1990: 85)

This process of desensitisation is also facilitated by the reification of the interrogation:

> For the torturers the sheer and simple fact of human agony is made invisible, and the moral fact of inflicting that agony is made neutral by the feigned urgency and significance of the question. For the prisoner, the sheer, simple, overwhelming fact of his agony will make neutral and invisible the significance of any question as well as the significance of the world to which the question refers. (Scarry 1985: 29)

Once a torturer has been 'created' there frequently follows a social-psychological process in which 'perpetrators develop an intense, fanatic commitment to some higher good and supposed higher morality in the name of which they commit atrocities' (Staub 1989: 64). This ideological commitment, coupled with what Staub has described as the development of the 'differentiated self', that is, an orientation which differentially excludes certain groups from one's own 'moral universe',[16] makes inflicting gross harm upon them much easier.

In an attempt to develop our understanding of the social psychology of torturers, and in particular the relevance of *masculinity* to this understand-ing, Huggins and Haritos-Fatouros (1998) derived what they describe as 'two modal masculinities' following interviews with police officers who had been institutionally involved in the torture and murder of suspects in Brazil. Their findings challenge the notion of a fixed and unidimensional masculinity so centrally embodied, they argue, in the term 'torturer'. The two modalities, the 'lone wolf police' and 'institutional functionaries' embodied very different degrees of 'masculinity'. The 'lone wolves' who were more prevalent before the imposition of the National Security State (that is, before 1969) shared the stereotypical characteristics of western masculinity, placing 'a premium on interpersonal (rather than structural) control, on individual responsibility and autonomy, on demanding respect, and on demonstrations of force to maintain others' deference and keep deviants in line' (Huggins and Haritos-Fatouros 1998: 51). By contrast the 'institutional functionaries' who held prominence between 1964 and 1985 displayed only 'muted' characteristics of individualised masculinity; rather they were representatives of the 'internal security bureaucracy' – true state functionaries subsumed by institutional authority.

The shift from one form of policing to another form less reliant on individual characteristics appears to have been a direct reflection of the structural needs of the changing Brazilian state. In post-1964 authoritarian Brazil, the security forces were increasingly required to identify with the impersonal bureaucracy structured to maintain internal security. There was little room for individual displays of initiative or character – in fact, such policing as was represented by 'lone wolf' officers was, in this period of military rule, considered dangerous to a regime which demanded a highly disciplined and obedient force completely subservient to the greater interests of the internal security bureaucracy.

The research of Huggins and Haritos-Fatouros (1998) suggests again the importance of understanding the relationship between institutional contexts, political economy and the character of torturers.

THE TORTURERS: TRADERS AND TRAINERS

Individual perpetrators of torture and their political masters are not the only culpable actors in the realm of torture. Hypocrisy is a central feature of foreign policy and practice. With astonishing ease, the US and other western powers employ a double discourse around torture. According to Human Rights Watch:

> Some of the Governments that are denouncing torture before [the UN Commission on Human Rights], including the United States, are at the same time providing extensive international assistance to the authorities which consistently engage in this practice.[17]

More sinister is the direct involvement of these governments in the trade in instruments of torture and in the training expertise they offer authoritarian regimes in counter-insurgency, despite claims of human rights considerations and 'ethical' foreign policy. Between 1998 and 2000, Amnesty International identified the United States as the country with the greatest number of manufacturers, distributors, suppliers or brokers of leg irons, shackles, gang chains or thumbcuffs. While Amnesty identified 22 such companies in the US, Germany was known to have three, the United Kingdom, South Africa and Taiwan two each, and France, Spain and China each had one such company (Amnesty International 2001f: 48).

Khiam Detention Centre in the former Israeli-occupied South Lebanon is a perfect illustration of the international nature of torture complexes. Khiam was operated and controlled by Israel's proxy militia, the South Lebanon Army with the support of the Israeli Army. When, in May 2000, the last remaining detainees of Khiam were released it became clear that US-manufactured handcuffs were used to suspend detainees from an electricity pylon in order to administer electric shocks. Torture was a routine and systematic occurrence in Khiam which was designed for interrogation and isolation. Mahmud Ramadan was detained in Khiam for seven years in the 1990s:

> He suffered electro-shock torture while suspended in painful positions and was held in solitary confinement for three years. By 1993 one of his hands had had to be amputated and he had lost an eye. By 1995 he was suffering from severe psychological problems. (Amnesty International 2001f: 45)

In Saudi Arabia, with its extensive history of gross human rights violations, torture equipment in the form of leg irons, shackles and handcuffs is supplied by well-known British and US companies. Ironically, it was the torture of a British businessman in 1992 which revealed the explicit use of these British exports: 'the next thing I knew they had attached leg shackles around my ankles ... my wrists were handcuffed. Now that I was completely shackled these nameless thugs started punching me around the

head, chest and stomach.'[18] The shackles were stamped with the UK
company brand Hiatts. Following these allegations a Hiatts director replied,
'We've stopped making legcuffs and those were dispatched as handcuffs
... I don't have to dictate or tell anybody what to do with the tools they get.
That's not my problem, they do exactly as they like.'[19] However, what had
actually transpired was that Hiatts were now exporting oversized handcuffs
from the UK to the US where Hiatt-Thompson added extra chain length to
transform them into legcuffs – the sale and export of legcuffs being legal
in the US.[20]

Training, as we have noted, plays a crucial role in the creation of professional torturers. The US, China, France, Russia and the UK provide the
bulk of training for police, military and security forces throughout the
world, and as Amnesty reveals,

> ... much of this training occurs in secret so that the public and legisla-
> tures of the countries involved rarely discover who is being trained,
> what skills are being transferred, and who is doing the training. Both
> recipient and donor states often go to great lengths to conceal the transfer
> of expertise which is used to facilitate serious human rights violations.
> (Amnesty International 2001f: 41)

Located in Fort Benning, Georgia is perhaps the most sinister and insidious
of all training centres. The School of the Americas (now the Western
Hemisphere Institute for Security Cooperation) has played a dominant role
in training torturers, particularly those from Latin American dictatorships.
Senior members of the Argentine and Chilean Juntas, military officers
from Panama and the officer corps of Guatemala's brutal counter-insurgency
military were all trained in the American art of counter-insurgency at the
SOA. The SOA's training manuals (1982–91) which came to light in 1996,
advocated torture, beatings, blackmail and executions as central to counter-
insurgency and were distributed for training purposes in Colombia, Ecuador,
El Salvador, Guatemala and Peru (Kepner 2001).

According to the Guatemalan Historical Clarification Commission (set
up to investigate human rights violations during the period of civil conflict),
the United States, in addition to promoting anti-communism,

> ... demonstrated that it was willing to provide support for strong military
> regimes in its strategic backyard. In the case of Guatemala, military
> assistance was directed towards reinforcing the national intelligence
> apparatus and for training the officer corps in counterinsurgency
> techniques, key factors which had significant bearing on human rights

violations during the armed confrontation. (cited in Amnesty International 2001f: 44)

The International Court of Justice has made clear that government responsibility lies within the nation-state unless there is evidence to demonstrate that a government 'exercised effective control' over torture or other prohibited conduct in another jurisdiction. This has significant implications when we consider the trade in instruments of torture. In effect, then, the legal responsibility of a country involved in the manufacture and/or export of torture devices and technologies ends at the border of the importing state and governments are able 'to alternate between facilitation of torture abroad and condemnation of governments on whose territory torture takes place' (Tomasevski 1998: 183).

TORTURING STATES AND INTERNATIONAL LAW

A range of widely framed and largely unenforceable anti-torture declarations, conventions and resolutions issued forth from the United Nations and related NGOs, following the horrific revelations which emanated from the Third Reich. These declarations, conventions and treaties represented an attempt to universalise and privilege a normative commitment to human rights over individual state concerns. They include:

- Article 55 of the UN Charter, 1945 which called for 'a universal respect for, and observance of, human rights and fundamental freedoms for all … ';
- The Universal Declaration of Human Rights in 1948 which declared, 'No-one shall be subjected to torture or to cruel, inhuman or degrading treatment or punishment';
- UN General Assembly Resolution 3452 (XXX), 1975, 'Declaration of the Protection of All Persons from being subjected to Torture and other Cruel, Inhuman or Degrading Treatment or Punishment';[21]
- UN General Assembly Resolution 2200 A (XXI), adopted in 1966, effected in 1976, The International Covenant on Civil and Political Rights, which declares, 'No one shall be subjected to torture or to cruel, inhuman or degrading treatment or punishment';
- The Helsinki Agreement, signed in 1975 by 35 nations, which committed signatories to act, 'in conformity with the purposes and principles of the Charter of the United Nations and with the Universal Declaration of Human Rights'.

These UN resolutions have been reinforced by regional organisations, most notably the Council of Europe with its European Convention on Human Rights.

There are no exceptions from the protection from torture – it retains the highest degree of protection afforded by international human rights and international humanitarian law. Neither war nor states of emergency provide grounds for derogation.[22] Torture is also subject to the principle of universalism under humanitarian law in order to protect against the emergence of 'safe-havens' for torturers.

Despite the high moral commitments embodied in all the UN and regional declarations, resolutions and conventions, they remain in practice politically bankrupt. Torture today is widespread and shamefully practised in some of the nations publicly committed to its end. The United States is the most blatant and hypocritical offender. Nowhere is this more evident than in the US prison camp in Guantanamo Bay, Cuba. Here 641 men (three of whom are children under the age of 15)[23] continue to be held under conditions which breach no fewer than 15 articles of the Geneva Convention (Monbiot 2003). In degrading and inhumane conditions these prisoners have been hooded, chained, manacled, sedated, forced to kneel and subjected to what has been described as 'torture lite' – a form of sleep deprivation induced by continuous exposure to bright light.

The *Washington Post* also described how many of the same prisoners, when held in the CIA interrogation centre at Bagram air base in Afghanistan, were subjected to 'stress and duress' techniques, including 'standing or kneeling for hours' and being 'held in awkward, painful positions'.[24]

Two of Staub's structural conditions of torture seem relevant here: the devaluation of a section of the community (manifest in 'Islamophobia'), and the clear identification of an enemy – the 'axis of evil'. The United States administration has been at pains since September 11 to equate various regions of the Islamic world with the terrorist attacks launched by Al-Qaeda; first the Taliban fell victim, then Iraq. Syria and Iran may become future targets. Torturing the enemy in these circumstances brings the United States in line with many other torturing regimes.

It would be naïve to imagine that international prohibition coupled with effective enforcement powers could make any real impact on the extent of torture when, as we argue in this chapter, the roots of torture lie beyond law in the complex realities of political economy, conflict and culture.

9
War Crimes

Fight in the cause of God, those who fight you. But do not transgress limits, for God loves not the aggressors.

> (Quran 2.90, quoted by Halliday 2002: 239, n. 12)

Warfare has always been characterised by some legal or conventional boundary, which distinguishes soldiering from crime:

> From the dawn of history to the present day, men – far from discarding all restraint when they went to war – have sought to regulate it and subject it to limitations ... It is true that different societies at different times and places have differed very greatly as to the precise way in which they draw the line between war and murder; however, the line itself is absolutely essential. Some deserve to be decorated, others hung. Where this distinction is not preserved society will fall to pieces, and war – as distinct from mere indiscriminate violence – becomes impossible. (van Creveld 1991: 87, 90)

War requires individuals to behave in ways quite contrary to their interests, risking death for their country or their cause. It therefore requires some legitimating ideology. The conventions or laws of war prescribe forms of conduct that are promoted as honourable, noble and manly. By condemning some forms of combat (for example, the use of 'dum-dum' bullets or chemical weapons) they make others (such as the bombing of cities) appear acceptable. There is virtually no limit to the degree of civilian death and suffering that can be legally defended on grounds of 'military necessity' (af Jochnick and Normand 1994), as the devastation of Iraq in the Gulf War illustrated (Normand and af Jochnick 1994). Legal rules also reduce the risks of war. In particular, by protecting prisoners they facilitate surrender. A force which is believed to treat prisoners well can defeat its enemy much more cheaply than one which is perceived (rightly or wrongly) as being likely to massacre them (Ferguson 2000).

The laws of war presuppose and reinforce the monopoly of states over the legitimate use of violence. Soldiers, duly licensed by the state, are supposed to bear their arms openly; civilians are to be left alone so long as they stay out of the fighting. As van Creveld points out, this convention has in the past permitted the utmost brutality against unlicensed combatants and against non-western peoples who did not wear uniforms to resist European colonists. It is a rule which appears increasingly obsolete in the context of 'people's wars', fought by insurgent forces which blend into the civilian population. International law now takes some account of these realities. Guerrillas must carry their arms openly only during an engagement or when deploying prior to an engagement (Geneva Conventions,[1] Protocol I, Art. 44). Common Article 3 of the Geneva Conventions extends the most basic protections of humanitarian law to those engaged in non-international conflicts. Protocol II lays down a more detailed code applicable to conflicts between states and other 'organised armed groups which, under responsible command, exercise such control over a part of [a state's] territory as to enable them to carry out sustained and concerted military operations and to implement this Protocol' (Art. 1). We include war crimes by entities of this nature ('proto-states') within the scope of this chapter.

In the negotiations leading to the codification of the rules of warfare by the Hague Convention (1907),

> ... a handful of powerful states succeeded from the outset in having the thorniest issues concerning means and methods of warfare (where they were obviously superior) legally uncontrolled, or at least in watering down the few rules they had to agree upon. (Cassese 1986: 257)

The regulation of methods of combat remains 'very defective indeed', and the principles regulating bombing that results in civilian casualties permit 'the most divergent interpretations' (Cassesse 1986: 271–2). This is evident from debates over US tactics in Vietnam (Trooboff 1975; O'Brien 1981) and the Gulf (Clark 1992; Normand and af Jochnick 1994; Smyth 1999); but perhaps the most striking example is the NATO bombing of Yugoslavia in 1999. NATO spokesperson Jamie Shea claimed that never in the history of modern warfare had more care been taken to comply with the laws of war. But the US General commanding the allied air forces acknowledged that 'There are nations that will not attack targets that my nation will attack. There are nations that do not share with us a definition of what is a valid military target' (quoted by Amnesty 2000a). The implication is that in particular instances – notably the bombing of the Serbian Television building in Belgrade – the US claimed to be acting with meticulous respect for law while committing what *their own allies* regarded as illegal acts.[2]

The Kosovo campaign illustrates another point about the international law of war. The law draws a sharp distinction between the legality of entering into war (*jus ad bellum*) and the lawful conduct of war (*jus in bello*). For example, it seems reasonably clear that NATO acted illegally in attacking Yugoslavia without the authority of the Security Council (Simma 1999). From a legal point of view this is a completely separate issue from whether, having launched the war, NATO conducted it in a lawful manner, that is, in compliance with *jus in bello*. Aggressive war is an international crime (Cassese 2003). It also falls within our definition of state crime unless, as some would argue in the case of Kosovo, it is a legitimate though technically unlawful act in defence of human rights (Pellet 2000).

The crime of aggression is a curious one in that if it succeeds, it virtually confers immunity from punishment. Why states commit aggression raises very large questions which we cannot discuss in any depth. Suffice it to say that the questions concern how far states act as rational calculators, how far their rationality is distorted by ideology and organisational pressures (see, for example, Kolko 1994b, 2002), and how far they are swayed by collective emotions (see especially Scheff 1994). Here we shall focus on manifestly criminal acts by military personnel against civilians, combatants who surrender, and prisoners of war.

A large part of this chapter will focus on the Vietnam War, and particularly the crimes of the US forces, which are the subject of a uniquely rich journalistic, autobiographical and scholarly literature.[3] Surprisingly little has been contributed to this literature by criminologists (with the exception of Bryant 1979). With the flowering of radical and 'conflict' perspectives in the 1970s, it might have been expected that US war crimes would have been high on the alternative criminological agenda. One reason why this was not the case may have been the reluctance of many on the US left to treat war crimes as crimes for which individuals as well as governments were in some degree responsible (McCarthy 1974; Bourke 1999: 192). Richard Quinney, who does discuss the Vietnam War in his critical textbook on criminology (1979: 174–81), focuses almost exclusively on the responsibility of the US government and senior policy makers. Lieut. Calley, the one soldier convicted for his part in the massacre of some 400 unresisting women, children and old men at My Lai in 1969, is dismissed as 'a scapegoat' (Quinney 1979: 180), whose individual responsibility is limited to his obedience to unlawful orders.

Paradoxically, too exclusive a focus on the state may have inhibited understanding of this branch of state crime. War crimes, like police crimes, are the product of an interaction between individual and organisational deviance: they are not *simply* 'crimes of obedience' (Kelman and Hamilton 1989). The motives of leaders who order or condone atrocities may be quite different from the motives of the actual perpetrators, which are often as much emotional as instrumental (Bloom 2001).

Feminist scholarship reinforces the objection to viewing war exclusively through a 'statist lens' (D'Amico 2000: 105) which obscures questions of gender and human agency. War is the ultimate 'masculine honour contest' (Polk 1994): a context in which men can prove their masculinity by demonstrating violent prowess against other men (van Creveld 2001), and also against *other men's* women (Brownmiller 1994; Seifert 1994; Kelly 2000). In recognising the plainly gendered character of military violence, however, it is important not to succumb to 'a "one size fits all" model of masculine aggression and female victimhood' (Jacobs et al. 2000: 12).

Like other forms of organisational crime, war crimes require analysis on three levels: structural or societal, institutional and individual. We can summarise the main explanatory factors in war crimes as:

- *'Criminal wars'*, where the nature of the war is such that for one or both sides there is little or no incentive to abide by the conventional rules.
- *'Criminal armies'*, where the commanders of an armed force decide to flout the rules as a matter of strategy. By an 'army' here we mean any military unit which is sufficiently autonomous to adopt a criminal course of conduct as a matter of policy.
- *'Criminal soldiers'*, where individual combatants have motives for breaking the rules which outweigh the reasons for following them.

CRIMINAL WARS

Writing during the Vietnam War, Kolko (1971: 415) denounced it as an 'intrinsically criminal war', in which the absence of conventional fronts or areas of uncontested American control 'makes "legal" combat impossible and necessitates endless crimes against civilians and combatants alike' (1971: 406). Similarly, Falk (1975: 37) argued that 'the methods and tactics of a large-scale counterinsurgent effort, especially if carried out with high-technology weaponry, necessarily violate' general principles of customary international law. Defenders of US tactics could respond that if the nature of guerrilla warfare made great destruction of civilian life and property by counter-insurgent forces inevitable, then such tactics reflected 'military necessity' and so were *not* crimes against international law (Jordan 1975; Lewy 1978). More recently, Kolko (1994a, 1994b) has argued that US tactics in Vietnam were not an inevitable or rational response to the nature of the war, but rather were the product of the structure and culture of the US military:

[A] kind of 'amoral' pragmatic conviction [prevailed] among US leaders that America could win the war more quickly if, by utilizing every form of warfare available to it short of nuclear weapons, it emptied vast regions of the population essential to sustaining the enemy ... In brief, as has happened so often in this century, nominally good and virtuous men ... committed consummately evil acts with the gravest human consequences because the system within which they operated made conformity to a dangerously narrow view the rule for decisive periods of time. In this case, such conduct was not only morally reprehensible; pragmatically too it was unjustifiable, save for the careers of individuals concerned. (Kolko 1994b: 431)

This is to explain American crimes at the level of 'criminal armies' (and soldiers) rather than as part of an 'intrinsically criminal war'.

Not only in Vietnam have insurgency and counter-insurgency been associated with massive levels of destruction of civilian life and property, but also in what Kaldor (1999) calls 'new wars'. 'New wars' are fought between factions seeking to control weak states which lack legitimate or effective government. The belligerents adopt some form of ethnic or religious 'identity politics' rather than the ideological or geopolitical goals characteristic of earlier wars. These ethnic conflicts are not necessarily the *cause* of 'new wars'; they may, rather, be useful pretexts for predatory violence (Mueller 2002). The warring factions have no claim to legitimacy *vis-à-vis* those who do not share their self-proclaimed identity, and even among those they identify as 'their' people their legitimacy is based largely on fear of the 'other' rather than on any positive benefits they have to offer. The result is a mode of warfare based on terror:

[W]hereas guerrilla warfare, at least in theory ... aimed to capture 'hearts and minds', the new warfare borrows from counterinsurgency techniques of destabilisation aimed at sowing 'fear and hatred'. The aim is to control the population by getting rid of everyone of a different identity (and indeed of a different opinion). Hence the strategic goal of these wars is population expulsion through various means such as mass killing, forcible resettlement ... [and] intimidation. This is why, in all these wars ... most violence is directed against civilians. At the turn of the [twentieth] century, the ratio of military to civilian casualties in wars was 8:1. Today, this has been almost exactly reversed; in the wars of the 1990s, the ratio ... is approximately 1:8. (Kaldor 1999: 8)

Whether wars of this kind are entirely without historical precedent (cf. Hirst 2001: 82–4) is not really the point. What is 'new' is that the predominant form of warfare in the world is one in which war crimes 'are not a side effect of war but a central methodology', and which is funded by looting, illegal trading, transnational criminal networks and corruption (Kaldor 2003: 121–2).

The career of the logging company executive turned warlord, turned president of Liberia, Charles Taylor provides a good example of the links between corruption, state-corporate crime, organised crime and 'new war'. Having won a civil war in his own country (1989–97), Taylor used embezzled funds to support rebel movements in Côte d'Ivoire and Sierra Leone, whose governments in turn supported the LURD (Liberians United for Reconciliation and Democracy) rebel movement, eventually forcing Taylor into exile in August 2003.[4] Taylor's supplies of illegally-imported guns and mercenaries were largely channelled through logging companies linked to organised crime (Global Witness 2003b; Chapter 6 above). International timber and diamond companies were willing to pay vast sums of money to Taylor while he was still a rebel, since his 'Greater Liberia' was the *de facto* ruler of the parts of Liberia that contained its natural resources (Ellis 1999).

Quite different from Kaldor's 'new wars' are the kind of wars fought by the US and its allies in Iraq in 1991 and 2003 (in Afghanistan and Kosovo, warfare of this type was superimposed on an existing 'new war'). These are wars between states of hugely different technological capacities, in which those on the (inevitably) victorious side are at more risk from 'friendly fire' and accidents than from the enemy.[5] Both in their asymmetrical nature, and in the way the technologically inferior belligerent is placed outside the pale of civilised nations, these wars recall the colonial conflicts and 'Indian wars' of the nineteenth century, in which the supposedly civilised conquerors often displayed the utmost barbarity (Maguire 2001). According to some military thinkers, such wars are only the beginning of a 'revolution in military affairs' (O'Hanlon 2000). Over a period of thirty years or so, according to Hirst (2001), the most advanced states could largely replace their conventional forces by remotely controlled missiles and vehicles transporting large numbers of small but deadly weapons guided by sensors. The only human beings needed on the battlefield would be the enemies the weapons were sent to kill. Alternatively, expendable soldiers could be recruited from poor countries, on the model of the British Army's Nepalese Ghurkas (Luttwak 2001: 75). War, as Paul Hirst puts it, would cease to be a 'moral struggle' and become 'a species of pest control' (2001: 91).

In such 'post-heroic' wars (Luttwak 2001), the conventional reasons for refraining from war crimes would no longer apply. There is no significant fear of retaliation by the enemy, and damage to morale (which van Creveld 1991, gives as the main reason for a strong force to exercise restraint against a weak but tenacious adversary) is less of a problem for those who kill at a distance (D. Grossman 1995). The NATO attack on Serbia in 1999, conducted entirely by high-altitude bombing, has been described as the first such 'post-heroic' war (Luttwak 2001: 76). The pressure to exercise restraint in post-heroic warfare comes not from the enemy but from civil society. If too many civilians are killed, the 'political costs of persisting may not be sustainable, and even if they are, they may exceed the gains of the enterprise' (Luttwak 2001: 77).

CRIMINAL ARMIES

Armed forces may adopt two types of criminal policy. In one, commanders explicitly direct or permit their subordinates to commit criminal acts. The German forces on the eastern front in the Second World War were an example (Bartov 1985). In the second type, the commanders adopt policies which lead to criminal conduct on the part of their troops, and persist in those policies despite clear evidence of their criminogenic effect.

US forces in Vietnam, Laos and Cambodia committed both these kinds of crimes.[6] Whatever legal arguments can be advanced in defence of the devastating US bombing campaigns (Lewy 1978; O'Brien 1981), the bombing was criminal in our sense: it grossly violated human rights and was effectively labelled as deviant by domestic and international audiences (de Saussure and Glasser 1975: 134; 256, n.75). These were crimes committed as a matter of explicit strategy. The crimes of soldiers on the ground exemplify the second type of criminal policy, as even Lewy (1978), who largely defends the legality of American tactics, acknowledges:

There is no evidence that MACV [Military Assistance Command, Vietnam] knew of the My Lai massacre, but MACV was undoubtedly aware of high civilian casualties resulting from fighting in and around hamlets and villages, of the existence of command pressure for a high body count and of the belief of many soldiers in the 'mere-gook rule' – that the lives of Vietnamese were cheap and not protected by the law of war ... [T]he fact that corrective measures were not taken until [after My Lai] indicates at least dereliction of duty and perhaps even criminal negligence on the part of MACV ... (1978: 241)

But as Gibson (2000) argues in a penetrating sociological analysis of the war, the institutional causes of atrocities went deeper than a failure to train soldiers adequately in the Rules of Engagement – which is what the 'remedial measures' Lewy mentions sought to address. Rather, war crimes were a product of what Gibson calls 'techno-war', a strategy which relied on US technical superiority to wear down the enemy by inflicting a high casualty rate. Managers demanded measurable outputs in the form of 'body counts', and subordinate officers hungry for promotion had every incentive to generate as high a body count as possible. Hence the working rule: 'If it's dead and Vietnamese it's a VC [Vietcong]' (Caputo 1999: xx; Gibson 2000: 141).

In theory, the Americans fought according to Rules of Engagement which reflected a strict interpretation of the law of war (Lewy 1978; Best 1994). There was no lack of pamphlets and pocket-sized cards to inform soldiers of the rules (Bourke 1999: 206). Such laws, however, functioned very largely as what in the sociology of policing are called 'presentational rules' (Smith and Gray 1985: 442).[7] They aimed to legitimise the conduct of the war in the eyes of domestic audiences but 'they corresponded as much to the world of the "common grunt" as road maps of Mars' (Bilton and Sim 1992: 376). As in the policing context, these presentational rules could be used to provide acceptable accounts of illegitimate behaviour. For example, some commanders interpreted the Rules as allowing anyone who took 'evasive action' to be fired upon (Lewy 1978: 235). Some soldiers and helicopter pilots deliberately frightened civilians into running away so that they could be shot under the 'evasive action' rule – thus adding to the 'body count' (Gibson 2000: 137–8). 'Shot while evading' was a phrase frequently used in officers' reports to account for the deaths of civilians (Lewy 1978: 346).

The rules forbidding rape and murder were not *purely* presentational. Particular political circumstances (such as villagers' grievances being taken up by an influential South Vietnamese officer) could lead to prosecutions, as Caputo (1999) discovered to his cost. (Prosecutions became much more frequent in the wake of My Lai: Lewy 1978: 348.) Arguably, such prosecutions were necessary to the presentational function of the rules: they allowed the killings of civilians to appear as deviations from the rules, rather than as products of the technowar strategy (Gibson 2000: 179–80). As in the case of policing, however, sporadic and arbitrary enforcement of the rules can generate further deviance. Van Creveld (1991: 92) attributes the 'disintegration' of US forces in Vietnam to a cycle of atrocities, cover-ups and scapegoating which left soldiers feeling unable to trust one another or their officers: '[T]ens of thousands went AWOL, and an estimated 30 per cent of forces were on hard drugs. Soon such an army will cease to fight, each man seeking only to save his conscience and his skin.'

CRIMINAL SOLDIERS

Even in the absence of orders or encouragement to 'take no prisoners', the killing of prisoners or enemies trying to surrender was a common form of crime in the two world wars, as well as Vietnam (Bourke 1999). As Ferguson (2000) argues, in the decision whether to capture or kill an enemy the interests of the individual soldier often conflict with those of the army as a whole. For the army, a prisoner represents a potential source of intelligence and possibly labour; and if the enemy becomes aware that prisoners are being killed or ill-treated this will discourage surrender and may lead to acts of retaliation. In the short term, however, the individual soldier may see little reason to take the trouble to capture an enemy and escort him back to his lines, especially if he suspects that the enemy might be bluffing or try to escape. In a recent documentary (Lewis 2001), a US marine who fought in the Pacific in the Second World War recalled:

> We had such intense hatred for [Japanese soldiers], and they were so tricky. I mean they'd have their hands up like that, and then when you got close enough they spread their arms out and out popped two grenades, one for each armpit. And so we just automatically shot them, unless some officer stopped us.

Australian officers, who attached a high value to taking Japanese prisoners and being seen to treat them well, had to make considerable efforts to persuade rank-and-file soldiers that this was the correct thing to do (Fedorovich 2000).

Soldiers trying to surrender are often killed in the heat of battle:

> No soldier who fights until his enemy is at close small-arms range, in any war, has more than perhaps a fifty-fifty chance of being granted quarter. If he stands up to surrender he risks being shot with the time-honoured comment, 'Too late, chum'. (Holmes 1987: 382)

Bryant (1979: 229) suggests that elite troops are particularly prone to kill prisoners as it is in keeping with their 'self-image of asking and giving no quarter'.

Perhaps the most salient emotional motive for killing or mistreating prisoners is revenge (Bryant 1979: 283–90; Holmes 1987: 385–6; Bourke 1999: 182–3). Revenge also appears to be the keynote of many acts of 'battlefield frenzy' (Browning 1998) including the slaughter of civilians and the mutilation of the dead (Shay 1995). As Scheff (1994: 62) notes, explaining vengeful emotions and behaviour is a complex task that has received surprisingly little attention in the social-scientific literature. From the work of Katz (1988) in criminology, Scheff (1994) in historical sociology and Lifton (1973) and Shay (1995) with Vietnam veterans, it appears that violent revenge arises from a process by which shame or grief are converted into rage. In its most extreme form this dynamic results in what Shay (1995) calls the 'berserk' state, in which the desire for revenge is pursued without restraint, without regard for the future, and sometimes with complete recklessness as to personal safety. The soldier may experience a momentary sense of transcendence (partly for physiological reasons, such as the body's release of pain-numbing opiates) but in retrospect often sees his own conduct as senseless or inhuman. Shay's account of 'berserking', and autobiographical accounts such as Caputo's, suggest a parallel with Katz's (1988) phenomenology of 'righteous slaughter': murders committed in a state of 'blind rage' against an acquaintance or intimate who has humiliated the perpetrator. The transformation of humiliation into rage gives the killer a sense of power and a momentary conviction that he or she is acting 'righteously', restoring the moral order which the victim has violated.

There are, however, two important differences between 'berserking' and 'righteous slaughter'. While the civilian killer's blind rage is described by Katz as a transient state, the vengeful rage of the soldier is sometimes a lasting or recurrent condition:

> Got worse as time went by. I really loved fucking killing, couldn't get enough. For every one that I killed I felt better. Made some of the hurt went away [*sic*]. Every time you lost a friend it felt like a part of you was gone. Got one of them to compensate what they had done to me. I got very hard, cold, merciless. I lost all mercy. (Vietnam veteran quoted by Shay 1995: 78–9, emphasis omitted)

Moreover, the soldier does not hold a specific individual responsible for his humiliation, but can identify any enemy soldier or civilian with 'the forces that have made him powerless', as Caputo (1999: 294) puts it in describing the 'violent catharsis' his unit achieved through the wanton destruction of a Vietnamese village. Such substitution of victims is not unique to war. For example, Scully (1990: 138–41) argues that a form of 'collective liability' enables a man to rape one woman as revenge for his humiliation by another woman. What *is* distinctive about war is the way in which some armies institutionalise collective liability as a means of channelling their soldiers' emotional energies. Some American officers in Vietnam used the advice, 'Don't get sad, get even!' as 'a conscious motivational technique' (Shay 1995: 81). Whether or not Captain Medina, in his briefing before the My Lai massacre of 1968, gave an explicit order to 'kill everything that moves', women and children included, he certainly conveyed the message that 'This was a time for us to get even. A time for us to settle the score. A time for revenge – when we can get revenge for our fallen comrades' (Sgt.

Hodges, quoted by Bilton and Sim 1992: 98). As Medina later explained, he wanted to keep the men 'jacked up' (McCarthy 1974: 351). A similar order led to the massacre at Son Thang in 1970. The Lieutenant who sent out a patrol to the village reminded them of comrades who had been killed over the past few days and told them to 'shoot first and ask questions later … I said, "Don't let them get us any more. I want you to pay the little bastards back"' (quoted by Solis 1998: 30).

The 'forces' that make the soldier 'powerless' are forces on both sides of the battle. Both Caputo (1999: 293–4) and the veteran quoted above from Shay (1995: 78) relate their lust for revenge to the experience of a helicopter landing in a 'hot landing zone': 'On the ground, the infantryman has some control over his destiny, or at least the illusion of it. In a helicopter under fire, he hasn't even the illusion' (Caputo 1999: 293). Physically propelled towards enemy fire, these soldiers became acutely aware of their condition as captives of their own side (Shay 1995: 35–7): 'It was then that I started hating the fucking government', says Shay's veteran (1995: 78). Many Americans in Vietnam vented their frustration by 'fragging' (murdering) their own officers (Kolko 1994a: 364; Shay 1995: 224–7; Gibson 2000: 210–11).

Violence against the enemy soldier or civilian provides a more acceptable outlet for the tensions generated by the humiliations of military life (Osiel 1999: 1041–4). Some armed forces, such as the Japanese in the Second World War (Tanaka 1996; Rees 2000; Lewis 2001) and some American units preparing recruits for Vietnam, employed training techniques such as collective punishments (Dyer 1986: 114), 'incessant demands for proof of obedience and loyalty, and intense pressure to ally with the power-holder by forcing recruits to sacrifice and victimise other recruits' (Shay 1995: 151). In the field too, many American commanders seem to have 'inflicted intentional injustice and humiliation on their subordinates to have inflamed their fighting spirit', believing 'that rage at superiors is usefully channelled into rage at the enemy' (Shay 1995: 151, 201). As Chang (1998: 217) illustrates in her account of the 1937 'rape of Nanking' by the Japanese army, such techniques may also bring about crimes against civilians as soldiers vent the humiliated rage engendered by brutal discipline on those 'even lower on the pecking order than themselves'.

Military training is, of course, designed to teach soldiers to kill. Between the Second World War and Vietnam, the US military (among others) recognised the need to overcome the widespread resistance against killing which (according to Marshall 1947) resulted in only 15–20 per cent of soldiers in Second World War battles firing at the enemy (Dyer 1986; D. Grossman 1995). Training techniques included repeated, realistic simulations of combat killing and instilling slogans such as 'AMBUSHES

ARE MURDER AND MURDER IS FUN' (Caputo 1999: 36). Training also involves induction into a moral order which distinguishes between legitimate and criminal killing (van Creveld 1991). According to Bourne (1971: 464), however, drill sergeants with experience of Vietnam often boasted to recruits about atrocities they claimed to have committed, as a way of breaking down any humanitarian beliefs the recruits might have brought with them (see also Lifton 1973: 42–4).

Even if moral distinctions between murder and legitimate killing are effectively communicated in training, the soldier in the field may find that such distinctions are not observed by his superiors. One of Shay's veterans, for example, was appalled to be given a medal for killing people he had been told were Vietcong but in fact were 'fishermen and kids':

> I'd be standing like a fucking jerk and they'd be handing out fucking medals for killing civilians ... I was sick over it ... but – see, it's all explained to you by captains and colonels and majors that 'that's the hazards of war. They were in the wrong place ... It didn't have anything to do with us ... They was suspects anyways.' ... All I could see was anger building up. And what they did is they played on my anger. (quoted by Shay 1995: 171)

While such rationalisations may resemble familiar 'techniques of neutralisation', the situation here is very different from that described by Sykes and Matza (1957). In the context of everyday crime, neutralisations serve to free the actor temporarily from what is assumed to be a stable moral order (Matza 1964). Here, it is the guardians of the moral order themselves who neutralise its injunctions, and who deny the actor's own perception of the reality of his actions (Lifton 1973, Ch. 6). It is the sense of betrayal this induces that explains (according to Shay 1995: 171) the soldier's 'anger building up', which his superiors 'played on' by channelling it into reckless, anomic violence.

All these descriptions relate to the violence of ground warfare. Aerial bombing is by all accounts a very different experience, embodying that separation of decision from action that Bauman (1989) sees as characteristic of modernity. Fred Branfman wrote of the US pilots bombing Laos:

> Men are freed from the hatred, doubts, greed or rationalisations that killing usually entails. The issue of guilt becomes meaningless ... One does not set out to kill and therefore, psychologically, one does not. (quoted by Lifton 1973: 347)

Grossman, a US military psychologist, writes that in years of research and reading he has not found a single instance of an individual who refused to kill by bombing, missile firing, artillery or naval gunning, nor a single instance of psychiatric trauma associated with this kind of killing (1995: 108). In the Gulf, Kosovo and Iraq (Layton 2003), American and British pilots could kill from a distance, at minimal risk to themselves, and with teams of lawyers to reassure them that the 'collateral damage' they were inflicting was strictly legal.

RAPE IN WAR

The interaction between 'criminal soldiers' and 'criminal armies' can be seen particularly clearly in the case of rape. Rape has been an element of warfare throughout history (Brownmiller 1976; Lilly and Marshall 2001), but recently has received particular attention as a result of the mass rapes in Bosnia-Herzegovina and Rwanda. One of many equally horrific but less publicised examples of mass rape has been inflicted on the Nuba peoples by government forces and their militia allies in the course of the Sudanese civil war. This is a typical 'new war' in which the main targets of the government troops are civilians regarded as potential supporters of the rebel forces. Villages are looted and burned ('combed'), villagers abducted and herded into so-called 'peace camps':

> Soldiers and militiamen are given a license to rape Nuba women and girls during 'combing', during abductions and in garrisons and peace camps … Often, every single one of the women who are captured or abducted from a village is raped. Every woman interviewed by African Rights who has been taken to a peace camp has been raped or threatened with rape. (African Rights 1995: 221)

African Rights (1995: 221) succinctly indicates some of the common military uses of rape: 'First, it seen as an "incentive" to soldiers and militiamen. Secondly, it terrorises and humiliates Nuba communities.' Thirdly, rape serves a purpose which African Rights accurately describes as 'genocidal' in the legal sense. It aims, in the words of the UN Convention on Genocide, to 'destroy an ethnic group as such', by breaking up families and causing women to have babies who will have no acceptable social identity. That rape can, legally, constitute genocide was confirmed by the International Criminal Tribunal for Rwanda in *Prosecutor* v. *Akayesu* (1998, paras 731–2).

The same functions of mass rape are apparent in the case of the Serb forces in Bosnia. According to testimony in the international tribunal case of *Prosecutor* v. *Kunarac, Kovac and Vucovic* (2001), soldiers were authorised or even ordered to rape women 'to improve their fighting spirit' (para. 39) or as 'rewards' for capturing a particular pass (para. 43). There is some evidence for a concerted strategy of raping Bosnian women as a means to undermine morale, but none that will 'stand up in court' (Sharlach 2002; see also Allen 1996). There is little doubt, however, that the 'blanket impunity' enjoyed by Serb rapists was part of a conscious strategy of 'expulsion through terror' (*Prosecutor* v. *Kunarac* ..., paras 568, 579). In the words of Cvijetin Makzimovic, a Bosnian Serb soldier who confessed to rape and murder: 'It's because of territory ... The rape is part of it; it spreads fear and terror so that people flee and don't come back' (quoted by Stiglmayer 1994: 157). In Kosovo, too, the fear of rape proved a highly effective means of 'ethnic cleansing'(Human Rights Watch 2000c).

Impregnating women so as to deny them and their babies a socially acceptable identity was a salient aspect of rape in Bosnia and Kosovo. Allen (1996: 97) describes the rapists' repeated taunts that their victims would bear 'Serb babies' as 'the uninformed, hallucinatory fantasy of ultranationalists'. Salzman (2000: 78), however, argues that the myth that the father determines a child's ethnic identity is not limited to Serbs. A Kosovo Albanian man told Helena Smith (2000) that 'in Kosovo, in our culture, death is better than rape. I could not accept my wife [if she were pregnant by a Serb]. She would be dirty, evil, the castle of the enemy.'

These three functions of rape – as an incentive or entertainment for soldiers, a means to demoralise the enemy combatants and civilians, and a means of destroying social identities – explain why armies tacitly license their soldiers to rape. The motives of individual soldiers for taking advantage of this licence are another matter. In a study of American college students (Briere and Malamuth 1983, cited by Scully 1990: 51), 28 per cent of men indicated some likelihood that they would commit rape using force if they were sure they would not be caught. This and similar studies suggest that, as Brownmiller (1976) and Seifert (1994) argue, many men's ordinary, peacetime attitudes towards women are sufficient to motivate them to rape if given a licence to do so. These attitudes may be heightened by the emphasis in military culture on a form of masculinity emphasising attributes such as dominance, aggressiveness, and the rejection of compassion and sensitivity, which have been found to be related to propensity to rape (Morris 1996). Seifert's (1994) thesis that wartime rape reflects a culturally rooted contempt for women is not necessarily called into question by the fact that some victims are men, because one way of displaying contempt for a man is to equate him with a woman. Hague (1997) argues that the male victims of rape in Bosnia were 'feminised' so that their rape was not seen as a 'homosexual' act and was consistent with the 'hegemonic masculinity' valued by the Serb forces. Inmates of a Russian detention camp in Chechnya report that guards gave the men they raped women's names (Human Rights Watch 2000e).

Scully (1990) identified four clusters of motives among the peacetime rapists she interviewed. For some, rape was a form of revenge, often based on 'collective liability'. For others, rape was an afterthought or 'bonus' added to another act of violence or theft when they found they had a woman in their power. A third group used rape as a means of sexual access to women. It is easy to see how any of these motives could readily arise in war. Scully's fourth type, however, is probably the most germane to war: namely gang rape as a form of male bonding (Seifert 1994). Some Serbs were clearly under intense pressure, even including the threat of death, to demonstrate that they were 'real men' and 'real Chetniks' by participating in rape (Stiglmayer 1994; Hague 1997). For Bosnian Serbs, rape was also a way of bonding them to their fellow Serbs and irrevocably dividing them from their fellow Bosnians. As the self-confessed murderer and rapist Maksimovic put it, 'The killing and raping were supposed to teach us to hate' (Stiglmayer 1994: 156). Similarly in Sudan, Nuba men who have been forced to join the pro-government militia have been coerced into raping Nuba women (African Rights 1995).

CHILD SOLDIERS

'At any one time, more than 300,000 children under 18 – girls and boys – are fighting as soldiers with government armed forces and armed opposition groups in more than 30 countries worldwide' (Coalition to Stop the Use of Child Soldiers 2001). Many of these children can be considered victims of crime. Under international law it is a war crime to enlist children under 15 or use them in combat.[8] They are usually recruited coercively, or have little genuine choice about whether to fight. The great majority of those recruited for combat are boys; girls are more often abducted for purposes of sexual slavery (Coalition 2001).

Children are also the perpetrators of many war crimes.[9] In the Liberian civil war, where some 30 per cent of combatants were children, the 'Small Boys Units' of Charles Taylor's ultimately victorious army were 'infamous for their lack of fear and brutality' (Ismail 2002: 127). Children as young as eight, trained (with the aid of drugs and purported magic) as fanatical and fearless fighters, took part in all manner of atrocities, including rape (Beauchemin 1998; Cain 1999; Dufkor 1999). Many children have committed atrocities only under extreme duress. For example, the Lord's Resistance Army, a Ugandan rebel force formerly supported by the Sudanese government, abducts boys and girls as young as eight and trains them as soldiers.[10] Any child who tries to escape is killed by other children with clubs and machetes. A child who refuses to participate in the killing faces being killed in the same manner (Human Rights Watch 1997b, 2003f).

Other children, however, become strongly committed to the forces that have recruited them. Cain (1999) describes the Liberian Small Boys Units as 'intensely loyal rebels, unburdened by the independence of thought or moral restraint of adulthood'. Several factions in the Sierra Leone civil war reportedly have their 'Small Boy Units,' with boys and girls of eleven or twelve trained in torture, mutilation and cannibalism (Sweeney 2000). Richards (1996: xix) describes how the RPF, the Sierra Leonean rebel movement backed by Taylor, initially terrorises its young recruits but then treats them generously and initiates them into the secrets of the movement. As in many West African cultures, initiation separates young people from their immediate families and establishes new, adult loyalties.

According to Ellis (1999), as the Liberian civil war went on the fighters of Taylor's National Patriotic Front of Liberia (NPFL), many of whom were teenagers, appeared increasingly to be motivated by the prospect of loot. As they were unpaid (despite the vast revenues at Taylor's disposal), they had to live off the land, but as the front reached the capital, they saw a chance to acquire something of value from a relatively wealthy city which many of them had never seen before. The NPFL also offered its teenage soldiers drink, drugs, arbitrary power and a chance to settle personal scores. Adolescents indulged in extremes of arbitrary violence, shooting people at random or, in one incident, using a monkey to pick out members of the ethnic group regarded as the enemy (Ellis 1999: 116–18). Some of their activities (like those of the RPF in Sierra Leone) appeared to be inspired by American action videos such as the *Rambo* films (Richards 1996; Ellis 1999: 121–2). Dr Edward Snoh Grant, apparently Liberia's only practising psychiatrist, gives the following pen-portrait of a typical child soldier:

> He is 15 years and may be as young as 9. He carries a gun that is sometimes heavier than his body weight … He is very *deadly.* He has been *programmed* to carry out orders without question … He is the one who will address you as 'papa' and at the same time order you to 'bring your ass here'. He enjoys the cracking of his gun and the sound of a gun going off, the menacing noise of a RPG [rocket propelled grenade] while oblivious to the destruction and the taking away of life this may cause. He is 'loved' by the 'Pape' [Taylor] for his bravery. At 12 years he is made a General (how deceitful!). (quoted by Ellis 1999: 131)

In a well-known passage from *Delinquency and Drift*, Matza (1964) argued that if youth crime were 'constrained by compulsion or commitment' in the way conventional theories envisaged, there would be much more of it than appeared to be the case. In West Africa's civil wars, we catch a glimpse of how children and adolescents can behave when they are so constrained.

NEW WARS – OLD CRIMES?

There is another side to this comparison between war criminals and the juvenile delinquents of conventional criminology. Van Creveld (1991: 204) predicted that as states lost their monopoly of organised violence, established distinctions between war and crime would break down. Cain (1999: 287) writes that the Liberian conflict exemplified van Creveld's prophecy: 'Military operations and criminal motivation have been so hopelessly intermingled as to be indistinguishable.' Mueller (2002) argues that 'new wars' are not really wars at all but a form of organised crime or banditry, with governments in some cases being among the 'criminal bands'. Cohen (1996), drawing on Ignatieff's (1994) writings on nationalism, suggests that:

> Nationalist violence offers young, marginalised, unemployable males –
> the old objects, remember, of criminological theory – an escape from the
> mediocrity and boredom of backward societies, dislocated by modern-
> isation. They assert their masculinity, entering a mythic realm of
> 'history', intoxicated by destruction and power. As the state monopoly
> on violence breaks down, the resulting chaos offers young men running
> the gun culture of checkpoints the chance, Ignatieff speculates, ' ... of
> entering an erotic paradise of the all-is-permitted'. (Cohen 1996: 17;
> Ignatieff 1994: 141)

Cohen's comment seems equally applicable to the checkpoints of Rwanda (see Chapter 10) or Liberia – although it is important to recognise that, especially in Rwanda, women also savoured 'the intoxicating pleasure of untrammelled sadism' (Jones 2002: 84). States or proto-states with little claim to legitimacy can offer an 'illegitimate opportunity structure' (Cloward and Ohlin 1966) to young people who have little prospect of achieving prosperity or prestige by legitimate means. In this respect, the criminality of new wars looks very much like familiar patterns of crime – only much more serious.

CONCLUSION

Traditionally, war was defined as an heroic, masculine enterprise. Killing 'honourably' in war was seen as a praiseworthy act and sharply differentiated from crime. There was always a large gap between the heroic mythology of war and its ugly reality. The disillusionment and *anomie* this gap induces is one of the reasons why war crimes occur.

The traditional ideology of war is now being eroded from two directions. The 'revolution in military affairs' offers a 'post-heroic' vision of war, in which notions of 'honour' will seem largely irrelevant. 'New wars' make killing, robbery and rape in war look much like killing, robbery and rape in ordinary life. In these circumstances, civil society, in both its domestic and transnational forms, becomes increasingly central to the prospects for preventing or restraining war. 'New wars' are unlikely to break out where civil society is strong (Kaldor 1999). The weakness of civil society in Yugoslavia, for example, was a major reason, according to Allcock's (2000) sociological analysis, for the rapid and violent disintegration of the state. And if anything is likely to make the US and its allies think twice before using their military high technology for new adventures, it is the reaction of the protest movements and the mass media to the death and suffering of civilians.

10
Genocide

Witness NN said one of the men told her that the girls had been spared so that they could be raped. She said her mother begged the men, who were armed with bludgeons and machetes, to kill her daughters rather than rape them in front of her, and the man replied that the 'principle was to make them suffer'.

(Prosecutor v. *Akayesu*, International Criminal Tribunal for Rwanda, para. 430)

When we confront the horrors of genocide in a particular country, two questions inevitably spring to mind: 'How is it possible?' and 'Why here?' The 'how' question seems to be the one that criminology is best equipped to answer, though Anglo-American criminology, at least, has made astonishingly few attempts to do so.[1] The 'why' question requires analysis of extremely complex issues of political economy, history and culture. In this chapter we offer the briefest sketch of an answer to the 'why' question, and a more sustained, but still tentative, examination of the 'how'. We focus chiefly on three cases: the genocides in the Third Reich (1941–45), Cambodia (1975–79) and Rwanda (1994). First, though, we must consider what we mean by genocide.

WHAT IS GENOCIDE?

The definition of genocide is the subject of a complex and sometimes acrimonious debate (see, for example, Andreopoulos 1994; Rosenbaum 1996). Some scholars confine the term to attempts to exterminate an ethnic group *in toto*. Only the Nazi extermination of Jews, and possibly the 1994 Rwandan genocide, are deemed to qualify (Katz 1994; Destexhe 1995). Others point out that under the Genocide Convention 1948, a range of actions short of deliberate killing constitute genocide if 'committed with intent to destroy, in whole or in part, a national, ethnical, racial or religious group, as such'. One such act is '[f]orcibly transferring children of the group to another group', giving rise to a strong *legal* argument that Australia committed genocide by removing 'half-caste' children from Aboriginal families from the 1900s to the 1960s (Bartrop 2001; Manne 2001). For *criminological* purposes, it does not appear helpful to put this form of institutionalised child abuse in the same category of crime as mass murder.

Turning from the legal to the historical and sociological literature, we find at least 13 different definitions of genocide (Straus 2001). Most, but not all, confine the term to mass killings of members of a group. The main points of disagreement are whether the killing must be intentional, and whether the group must be defined by ethnicity, or whether the criterion of selection may be political (for example, Communists in Indonesia: Cribb 2001) or economic (for example, Kulaks – relatively wealthy peasants – in the USSR).

To keep our discussion within manageable limits we shall adopt a relatively narrow definition, based on those by Chalk and Jonassohn (1990) and Levene (1994): *genocide is the systematic, one-sided mass killing of persons selected on the basis of their perceived membership of an ethnic or communal group, with the aim either of eliminating the group in its entirety, or of eliminating whatever threat it is perceived to pose.*

In terms of the classification adopted by Harff and Gurr (1998), this definition embraces both 'genocide' and 'politicide against politically-active communal groups'. However, it excludes the mass deportations of ethnic minorities in the USSR, which account for three of the seven 'pure' genocides Harff and Gurr identify between 1945 and 1995, since few of the hundreds of thousands who died were deliberately murdered. The other four cases involved the Aché in Paraguay (about 900 victims, a substantial proportion of this small tribe, 1962–72); the Ibo in Northern Nigeria (9,000–30,000 victims, 1966); Muslims in the border region of Burma (under 10,000 victims, 1978); and Muslims in Bosnia (c. 200,000 victims, 1992–94). The 1988 massacres of 50–100,000 Hutus in Burundi are mentioned as a 'possible' eighth case.

The twelve instances of 'politicide against politically-active communal groups' include the mass killings of Maya in Guatemala (see Chapter 9) and Kurds and Marsh Arabs in Iraq which will be discussed in Chapter 12.

Among the seven episodes that Harff and Gurr class as 'mixed genocide and politicide' are the three greatest post-war genocides: those in Cambodia, Rwanda and Sudan. In Cambodia, the Khmer Rouge regime (1975–79) murdered many of the Cham minority and virtually all ethnic Vietnamese. It also persecuted and murdered members of two categories that its ideology defined as not being 'true Khmer'. These were the 'new people', who had lived in the cities, and people living in the areas bordering Vietnam who were condemned as 'Khmer bodies with Vietnamese minds' and systematically killed. At least 100,000 people were executed and (at a moderately conservative estimate) around a million – one in eight of the population –

died from malnutrition, overwork and disease (Kiernan 1996; Chandler 1999). Cambodia is therefore a mixed case of genocide and state-induced disaster, but the two phenomena are so closely interwoven that there is little sense in trying to separate them.

In Rwanda at least 500,000 people (des Forges 1999), and possibly twice that number (Melvern 2000), were killed in 100 days in 1994. The victims were predominantly (actual or supposed) Tutsi and the perpetrators Hutu,[2] but Harff and Gurr class Rwanda as a 'mixed' case because many 'moderate' Hutu were also killed.

In Sudan, Burr (1998) calculates that 1.9 million civilians have been killed in the civil war since 1988. A large proportion of these deaths, particularly among the Nuba and Dinka peoples, can be classed as genocidal (see also African Rights 1995).

'WHY HERE?'

If we compare different genocides and try to identify common features of the societies and historical conjunctures where they occur, we end up with very broad and abstract answers, because the political and economic contexts of different genocides are so different. For example, Kuper (1981) argues that genocides tend to occur in ethnically-stratified nation-states. Levene (1999b) tentatively locates genocide in the context of twentieth-century nation-building. Dadrian (1998: 206) points to three factors: the absence of a parent state or deterrent force to protect the victims, the opportunity structure of war, and 'the substitution of a more or less homogenous social system for a heterogenous one that is ideologically vilified'.

It may be more productive to break down the question of 'Why here?' into the following two questions. First, what was there in the political economy of the state that made it prone to a high level of state crime? Secondly, what in the specific cultural and political circumstances of that state led the crime to take a genocidal form? We suggest that the three cases on which we shall focus – Germany, Cambodia and Rwanda – are examples of three very different kinds of crime-prone state, but that each had marked peculiarities that led state violence to take a genocidal form.

Germany between 1933 and 1945 was an extreme example of a capitalist state where an authoritarian government set out to crush working-class resistance, and revitalise the economy through military spending and infra-structure projects. As in any fascist state, the violent repression of all those who did not wholeheartedly identify with the project of national reconstruction was integral to the Nazi project. But fascism *per se* is not inherently genocidal (Steinberg 1992). The genocidal nature of the regime can only be explained by features peculiar to Germany, including the trauma of defeat in the First World War and the subsequent scapegoating of the Jews; the particular forms of romantic nationalism, anti-Semitism and militarism inherited from nineteenth-century German culture, and the demographic and economic consequences of the German conquest of eastern Europe.[3]

The complex relationship of the genocide to the underlying political economy is perhaps best explained by Ian Kershaw:

> 'Big business' was largely indifferent to early anti-Jewish measures ... Under the growing pressure of the armaments economy, however, 'big business' had a direct interest in the acquisition of Jewish capital and keenly promoted the 'aryanization' of Jewish concerns in late 1937 and 1938. Moreover, the expanding power and autonomy ... of the SS-Police-SD complex ... meant that anti-Jewish measures now acquired a rapidly increasing momentum of their own. With the massive extension of the 'Jewish question' in the Occupied Territories and the administratively insoluble character of the 'problem', the inner dynamic of a course of development which could by now only logically end in physical extermination could not be checked. In any case, there was still at this stage no contradiction between the relative autonomy of the SS apparatus within the regime and the interests of German capital. (Kershaw 2000b: 55–6)

German businesses exploited slave labour and could tolerate 'wastage'; and, as we noted in Chapter 3, there was money to be made from the process of extermination itself. Kershaw concludes that though the genocide itself was economically irrational, 'it emerged as the final stage of a process which for long was compatible with, even where not directly in the interests of, German capital' (2000b: 56).

Cambodia is in some respects a clear example of a state capitalist regime (Cliff 1988) coming to power in a backward peasant economy devastated by war. As in the USSR and China, the regime aimed to accumulate the surplus necessary for industrialisation by a brutal exploitation of the rural economy (Burgler 1990). What was different about Cambodia was that the US's bombing and subsequent abandonment of Cambodia created a social vacuum which was filled by a revolutionary movement with a very narrow base of support and no realistic strategy for governing the country. Faced with the difficulty of establishing control over the cities, where it had virtually no support, the regime resorted to the unprecedented expedient of evacuating the entire urban population, which it saw as corrupted by foreign influences, into the countryside. The regime then attempted to put into practice an absurdly over-ambitious plan to transform the economy by abolishing money and markets and using agricultural exports to subsidise industrialisation. The plan 'owed nothing to sustained research' but rather reflected a blind faith, as one official put it, that 'When a people is awakened by revolutionary consciousness, it can do anything' (Chandler 1999: 115). As we argued in Chapter 7, this 'substantive irrationality' (O'Kane 1996) could not be corrected because of the all-pervasive terror created by the regime. Cadres had to meet the Party's demands for a rice surplus or be accused of incompetence, which was 'tantamount to treason' (Burgler 1990: 102). In this respect Cambodia resembled China during the 'Great Leap Forward' (see Chapter 7). But unlike Mao, beneath its 'red' veneer the Khmer Rouge had a profoundly reactionary nationalist agenda – nothing less than to restore the power of the ancient empire which built the great temples of Angkor Wat. Kiernan (1996) argues that this determination to turn back the historical clock explains some of the most brutal features of the regime. In addition, the devastating American bombing campaign heightened a desire for revenge (Burgler 1990: 211) which according to Hinton (2002) also had deep roots in Cambodian culture.

Rwanda is a particularly instructive case in that its economic and political trajectory is in some ways typical of much of Sub-Saharan Africa (Newbury and Newbury 2003). Indeed several states in Eastern and Central Africa have experienced levels of state violence arguably amounting to genocide: de Waal lists examples in Burundi, Eritrea, Ethiopia, Somalia, Sudan, Uganda and Zaire (2000: 38). Rwanda is a desperately poor country: Uvin (2000) estimates that half the population in the 1980s and 1990s were too poor to feed themselves decently. Overseas aid projects, according to Uvin, increased inequality and clientelism without benefiting the poor. Rwanda was further impoverished by the falling price of its main export, coffee, the collapse of its mining industries, and a stringent Structural Adjustment Programme imposed by the IMF (Newbury 1998). As noted in Chapter 2, this created a 'crisis of clientelism' (Hintjens 1999: 261). The power base of the regime was reduced to a narrow patron–client network (known as the *Akazu*) based on the family of President Habyarimana's wife. De Waal (2000: 53) describes this 'shadowy mafia-type network' as 'a classic instance of the "criminalisation" of the state', With its income derived from corruption and its power sustained by paramilitary forces, the *Akazu* amounted to a kind of 'shadow state' (cf. Reno 1995). A further consequence of the economic crisis and Structural Adjustment was to create a cohort of homeless, landless, jobless and unmarriageable young men, from which many of the genocidal militia groups were recruited (International Panel 2000: para. 5.12). Thus the economic conditions in Rwanda created both 'a deep-rooted crisis of state legitimacy' (Hintjens 1999: 251) and a pool of ready recruits for a violent solution to the crisis.

But to understand why that solution took a genocidal form we have to look at some of the peculiarities of Rwandan society.

In common with neighbouring Burundi, Rwanda had long had a Tutsi elite and a Hutu majority. Unlike Burundi, where the Tutsi elite remained in power, Rwanda's independence from Belgium was engineered in such a way as to transfer power to the Hutus. Many Rwandan Tutsis were driven into exile by Hutu violence in 1959. In Burundi, the Hutus were the victims of genocidal violence by the Tutsis in 1972 and the country's first democratically elected Hutu president was murdered by Tutsi extremists in 1993. So after the Rwandan Patriotic Front (RPF), a rebel force dominated by Tutsi exiles, invaded Rwanda from Uganda in 1990, it was easy for the regime not only to blame the invasion for the disastrous state of the economy, but to arouse real fears of a genocide in which Hutus would be the victims (Prunier 1995; Lemarchand 1998; Mamdani 2001). It was to sabotage a peace accord with the RPF that the ruling clique launched the 1994 genocide, following a still mysterious incident in which both the Rwandan and Burundian presidents were killed when the plane in which they were travelling was shot down.

For a rural society, Rwanda has an exceptionally dense population (Prunier 1995). The shortage of land was one incentive for people to kill their neighbours, though Rwanda scholars appear unanimous in rejecting any crude demographic determinism. The density of population also helps to explain why Rwanda has been characterised since pre-colonial times by markedly authoritarian patterns of social control. As Hintjens argues: 'Deference to authority is certainly not a pathology of particular peoples, but it does have some material basis in the extremely hierarchical social structure that has characterised Rwanda for centuries' (1999: 271).

Hintjens alludes here to the evidence that, across a wide range of cultures, authorities can issue commands that appear self-evidently contrary to accepted moral standards, and yet be obeyed; that 'people can treat [morally] corrupt institutions as legitimate in cases in which it would not seem possible to do so' (Sabini and Silver 1980: 337). This brings us to our second question: how is such behaviour possible?

GENOCIDE IN SOCIOLOGICAL THEORY

All societies have norms which limit killing and other forms of violence, but those norms do not necessarily accord protection to all human beings. Fein (1990) argues that one crucial feature which all genocides have in common is that the victim group is excluded from the *universe of obligation* as defined by the perpetrators. What this means was simply put by Heinrich Himmler, the Chief of the SS: 'We must be honest, decent, loyal and comradely to those of our own blood, and to nobody else' (quoted by Fein 1979: 25). Fein (1977; 1979: 33) argues that an offence against humans outside this moral 'universe' is not a 'crime' in a Durkheimian sense: it does not 'shock the common conscience' and will not be 'labelled' as criminal.

Palmer (1998) points to an important difference between the genocides of Armenians (in Turkey in 1915) and Jews on the one hand and colonial genocides of indigenous peoples on the other. In the former cases the victims and perpetrators had previously been integrated into the same society and a policy of formal and systematic exclusion was necessary to define them as outside the perpetrators' universe of obligation. Where there is no such tradition of integration, for example between settlers and aborigines in nineteenth-century Australia, genocide may require only 'passive consent' (Palmer 1998: 104) rather than active instigation by the state. The genocide against the Aché Indians in Paraguay in the 1960s and 1970s (Kuper 1981: 40) is a more recent example of this 'developmental' type of genocide (Fein 1990).

It is not difficult to understand why political leaders in a state facing a crisis of legitimacy might seek to construct a form of solidarity based on a restrictive universe of obligation. If a major part of a state's population can be persuaded to identify itself as an ethnic group whose interests, as defined by an elite, override any obligations towards others, then from the perspective of that group the elite will have a strong claim to legitimacy. If those inhabitants of the state either excluded from the group or insufficiently loyal to it ('moderate' Hutus in Rwanda, city-dwellers in Cambodia) are portrayed as a threat, the members of the dominant group will have reason to reaffirm their solidarity and reinforce the exclusion of the 'other'. If they repudiate any obligation to the 'other' group, destroying that group in whole or in part may appear a rational response to whatever threat it is deemed to pose. This logic of exclusion and solidarity (Jamieson 1999) was followed by the Young Turks (who sought to redefine the multi-national Ottoman empire as a Turkish nation-state: Hovannisian 1994); by the Nazis in Germany; by the ultranationalist Khmer Rouge and by the 'Hutu Power' faction in Rwanda. In each case, 'the need to define enemies and the urge to make victims' (Bartov 2000: 92) were integral to the process of redefining a national identity.

Genocide or 'ethnic cleansing' is not simply the *result* of an ethnically exclusive national identity. It can (as in former Yugoslavia) be a means of creating such an 'imagined community' by 'making existing heterogeneous [communities] unimaginable' (Hayden 2002: 232). The Rwandan genocide aimed to bind the Hutus together, despite their regional differences, and rule out any future coexistence, let alone power-sharing, with the Tutsis (African Rights 1994).

The exclusion of the victims from the perpetrators' universe of obligation is a necessary but not a sufficient condition for genocide (Fein 1979: 9). It allows ruling elites to use genocide as a strategy

> ... to resolve real solidarity and legitimacy conflicts or challenges to their interests ... in situations where a crisis or opportunity is caused by or blamed on the victim (or the victim impedes taking advantage of an opportunity) and the perpetrators believe they can get away with it. (Fein 2000: 158)

The combination of crisis or opportunity and ability to 'get away with it' usually occurs in war (Dadrian 1998), as it has in several of the 'new wars' (in Sudan, Burundi, Rwanda, Liberia, Bosnia, Iraqi Kurdistan, and arguably Chechnya) fought over issues of ethnically based 'identity politics'.

In the case of Germany, the Jews and Gypsies were excluded from the Nazi 'universe of obligation' (along with homosexuals, the mentally ill, and others) long before their systematic physical extermination began in 1941. Nazi ideology, a heady synthesis of apparently rational science and quasi-religious mysticism (Burleigh 2001), left no room for any obligation towards those defined as racial enemies. Exactly when and why the decision to embark on systematic genocide was taken is matter of intense and complex debate (for a judicious review see Kershaw 2000b). The most rational of the perpetrators' motives was to resolve the problems created by the German state itself through its conquests, enforced population movements and ghet-toisation of the Jews (Bauman 1989; Kershaw 2000a, 2000b; Gerlach 2000). Once adopted as an organisational goal, the genocide took on a momentum of its own and was pursued even when it conflicted with important economic and military interests (Hilberg 1985; Bauman 1989).

Fein's concept of the universe of obligation has great explanatory power. Indeed, it is almost *too* powerful: it makes genocide seem too easy. If the perpetrators see themselves as owing no obligation whatever to the victims, killing them becomes – as one survivor described the attitude of Khmer Rouge – of no more consequence than swatting a fly (Ngor 1987, quoted by Hinton 1996: 825). It is not, however, an easy matter for most people to adopt such an attitude consistently. Hitler himself 'could not bring himself to speak with outright frankness about the killing of the Jews', even to his inner circle (Kershaw 2000a: 487). When Himmler did speak frankly about it, in the speech to the SS quoted above, it was in these terms:

> Most of you must know what it means when 100 corpses are lying side by side, or 500, or 1,000. To have stuck it out and – apart from exceptions caused by human weakness – to have remained decent fellows, this is

what has made us hard. This is a page of glory in our history which has never been written and is never to be written. (quoted by Fein 1979: 25)

No one would speak in such heroic terms about killing bedbugs or rats, which Himmler in another speech equated with the slaughter of Jews (Hilberg 1985, I: 333). Paradoxically – but expressing what seems to have been a widely-held view among the perpetrators (Bartov 2000) – Himmler at once glorified genocide as an awesome proof of absolute dedication to the *Volk* and *Führer*, and recognised it as a deviant act that must be forever concealed.[4]

The extraordinary and deviant character attributed to modern genocide differentiates it from many mass atrocities in earlier historical periods, including the transatlantic slave trade:

There was no need for concealment and no international declaration against the Atlantic slave trade until more than three centuries into the duration of the system ... Participants in the Atlantic system operated within the comforting context of doing or seeing ordinary and customary things. *The Nazis were cognizant that they were radical innovators and directors of an operation that they themselves had begun and that they alone were capable of seeing through to completion.* Indeed they knew that they had bet their lives on a project that would be considered a war crime were they to be defeated. (Drescher 1996: 79)

The sense that genocide is a crime as well as a duty is stronger in some cases than others. The young soldiers of the Khmer Rouge, according to Becker (1986: 286), were compared by many Cambodians to 'trained guard dogs', who would kill others or risk their own lives 'without a second thought, or so it appeared'. Many were the children of poor peasants, taken from their villages as children and trained as ascetic militants whose only loyalty was to the revolution (Burgler 1990: 48, 140, 213). Similarly, Browning (1998: 182) points out that many Nazi perpetrators were very young men, some of whom may have known no alternative value system to that of the Nazis (see also Bartov 1985; Kershaw 2000b: 467). By contrast, both the police units whose participation in genocide was studied by Browning (1998), Matthäus (1996) and Haberer (2001), and the Auschwitz doctors interviewed by Lifton (1986), had been socialised into a more humane morality and experienced serious psychological difficulties in adjusting to genocide (Kren and Rappoport 1994: 71). So too did many among the more ideologically driven *Einsatzgruppen* (MacNair 2001) and SS: 'at least one psychiatric hospital specialised in treating SS men "who have broken down while executing women and children"' (Burleigh 2001: 604).

These accounts suggest that genocide offends against values which have been learnt through early socialisation and are not easily eradicated. Mass slaughter also arouses what Arendt (1965) calls 'animal pity' or physical revulsion. In addition, Arendt (1965) and Fein (1979) highlight the varying role played by different churches in Axis countries – virtually all that remained of civil society – in maintaining or betraying traditional values. In Rwanda, 'the church hierarchies were at best useless and at worst accomplices in the genocide.' (Prunier 1995: 250).

Bauman (1989) rejects these explanations of the persistence of anti-genocidal values. Agreeing with Fein that genocide is not deviant or criminal in a Durkheimian sense, he takes this to indicate a fundamental flaw in the Durkheimian view of morality. Both in his influential study of the Holocaust[5] (1989) and in his subsequent work on the sociology of morality (1993, 1995), Bauman argues that sociologists since Durkheim have mistakenly assumed that morality is a product of society. Bauman distinguishes between *morality*, which is founded upon a sense of responsibility towards another person, and *ethics*, or prescriptive general rules of behaviour. He argues that while ethical codes are a product of societal agencies of training and enforcement, morality is not; on the contrary, socialisation channels, manipulates or suppresses an innate moral impulse or capacity (1989: 178). Not morality but immorality – 'conduct which forsakes and abdicates responsibility for the other' (1989: 183) – is 'socially produced'. Modern bureaucracies produce immorality through the distance they create between decisions and their implementation. Bureaucrats or political leaders can give instructions for mass killing without knowledge of their individual victims, while those who operate the gas chambers (a technological device for creating distance between victim and executioner) can shelter behind the idea that they are 'only obeying orders'.

Bauman's notion of a 'pre-societal' morality fills the same gaps in orthodox sociological theory as are filled in our approach by the concept of human rights. It restores the evaluation of specific social moralities, on the basis of human needs, to the sociological agenda (1989: 172); and it provides 'some justification for conceiving of disciplined behaviour, totally conforming to the moral norms in force at that time and in that place, as criminal' (1989: 177). From our perspective, the Nazis' behaviour was criminal because their gross violations of human rights were deviant by the standards of international society, and they knew it. We do not need, either, to invoke 'primeval moral drives' to explain the important contrast pointed out by Bauman between abstract racist stereotypes of 'the Jew' and many ordinary Germans' attitudes towards 'the Jew next door' (1989: 187). The 'Jew next door' was included within the universe of moral obligation because one cannot deal with a Jew or anyone else as a neighbour, social acquaintance or business contact without at least a minimal level of respect for his or her rights. Especially among the bourgeoisie (Burleigh 2001: 292–3; Kershaw 2002), moral obligations towards individual Jews were woven into the fabric of social relations, which is why it required a concerted effort by the state bureaucracy to neutralise them.

Bauman's (1989) analysis focuses on practices that were unique to the Nazi genocide. His argument about the 'modernity' of the Holocaust rests on the bureaucratic, quasi-industrial system of camps and the use of gas chambers to create physical and emotional distance between killers and victims. As Herbert (2000) notes, however, only about 60 per cent of Jewish victims were gassed in the camps, and death in the camps was by no means a completely impersonal, factory-like process: 'The Holocaust meant, to a considerable degree, exterminating human beings in very traditional, even archaic, ways, with a correspondingly high number of direct perpetrators' (Herbert 2000: 37). Herbert's remark is even more true of Rwanda, Bosnia, Sudan, Cambodia and other post-war genocides, in which the killers have often shown a positive preference for 'traditional' and 'archaic' means of slaughter. In highlighting the uniquely cold, bureaucratic, methodical aspects of the Holocaust, Bauman neglects what it has in common with other cases (Burleigh 1997).

GENOCIDE AND 'ORDINARY' CRIME

The idea that all human beings (or all inhabitants of a particular country) share a common 'universe of obligation' may not be 'pre-societal', but it is one that was culturally established, to a greater or lesser extent, in most of the societies where genocide occurred in the twentieth century. In a society where most people have learned humane values through early socialisation, the adherents of a 'new' morality which restricts the universe of obligation need to free themselves and their followers from the inhibitions created by the 'old' morality, if they are to carry out genocide without great psychic distress. In this respect, their position is not dissimilar to that of more mundane deviants from conventional morality. In particular, it resembles that of members of a 'subculture of delinquency' who ostensibly reject the prevailing values of their society. Several writers have suggested that Sykes and Matza's (1957) 'techniques of neutralisation', developed originally in the context of youth crime may also be relevant to genocide (Hazani 1991; Alvarez 1997; Day and Vandiver 2000; Cohen 2001). A number of further parallels can be drawn.

Matza's work suggests that members of subcultures often remain attached to conventional values, but are afraid to admit this attachment publicly. The reasons may have less to do with fear of physical punishment than with what Matza calls *masculinity anxiety* – the fear that they will be seen to lack the toughness to join in the group's activities – and *membership anxiety,* the fear of admitting less than total commitment to the group. This anxiety may be reinforced by 'pluralistic ignorance' – a situation in which each member of the group professes allegiance to values to which they believe the other members are committed (Matza 1964; Kelman and Hamilton 1989).

Cohen (1956) argued that the anxiety of members to demonstrate their repudiation of conventional values led them to engage in 'malicious, negativistic, non-utilitarian' behaviour. Genocide, far from being a cold and rational process, seems always to be accompanied by acts of an extremely malicious, non-utilitarian kind. Though nearly all youth crime is utterly trivial by comparison, it does not seem far-fetched to suggest that similar psychological mechanisms might be at work.

Finally, members remain aware of the possibility of condemnation by the wider society, or international society in the case of genocide. This awareness may lead them to moderate, to conceal or to increase their deviant activity.

There is, however, an obvious objection to the suggestion that genocide, like youth crime, is an activity that individuals 'drift' into 'through a series of choices that reflect conventional, though sometimes "subterranean" values' (Day and Vandiver 2000: 46). Matza developed the theory of 'drift' because most youth crime seemed to him more trivial and transient than it would be if delinquents were 'constrained by compulsion or commitment'. One cannot say the same about genocide. It is clear that some of the perpetrators of genocide in the Third Reich, Cambodia, Bosnia and Rwanda were subject to high degrees of compulsion and/or commitment, but there is also clear evidence that this was not true of all perpetrators. Neither compulsion, commitment nor drift provides, by itself, a sufficient explanation of genocide. We need, rather, to see how these pressures combine to produce a breakdown of previously accepted moral constraints.

Pressures to Conform

Browning (1998) provides a remarkable instance of the effects of membership and masculinity anxieties in *Ordinary Men: Reserve Police Battalion 101 and the Final Solution in Poland*. This group of middle-aged policemen, few of whom are likely to have been fervent Nazis, was ordered to carry out a series of massacres and deportations of Jews. Most unusually, their commander, who made no secret of his distaste for the order, allowed any of the 'older men' who felt unable to participate to opt out. A few did so, but

80 to 90 percent of the men proceeded to kill, even though almost all of them – at least initially – were horrified and disgusted by what they were doing. To break ranks and step out, to adopt overtly nonconformist behaviour, was simply beyond most of the men. It was easier for them to shoot. (Browning 1998: 184)

Not to shoot was to shirk one's share of the 'dirty work' of the battalion. It implied either that one disapproved of the actions of those who did shoot, or that one was 'too weak' to shoot. Most non-shooters presented themselves as being 'too weak' and thereby

... reaffirmed the 'macho' values of the majority – according to which it was a positive quality to be 'tough' enough to shoot unarmed, non-combatant men, women and children – and tried not to rupture the bonds that constituted their social world ... Only the very exceptional remained indifferent to the taunts of 'weakling' from their comrades and could live with the fact that they were considered to be 'no man'. (Browning 1998: 186)

Goldhagen (1997), in a highly controversial study of the Holocaust, has forcefully challenged Browning's account. He maintains that explanations appropriate to 'mundane' deviant acts cannot plausibly be applied to acts which were both extraordinarily gruesome and infringed fundamental taboos (1997: 21–2). Ordinary Germans, he argues, accepted such barbaric orders as legitimate because they and their leaders shared a deep commitment to 'eliminationist anti-semitism'. In short, Goldhagen's argument is the converse of Matza's. Because their crimes were so serious, the Germans must have been driven by commitment or compulsion, and because in many situations they were not compelled to act as they did, they must have acted from commitment.

That anti-Semitism (not only among Germans, but among many of the states occupied by or allied to Germany) is a major factor in explaining the Holocaust is beyond dispute (see, for example, Fein 1979; Friedländer 1998). What is very much in dispute is Goldhagen's claim that the peculiarly virulent character of German anti-Semitism provides a 'monocausal' and 'sufficient' explanation of the motivation of both the instigators and the ordinary perpetrators of the Holocaust (though not of the historical conditions that made their actions possible) (1996: 416–17). Neither atrocious violence against those seen as racially other, nor 'malignant indifference' to their suffering, was unique to Nazi Germany (Finkelstein and Birn 1998: 53–4; Traverso 1999); nor was obedience to flagrantly immoral orders from those in authority.

Evidence for the last proposition comes from the famous experiments of Stanley Milgram (1974), on which both Bauman and Browning rely. Milgram sought to test the strength of internalised sanctions against disobeying a legitimate authority (1974: 141): specifically the authority vested, in 1960s America, in scientific expertise. He found that nearly two-thirds of experimental subjects[6] could be induced to administer what they believed were extremely painful and dangerous electric shocks to another supposed volunteer (actually an actor) simply by the experimenter, playing the role of a scientist, insisting that they must do so as part of an experiment. Milgram introduced variations into the design of the experiment, producing results which, Browning (1998) argues, broadly fit the actions of the police battalion he studied. Physical proximity to the victim made compliance less likely; so did the absence of direct supervision. Peer pressure (by actors playing the part of fellow-volunteers) reinforced the authority's demands.

If such dramatic effects could be achieved by a relatively informal and non-coercive exercise of authority in an ostensibly democratic culture, it is little wonder that widespread obedience is accorded to formal authorities, in authoritarian cultures, backed by formidable coercive power and locked in a state of war. This applies to the Third Reich and even more to Rwanda, where there was both a strongly authoritarian culture, and a very real threat of death for those who did not conform (Prunier 1995; Hintjens 1999).

Sabini and Silver (1980), in applying Milgram's findings to the psychology of genocide, argue that 'conscience' is not an effective check on behaviour in such situations. Our conscience tells us to resist the temptation to follow our own inclinations rather than a legitimate rule; but in Milgram's experiments the 'temptation' the subjects had to resist was the temptation to *stop* giving electric shocks. Similarly, as Arendt (1965: 150) put it, 'Evil in the Third Reich had lost the quality by which most people recognise it – the quality of temptation.' The temptation which had to be resisted was the temptation *not* to kill.

Neutralising Humane Values

Nevertheless, conscience rears its head in the shape of what some psychologists call 'cognitive dissonance' – an awareness of the incompatibility between what one is doing and the kind of person one takes oneself to be (Hinton 1996). Milgram reported that subjects coped with this dissonance by entering an 'agentic state' in which they defined themselves as non-responsible 'instrument[s] for carrying out the wishes of others' (1974: 134). As one of the German policemen studied by Haberer put it, 'most reconciled themselves with their fate' of shooting Jews (2001: 399).

Another tactic noted by Milgram was ineffectual protest: the subject expresses dissent, thereby defining his or her 'true' self as opposed to the authority's orders, but obeys anyway. Lifton (1986) found that doctors at Auschwitz were permitted and even encouraged to give vent to their disgust at their work during drinking sessions at the officers' club. These sessions also provided the occasion for new recruits to learn the vocabulary of 'interpretive denial' (Cohen 2001) or neutralisation. According to 'Dr B.', one of the participants, every new doctor

> ... would ask, 'How can this be done here?' Then there was something like a general answer ... which clarified everything. What is better for him [the prisoner] – whether he croaks [*verreckt*] in shit or goes to heaven in [a cloud of] gas? And that settled the whole matter for the initiates. (Lifton 1986: 186; ellipsis and square brackets in original)

So, rather than murdering prisoners, the doctors were merely putting them out of their misery. Another rationalisation was to compare the selection of prisoners for death with triage on the battlefield: a harsh but necessary medical procedure.

Another well-known 'technique of neutralisation' is denial of the victim, the claim that one is really acting in self-defence:

> That the Jews *appeared* defenceless seems only to have enhanced the need among the perpetrators to view themselves as the 'real' victims and those they were murdering as the culprits. The children, if allowed to survive, would take revenge; the women would bear more children; the elderly would tell the tale. (Bartov 2000: 109–10; original emphasis)

What Bartov refers to as the image of the 'elusive enemy' also featured prominently in Rwandan propaganda inciting Hutus to genocide (des Forges 1999). In Cambodia, too, whole families were executed in the belief that young children would grow up to seek revenge (Ung 2001; Hayden 2002).

Prunier argues that even for those who were forced to take part in the Rwandan genocide, the belief that they were participating in a collective act of self-defence served as a 'mental and emotional lubricant' (1995: 247). He quotes the confession of one perpetrator:

> 'I am ashamed, but what would you have done in my place? Either you took part in the massacre or else you were massacred yourself. So I took weapons *and I defended the members of my tribe against the Tutsi.*'

Even as the man pleads compulsion, in the same breath he switches his discourse to adjust it to the dominant ideology. (Prunier 1995: 247; original emphasis)

Participation in genocide is not always an unequivocally distressing experience: it can offer tempting rewards. In the Rwandan genocide, for example, the core of the *Interahamwe* militia was made up of unemployed, uneducated, landless young Hutu men who, 'previously scorned in their communities, seized on the genocide as an opportunity to gain stature as well as wealth' stolen from their Tutsi victims (des Forges 1999: 261). In these circumstances, rather than redefining what they are doing, perpetrators may temporarily redefine themselves. While they are playing their roles, they are not the kind of people to whom conventional values apply. As the famous Stanford prison experiment showed (Haney et al. 1973), when people are given roles which they find psychologically rewarding, they may enter into them so completely that their personality appears completely changed.

Steiner, in his study of former SS-men, proposes the concept of the 'sleeper', a person whose sadistic personality 'lies dormant until circumstances or specific events will activate him or her and produce behavioural traits not apparent before' (1980: 431). But there is little evidence for such sadistic traits pre-dating the perpetrators' involvement in SS work. Hatred of the victims, rage, or cruelty, rather than being a cause of genocide, may 'serve to provide the perpetrators with an explanation and rationalisation for their violent behaviour' (Kelman and Hamilton 1989: 15). In Jan-Phillip Reemstma's phrase, many perpetrators of the Nazi genocide 'were doing it because they wanted to. But the others wanted to because they were doing it' (quoted by Herbert 2000: 33).

Lifton (1986) describes the doctors in Auschwitz as engaging in a process of 'doubling': the development of an 'Auschwitz self' that could carry out their murderous duties while leaving the 'normal self' (the loving, kindly family man, for example) relatively intact. Hinton (1996), in his study of Cambodia, similarly talks about the emergence of a 'genocidal self' in response to 'psycho-social dissonance'. Whereas Lifton regards 'doubling' as a special psychological mechanism, Hinton regards it as one aspect of the generally context-dependent nature of the 'self'. Having one concept of ourselves at work and another at home is not unusual. As Kren and Rappaport (1994: 153) suggest, it can be regarded as characteristic of the alienation of labour in modern industrial societies. Cohen (2001: 93) argues that terms like 'doubling' are 'too dramatic to convey the everyday forms of role distancing, compartmentalisation and segregation by which people segregate themselves from what they are doing'.

EXCESSES

The most telling objection which Goldhagen (1997) raises to 'conventional explanations' such as obedience to authority and peer pressure is that they do not account for the element of gratuitous cruelty, of zeal beyond the call of official duty, displayed by many participants in the Holocaust. As Hannah Arendt observed:

> No one had issued orders that infants should be thrown into the air as shooting targets, or hurled into the fire alive or have their heads smashed against walls ... Innumerable individual crimes, one more horrifying than the next, surrounded and created the atmosphere of the gigantic crime of extermination.[7]

Victims of the Rwandan genocide also suffered appalling torments – in Sofsky's (1997) sense of 'torment' as pain and degradation inflicted for its own sake, not instrumentally as in the case of torture: '[T]he care with which thought was given as to ways to inflict maximum physical suffering and to sow maximum psychological terror defies belief' (African Rights 1994: 335). Victims were mutilated with machetes and left to die, burnt alive, buried alive, thrown living into pit latrines, or forced to kill members of their families. Women and girls were systematically raped and humiliated, and then often killed or thrown into latrines (African Rights 1994; International Panel 2000).

We believe that pressures from authorities and peers, in the context of the specific social dynamics of genocide, do allow us to make a degree of sense of such excesses. The most important common thread linking different genocides is that by excluding victims from the perpetrator group's universe of obligation, a new form of solidarity is forged among the perpetrators. Apparently 'gratuitous' violence may contribute to that process in three ways.

First, excesses take the genocidal ideology to its 'logical' conclusion, and thereby demonstrate the perpetrator's commitment to the ideology. As we have observed, if the victims are totally excluded from the universe of obligation, killing one should be of no more consequence than swatting a fly. It may not be easy for most people to act on this assumption, but some perpetrators do – Amon Goeth, the labour camp commandant portrayed by Thomas Keneally in *Schindler's Ark* (1982), seems to have been an example. According to Sofsky (1997: 225), violence by concentration camp guards was routinised to such an extent that they could 'do without reasons for their actions'.[8] If there is no valid reason *not* to kill or torment a member of the victim group, no positive reason for doing so is needed.

Second, excesses display commitment – both to the institution and to the perpetrators' peer group – precisely because they go beyond what is demanded. A committed subordinate is expected to show initiative and enthusiasm rather than merely to obey orders. Rather than being a product of the perpetrators' convictions, excesses may be a way of producing and sustaining conviction (Kamber 2000: 174). In 'a subculture of violence, demonstrative deeds earn the actor respect and standing' (Sofsky 1997: 105, 229). In the Rwandan genocide, status depended on commitment to killing more than on formal rank (des Forges 1999).

Third, by degrading the victims, excesses reinforce their status as different and inferior beings beyond the scope of moral concern. Franz Stangl, the commandant of Treblinka, told Gita Sereny that the degradation of inmates was necessary to 'condition those who actually had to carry out the policies … To make it possible for them to do what they did' (Sereny 1995: 101). The fact that many or all Jews, Tutsis, Muslims or Cambodians with 'Vietnamese minds' were physically indistinguishable from Aryans, Hutus, Serbs or 'true' Khmer may, as Appadurai (2002) suggests, have added to the need for an extreme form of degradation ceremony, in which difference was ritually inscribed upon the victims' bodies.

Taylor (1999), an anthropologist who witnessed the outbreak of the Rwandan genocide, argues that the torments inflicted on the victims were intelligible in terms of a Rwandan cosmology that attributed bodily disorders (and, by extension, disorders in the 'body of the state') to 'blocked' or 'blocking beings'. For example, one category of 'blocked being' is a woman whose breasts fail to develop; by cutting off women's breasts, the perpetrators marked them out as 'blocked beings'. By forcing victims to commit incest, 'their bodies were transformed into icons of asociality' (C. Taylor 1999: 143, 141).

While extreme cruelty has a social meaning and purpose, it is possible that for some perpetrators it is also pleasurable. As often happens in war (Bourke 1999), participants may learn to derive pleasure from extreme violence as a way of 'making the best' of the situation in which they find themselves. Cruelty can provide a relief from boredom, a measure of creativity or craftsmanship in devising new torments, even 'a sense of joy and festivity' (Browning 1998: 208, paraphrasing Katz 1993). Absolute control over the body and the life of another, absolute freedom from all ordinary restraints, may produce a state of 'transcendence' (Cameron and Fraser 1987), 'ecstatic joy' (Steiner 1980: 431), 'or perhaps the experience of both abandonment and strength as in an intense sexual experience' (Staub 1989: 139).

COLLECTIVE DEVIANCE AND INTERNATIONAL SOCIETY

When Himmler made his speech about 'an unwritten page of glory in our history', it was clear that Germany was losing the war. Despite Himmler's emphasis on secrecy, his two speeches at Posen (one to SS members and one to senior Party officials) were part of a deliberate policy of making the German elite, the leaders of their allies, and to a lesser degree the German people, aware that by their crimes against the Jews they had 'burnt their bridges behind them' (Bankier 1992: 225; Sereny 1995: 388–92; Kershaw 2000a: 582–4, 604–6). At another meeting of senior officials in 1943, Hans Frank (the governor of a large part of Poland) 'announced that all those assembled were on Mr Roosevelt's war criminals list and that he had the honour of occupying first place on that list' (Hilberg 1993: 49). According to Bankier (1992), there was a widespread awareness that something terrible had been done to the Jews, and a widespread fear of the retribution that Germany would suffer at the hands of the supposedly Jewish-dominated allies. The torrent of anti-Semitic propaganda, which intensified as defeat grew closer, not only played on the fear of Jewish revenge but reminded people what that revenge would be *for*. At the same time, by portraying Germany as the potential victim of Jewish vengeance, it contributed to the reversal of perpetrator and victim roles which helped rationalise the genocide (Bartov 2000). The leadership attempted to bind its followers together in a 'community of fate' (Kershaw 2000a: 604), a collective deviant identity: aware that they were criminals in the eyes of the outside world, aware of the prospect of retribution and, for that reason, all the more determined to persevere to the bitter end.

→ In Rwanda, the leadership's concern about the reactions of foreign governments led them to order the militias to kill 'in a more discreet and disciplined fashion. No survivors were to be left to tell the story. The clean-up operation was much different than the large-scale killings; victims now knew their killers as neighbours, colleagues, or one-time friends' (International Panel 2000, para. 14.31). 'The extremists wanted everyone to be tainted with the blood of those who had died. Then there could be *no going back*' (African Rights 1994: 568). This 'community of fate' led more than a million Hutus to join their defeated army in exile. The fear of justice, or revenge, which at the same time confirms that the perpetrators of genocide are really victims (Gourevitch 1999: 161) is strikingly reminiscent of Bankier's description of the mood of ordinary Germans as defeat loomed.

Des Forges (1999) and Melvern (2000) argue strongly that the Rwandan genocide was a direct result of the lack of decisive action by the UN and western governments, who were reluctant even to use the word 'genocide', let alone do anything to stop it. Perhaps the most telling piece of evidence is that the interim government in Rwanda took a decision to extend the genocide on the day after the US announced its support for total withdrawal of UN forces from Rwanda (des Forges 1999: 630). With the exception of France, no major power considered its national interests to be significantly affected by events in Rwanda, and France's perceived interests lay in maintaining the genocidal regime in power, or at least forestalling an RPF victory. The main source of pressure on governments to defend human rights was transnational civil society – Human Rights Watch, Oxfam, the Red Cross and other groups. But though they did what they could, they failed to arouse sufficient support in domestic civil society, especially in the US (des Forges 1999: 624). Without pressure from 'public opinion', western governments saw no reason to act. The perpetrators were able, in Fein's (2000: 158) simple phrase, 'to get away with it'.

CONCLUSION

Let us summarise what seems to be the common pattern linking at least three of the major genocides of the twentieth century. Its key features are: (1) the propagation by the ruling elite of an ideology excluding the victim group from the perpetrators' universe of obligation; (2) the elite's perception of the victim group as a threat or obstacle in a context of economic and political crisis, generally against a background of war; (3) a competing ideology, rooted in national and/or international culture, that does recognise the victims as worthy of moral concern; (4) the use of psychological mechanisms of denial and neutralisation to overcome the inhibitions created by the more inclusive ideology, and (5) the perpetration of excesses that reaffirm the banishing of those inhibitions.

These common features explain *how*, but not *why*, genocide occurs. To explain *why* it occurs, we have argued, requires an analysis both of the economic and political factors that make states prone to extreme violence, and the specific cultural factors and historical circumstances that lead that violence to take a genocidal form. In the following chapter we discuss further common economic and political factors leading to state crime.

11
The Political Economy of State Crime

In the preceding chapters we have focused on a range of what we identified as the more significant state crimes on a number of different levels. In this chapter we tie together some threads from our earlier discussion by examining the relationship between the state and the economy, and how this relationship shapes patterns of criminal behaviour in different kinds of states. For this purpose we can classify states according to their relationship to the forces and relations of production. First, however, it is important to understand states in the context of the wider international political economy.

We make no attempt here to develop any general theory of the state, but simply to group states together in a way that allows us to recognise certain common patterns of crime that emerge from the empirical work in the earlier chapters.[1]

For our purposes, then, it makes sense to talk about three categories of states. By 'states', we refer primarily to those institutions which exert a monopoly (or near-monopoly) of coercive force and the extraction of revenue in some substantial tract of territory. The first category comprises capitalist states, which can be subdivided into the advanced industrialised democracies (the US, the UK, Japan, etc.); and the developing or transitional states such as Honduras, Turkey, Kazakhstan and Bangladesh. The second comprises state-capitalist states (Cliff 1988), where the state owns and controls the means of production. (A socialist state, by contrast, would be one where the workers control the means of production.) The third, and perhaps less obvious, category comprises what we shall call 'predatory states'. These are states, where the state elite rules essentially for its own benefit, rather than for that of any class outside itself. Such elites do not directly control the means of production, but rather enrich themselves primarily by extortion. Some of these states (for example, Democratic Republic of Congo) have the legal trappings of statehood but control only limited areas within their territory; others (such as the FARC in Colombia, and formerly the Taliban) are not legally recognised as states but in fact control substantial territory.

CAPITALIST STATES

The distinction we have drawn between 'advanced' and 'transitional' countries is not clear-cut. On which side of the line does the Czech Republic fall, for example? The essential point of the distinction, for our purposes, is that in the 'transitional' countries, transnational financial institutions and global powers play a greater role in the genesis of state crime. There are, however, many factors that are equally relevant to both kinds of state.

In some forms of state crime we can see a very direct relationship between political economy and the motivation of the perpetrators. In all three of the case studies explored in Chapter 3, both state agencies and corporations (and some individual state officials) stood to gain financially from collusion in criminal enterprises. In developing countries the imperative to raise revenue by any means available is especially pressing, particularly given the need for international debt repayments. The crimes associated with the development of shrimp aquaculture in Latin America are very directly driven by this kind of pressure. In other instances of state-corporate crimes the economic motivation appears secondary to political concerns, as illustrated by the Al-Yamamah scandal and the *Challenger* disaster (Kramer 1992; Vaughan 1997; Chapter 3 above). In examples of state collusion with organised crime, economic and political goals are often merged as with US support for right-wing narco-guerrilla movements in Latin America (Chapter 6). Similarly when we examine torture and state terror in Argentina, we can see a direct connection to economic interests at least in the early stages, whereas in Turkey (Poulton 1997) and Northern Ireland the determination to maintain territorial integrity conflicts with economic interests.

At the beginning of the twenty-first century, if we exclude China[2] all the major capitalist states except the oil-rich countries of the Middle East can be characterised as 'democratic', or at least as having 'restricted democratic practices' (Freedom House 1999). Rummel (1994) argues strongly that democracies do not make war on one another, and commit less state murder than other regimes (see also Gurr, 1986). Nevertheless, as we have seen in Chapters 7, 8 and 9, democracies have been responsible for many instances of torture, murder and war crimes; and they have been implicated in numerous deaths through state-corporate offending, illegal trading and natural disasters (Chapters 3, 4 and 6). Democracy in itself affords only limited protection against state crimes: elected governments in Colombia, Guatemala and Russia have pursued policies arguable amounting to genocide (see Chapters 9 and 10).

If there is one factor that emerges throughout this book as a major constraint on state crime it is a strongly developed civil society. States with strong civil societies are generally democracies, but some (particularly the more liberal eastern European states) have become democracies precisely because they had already developed strong civil societies (Held et al. 1999; Keane 1998; Harman 1996). In particular our analysis suggests that the existence of a strong civil society places important curbs on torture, state terror, war crimes and genocide. In Turkey the growth of domestic civil society is seen as essential in ensuring the stability of recent human rights reforms (for example, abolition of the death penalty in 2002 and a curtailment in the restrictions imposed on the Kurdish minority) initiated by the Turkish government in response to European demands for compliance with international norms.

As indicated in Chapter 1, civil society is made up of a range of associations that are independent of the state and are capable of articulating norms against which the legitimacy of state actions can be judged. The role of civil society in collectively and publicly communicating demands and expectations to the state can be contrasted with clientelism, in which people individually and privately seek to influence state decisions through relationships with powerful patrons. Clientelism is likely to flourish where civil society is weak (Putnam 1993). State crime is likely to flourish where clientelism is strong. As we argued in Chapter 2, this is especially true of corruption, because clientelism contributes to a political culture in which informal exchanges between state and non-state actors flourish. Corruption, in turn, is an element in other forms of state crime: state-corporate crime, state links to transnational crime, natural disasters and police crime. The relation of clientelism to violence is more equivocal. Patron/client networks enable rulers to obtain a degree of consent for their rule and in that way avoid violence (Clapham 1982). But clientelism militates against the development of civil society and of concepts of citizenship and equal rights. In that way, as Allcock's (2000) sociology of former Yugoslavia and Chevigny's work on policing (1995) suggest, it may make civil conflict and violent repression more likely.

Even in states characterised by vibrant civil societies there are still significant sections of the population which may be marginalised in economic, political and social terms.[3]

It is a truism within criminological discourse that the socially marginalised are most likely to be both criminalised and victimised (Young 2002). As such they become exposed (through criminalisation), and in consequence more vulnerable, to state violence. The marginalised are also less likely to be able to mobilise the resources of civil society (for example, the law, media) in exposing state deviance. In weak democracies such as Brazil and Jamaica (see Chapter 5) there may be considerable public support for repressive actions against the poor. To a lesser degree, this process is also evident in strong democracies where certain social groups may become scapegoats for more fundamental social fissures (for example, asylum seekers in Britain: see Green and Grewcock 2002).

In considering the political economy of capitalist states, it is essential to examine illegal as well as legal markets. Organised crime, like corruption, tends to flourish in clientelist states where informal exchange practices facilitate the development of a shadow economy. There are also a number of important global economic and political policies and practices (usually initiated and led by the US) that have impacted on the development of illicit markets throughout the world. The deregulation of legitimate financial markets has, for example, led to an increase in money laundering (Andreas 1999) but two further state policies have been particularly central to creating the conditions for the growth of organised crime, and therefore illustrate the degree to which the aetiology of organised crime must be understood in relation to the state. These strategies are prohibition and the imposition of economic sanctions. Prohibition has provided one of the most popular explanatory paradigms of organised crime (see Chapter 6). It is, as Berdal and Serrano (2002) argue, 'at the nub of transnational organised crime' largely because (as in the case of economic sanctions) existing markets do not simply disappear when they become illegal. For a variety of reasons these services and commodities became prohibited but prohibition does little by way of impacting on demand. Illegality creates a market tendency toward profit inflation. Illegal industries develop and flourish under a climate of prohibition. When a state prohibits certain commodities and services it also 'de facto abrogates the enforcement of many other regulatory laws in these illicit economic spheres' (Berdal and Serrano 2002: 15). Organised crime fills the vacuum thus created in certain arenas of economic power.

Transnational financial institutions play a significant role in the encouragement of state crime. Debt repayments represent a crippling burden for states with weak economies. The demands of Structural Adjustment Programmes (a condition of World Bank and IMF loans) lead to the domestic imposition of austerity packages which in turn require increasingly repressive policing measures on the part of the cooperating state. Loan repayments, as we have seen, also encourage deviant alliances between states and corporations, and states and organised crime. This opportunity structure fosters short-term economic returns normally at great cost to human rights and the environment.

STATE-CAPITALIST STATES

Although seemingly in transition to free-market capitalism China remains the most significant example of state capitalism with a strong market orientation. State capitalism is characterised by state ownership and control over the means of production. Under state-capitalist arrangements, workers are exploited in largely the same manner as under capitalist exploitation.

As Harman writes of the Soviet Union:

> The only significant difference was that while Western capitalism took hundreds of years to complete its primitive accumulation,[4] Stalin sought to achieve Russia's in two decades. Therefore the brutality and barbarity was more concentrated. (Harman 1999: 478)

As Chapter 10 suggests, this analysis applies equally well to Pol Pot's Cambodia.

Both the USSR and China sought to achieve their economic goals through widespread state terror. Both also created the conditions for catastrophic famine. While recent scholarship suggests that Stalin's 'great terror' killed 'only' about 2 million people (Getty and Naumov 2000), the Ukrainian famine is estimated to have killed between 7 and 8 million in 1933 alone, and the Chinese famine of 1958–61 over 30 million (Becker 1996; Chapter 4 above).

Much of this destruction, far from being deviant, was entirely in accordance with state norms and ideologies. State-capitalist societies have, however, been characterised by two forms of organisational deviance. First, local economic and administrative agencies violate the rules and policies laid down by the central state. Given the nature of some of those policies, deviation from them can sometimes be relatively benign (see Chapter 2), but more often deviation has exacerbated the level of famine and state violence. Second, the central state violates its own rules (such as the 1936 Soviet constitution), which no agency within or outside the state has the capacity or political will to enforce. Scholars are now learning a great deal about the detailed history of the Soviet terror (see, for example, Getty and Naumov 2000), and it should be possible to analyse this history within a state crime framework. This task is clearly beyond the scope of the present book.

PREDATORY STATES

Many writers have arranged states on a continuum from 'strong' (effective and legitimate) to 'weak', and have argued that weak states are particularly prone to rule through terror or collapse into civil war. As we discuss in Chapter 4, some weak states in Africa have become, in Bayart et al.'s (1999) term, 'criminalised'. Their elites are essentially murderous organisations of thieves and smugglers: for example, Liberia, Equatorial Guinea and the Congo. Reno (1999) distinguishes between weak states and warlordism. Warlords abandon 'almost entirely many internal components of conventional states, such as bureaucratic hierarchies or any autonomous definition of an interest of state' (Reno 1998: 222). We use the term 'predatory states' to embrace both very weak and kleptocratic states, such as Mobuto's Zaire and Abacha's Nigeria, and the warlord politics characterising Liberia, Somalia and Congo (Kinshasa).

The economies of these states rest, in varying combinations, on natural resources such as diamonds, minerals and timber, overseas aid, and illegal trade. William Reno documents the process by which weak states, faced with an increasingly desperate economic position, abandon many of the conventional activities of government, 'jettisoning bureaucracies, abjuring pursuit of a broad public interest, and militarising commerce' (1998: 218). Such governments appear increasingly indistinguishable from other 'warlords' vying for control over their territory and resources, except that they enjoy the benefits of internationally recognised sovereignty. One such benefit is eligibility for foreign aid. Moreover, the 'trappings of sovereignty – such as the capacity to manipulate enforcement of laws, to generate globally accepted documents, and to hide clandestine activity beyond diplomatic immunity' provide enhanced opportunities for both legal and illegal commerce (Reno 1998: 21).

The colonial legacy of these states plays a significant role in their criminogenic nature (Sumner 1982). As Tilly (1985) argues, the former colonies acquired their military and policing structures from the colonial powers, and were able to maintain them through the Cold War period by alliances with one or other superpower. They never perceived the same need as the European states to establish domestic legitimacy as a foundation for military power. The decline of the Cold War, however, effectively cut these states adrift. At the same time, international creditors forced weak states to pursue policies of economic liberalisation that failed to revive their economies but undermined the patronage networks on which their fragile political stability depended (Chabal and Dalloz 1999; Reno 1998; Bayart et al. 1999).

STATE CRIME AND GLOBAL POLITICAL ECONOMY

According to Held et al. (1999) there has been little in the way of a systematic process of integration within the world economy.[5] Capital takes different forms: finance capital, trade and productive capital; and to generalise from the developments in relation to finance capital, for example, to all of the workings of the world economy – as is frequently done by globalisation enthusiasts – is methodologically untenable and therefore misleading. The system is not integrated in this way and capital remains primarily rooted in 'discrete national formations' (Held and McGrew 2002: 41).

⇒ Thus, while there has been an unprecedented growth of global finance capital flows, the growing networks of trade have not been distributed evenly across the planet. Rather, processes of regionalisation (centred on the 'core blocs' of North America, western Europe and South-East Asia) and marginalisation (in most of Africa and much of South and Central Asia and Latin America) have taken place (Ellwood 2001: 33; Harman 1996: 7; Held and McGrew 2000: 177–82; Hirst and Thompson: 1996).

Similarly foreign direct investment has, by and large, favoured those developing countries with a relatively skilled and well-paid labour force such as India or Malaysia.[6] African and other poorer countries remain at the margins of international finance, heavily reliant on the flow of aid.

These processes, exacerbated by the debt crisis and recession, have led to increasing inequality. Between 1960 and 1997, the ratio of the income of the richest fifth of the world's population to that of the poorest fifth increased from 30:1 to 74:1 (Human Development Report 1999: 3).

Thus the relation of the developing world to that of the developed world in global economic terms has changed little in over a century: 'The present international division of labour is one Marx would instantly recognize' (Held and McGrew 2002: 45).

According to World Bank figures, by 2000, there was evidence that the world economy was slowing down.[7] This sharpened the level of crisis internationally. Western military intervention in the Gulf, the Balkans, Afghanistan and again in Iraq illustrates the extent to which the major imperialist powers are prepared to use force, particularly if oil or other multinational corporate interests are at stake. The 'War on Terror' has become the key strategic device through which the United States is enforcing its hegemony through a series of military incursions in some of the world's most unstable regions.

As we have already mentioned, the state apparatus in many of the poorest countries has, at the same time, become more militarised and fragmented. Between 1985 and 1999, the total number of armed forces in the least developed countries rose by 81 per cent (Human Development Report 2001: 207). This is in the context of a substantial change in the pattern of warfare, resulting in much higher rates of civilian casualties (Kaldor: 2003).

The implications of this global economic landscape for states and state crime are considerable. The continued marginalisation of much of the developing world creates a crisis of political legitimacy and instability for struggling states. We have demonstrated how poverty, corruption and authoritarianism foster many of the worst forms of state crime but we have also shown how the hegemonic supremacy of one superpower, the United States, produces dangerous criminogenic tendencies.

The 'informal elite networks of global governance' (the World Bank, the IMF, the WTO, G7 and the Bank of International Settlements) play a central political role in linking the developed world with the underdeveloped, albeit in a grossly uneven manner, 'enslaving the world and its peoples to neoliberal ideology and global corporate capitalism' (Held and McGrew 2002: 58).

Engagement with institutions of global finance and the political conditions they impose has had a significant impact on the criminal activities of some states, particularly those with developing industrial economies and those which we have characterised as 'weak'. Bayart et al. go so far as to say that the resulting process of criminalisation has now become the 'dominant trait' of Sub-Saharan Africa, 'in which the state has literally imploded under the combined effects of economic crisis, neoliberal programmes of structural adjustment and the loss of legitimacy of political institutions' (Bayart et al. 1999: 19). World Bank loans, since the early 1990s, have been accompanied by a set of political conditions relating to 'good governance' and human rights (George 1992; Toussaint 1999). And increasingly, following the 2001 attacks on the World Trade Center, they have been accompanied by US-driven security agendas. The imposition of austerity packages underpinning these conditions and agendas, however, directly violate human rights: 'IMF and World Bank conditions for loans to distressed borrowers invariably impose cuts in nutrition, health and educational expenditures for the lower 60 per cent of income receivers' (Herman 2002: viii). As an inevitable consequence, they undermine state legitimacy and lead to increased authoritarianism and ironically to further violations of human rights (Toussaint 1999; Bayart et al. 1999).

This is one of several paradoxes inherent in the way human rights and 'good governance' norms are used by the international financial institutions to legitimise their global hegemony. We are using the term 'hegemony' here in a specific, Gramscian sense (see Chapter 1). It refers to the dissemination and acceptance as an almost unchallengeable 'common sense' – 'what all humankind believes and desires'[8] – of a set of ideas that make the ruling institutions of global society appear to serve universal interests, when in fact they are serving the interests of the economically powerful. Human rights serve this purpose so well – this is the second paradox – because they genuinely do embody universal interests. Not to be killed or tortured, to have access to education, freedom to participate in the political process and so on, really are fundamental human needs (Doyal and Gough 1991). These norms have provided a language and an international organising tool for domestic civil society in many repressive societies.

Global institutions and powerful democracies do not, however, promote such universal interests in a consistent or neutral fashion. They uphold a selection of human rights (civil and political rather than economic, social or cultural) against a selection of rights violators (Chomsky 1999b). The third paradox, raised in our introduction, arises when those states and institutions deploying global authority take it upon themselves to uphold human rights norms by force. Nowhere is this more clearly illustrated than in the case of Iraq.

12
Every Crime in the Book:
Iraq and its Liberators

Two days before the US and the UK launched their war against Iraq in March 2003, we sat in a Turkish café in Stoke Newington wondering how to finish this book. We soon realised that it could only end with a discussion of the impending war. The history of Saddam Hussein's regime epitomised much of what we have said about criminal states. Equally, however, the conduct of the US and the UK throughout Saddam's period in power, as well as in his overthrow, epitomises what we have said about the crimes of advanced democracies.

THE NATURE OF THE IRAQI REGIME

As Charles Tripp writes in his *History of Iraq* (2000), three factors have dominated the state since (and indeed before) its independence in 1932: patrimonialism, the political economy of oil, and the use of violence. Throughout Iraqi history,

> ... the idea of politics as civility ... has generally been overwhelmed by people organized according to very different notions of trust, where the community is not one of citizens, but of family and clan members, fellow tribesmen and conspirators. They have tended to see the state as the guarantor of their own privileges ... (Tripp 2000: 2)

Iraq's oil reserves have placed great wealth in the hands of the state, especially since the nationalisation of the Iraqi Petroleum Company in 1972 was followed by the sharp increases in oil prices in 1973 (Farouk-Sluglett and Sluglett 2001: 230). This made possible the creation of a quite generous state welfare system, alongside a massive apparatus of state repression. According to Makiya (1998: 38), by 1980 one in five of the economically active labour force – 677,000 people – were employed by agencies charged 'with one form or another of violence'.

The salience of violence in Iraqi politics can be partly explained by the way the state was created by the British, when the Ottoman Empire was dismembered after the First World War. The predominantly Kurdish province of Mosul was welded on to the provinces of Baghdad and Basra, ensuring that the Kurds (and the Assyrian Christians) would always be 'a thorn in the flesh' of Iraqi nation building (Levene 1998). The British also followed the Ottoman example of ruling the predominantly Shi'a Muslim population through a Sunni elite. It was never likely that such a state could be ruled by consent. Not surprisingly, successive regimes have fallen back on the combination of patron–client networks and violence typical (as noted in Chapter 2) of so many artificially created, internally fragmented post-colonial states (Tripp 2000).

Both the patrimonialism and the violence of the regime increased during the long, bloody and futile war with Iran from 1980 to 1988. Continuing a process already begun before the war, Saddam Hussein concentrated power in the hands of a small circle of relatives and trusted cronies, and also relied increasingly on tribal leaders for support (Tripp 2000; Farouk-Sluglett and Sluglett 2001; Cockburn and Cockburn 2002; ICG 2002a). To secure his family's loyalty they were allowed to line their pockets by corruption on a large scale (Aburish 1999: 234–5). Similarly, the loyalty of the security services appears to have been secured by material benefits (backed up by blackmail) rather than ideological conviction (al-Khafaji 1994).

In many respects, the combination of patronage and terror that kept Saddam in power was typical of many of the countries studied in this book. The might and ruthlessness of the security apparatus, however, undeniably marked out Iraq as among the worst of the world's criminal regimes, guilty of torture, disappearances, extra-judicial executions, inhuman judicial punishments, war crimes and genocide.

TORTURE AND TERROR

Mustafa Kothair's uncle Mohammed was 'disappeared' following his refusal to join the Iraqi army in 1988. A month later the family learned that Mohammed had been executed. Mustafa and his mother travelled from Shuaba to Baghdad to collect his body. They found him dirty and covered in blood with five bullet holes to his chest. Before his body could be claimed, however, Mustafa's mother was forced to pay 25 dinar for the bullets used by the Iraqi state to kill her brother – 5 dinars each (*Observer*, 13 April 2003).

Like a number of other torturing states, Iraq is a state party to the International Covenant on Civil and Political Rights (ICCPR) and the terror, torture, forced disappearances and extra-judicial executions and forcible expulsions on the basis of ethnicity violate Iraq's own 1990 Interim constitution (Article 2002(a)), and Article 127 of the Code of Criminal Procedure. Yet, as Amnesty International declared in 2001, the systematic nature, scale and severity of torture in Iraq 'can only result from the acceptance of its use at the highest level' (Amnesty 2001e: 1). Those targeted also reveal a degree of state coordination – Shi'a Muslims in southern Iraq and in Baghdad and Kurds in the north – that is, the main internal forces of opposition to Saddam's regime. Mass executions of Shi'ite Arabs (some of whom had been involved in the 1991 uprising) took place at the Al Radwaniyah and Abu Ghraib prisons in central Iraq during 1993. Such was the scale of terror that some members of Saddam's ruling family had their own private torture chambers. Forms of torture included eye-gouging, electric shocks, the piercing of hands by electric drilling, rapes and the rape of family members, 'falaqa', acid baths and mock executions (Amnesty International 2001e). In 1994 Iraq introduced new forms of torture involving the amputation of ears and the branding of foreheads for certain economic crimes and desertion from the army. These barbaric developments, did however, produce anti-regime demonstrations (Cordesman and Hashim 1997: 113). Hundreds of thousands of Kurds and Shi'as are said to have 'disappeared'. As Amnesty International has illustrated, this 'climate of terror' has led to thousands of Iraqis fleeing to seek asylum in bordering countries and beyond.

GENOCIDE

Iraq has been accused of genocide against two ethnic groups: the Marsh Arabs in the south,[1] and the Kurds in the north. Since 1988 the Marsh Arabs have been subject to brutal repression, coupled with the destruction of the wetland ecosystem in which they live. This has resulted in an enormous reduction in the population living in the area – possibly from 400,000 to as few as 20,000 (Human Rights Watch 2003d). Dellapenna (2003) has called this process 'ecocide as genocide'. The reduction in population seems, however, to be mainly the result of internal migration, though mass executions have also played a part. The brutality of the repression directed against the Marsh Arabs is not in question, but it does not appear to amount to genocide in the sense used in this book.

The repression of the Kurds is another matter. In the 1970s and 1980s, the regime conducted a counter-insurgency campaign in Iraqi Kurdistan, using tactics that included the destruction of villages and mass resettlement of the inhabitants. This is a common counter-insurgency tactic, used by the French in Algeria, the British in Malaya and South Arabia, and the Americans in Vietnam (McCuen 1966; McClintock 1992; Mockaitis 1995).

In 1983, when the KDP (Kurdish Democratic Party) resistance movement allied itself with Iran, the Iraqi army abducted between 5,000 and 8,000 males aged twelve and over who belonged to the clan of the KDP leader; it is believed that all were killed. In 1987, Saddam Hussein's cousin Ali Hasan al-Majid was appointed Supreme Commander of the North. By this time most of the countryside was under the effective control of the two rival resistance groups, the KDP and PUK (Patriotic Union of Kurdistan). He intensified the counter-insurgency campaign, using tactics of massacre and the destruction of villages similar to those employed in Guatemala (see Chapter 7). As in Guatemala, inhabitants of 'prohibited areas' were presented with a choice:

> ... either they could 'return to the national ranks' – in other words, abandon their homes and livelihoods and accept compulsory relocation in a squalid camp under the eye of the security forces; or they could lose their Iraqi citizenship and be regarded as military deserters. The second option was tantamount to a death sentence ... (Human Rights Watch 1993: 6)

In effect, those who refused to comply were explicitly excluded from the army's 'universe of obligation' – the Iraqi nation. In meetings with subordinates which were secretly tape-recorded, al-Majid made no secret of his racist contempt for the Kurds:

> 'Why should I let them live there like donkeys who don't know anything?' al-Majid asks in one meeting. 'What did we ever get from them?' On another occasion, speaking in the same vein: 'I said probably we will find some good ones among [the Kurds] ... but we didn't, never.' And elsewhere, 'I will smash their heads. These kind of dogs, we will crush their heads.' And again, 'Take good care of them? No, I will bury them with bulldozers.' (Human Rights Watch 1993: 9)

Human Rights Watch estimates the numbers killed in al-Majid's operations at between 50,000 and 100,000. These include the victims of chemical weapons which were used against many villages, as well as the city of Halabja (and were also deployed, very effectively, against Iranian forces). Not only does the campaign against the Kurds meet the legal definition of genocide, as Human Rights Watch argues; it also fits squarely into the sociological account of genocide provided by Fein (1990) and, with specific reference to Iraq, by the historian Mark Levene (1998, 1999a). As in Guatemala (and East Timor), partial genocide (the killing of a substantial part of an ethnic group) was used as a means of terrorising those who survived. One of the preconditions for genocide, according to Fein (2000) is that 'the perpetrators believe they can get away with it'. This raises the issue to which we now turn: why was the regime allowed to get away with so much, for so long? And why was the country then punished so brutally?

WESTERN COMPLICITY IN SADDAM'S CRIMES

While the case has been made of the criminal nature of the Iraqi state, the focus on Iraq is equally important for illuminating the criminal complicity of western states in the range of human rights violations perpetrated by the regime of Saddam Hussein.

The determination to punish the régime's crimes in 1991 and 2003 is in marked contrast to the West's attitude when Saddam's worst crimes were committed. In terms of the human calamity it caused, by far the worst crime of the regime was its aggression against Iran in 1980: a crime not only condoned, but covertly encouraged, by the US (Hiro 1990: 71–2). As Farouk-Sluglett and Sluglett aptly put it, the chemical bombing of Halabja and the genocide against the Kurds 'occasioned little reaction on the part of Iraq's patrons in the West beyond some feelings of unease, a feeling, perhaps, that a headstrong and wayward child had gone a little too far' (2001: 270). Only one non-Iranian diplomat – Rolf Ekeus of Sweden, later a chief weapons inspector – protested against the bombing of Halabja, and that was in defiance of his government's wishes (Cockburn and Cockburn 2002). The Americans' initial reaction to the Halabja bombing was to to try to blame the Iranians (Aburish 2000: 249).

In November 2002 the British government published a dossier on torture in Iraq. As the government had never been concerned about human rights abuses inside Iraq in the past, the dossier was nothing more than a calculated strategy to encourage public support for the coming war on Iraq. The hypocrisy of the government's move infuriated human rights organisations whose work had been exploited by the dossier. Amnesty International's secretary general, Irene Khan retorted:

> Let us not forget that these same governments turned a blind eye to Amnesty International's reports of widespread human rights violations in Iraq before the Gulf War. They were silent when thousands of unarmed Kurdish civilians were killed in Halabja in 1988. (*Guardian*, 2 December 2002)

One example of the hypocrisy embedded within Britain's condemnation of the 'pariah state' has been its less than welcoming approach to Iraqi asylum seekers – victims of torture and terror – fleeing the 'pariah' regime. As Melanie McFadyean recently reported:

> It is an unpalatable irony that the UK government, in the midst of its crusade to liberate the people of Iraq from Saddam Hussein's tyranny, should be giving such a wretched welcome to many of those who escaped his regime, condemning them to misery in our cities or sending them back where they came from. (McFadyean 2003)

This is less surprising, but no less hypocritical, in the context of the isolation forced upon Iraqi Kurds and Shi'as by the US and Britain during their doomed uprisings in 1991. It also follows from the tremendous support offered by both Britain and the US in the years prior to Saddam's invasion of Kuwait. John Pilger reports a succession of British ministers 'bowing before the tyrant, the renowned interrogator and torturer of Qasr-al-Nihayyah, "the palace of the end". The gassing of 5,000 Kurds in Halabja in the same period was not to be a barrier to securing arms and "dual purpose" equipment deals' (Pilger 2002: 63).

'Liberated' Iraq is now revealing the hollowness of US and British claims that human rights concerns in any way motivated their invasion. Robert Fisk's powerful reports throughout the conflict shed material light on the allies' primary motivations. Why, Fisk challenged, as he personally toured the Baghdad ministries in the days following 'liberation', had the US secured only the Ministry of Oil and the Ministry of the Interior, while leaving hospitals, UN offices, national museums, and all other ministries unprotected against the attacks of looters, vandals and arsonists? (*Independent*, 14 April 2003).

In a report filed for the *Independent* newspaper on 17 April 2003, Fisk describes visiting the torture chambers of Qasimiyeh security station where torture took place in the office of Captain Amar al-Isawi. Prisoners would remain suspended on hooks in the ceiling screaming in agony while the captain waited, smoking and conducting his barbarous administrative tasks until the victim broke. More terrible still is the whole Iraqi intelligence complex: 'a massive grey painted block ... and a series of villas and office buildings that are stashed with files, papers and card indexes'. Here Fisk found piles of bags filled with the shredded records of millions of the regime's worst excesses. Yet the Americans and British have displayed no interest in seeking to discover the contents of those documents, no interest in reconstituting them and discovering the names of the senior intelligence officials guilty of crimes against humanity. This is true of all Baghdad's torture centres and prisons, and those who carried out the torture and executions and those who issued the orders are now free to enrol as Iraqi police under the tutelage of the American military (*Independent*, 17 April 2003).

SANCTIONS AND THE WEAPONS INSPECTORS

On 6 August 1990, four days after Iraq invaded Kuwait, the United Nations Security Council (by Resolution 661) imposed a regime of stringent economic sanctions on Iraq. That regime was 'proudly' described by US National Security Adviser, Sandy Berger, as 'unprecedented for its severity in the whole of world history' (Said 2002: 210–11). On 3 April 1991, these sanctions were reinforced under Resolution 687, the lifting of which, it was declared, was to be conditional on the regime's disarmament of weapons of mass destruction and long-range missiles. The United Nations Special Commission (UNSCOM) was created to oversee the disarmament process. This condition, as the allied invasion of Iraq in March 2003 and a series of events leading up to it, so clearly demonstrated, was a hollow one. Both the British and American governments made it clear that they would oppose the lifting of sanctions as long as Saddam Hussein remained in power (Hiro 1992; Cockburn and Cockburn 2002). As the events of 2003 unfolded, it became clear that nothing short of Saddam's demise could have influenced the Security Council to lift sanctions. Concomitantly the evidence suggests that the failure or discrediting of UNSCOM (and its successor UNMOVIC) was to become an organisational goal of those states on the security council determined to effect regime change in Iraq.

Until the withdrawal of UNSCOM's inspectors and the whole monitoring team in 1998, UNSCOM had produced countless reports documenting that 90–95 per cent of Iraq's proscribed weaponry had been accounted for. Contrary to allied propaganda, UNSCOM was not expelled by the Iraqi regime; they were withdrawn at the order of the United States following a scandal which revealed that UNSCOM had been penetrated by the US Intelligence Service and used to spy on and relay information acquired on Saddam's minders to the US administration (Rai 2002: 73, 68).

By using UNSCOM for intelligence purposes, Washington placed its own intelligence and foreign policy goals above the integrity and survival of UNSCOM. Spying on the leader of Iraq – presumably in order to arrange his assassination – was more important to the US than securing the disarmament of Iraq (Rai 2002: 56). According to Scott Ritter, former UN weapons inspector, a Republican and a defiantly outspoken critic of the war:

> ... since 1998 Iraq has been fundamentally disarmed: 90–95 per cent of Iraq's weapons of mass destruction capability has been verifiably

eliminated. This includes all of the factories used to produce chemical, biological and nuclear weapons, and long-range ballistic missiles; the associated equipment of these factories; and the vast majority of the products coming out of these factories. (Ritter and Pitt 2002: 23)

Two years earlier he had written:

Given the comprehensive nature of the monitoring regime put in place by UNSCOM, which included a strict export-import control regime, it was possible as early as 1997, to determine, that from a qualitative standpoint, Iraq had been disarmed ... As long as monitoring inspections remained in place, Iraq presented a WMD-based threat to no one. (Ritter 2000)

Yet these were facts that the US and Britain categorically would not hear. Iraq's possession of weapons of mass destruction had become a supreme truth – a mantra to justify war. If the overriding goal of the US and Britain was to effect regime change inside Iraq through war on Iraq, then the inspection teams and their finding had to be discredited.

The disingenuous obsession with Iraq's weapons of mass destruction has somehow erased some very chilling facts about the United States. The US has, for example, the full arsenal of biological, chemical and nuclear weapons of mass destruction. Moreover it is the only state in the world to have ever used nuclear bombs against a civilian population.

In 1997, the US Senate passed an act to implement the Chemical Weapons Convention. Section 307 states that 'the President may deny a request to inspect any facility in the United States in cases where the President determines that the inspection may pose a threat to the national security interests of the United States'. Wherein lies the difference with Iraqi refusals to allow inspections of the Presidential Palaces?

Similarly the same Act (section 303) stipulates that if the President of the United States objects to any individual acting as an inspector then this objection cannot be reviewed in court (Blum 1998: 3). The Iraqis were afforded no equivalent right of objection and given that the majority of inspectors were frequently from Britain and the US – countries which had systematically bombed Iraq from 1998 – the partisanship of inspectors would have been a reasonable objection.

SANCTIONS AND VIOLATIONS OF HUMAN RIGHTS

Sanctions created untold misery for the people of Iraq. The list of banned items (prior to the lifting of sanctions in May 2003) was unusually cruel and contributed to the scarcity of commodities essential for purposive existence of millions of Iraqi people. Banned items included: all electrical equipment, ambulances, baby food, bandages, blankets, cannulas for intravenous drips, infant catheters, chlorine and other water purification chemicals, cleaning agents, dialysis equipment, angina and epilepsy medication, incubators, medical swabs, medical journals, medical syringes, naso-gastric tubes, flour, oxygen tents, paper, pencils, pencil sharpeners, school books, soap, shampoo, steel plate stethoscopes, surgical instruments, toilet paper, toothpaste and brushes (Simons 2002, 2003). The consequences of these deprivations have been unconscionable.

According to two senior policy analysts for the US government the impact of sanctions has permeated the very core of Iraqi society. It is clear, however, that Iraqi living standards have declined precipitously since 1990; and that this decline has reached the 'centre' as well as Shi'ite and Kurdish areas. Prices have increased sharply while wages and salaries have not risen for the past six years. Poverty is widespread even in Sunni areas, and much of Iraq's prosperous middle class has been wiped out. Many Iraqis have had to sell or pawn their valuables, and take second jobs – driving cabs or hawking their wares on the streets (Cordesman and Hashim 1997: 14).

UNICEF reported in 1999 that between the periods 1984–89 and 1994–99 infant mortality had increased from 47 to 108 per 1,000 live births and the death rate among children under five had more than doubled. In April 1999 a panel, established to assess the humanitarian situation following sanctions, reported that under-five child mortality had more than trebled between 1989 and 1997 and maternal mortality had more than doubled (UN 1999, Annex II).

Over 500,000 children are estimated to have died as a direct result of sanctions. Malnutrition has soared. Prior to the advent of sanctions, malnutrition was not a problem in Iraq; by 1997, UNICEF estimated that around a million children under five were chronically malnourished (UNICEF 1997: 23).

In January 2003, the *New York Times* quoted Farid Zarif, deputy director of the UN humanitarian aid programme:

> We are told that pencils are forbidden because carbon could be extracted from them that might be used to coat airplanes and make them invisible to radar,' Zarif said, 'I am not a military expert, but I find it very disturbing that because of this objection we cannot give pencils to Iraqi schoolchildren.'

Epidemiologist Richard Garfield reports over the same period a decline in adult literacy from 80 per cent to 58 per cent, a decline he describes in humanitarian terms as a fundamental loss of 'long-term assets' (Garfield 2000: 47).

The *Economist* summed up the consequences of the UN's sanctions policy: 'Slowly, inexorably, a generation is being crushed in Iraq. Thousands are dying, thousands more are leading stunted lives, and storing up bitter hatreds for the future' (8 April 2000, cited in Rai 2002: 179).

Sanctions have also created an anomic criminal climate inside Iraq, what Cordesman and Hashim (1997) have described as 'the calamitous decline in social and moral mores', evidence of which most visibly came to light with the wholesale looting of Baghdad once US troops had occupied the city in April 2003. This was something of which the Security Council was well aware. In 1999 the Security Council's Humanitarian panel reported that sanctions had created a climate of:

> Juvenile delinquency, begging and prostitution, anxiety about the future and lack of motivation ... the development of a parallel economy replete with profiteering and criminality, cultural and scientific impoverishment, disruption of family life. (UN 1999, Annex II)

The sanctions programme has also led to increased corruption within Iraq as officials and professionals resort to bribery in an effort to make ends meet; however, in some respects the government's rationing system was remarkably equitable (and served to increase the population's dependence on the regime) (Cockburn and Cockburn 2002: 120, 123). Smugglers, middlemen and tribal leaders close to the regime have made fortunes from the rationing system, illegal oil sales and other black market activities (Farouk-Sluglett and Sluglett 2001: 294; Hiro 2003: 16; Cockburn and Cockburn 2002: 150; ICG 2002a).

Iraq's acceptance of UN Resolution 986 in 1996 finally created an (albeit wholly inadequate) 'oil for food' programme. Iraq was allowed to sell $330 million worth of oil per month for a period of six months with less than half the proceeds going to providing food and medicine in areas under Ba'ath Party control (30 per cent on war reparations to Kuwait, 15 per cent on food and medicine for the semi-autonomous Kurdish region and 10 per cent to pay for the costs of UN operations inside Iraq, such as the loathed weapons inspections) (Cordesman and Hashim 1997: 15). While the ceiling for Iraqi oil sales was increased over the years humanitarian commentators made clear it was simply not enough to counter the appalling social and health costs of sanctions (Cappacio 2000: 137).

The sanctions saga has a dual significance from a state crime perspective. On the one hand, it exemplifies the injustice of punishing an entire nation for the crimes of its ruler. On the other, although the sanctions were undoubtedly *legal*, they can be considered criminal in view of their gross violation of the very human rights that the UN was supposed to uphold. In this respect it seems particularly significant that the resolutions for an oil-for-food deal proposed by the Security Council prior to Resolution 986 imposed humiliating limitations described by Milan Rai as 'designed to be refused' (2002: 182). As a result of Iraq's refusal, which Graham-Brown (1999: 77), among others, had predicted, 'negotiations were stalemated for over four years of suffering' (Rai 2002: 183). It is also significant that two successive heads of the UN Office for the Co-Ordination of Humanitarian Affairs in Baghdad, Dennis Halliday and Hans von Sponeck, as well as the World Food Programme's Jutta Berghardt, felt driven to resign (Farouk-Sluglett and Sluglett 2001: 295).

THE ARMS TRADE – WESTERN COMPLICITY

The illegal trade of arms and weapons technologies from Britain and the United States to the Iraqi regime, particularly through the 1980s, played a crucial role in developing Iraq's weapons of mass destruction capability. During the early 1990s, government inquiries in both the US and Britain revealed covert support for the regime of Saddam Hussein. False 'end user' certificates and the facilitation of 'third countries' were used extensively by western states, not least the US and Britain, to conceal illegal weapons and weapons technology exports to Iraq. The US also maintained a close monitoring of 'third country' arms sales to Iraq to ensure that Iraq was being adequately supplied with weapons for the war against Iran (Teicher 1995). While Russia and France were Iraq's largest exporters of arms between the 1970s and 1990, the United States, Britain and Germany (McDowall 1996: 361–7; Hooper 2003) also supplied Iraq with a wide and deadly range of arms equipment and technologies including the actual ingredients for biological weapons during the same period.

A US General Accounting Office investigation into US exports and transfers of military items reported:

> [Department of] Commerce officials told us that because Iraq was removed from antiterrorism controls [in 1982] and because controls on missile technology and chemical and biological warfare were not in place until the late 1980s, few foreign policy controls were placed on exports to Iraq during the 1980s. They said that this, along with the threat of national security controls, resulted in a long list of high-technology items being sold to Iraq during the 1980s. (GAO 1994: 5)

In October 1992, the US Committee on Banking, Housing, and Urban Affairs, which has Senate oversight responsibility for the Export Administration Act (EAA), conducted an inquiry into US export policy to Iraq in the years leading up to the Persian Gulf war (September 1980–August 1988). Evidence submitted to the inquiry revealed that UN inspectors had identified

> ... many US-manufactured items exported pursuant to licenses issued by the US Department of Commerce that were used to further Iraq's chemical and nuclear weapons development and missile delivery system development programs. (US Senate 1994: Introduction)

An excerpt from the Senate Committee's inquiry demonstrates how the US government ensured Iraq's biological weapons capability:

> After receiving this information, we contacted a principal supplier of these materials to determine what, if any, materials were exported to Iraq which might have contributed to an offensive or defensive biological warfare program. Records available from the supplier for the period from 1985 until the present show that during this time, pathogenic (meaning 'disease producing'), toxigenic (meaning 'poisonous'), and other biological research materials were exported to Iraq pursuant to application and licensing by the U.S. Department of Commerce ... These exported biological materials were not attenuated or weakened and were capable of reproduction. The inquiry found that export licences, sanctioned by the State Department, were issued to US companies to export both anthrax (*Bacillus Anthracis*) and botulism (*Clostridium Botulinum*) between 1985 and 1990. (US Senate 1994: Ch. 1: 10)

In 1992 the Department of Defense's *Report to Congress on the Conduct of the Persian Gulf War*, revealed the direct consequences of America's active support of Iraq's biological warfare programme:

> By the time of the invasion of Kuwait, Iraq had developed biological weapons. Its advanced and aggressive biological warfare program was the most advanced in the Arab world ... The program probably began late in the 1970s and concentrated on the development of two agents, botulinum toxin and anthrax bacteria ... (cited in US Senate 1994: Ch. 1: 10–11)

The US was not alone in duplicitously building Iraq's biological arsenal. Anthrax was also supplied to the Iraqi state by the government-owned Porton Down laboratories in Britain (Pilger 2002: 67). Despite the knowledge that Iraq had been engaging in chemical (and possibly biological) warfare against its own Kurds, Shi'ites and the Iranians, these deadly exports continued until late November 1989.

The scandal surrounding Britain's role in arming the Iraqi regime (see Chapter 3) illustrated, not only that the British state was 'knee deep in dishonour', but that it had breached its own rules, acted illegally and employed deception to conceal those breaches from the public.

The British government inquiry led by Sir Richard Scott was to demonstrate the wholesale complicity and duplicity of the British state in arming Iraq. As Paul Foot argued, 'Scott shows how the civil service and the politicians, either together or separately, combined to deceive the public about what really went on' (Foot 1996).

The Scott Inquiry demonstrated that Britain had never adopted the policy of impartiality during the 1980–88 Iran–Iraq war that it had always publicly maintained. Rather it favoured Iraq from the outset. From 1985 the Export Credits Guarantee Department (responsible for guaranteeing all British exports) guaranteed defence equipment sales to Iraq of at least £25 million. The same did not apply to Iran and when the war came to an end in 1988 the guarantee for Iraq was dramatically increased to £100 million. Scott also revealed a deep and prolonged hypocrisy relating to the apparently 'restricted' policy Britain maintained during the years of the Persian Gulf war. What emerged from the Scott Inquiry was that Britain had covertly and illegally exported a whole range of lethal weaponry to Iraq throughout the 1980s through the use of third countries and false 'end user' certificates. Jordan was the main diversionary route for British arms (Norton-Taylor et al. 1996). According to Paul Foot, arms sales from Britain to Jordan were 3,000 per cent (in the region of £500 million) higher in the 1980s than they had been in the preceding decade. This was not a function of Jordanian arms expansion – which throughout the 1980s was actually contracting. Jordan was simply a conduit for the covert transfer of British arms exports to Iraq (Foot 1996).

Arms dealers were also encouraged by the Minister of State for Defence, Alan Clark (when he was Minister for Trade) to imply that their machinery and equipment were for civil use only when applying for an export licence.

HEGEMONY

In our introduction we proposed the concept of global hegemony as one useful for understanding the way in which key international institutions facilitate the expansion of dominant economic, political and social forces. Cox has described a 'hegemonic concept of world order ... founded upon not only the regulation of inter-state conflict but also upon a globally conceived civil society' (1993: 61). World or global hegemony is a particularly important concept in the study of state crime because it embodies not only universal norms but also the institutions and mechanisms which define how states should behave.

The US and its allies exercise hegemony in that their dominance appears to serve universal interests (ridding 'dangerous' states of tyrannical leaders and their weapons of mass destruction, liberating oppressed peoples, restoring human rights, bringing 'stability' and 'democracy' to the Middle East, and so on), rather than serving the sectional interests of transnational capital and global political supremacy. As the historian Gabriel Kolko puts it, there are 'mystical elements in the United States' vaguely defined mission to reform the way the World has existed and operated, but at its core these always identify the world's interests and America's as one and the same' – 'regional or global order' equals 'the freedom of American businessmen to make money' (2002: 109, 143). As we have argued, human rights norms (selectively interpreted and enforced) offer an ideal basis for a global hegemonic consensus because they are founded upon genuinely universal interests. No one can dispute that human beings are better off when they are not tortured or threatened with genocide.

In recent years, these universalist norms have been mixed with something very different: a concerted anti-Arab Islamophobia: 'Arabs are dehumanised ... seen as violent irrational terrorists always on the lookout for murder and bombing outrages' (Said 2002: 212).

The singular and isolated demonisation of Saddam Hussein (in marked contrast, for example, to his Guatemalan counterpart General Rios Montt), Britain and America's disingenuous obsession with absent weapons of mass destruction, and the unfounded conflation of Iraq and Al-Qaeda are underscored by a deeply ingrained, politically cultivated fear of the Arab and Islamic world. And it is this racism that has prepared domestic populations (though by no means wholly successfully) to tolerate a brutal, punitive and expensive war.

As Edward Said reported, 'The notion of "justified punishment" for Iraq is now uppermost in the minds of most American consumers of news' (2002: 213). This punitive motivation was also evident in the 1991 Gulf War:

As a 'police action,' the Coalition War implicitly meant that Iraq was liable to punishment for its aggression against another state. Indeed, the manner the Coalition War was prosecuted seemed not only to drive Iraq's forces out of Kuwait, as it was announced, but also to punish a nation by the destruction of its industrial and infra-structure centers contrary to the norms governing war as defined under International Law ... (Khadduri and Ghareeb 1997: 169)

But the legitimacy of both the United States and Britain has been gravely damaged in the war waged against Iraq. The evidence of twelve years of crippling and impoverishing sanctions, mass demonstrations against the invasion of Iraq around the world, the exposure of governmental lies and deceits relating to Iraq's weapons capabilities, and US control over contracts relating to the rebuilding of Iraq have all challenged the neutrality and consistency of such universal interests. Instead the fissures now visible in that global hegemony reveal the primary motivations for war as protection of US oil interests in the region and the unashamed drive for US political control of the Middle East.

CONCLUSION

Writing in the *Independent on Sunday* (4 April 2003), John Pilger lists some of the incidents in which civilians were recklessly killed by American and British forces, and adds that such deaths would have occurred 'in industrial quantities now were it not for the voices of the millions who filled London and other capitals, and the young people who walked out of their schools; they have saved countless lives'. In the 1991 Gulf War, civilians were indeed killed 'in industrial quantities' by the deliberate destruction of the country's infrastructure, particularly the water and electricity supplies (Khadduri and Ghareeb 1997; Cockburn and Cockurn 2002). That did not happen in 2003.[2] Was it because the American and British suddenly became more humane? Or because their weapons were more accurate? Or was it because they faced a more critical domestic public than in 1991? Paraphrasing the American journalist Patrick Tyler, Pilger concludes that 'we are entering a new bi-polar world with two new superpowers: the Bush/Blair gang on one side, and world opinion on the other, a truly popular force stirring at last and whose consciousness soars by the day.' Perhaps this errs on the side of optimism but it captures the essential point. To control the crimes of our rulers we must look not to international courts – where only the defeated are ever likely to face trial – but to civil society: the organised voice of ordinary working people.

In stressing the role of civil society we are being deliberately vague. Civil society takes a multitude of forms, from trade unions to television channels to single-issue pressure groups to revolutionary movements. In broad terms, the political implication of our position is clear: what is needed is a strong, transnational network of organisations – a united front – that will oppose and denounce state crimes by any means, consistent with human rights, that can provide an effective sanction against the perpetrators.

This perspective (influenced by Kaldor 1999, 2003, and Risse et al. 1999) does not entail a complete rejection of courts or truth commissions but it gives them only a secondary role. To argue for international justice on grounds of deterrence (as does Robertson 2002: xxv) is unconvincing, at least as far as political leaders are concerned, because the one sure way to avoid punishment by an international tribunal (or, what is probably a greater concern for most tyrants, by one's political enemies) is to stay in power at all costs. A more credible case for courts and truth commissions sees them as a way of shaping 'collective memory' (Osiel 1997). They are a way of impressing upon civil society that state crimes are indeed crimes, and are not to be tolerated. It is organised public intolerance that provides the deterrence: the prospect, in a democracy, of being voted out of office, or in an authoritarian state, of the country's becoming ungovernable (and one's overseas bank accounts being frozen). To resist the worst tyrannies, where civil society has been systematically destroyed, requires acts of almost unimaginable courage. Nevertheless, recent history – in eastern Europe, Latin America, Indonesia, the Philippines, South Africa – suggests that civil society has a much better record than 'humanitarian bombing' in bringing state crime under control.

Notes

CHAPTER 1

1. Some hospitals, schools, power stations, etc., are state agencies but for criminological purposes it is not obvious why this should put their organisational crimes in a different category from those of private hospitals, etc. Conversely, some technically private bodies such as private prisons, which form part of Engels' 'public power', can be considered as state agencies.
2. The conceptual puzzles mainly centre on the relation between actual and perceived legitimacy, and between legitimacy and consent. See Beetham (1991), Ward and Green (2000).
3. There were many rumours of covert military involvement in policing operations.
4. For example, a state agency's goals may be served *both* by generally tolerating petty corruption *and* by sometimes prosecuting it (see Chapter 2).
5. Exceptions include Bahrain, Brunei, Cuba, Fiji, the Holy See, Indonesia, Kazakhstan, Myanmar (Burma), Pakistan, Qatar, Singapore, and the United States, which has signed the Covenant on Social, Economic and Cultural Rights but not ratified it.
6. For a more detailed discussion see Green and Ward (2000). Our view is influenced by liberal political philosophy, particularly Rawls (1971) and Gewirth (1982), and by R. G. Peffer's (1990) argument that the gap between such left-liberal theories and Marxism is much narrower than is often supposed.
7. There are enormously difficult issues about whether some human beings with extremely severe disabilities, and some non-human beings (for example, the great apes: Cavalieri and Singer 1993) are prospective purposive agents, and what rights they have.
8. One of us (P.G.) is a Marxist; we believe our analysis is at least consistent with Marxism.
9. In its context, the phrase specifically refers to 'the first phase of a communist society'.
10. On the symbolic goals served by international criminal justice see Osiel (1997), Minow (1998), Bass (2000). On the law of the International Criminal Court see Cassese (2003). On truth commissions see Hayner (2001) and, on the limitations of the South African model, Stanley (2001).

CHAPTER 2

1. The study, by G. A. Satarov et al., is summarised at <www.rand.org/nsrd/cre/events/corruption.html>; this detail is taken from the report in the *Helsingen Sanomat* 13 August 2002 <www.helsinki-hs.net/news.asp?id=20020813IE15>
2. Those of Taca's activities which were less than open did give rise to accusations of corruption: see Keena (2003).
3. What makes corruption 'obvious' is itself an interesting sociological question, which we pass over here. See, for example, Chibnall and Saunders (1977).
4. For two contrasting assessments of the role of the Italian judiciary, see Nelken (1996), Burnett and Mantovani (1998).

5. For more on the benefits of funding New Labour, see <www.red-star-research. org.uk>
6. We owe this description, and other valuable insights into Irish political life, to the investigative journalist Frank O'Connor (interview, 11 October 2000).
7. Cf. Nickson's (1996) description of Stroessner's Paraguay as a sultanist regime, and Perlmutter (1977) on the generally sultanist nature of military regimes.

CHAPTER 3

1. The Convention on Wetlands of International Importance Especially as Waterfowl Habitat.
2. Note that this estimate was made in 1995, before the widespread militia attacks on the population in 1999 surrounding the referendum ballot on independence.
3. April 1996 Session of the Shrimp Tribunal, at <www.earthsummitwatch.org/shrimp/ national_reports/ecua96.html>

CHAPTER 4

1. This chapter is dedicated to the memory of Aykut Barka (1952–2002), the Turkish seis-mologist who first stimulated us to think about natural disasters. His commitment to his science and to the life-safety of Turkish people was inspirational.
2. '*Bu deprem, Türk siyasi idare yapısının iflasıdır. Türk siyasi ve idari sistemi yeniden sorgulanmalıdır*', Erkan Mumcu, Tourism Minister, quoted in *Sabah* newspaper, 24 August 1999.
3. '*Şu anda altyapı sorunlarını gündeme getirme ve suçlama zamanı değil*', *Sabah* newspaper, 20 August 1999, p. 2.
4. For example, parts of India and newly industrialising countries such as Malaysia.
5. In absolute terms, the figures are stark. Between 1990 and 1998, foreign direct investment in 'low-income' countries rose from $2,201 million to $10,674 million; in 'middle-income' countries from $21,929 million to $160,267 million; and in 'high-income' countries from $169,252 million to $448,316 million. See World Bank (2000: 315).
6. Economic losses, using Abramovitz's definition, include insured property losses, the costs of repairing physical infrastructure such as roads and power, and certain agricultural losses. There are, however, very significant indirect consequences, 'such as the costs of business failures or interruptions, suicide due to despair, domestic violence, human health effects, or lost human and development potential' (2001: 12). Damage figures employed by all assessors, reinsurers and the majority of commentators also exclude the destruction of natural resources.
7. The NAFZ is a strike-slip fault that traverses approximately 1,500 km, and has been frequently active in the last century, the most destructive earthquakes occurring in Sakarya in 1967 (moment magnitude 7.1), Abant in 1957 (moment magnitude of 7.0) and Izmit Gulf (between Istanbul and Adapazari) in 1894 <www.koeri.boun.edu.tr/ earthqk/eqhistory.htm>
8. What is most striking about the media and official coverage of the earthquake is the total dearth of information about the number of missing. A year following the earthquake one columnist stated: 'There has been no other earthquake on the face of the earth where the number of dead and missing is unknown. We call on those concerned to explain the real figures' (*Cumhuriyet*, 16 August 2000). The official estimates of the number of deceased stand at 17,840 deaths, 43,953 wounded and 505 permanently disabled. However, the unofficial estimates of number of deaths stand much higher. Originally, government

sources were quoted as saying that they believed the death toll would stand at well over 35,000, given that at least 35,000 buildings had been destroyed (and bearing in mind that each building is approximately 16 homes).

9. Afet ve Afet İşleri Genel Müdürlüğü Eğetim Haber Bilim Dergisi, 2000 (2). T.C. Bayındırlık ve İskan Bakanlığı. ['Disaster and the Directorate for Disaster Affairs', *Education, News and Science Journal*: Ministry for Public Works and Housing].

10. Eastern Marmara Earthquakes and the Following Planning and Reconstruction Efforts towards Sustainable Future, Ministry of Public Works and Settlement, Turkey.

11. The regions that sustained loss of life and damage to structures in this earthquake were nine of Turkey's (then) 80 provinces. It has been estimated that Turkey's Ministry of Public Works and Housing (MOPWH) has reconstructed an average of 3,500 earthquake-affected housing units a year since 1965 (Coburn 1995: 67).

12. Infill is the material used to fill in a space or cavity: in this instance, the wall space between columns, floors and ceilings.

13. EQE International, 1999; this was consistent with the situation in previous earthquakes, for example, the 1992 Erzincan earthquake (EERI 1999).

14. Despite improvements in the building code, which has not been updated since the Marmara earthquake, but is based on the US building code and is consistent with recommended practice for the design of buildings in earthquake regions (US Geological Survey Circular, 2000) The building specifications for structures to be built in disaster areas were first implemented by the Ministry for Public Works and Housing in 1997 (Ministry for Public Works and Housing 1997).

15. The standard practice in civil engineering of deep bore hole investigations would have informed the contractors, consultant engineers and the municipal authority about the consequences of building on a particular site. According to the earth scientists and earthquake engineers interviewed, the suitability of a particular foundation type for a weak soil condition is not difficult to assess and was knowledge available to local government officials prior to the earthquake. There was no available evidence of bore tests being carried out prior to the earthquake (Municipal Officials, Mayor's office Adapazarı, personal communication, December 2000).

16. A recent building census (Mustafa Erdik, personal communication) estimates that there are 1 million freestanding buildings in Istanbul.

17. For a discussion on penal amnesties see Green (2000).

18. 'We are paying the price with negative outcomes for those who undervalue practitioners, who always put business interests first, who don't see the value of our aesthetic, evolutionary, and architectural environment. How shameful, development amnesties and those who see fit to commit crimes of procedure against construction laws, are creating large wounds to our way of life that are difficult to close' (Ahmet Necdet Sezer, quoted in *Cumhuriyet*, 8 November 2001).

19. *Cumhuriyet*, 1 November 2000, 'The Ceyhan group fed by the government'.

20. Originally, government sources were quoted as saying that they believed the death toll would stand at well over 35,000, given that at least 35,000 buildings had been destroyed (*Turkish Daily News*, 21 August 1999). The United Nations estimate on 23 August was of over 40,000 deaths (*Turkish Daily News*, 23 August 1999), based on figures given to them by the Turkish government. However, one week later the UN announced that the government had 'reassessed its need' (for body bags, of which 45,000 were requested), and declined to issue an official toll (*Turkish Daily News*, 27 August 1999). The government death toll was revised down to 12,514 and later to the official 17,840 deaths within a matter of days, with the discrepancies being accounted for as 'computer error' (*Turkish Daily News*, 26 August 1999).

21. A year following the earthquake one columnist stated 'There has been no other earthquake on the face of the earth where the number of dead and missing is unknown. We call on those concerned to explain the real figures' (*Cumhuriyet*, 16 August 2000).

22. The tragic Bingöl earthquake in which 85 school children died while sleeping in a school dormitory illustrates this point even more sharply. Here in the heart of Kurdish Turkey the consequences of political dispossession and war were revealed. This is an impoverished region where desperately needed national resources have been diverted into the prosecution of war and maintaining institutions of repression. Most of the children sleeping in the school lived in villages without local schools and were forced to board because of the failure of the Turkish government to invest in regional infrastructure and services in the region. As an uncle of one of the victims told a *Guardian* journalist, 'I am angry at the dishonest builders who built this trap for our children and their political allies who let them get away with it' (*Guardian*, 3 May 2003).

CHAPTER 5

1. In England the key studies are by Holdaway (1983), Smith and Gray (1985), Young (1991) and Choongh (1997). Reiner (2000) provides an excellent overview of the Anglo-American literature, and Waddington (1999c) contains much of interest on police violence and corruption. For the US, see especially Geller and Toch (1996), Kappeller et al. (1998), Manning (1997) and Cancino (2001). Australia offers less in the way of detailed ethnography, but Cunneen (2001) and McCulloch (2001) have published excellent studies of police violence and racism.

2. Thanks to Deborah Coles and her colleagues at INQUEST <www.inquest.org.uk>, for the information on which these case studies are based.

3. The Police Complaints Authority, however, has recently issued guidance stating categorically that CS spray should not be used against people with 'acute behavioural disturbance', because 'It may not subdue the individual and it could create needless liability' (2002: 7).

4. *R (on the application of Stanley)* v. *Inner North London Coroner*, BLD 3004031495. A new inquest is pending at the time of writing.

5. We deliberately use the term which excludes Northern Ireland.

6. The adoption of 'paramilitary' tactics by the regular police should be distinguished from the existence of paramilitary forces distinct from the regular police, which has a long history in many European states (Hills 1995; Waddington 1999c).

7. The 30 per cent estimate is Walker's (1993); Sherman et al.'s (1986) findings, quoted in Alpert and Fridell (1992: 37), indicate a fall of at least 50 per cent in large cities between 1971 and 1984.

8. Though we cannot vouch for its sociological accuracy, the Brazilian film *City of God* (2002) paints a compelling picture of the interplay of policing, poverty, gang warfare and vigilantism. Human Rights Watch (2002c, 2003e) presents a complex picture of the relation between police, vigilantes and state and local government in Nigeria, with the police sometimes clashing violently with vigilantes, but often tolerating their vicious crime-fighting activities.

CHAPTER 6

1. Tilly's remark has a particular resonance after the invasion of Iraq to 'protect' us against a 'threat' that appears daily more imaginary as we write: see Chapter 12.

2. Later described as 'shifting coalitions' by Block and Chambliss (1981).
3. In 1989, for example three Colombian presidential candidates were assassinated.
4. This model was developed by Naylor (1995) to examine organised crime in relation to economic relations.
5. On the parliamentary list of Jairo Ortega Ramirez.
6. At the time Deputy Prime Minister.
7. 'Ciller: Devlet İçin Kurşun Atan Şereflidir', cited in *Sabah* newspaper, 27 November 1996.
8. The information presented is taken from the newspapers *Hurriyet*, *Sabah*, *Radikal*, *Milliyet*, *Yeniyuzyil* and *Demokrasi*, from the period December 1996 to February 1997.
9. Sedat Bucak in his testimony to the Susurluk parliamentary commission, cited in *Hurriyet*, 23 January 1997.
10. Cited in *Sabah* newspaper, 1 January 1997.
11. Erbakan, cited in *Radikal*, 2 January 1997.
12. Cited in the *Washington Post*, 1 January 1997.
13. Cited in *Hurriyet*, 31 December 1996.
14. Cited in *Hurriyet*, 26 December 1997.
15. Çarkin admitted this to reporters at the Commission, cited in *Milliyet*, 22 January 1997.
16. Cited in *Milliyet*, 22 January 1997.
17. Cited in *Radikal*, 11 January 1997.
18. Cited in *Radikal*, 24 January 1997.
19. Cited in *Cumhuriyet*, 27 December 1996.
20. Photographs in *Radikal*, *Hurriyet*, *Milliyet*, 24 January 1997.
21. Cited in *Radikal*, 9 January 1997.
22. Sedat Bucak in his testimony to the Susurluk Parliamentary Commission, cited in *Hurriyet*, 23 January 1997.
23. Cited in *Milliyet* newspaper, 23 January 1997, referring to the following 1993 conversation. Gurdal Mumcu (the journalist's widow): 'So many errors [made by police investigating the bomb blast] have piled up. These stand before us as a wall.' Agar: 'If you took one brick from the base, it would all collapse.' Mumcu: 'Then do it.' Agar: 'I can't. Impossible.' Mumcu: 'Pull out that brick and let the wall collapse on them.' Agar: 'I can't.' Mumcu: 'Then it will collapse on you.'
24. Mesut Yılmaz, opposition leader, cited in *Hurriyet*, 26 December 1996.
25. *Radikal* newspaper, cited in *Turkish Daily News*, 24 December 1996.
26. Cited in *Hurriyet*, 11 January 1997.

CHAPTER 7

1. For criticisms of such complicity on the part of academic 'terrorology', see Herman (1982); George (1991); Chomsky (2002).
2. See Fisk 2001, for examples of the use of death squads against émigrés from Iran, Israel, Libya and Iraq.
3. See in particular the comments of Tony Blair, reported in the *Observer*, 1 June 2003, praising the referendum held under Russian martial law.
4. Barbara Crosette wrote in 1993 that the Indian police and security apparatus were then killing more people *each year* than were killed during the entire 17-year dictatorship of Pinochet in Chile (cited by Mahmood 2000: 82).
5. In 1987–89, the Sri Lankan government made highly effective use of death squads against the JVP, a Sinhalese organisation that threatened to overthrow it for being too conciliatory towards the Tamils (Uyangoda 1996). More recently the armed forces and

government-funded paramilitaries have been implicated in disappearances, torture and gang rape (Amnesty 2001a, 2002) in their campaign against Tamil separatist forces.

6. Northern Ireland (and previously Ireland as a whole) has long occupied an ambiguous position between the colonial and metropolitan spheres of the UK (Ruane and Todd 1996, Ch. 8).

7. Stalin's terror of the 1930s, also discussed by O'Kane, broadly fits the same pattern: unable to govern the countryside effectively, the regime 'decided to lash out brutally and wholesale' (Getty and Naumov 2000: 472). But the Bolsheviks' extraordinarily self-destructive purge of 1937–38 'defies explanation, let alone comprehension', according to the historian Arno Mayer (2000: 660).

8. The estimate of 25,000 is from National Commission on Disappeared People (1986); the figure of 30,000 'has the greatest currency in Argentine human rights circles' according to Feitlowitz (1998: 257, n.1).

9. Chomsky (1999b: 30) credits Israeli Labour politicians of the 1950s with devising this 'madman theory', later taken up by Richard Nixon.

10. Scilingo would have done well to read the original parable. When the owner of the field is asked by his servants whether they should pull up the weeds, he replies, 'Nay: lest while ye gather up the tares, ye root up the wheat with them' (Matthew 13: 29).

CHAPTER 8

1. Muzzafer Orucoglu is a Turkish Kurd poet and writer currently living in Australia. Orucoglu was sentenced to 37 years of imprisonment in the 1970s for his opposition to the military government, and a further seven for the publication (while in prison) of his cycle of poetry, *The Blacksmith*.

2. See, for example, Gordon and Marton (1995); Amnesty International (2000d); Conroy 2000; Human Rights Watch (2001b).

3. Resolution 39/46.

4. See for example, Rutherford and Hodgkinson (1996).

5. See in particular Amnesty International (2001), 'Broken Bodies, Shattered Minds: Torture and ill-treatment of women' London: Amnesty International Publications, which argues strongly for the incorporation of private individuals as agents of terror in the definitional category of torture.

6. This is not to deny that, for example, the Belgian state through its incompetence was culpable for the fate of the children Marc Dutroux abducted, sexually abused and in some cases murdered (Punch 2003). In everyday language these children were indeed tortured but the *state* crime of which they were victims was one of gross negligence.

7. Compare Bauman's (1989) juxtaposition of bureaucracy and morality, which we criticise in Chapter 10.

8. See Michael Levin (1982, 1990) for a philosophical (and highly problematic) justification for the practice of torture. For a critique of utilitarian justifications of torture, see Morgan and Evans (2001).

9. Kurdistan Workers Party, led by Abdullah Öcalan until his arrest, imprisonment and sentence of death by the Turkish authorities in June 1999.

10. Front Libération Nationale.

11. 1970s pro-independence movement in Indonesian-controlled East Timor.

12. Renamed in January 2001 'The Western Hemisphere Institute for Security Cooperation'.

13. In an attempt to reduce the export of torture to repressive regimes the European Parliament has called for the inclusion of 'repressive technologies' in the control of arms exports (in *Human Rights Law Journal*, Vol. 16, nos 1–3, 1995, paras 3, 74).

14. See Peters (1996: 172–6) for an extensive survey of torture sequelae.
15. OMCT, 1992, 'El Terrorismo de Estado en Colombia', Brussels: NCOS (cited in Sottas 1998).
16. See also Helen Feins' 'universe of obligation' in relation to the perpetrators of genocide (discussed in Ch. 11 of this volume).
17. Commmission on Human Rights: Military Aid to Governments Practicing Torture: Written Statement Submitted by Human Rights Watch, UN Doc. E/CN.4/1995/NGO/ 6 of 31 January 1995, para. 1.
18. 'The Torture Trail', Channel 4, *Dispatches*, 11 January 1995.
19. *Ibid.*
20. In July 2000, Peter Hain, the UK Foreign Office Minister, introduced new controls over the export of 'oversize' handcuffs to prevent their use as leg restraints; however, the case of Hiatts illustrates how readily and creatively arms manufacturers will break the rules in order to achieve market sales.
21. Accompanying this Declaration is an Annex consisting of twelve Articles attempting to define the precise nature of torture and cruel and inhuman punishment.
22. United Nations: World Conference on Human Rights, Vienna: Vienna Declaration and Programme of Action, 14–25 June 1993, UN Doc A/CONF.157/23 of 12 July 1993, Part II, para. 56; Article 2.2 of the Convention Against Torture and Other Cruel, Inhuman or Degrading Treatment or Punishment (adopted by the UN 10 December 1984) states, 'No exceptional circumstances whatsoever whether a state of war or a threat of war, internal political instability or any other public emergency, may be invoked as a justification for torture.'
23. Only Somalia and the United States have refused to ratify the UN Convention on the Rights of the Child.
24. The *Washington Post*, 2002, 'U.S. Decries Abuse but Defends Interrogations', <www.washingtonpost.com/wp-dyn/articles/A37943-2002Dec25.html>

CHAPTER 9

1. These and all other relevant international instruments can be found at: <www.unhchr.ch/html/intlinst.htm>
2. Particularly the French (Human Rights Watch 2000a; Robertson 2002) and also British legal advisers according to a report cited by Amnesty (2000a). While both Amnesty and HRW find bombing the TV station to have been illegal, only Amnesty labels it a 'war crime'. HRW, along with Robertson (2002) consider that it was not a 'grave breach' of the Geneva Conventions. Being criminologists not international lawyers, we are accustomed to ranking multiple murder rather high on the scale of gravity.
3. From 1965 onwards, the US sent troops to defend the repressive government of South Vietnam against the Vietcong rebels and the Communist state of North Vietnam. After the US withdrew in 1973 the South crumbled and was finally defeated in 1975. The US had no monopoly of war crimes: the North Vietnamese and Vietcong committed numerous assassinations, summary executions, acts of terror and at least one large-scale massacre (at Dak Son in 1967: Lewy 1978: 245, 272–9).
4. According to Global Witness (2003b), Taylor's prime motive for intervening in Sierra Leone was to disrupt the work of the Special Court set up to try war criminals. In June 2003, Taylor's fears that the Court would indict him proved correct. On 11 August, Taylor was induced to resign by an offer of 'asylum' from the Nigerian government, but the Nigerians have since hinted that he could still be prosecuted if he fails to keep a low

profile (*Reuters*, 17 September 2003). The episode starkly illustrates the dilemmas involved in attempting to deter state crime by the threat of legal punishment.

5. Of approximately 400 Americans killed in the 1991 Gulf War or the build-up to it, nearly 100 died during deployment or training. Of about 150 killed in action, 35 died by 'friendly fire'; another 150 were killed accidentally or by unexploded ordnance and mines (O'Hanlon 2000: 125). NATO incurred no combat casualties at all in the Kosovo war (Luttwak 2001: 76). Probably 1,500–2,000 Serbian civilians were killed by NATO, and 5,000–11,000 Kosovar Albanians were killed by the Serbs. Serbian military losses were 264 according to Belgrade, nearly 5,000 according to NATO (Cohen 2002: 328).

6. Having manipulated the Laotian government into a civil war against the Communist Pathet Lao, the US bombed rebel-controlled areas from 1964 onwards, culminating in a campaign in 1968–69 which devastated the Plain of Jars but failed to defeat the Pathet Lao. American bombing of Cambodia began secretly in April 1969 and continued, despite congressional legislation prohibiting intervention, in support of the pro-American regime of Lon Nol who overthrew the neutralist government of Prince Sihanouk in 1970. The most devastating bombing occurred in 1972–73, when the US and North Vietnam were on the brink of peace (Gibson 2000). The terrible aftermath of the communist/nationalist Khmer Rouge's victory is discussed in Chapter 10.

7. The same appears to be true of the role of legal advisers in the 1991 Gulf War: Clark (1992: 178–81).

8. International Criminal Court Statute, Art. 8(2)(e)(vii). It is also a contravention of the International Convention on the Rights of the Child. An Optional Protocol raising the minimum age of enlistment to 18 has so far been signed by 111 states.

9. Curiously, there is no age of criminal responsibility under the laws of war (Cassese 2003: 229). Tim Hillier (personal communication) has suggested that as those enlisted before the age of 15 are, by definition, victims of war crimes, there is an implicit duty to refrain from prosecuting them.

10. Dolan (2002) points out the Ugandan government forces have also used child soldiers, and numerous families have married their underage girls to soldiers in the hope of gaining greater protection from the army.

CHAPTER 10

1. The most important exception, Alex Alvarez's *Governments, Citizens and Genocide* (2001), begins with an excellent discussion of the reasons for such neglect, but is not easy to obtain in Britain – a copy finally reached us on the day we submitted our manuscript. Other honourable exceptions include Brannigan (1998) (adopting an 'evolutionary psychology' perspective), Jamieson (1998, 1999), and Day and Vandiver (2000).

2. The Tutsis are descended from the cattle-herders who constituted a social elite in precolonial Rwanda and Burundi; the Hutus make up the majority of the population.

3. The literature on these issues is immense. See in particular the magisterial works of Hilberg (1985), Mayer (1990), Kershaw (2000a, 2000b) and Burleigh (2001), and the collection edited by Herbert (2000). Benz (2000) is a useful primer.

4. Allcock notes a similar paradox in Serbian responses to the genocidal atrocities in Bosnia, which are both denied and embraced 'as part of the eternal mission of the Serbian people' (2000: 399).

5. We shall use this now conventional term, although its quasi-religious overtones are hideously inappropriate.

6. This refers to the versions of the experiment where the subject and 'victim' were physically separated.

7. Introduction to Bernd Naumann, *Auschwitz* (1966), quoted by Blass (1993: 36). As Blass points out, this passage suggests an important qualification to Arendt's better-known comments (1965) on the 'banality of evil'.

8. Our account draws heavily on Sofsky's compelling analysis; but our interpretation is somewhat different as we are seeking to explain excesses as part of the genocidal process, whereas Sofsky locates them in the specific form of power that was the concentration camp.

CHAPTER 11

1. Theorists who have influenced us include Gramsci (1971); Tilly (1985); Jessop (1982); Cliff (1988); Reno (1999); and Schatzberg (1988).

2. Succinctly described by Hirst (2001: 107) as 'a state capitalist autocratic regime based on the party elite in alliance with prominent overseas Chinese capitalists'. See below.

3. There is a huge criminological literature examining these processes of exclusion – see, for example, Cohen (1979); Hall et al. (1978); Young (1999).

4. Primitive accumulation lays the foundation for a capitalist economy through the accumulation of wealth by a nascent capitalist class and – crucially in the Soviet context – the separation of peasants from their traditional livelihoods.

5. And, according to their extensive review of the globalisation literature, little in the way of agreement as to what it means.

6. In absolute terms, the figures are stark. Between 1990 and 1998, foreign direct investment in 'low-income' countries rose from $2,201 million to $10,674 million; in 'middle-income' countries from $21,929 million to $160,267 million; and in 'high-income' countries from $169,252 million to $448,316 million. See World Bank (2000), *Selected World Development Indicators*, 315.

7. Europe and Central Asia fell by 0.1 per cent, Latin America and the Caribbean by 2.4 per cent, and Sub-Saharan Africa by 0.3 per cent. There were some spectacular individual falls: Angola 37.4 per cent, Ecuador 14.2 per cent, Sierra Leone 9.8 per cent, and Turkey 7.8 per cent. See World Bank (2000), *Selected Development Indicators*, 274–5.

8. The President of the UN General Assembly speaking in 1998, quoted by Chandler (2002: 14).

CHAPTER 12

1. Emma Nicholson MEP has repeatedly made this charge: see her press statements on <www.emmanicholson.net>

2. According to the independent organisation, Iraq Body Count, the number killed in the 2003 war against Iraq is between 5,425 and 7,041. This estimate was derived from meticulous checks of casualty reports but is almost certainly an underestimate.

References

Abramovitz, J. N. (2001) *Unnatural Disasters*, Worldwatch Paper 158.

Aburish, S. (2000) *Saddam Hussein: The Politics of Revenge*, London: Bloomsbury.

Ackroyd, C., Margolis, K., Rosenhead, J. and Shallice, T. (1980) *The Technology of Political Control* (2nd edn), London: Pluto.

Adamoli, S., Savona, E., Di Nicola, A. and Zofi, P. (1998) *Organised Crime Around the World*, Helsinki: HEUNI.

Adamson, W. L. (1987/8) 'Gramsci and the Politics of Civil Society', *Praxis International*, 7, 320–29.

af Jochnick, C. and Normand, R. (1994) 'The Legitimation of Violence: A Critical Analysis of the Gulf War', *Harvard International Law Journal*, 387.

African Rights (1994) *Rwanda: Death Despair and Defiance*, London: Author.

—— (1995) *Facing Genocide: The Nuba of Sudan*, London: Author.

—— (1999) *Rwanda: Insurgency in the Northwest*, London: Author.

al-Khafaji, I. (1994) 'State Terror and the Degradation of Politics' in Hazleton, F. (ed.), *Iraq Since the Gulf War*, London: Zed.

Allcock, J. (2000) *Explaining Yugoslavia*. London: Hurst.

Allen, B. (1996) *Rape Warfare: the Hidden Genocide in Bosnia-Herzegovina and Croatia*, Minneapolis: University of Minnesota Press.

Alpert, G. P. and Fridell, L. A. (1992) *Police Vehicles and Firearms: Instruments of Deadly Force*, Prospect Heights, IL: Waveland.

Alvarez, A. (1997) 'Adjusting to Genocide: The Techniques of Neutralization and the Holocaust', *Social Science History*, 21, 139–78.

—— (2001) *Governments, Citizens and Genocide: A Comparative and Interdisciplinary Approach*, Bloomington: Indiana University Press.

Amnesty International (1973) *Report on Allegations of Torture in Brazil*, London: Duckworth.

—— (1975) Unpublished transcript of the 1975 trial of tortures under the regime of the Greek Colonels, in Amnesty International archives.

—— (1998) *Annual Report*, London: Author.

—— (1999) 'Spain: A Briefing on Human Rights Violations in Relation to the Basque Peace Process. EUR 41/01/09', London: Author.

—— (2000a) *'Collateral Damage' or Unlawful Killings? Violations of the Laws of War by NATO during Operation Allied Force*, London: Author.

—— (2000b) *Torture – A Modern Day Plague*. London: Author.

—— (2000c) 'United Kingdom. Patrick Finucane's Killing: Collusion and Cover-Up', EUR 45/26/00.

—— (2000d) 'United States of America: A Briefing for the UN Committee Against Torture', AI Index: AMR 51/56/00.

—— (2001a) *Annual Report*, London: Author.

—— (2001b) *Broken Lives: A Year of Intifada*, London: Author.

—— (2001c) 'Colombia: Stop the Massacres, Stop the Aid!', London: Author.

—— (2001d) *Crimes of Hate, Conspiracy of Silence: Torture and Ill-Treatment Based on Sexual Identity*, London: Author.

—— (2001e) 'Iraq: Systematic Torture of Political Prisoners', AI Index MDE 14/008/2001 15 August 2001.

—— (2001f) *Stopping the Torture Trade*, Amnesty International Publications, London, Author.

—— (2002) 'Sri Lanka:Rape in Custody', AI Index: ASA 37/001/2002.

—— (2003) *Turkey. End Sexual Violence Against Women in Custody!* <http://web.amnesty.org/library/print.ENGEUR440062003>

Andersen, M. E. (1993) *Dossier Secreto: Argentina's* Desaparecidos *and the Myth of the 'Dirty War'*, Boulder, CO: Westview.

Anderson, N. G. (1999) *Sudan in Crisis: the Failure of Democracy*, Gainesville: University Press of Florida.

Andreas, P. (1999) 'When Policies Collide: Market Reform, Market Prohibition and the Narcoticization of the Mexican Economy', in Friman, H. R. and Andreas, P. (eds) (1999) *The Illicit Global Economy and State Power*, Lanham, MD: Rowman & Littlefield.

Andreopoulos, G. (ed.) (1994) *Genocide: Conceptual and Historical Dimensions*, Philadelphia: University of Pennsylvania Press.

Andvig, J.-C., Feldstad, O.-H., Amundsen, I., Sissener, T. and Søreide, T. (2000) *Research on Corruption: A Policy Oriented Survey*, Oslo: Chr. Michelsen Institute/Norwegian Institute of Foreign Affairs.

Appadurai, A. (2002) 'Dead Certainty: Ethnic Violence in the Era of Globalization', in Hinton, A. L. (ed.) *Genocide: An Anthropological Reader*, Oxford: Blackwell.

Arendt, H. (1965) *Eichmann in Jerusalem*, rev. edn, Harmondsworth: Penguin.

—— (1973) *The Origins of Totalitarianism*, New York: Harcourt Brace Jovanovich.

—— (1995) *Reflections on Violence*, New York: Harcourt Brace.

Aretxaga, B. (2000) 'A Fictional Reality: Paramilitary Death Squads and the Construction of State Terror in Spain', in Sluka, J. A. (ed.) *Death Squad*, Philadephia: University of Pennsylvania Press.

Arlacchi, P. (1988) *Mafia Business: The Mafia Ethic and the Spirit of Capitalism*, New York: Verso.

Arnold, G. (1996) *The Maverick State: Gaddafi and the New World Order*, London: Cassel.

Arnove, A. (ed.) (2000) *Iraq Under Siege: The Deadly Impact of Sanctions and War*, London: Pluto Press.

Baker, B. (2003) 'Policing and the Rule of Law in Mozambique', *Policing and Society*, 13(2), 139–58.

Bamber, H. (1995) 'The Medical Foundation and its Commitment to Human Rights and Rehabilitation', in Gordon, N. and Marton, R. (eds) *Torture: Human Rights, Medical Ethics and the Case of Israel*, New Jersey: Zed Books.

Bangladeshi Rehabilitation Centre for Trauma Victims (2000) *Annual Report*, Bangladesh: Author.

Bankier, D. (1992) *The Germans and the Final Solution. Public Opinion under Nazism*, Oxford: Blackwell.

Barak, G. (1991) *Crimes by the Capitalist State: an Introduction to State Criminality*, New York: SUNY Press.

Barbedo de Magalhaes, A. (1992) *East Timor: Indonesian Occupation and Genocide*, Oporto: Oporto University.

Barber, C. V. and Schweithelm, J. (2000) *Trial by Fire: Forest Fires and Forestry Policy in Indonesia's Era of Crisis and Reform*, Washington, DC: World Resources Institute.

Barnhizer, D. (2001) 'Trade, Environment and Human Rights: The Paradigm case of Industrial Aquaculture and the Exploitation of Traditional Communities', in D. Barnhizer (ed.) *Effective Strategies for Protecting Human Rights*, Aldershot: Ashgate Dartmouth.

Bartov, O. (1985) *The Eastern Front, 1941–45*, London: Macmillan.

—— (2000) *Mirrors of Destruction*, Oxford: Oxford University Press.

Bartrop, P. (2001) 'The Holocaust, the Aborigines and the Bureacracy of Destruction; An Australian Dimension of Genocide', *Journal of Genocide Research*, 3(1), 75–87.

Bass, G. J. (2000) *Stay the Hand of Vengeance: The Politics of War Crimes Tribunals*, Princeton, NJ: Princeton University Press.

Bauman, Z. (1989) *Modernity and the Holocaust*, Cambridge: Polity.

—— (1993) *Postmodern Ethics*, Oxford: Blackwell.

—— (1995) *Life in Fragments: Essays in Postmodern Morality*, Oxford: Blackwell.

Bax, M. (1976) *Harpstrings and Confessions: Machine Style Politics in the Irish Republic*, Assen, Netherlands: Van Gorcum.

Bayart, J.-F. (1993) *The State in Africa: The Politics of the Belly*, Harlow: Longman.

Bayart, J.-F. Ellis, S. and Hibou, B. (1999) *The Criminalization of the State in Africa*, Oxford: James Currey.

Bayley, D. H. (1969) *The Police and Political Development in India*, Princeton: Princeton University Press.

Beauchemin, E. (1998) 'Faceless Warriors', Radio Netherlands documentary, <www.rnw.nl/en/liberia>

Becker, E. (1986) *When the War was Over: the Voices of Cambodia's Revolution and its People*, New York: Simon & Schuster.

Becker, H. (1963) *Outsiders*, Glencoe, IL: Free Press.

Becker, J. (1996) *Hungry Ghosts: China's Secret Famine*, London: John Murray.

Beetham, D. (1991) *The Legitimation of Power*, Basingstoke: Macmillan.

Bell, J. B. (1996) *In Dubious Battle: The Dublin and Monaghan Bombings 1972–1994*, Dublin: Poolbeg.

Benz, W. (2000) *The Holocaust: A Short History* (4th edn), London: Profile.

Bequai, A. (1979) *Organized Crime*, Lexington: MA: Lexington Books.

Berdal, M. and Serrano, M. (eds) (2002) *Transnational Organized Crime and International Security: Business as Usual?*, Boulder, CO and London: Lynne Rienner.

Berrigan, F., (2001) 'Indonesia at the Crossroads: U.S. Weapons Sales and Military Training', *Arms Trade Resource Center*, The World Policy Institute, New York, at <www.worldpolicy.org/projects/arms/reports/indo101001.htm>

Best, G. (1994) *War and Law Since 1945*, Oxford: Clarendon.

Bilton, M. and Sim, K. (1992) *Four Hours in My Lai*, Harmondsworth: Penguin.

Binder, A. and Scharf, P. (1980) 'The Violent Police-Citizen Encounter', *Annals of the American Academy of Political and Social Science*, 452, 111–21.

BIRW (2000) *Justice Delayed ... Alleged State Collusion in the Murder of Patrick Finucane And Others*, Belfast: British Irish Rights Watch.

Bittner, E. (1975) *The Functions of Police in Modern Society*, New York: Jason Aronson.

Black, E. (2001) *IBM and the Holocaust*, New York: Little, Brown.

Blaikie, P., Cannon, T., Davis, I. and Wisner, B. (1994) *At Risk*, London: Routledge.

Blass, T. (1993) 'Psychological Perspectives on the Perpetrators of the Holocaust: The Role of Situational Pressures, Personal Dispositions and Their Interactions', *Holocaust and Genocide Studies*, 7, 830–50.

Block, A. A. (1997) 'The Origins of Iran-Contra: Lessons from the Durrani Affair', *Crime, Law and Social Change*, 33, 53–84.

—— (1999) 'Bad Businss: A Commentary on the Criminology of Organized Crime in the United States', in Farer, T. (ed.) *Transnational Crime in the Americas*, London: Routledge.

Block, A. A. and Chambliss, W. J. (1981) *Organizing Crime*, New York: Elsevier.

Bloom, M. (2001) 'Atrocities and Armed Conflict: State Consolidation in Israel, 1948–56', *Conflict, Security & Development*, 1(3), 55–78.

Blum, W. (1998) 'The United States vs. Iraq: A Study in Hypocrisy', *Third World Traveller*, 9 February 1998.

Borkin, J. (1978) *The Punishment and Crime of IG Farben*, New York: Free Press.

Bouhoutsos, J. C. (1990) 'Treating Victims of Torture: Psychology's Challenge', in Suedfeld, P. (ed.) *Psychology and Torture*, New York: Hemisphere.

Bouissou, J.-M. (1997) 'Gifts, Networks and Clienteles: Corruption in Japan as a Redistributive System', in della Porta, D. and Mény, Y. (eds) *Democracy and Corruption in Europe*, London: Pinter.

Bourdieu, P. (1977) *Outline of a Theory of Practice*, Cambridge: Cambridge University Press.

—— (1990) *In Other Words*, Cambridge: Polity.

Bourke, J. (1999) *An Intimate History of Killing*, London: Granta.

Bourne, P. G. (1971) 'From Boot Camp to Me Lai', in Falk, R. A., Kolko, G. and Lifton, R. J. (eds) *Crimes of War*, New York: Vintage.

Box, S. (1983) *Power, Crime and Mystification*, Basingstoke: Macmillan.

—— (1988) *Recession, Crime and Punishment*, Basingstoke: Macmillan.

Braithwaite, J. (1989) *Crime, Shame and Reintegration*, Cambridge: Cambridge University Press.

Brand, S. and Price, R. (2000) *The Economic and Social Costs of Crime* (Home Office Research Study 217) <www.homeoffice.gov.uk/rds>

Brannigan, A. (1998) 'Criminology and the Holocaust: Xenophobia, Evolution, and Genocide', *Crime and Delinquency*, 44, 257–76.

Bread for the World Institute (2001) *Foreign Aid to End Hunger: 11th Annual Report on the State Of The World's Hunger*, Washington DC: Author.

Brockett, C. D. (1991) 'Sources of State Terrorism in Rural Central America', in Bushnell, P. T. Shlapentokh, V., Vanderpool, C. K. and Sundram, J. (eds) *State Organized Terror*, Boulder, CO: Westview.

Brown, A. D. and Jones, M. (2000) 'Honorable Members and Dishonourable Deeds: Sensemaking, Impression Management and Legitimation in the "Arms to Iraq Affair"', *Human Relations*, 53(5), 655–89.

Browne, V. (2000) 'Do us all a favour Sean, tell us what you know', *Irish Times* (3 May).

Browning, C. (1998) *Ordinary Men: Reserve Police Battalion 101 and the Final Solution in Poland*, New York: Harper Perennial.

Brownmiller, S. (1976) *Against Our Will: Men, Women and Rape*, Harmondsworth: Penguin.

—— (1994) 'Making Female Bodies on the Battlefield', in Stiglmayer, A. (ed.) *Mass Rape: The War Against Women in Bosnia-Herzegovina*, Lincoln: University of Nebraska Press.

Bruce, S. (1994) *The Edge of the Union. The Ulster Loyalist Political Vision*, Oxford: Oxford University Press

Bryant, C. D. (1979) *Khaki-Collar Crime: Deviant Behaviour in the Military Context*, New York: Free Press.

Bufacchi, V. and Burgess, S. (1998) *Italy Since 1989: Events and Interpretations*, Basingstoke: Macmillan.

Burgler, R. A. (1990) *The Eyes of the Pineapple: Revolutionary Intellectuals and Terror in Democratic Kampuchea*, Saarbrücken, Germany: Breitenbach.

Burleigh, M. (1997) *Ethics and Extermination: Reflections on Nazi Genocide*, Cambridge: Cambridge University Press.

—— (2001) *The Third Reich*, London: Macmillan.

Burnett, S. H. and Mantovani, L. (1998) *The Italian Guillotine: Operation Clean Hands and the Overthrow of Italy's First Republic*, Lanham, MD: Rowman & Littlefield.

Burr, J. M. (1998) *Quantifying Genocide in Southern Sudan and the Nuba Mountains* <www.refugees.org/news/crisis/sudan.pdf>

Cain, K. L. (1999) 'The Rape of Dinah: Human Rights, Civil War in Liberia, and Evil Triumphant', *Human Rights Quarterly*, 21, 265–307.

Calavita, K., Pontell, H. N. and Tillman, R. N. (1997) *Big Money Crime*, Berkeley: University of California Press.

Callinicos, A. and Simons, M. (1985) *The Great Strike*, London: Socialist Workers Party.

Cameron, D. and Fraser, E. (1987) *The Lust to Kill*, Cambridge: Polity.

Campaign Against the Arms Trade (1991) *Arming Saddam* <www.caat.org.uk/information/issues/iraq.php>

Campbell, B. B. (2000) 'Death Squads: Definition, Problems and Historical Concept', in Campbell, B. and Brenner, A. D. (eds) *Death Squads in Global Perspective*, London: Palgrave Macmillan, 1–26.

Campbell, T. (1983) *The Left and Rights*, London: Routledge & Kegan Paul.

Cancino, J. M. (2001) 'Walking Among Giants 50 Years Later: An Exploratory Analysis of Patrol Officer Use of Violence', *Policing: An International Journal of Strategies and Management*, 24, 144–61.

Capaccio, G. (2000) 'Sanctions: Killing a Country and a People', in Arnove, A. (ed.) *Iraq Under Siege: the Deadly Impact of Sanctions and War*, London: Pluto Press.

Caputo, P. (1999) *A Rumor of War*, London: Pimlico.

Carson, W. G. (1970) 'White-collar Crime and the Enforcement of Factory Legislation', *British Journal of Criminology*, 10, 383–98.

Cartier-Bresson, J. (1997) 'Corruption Networks, Transaction Security and Illegal Social Exchange', *Political Studies*, 45, 463–76.

Cassels, J. (1993) *The Uncertain Promise of Law: Lessons From Bhopal*, Toronto: University of Toronto Press.

Cassese, A. (1986) *International Law in a Divided World*, Oxford: Clarendon.

—— (2003) *International Criminal Law*, Oxford: Oxford University Press.

Cavalieri, P. and Singer, P. (eds) (1993) *The Great Ape Project. Equality beyond Humanity.* London: Fourth Estate.

CEH (1999) *CEH Online Report. Guatemala: Memoria de Silencio* <http://shr.aaas.org/guatemala/ceh/>

Chabal, P. and Dalloz J.-P. (1999) *Africa Works: Disorder as a Political Instrument*, Oxford: James Currey.

Chalk, F. and Jonassohn, K. (1990) *The History and Sociology of Genocide: Analyses and Case Studies*, New Haven, CT: Yale University Press.

Chambliss, W. (1978) *On the Take: From Petty Crooks to Presidents*, Bloomington: Indiana University Press.

—— (1994) 'Policing the Ghetto Underclass: the Politics of Law and Law Enforcement', *Social Problems*, 41(2), 177–94.

—— (1999) *Power, Politics and Crime*, Boulder, CO: Westview Press.

Chan, J. (1996) 'Changing Police Culture', *British Journal of Criminology*, 36, 109–34.

—— (1997) *Changing Police Culture*, Cambridge: Cambridge University Press.

—— (2000) 'Backstage Punishment: Police Violence, Occupational Culture and Criminal Justice', in Coady ,T., James, S. Miller, S. and O'Keefe, M. (eds) *Violence and Police Culture*, Carlton South, Victoria: Melbourne University Press, 85–108.

Chandler, D. P. (1999) *Brother Number One: A Political Biography of Pol Pot* (rev. edn), Boulder, CO: Westview.

Chandler, D. (2002) *From Kosovo To Kabul: Human Rights and International Intervention*, London: Pluto.

Chang, I. (1998) *The Rape of Nanking*, London: Penguin.

Charny, I. W. (ed.) (2000) *Encyclopedia of Genocide*, Oxford: ABC Clio.

Chevigny, P. (1995) *Edge of the Knife: Police Violence in the Americas*, New York: New Press.

—— (1996)'Changing Control of Police Violence in Rio de Janeiro and São Paolo, Brazil', in Marenin, O. (ed.) *Policing Change, Changing Police*, New York: Garland.

Chibnall, S. and Saunders, P. (1977) 'Words Apart: Notes on the Social Reality of Corruption', *British Journal of Sociology*, 28, 141.

Chin, G. J. (ed.) (1997a) *New York City Police Corruption Investigation Commissions, 1894–1994. V: Knapp Commission Report*, Buffalo, NY: William S. Hein.

—— (1997b) *New York City Police Corruption Investigation Commissions, 1894–1994. VI: Mollen Commission Report*, Buffalo, NY: William S. Hein.

Chomsky, N. (1994) 'East Timor', *Guardian*, 5 July <http://monkeyfist.com/ChomskyArchive/essays/timor_html>

—— (1999a) *The New Military Humanism: Lessons from Kosovo*, London: Pluto.

—— (1999b) 'Rogue States', in Chomsky, N., Clark, R. and Said, E. W. (eds) *Acts of Aggression*, New York: Seven Stories.

—— (2002), *Pirates and Emperors, Old and New: International Terrorism in the Real World*, London: Pluto Press.

Chomsky, N. and Herman, E. (1979) *The Political Economy of Human Rights*, Nottingham: Spokesman Books for the Bertrand Russell Peace Foundation Ltd.

—— (1988) *Manufacturing Consent: The Political Economy of the Mass Media*, New York: Pantheon.

Choongh, S. (1997) *Policing as Social Discipline*, Oxford: Clarendon Press.

Cisin, I. H. and Clark, W. B. (1962) 'Methodologial Challenges of Disaster Research', in Baker, G. W. and Champman, D. W. (eds) *Man and Society in Disasters*, New York: Basic Books.

Cissna, K. (1997) *Presentation to UN Commission on Sustainable Development*, New York, NY, 11 April <www.earthsummitwatch.org/shrimp/national_reports/ecuacissna.html>

Clapham, C. (ed.) (1982) *Private Patronage and Public Power*, London: Pinter.

Clark, R. (1992) *The Fire This Time: US War Crimes in the Gulf*, New York: Thunder's Mouth Press.

Clarke, L. (2000) 'RUC Held Back Finucane Murder Confession to Protect Informants', *Sunday Times* (Irish edn, 15 Oct).

Clawson, P. L. and Rensselaer, W. L. (1998) *The Andean Cocaine Industry*, New York: St Martin's Griffin.

Cliff, T. (1988) *State Capitalism in Russia*, London: Bookmarks.

Cloward, R. and Ohlin, L. (1966) *Delinquency and Opportunity*, London: Collier-Macmillan.

Coakley, J. (1999) 'Society and Political Culture', in Coakley, J. and Gallagher, M. (eds) *Politics in the Republic of Ireland*, 3rd edn, London: Routledge, 32–70.

Coalition to Stop the Use of Child Soldiers (2001). *Child Soldiers Global Report* <www.child-soldiers.org>

Coburn, A. (1995) 'Disaster Prevention and Mitigation in Metropolitan Areas: Reducing Urban Vulnerability in Turkey', in Parker, R., Kreimer, A. and Munasinghe, M. (eds)

Informal Settlements, Environmental Degradation and Disaster Vulnerability: the Turkey Case Study The World Bank and The International Decade for Natural Disaster Reduction (IDNDR), Washington DC, 65–94.

Coburn, A. and Spence, R. (1992) *Earthquake Protection*, Chichester: Wiley.

Cockburn, A. and Cockburn, P. (2002) *Saddam Hussein: An American Obsession*, London: Verso.

Cockroft, L. (1998) *Corruption and Human Rights: A Crucial Link. TI Working Paper*, Berlin: Transparency International.

Cohen, A. K. (1956) *Delinquent Boys*, London: Routledge & Kegan Paul.

Cohen, L. J. (2002) *Serpent in the Bosom: The Rise and fall of Slobodan Milosevic* (rev. edn), Boulder, CO: Westview.

Cohen, P. (1979) 'Policing the Working-Class City', in NDC/CSE (eds) *Capitalism and the Rule of Law*, London: Hutchinson.

Cohen, S. (1993) 'Human Rights and Crimes of the State: the Culture of Denial', *Australian and New Zealand Journal of Criminology*, 26, 97–115.

—— (1996) 'Crime and Politics: Spot the Difference', *British Journal of Sociology*, 1.

—— (1998) 'Government Responses to Human Rights Reports: Claims, Denials and Counterclaims', in Friedrichs, D. O. (ed.) *State Crime*, Vol. 2, Aldershot: Ashgate, 3–29.

—— (2001) *States of Denial*, Cambridge: Polity.

Colazingari, S. and Rose-Ackerman, S. (1998) 'Corruption in a Paternalistic Democracy: Lessons from Italy for Latin America', *Political Science Quarterly*, 113(3), 447–70.

Cole, B. A. (1999) 'Post-Colonial Systems', in Mawby, R. I. (ed.) *Policing Across the World: Issues for the Twenty-first Century*, London: UCL Press.

Collins, N. and O Raghallaigh, C. (1997) 'Ireland', in Ridley, F. F. and Doig, A. (eds) *Sleaze: Politicians, Private Interests and Public Reaction*, Oxford: Oxford University Press.

Collins, N. and O'Shea, M. (2000) *Understanding Corruption in Irish Politics*, Cork: Cork University Press.

Comfort, A. (1950) *Authority and Delinquency in the Modern State*, London: Routledge & Kegan Paul.

Conroy, J. (2000) *Unspeakable Acts, Ordinary People: The Dynamics of Torture*, Los Angeles: University of California Press.

Coogan, T. P. (1996) *The Troubles*, London: Arrow.

Cook, R. (1997) 'Human Rights into a New Century' <www.fco.gov.uk>

Coolidge, J. and Rose-Ackerman, S. (1997) 'High-Level Corruption and Rent-Seeking in African Regimes: Theory and Cases', World Bank working paper.

Cooley, J. (2000) *Unholy Wars* (2nd edn), London: Pluto.

Cordesman, A. (1999) *Iraq and the War of Sanctions: Conventional Threats and Weapons of Mass Destruction*, Westport: Praeger.

Cordesman, A. and Hashim, A. (1997) *Iraq: Sanctions and Beyond*, Boulder, CO: Westview.

Corporate Watch (2002) 'BAe Systems: A Corporate Profile', <www.corporatewatch.org.uk/profiles/bae/bae1.htm>

Cowan, D. (2003) '"Rage at West*sinster*": Sociolegal Reflections on the Power of Sale', *Social & Legal Studies*, 12, 177–98.

Cover, R. (1986) 'Violence and the Word', *Yale Law Journal*, 95, 1601.

Cox, B., Shirley, J. and Short, M. (1977) *The Fall of Scotland Yard*, Harmondsworth: Penguin.

Cox, R. W. (1993) 'Gramsci, Hegemony and International Relations' in Gill, S. (ed.) *Gramsci, Historical Materialism and International Relations*, Cambridge: Cambridge University Press.

Crank, J. P. and Caldero, M. A. (2000) *Police Ethics: The Corruption of Noble Cause*, Cincinnati: Anderson.

Cribb, R. (2001) 'Genocide in Indonesia, 1965–66', *Journal of Genocide Research*, 3(2), 219–39.

Crowley, D. (2000) 'Survival of the Richest', *Magill* (October) 12–16.

Cruz-Torres, M. L. (2000) 'Pink Gold Rush: Shrimp Aquaculture, Sustainable Development, and the Environment in Northwestern Mexico', *Journal of Political Ecology*, 7, 63–90.

Cullen, P. (2002) *With a Little Help from my Friends: Planning Corruption in Ireland*. Dublin: Gill & Macmillan.

Cunneen, C. (2001) *Conflict, Politics and Crime*, Crows Nest, NSW: Allen & Unwin.

Dadrian, V. H. (1998) 'The Anticipation and Prevention of Genocide in International Conflicts: Some lessons from History', in Friedrichs, D. O. (ed.) *State Crime*, Vol. 2, Aldershot: Ashgate.

D'Amico, C. (2000) 'Citizen-Soldier? Class, Race, Gender and Sexuality in the US Military', in Jacobs, S., Jacobson, R. and Marchbank, K. (eds) *States of Conflict*, London: Zed.

Davies, N. (1999) *Ten-Thirty-Three: The Inside Story of Britain's Secret Killing Machine in Northern Ireland*, Edinburgh: Mainstream.

Davis, J. S. (1989) 'Prosecutions in their Context: The Use of the Criminal Law in Later Nineteenth-Century London', in Hay, D. and Snyder, F. (eds) *Policing and Prosecution in Britain 1750–1850*, Oxford: Clarendon.

Davis, M. (2001). *Late Victorian Holocausts: El Nino Famines and the Making of the Third World*, London: Verso.

Day, E. L. and Vandiver, M. (2000) 'Criminology and Genocide Studies: Notes on what Might have Been and what Still could Be', *Crime, Law and Social Change*, 34, 43–59.

deLeon, P. (1993) *Thinking About Political Corruption*, Armonk, NY and London: M.E. Sharpe.

della Porta, D. and Mény, Y. (1997) 'Conclusion: Democracy and Corruption: Towards a Comparative Analysis', in della Porta, D. and Mény, Y. (eds) *Democracy and Corruption Europe*, London: Pinter, 166–80.

della Porta, D. and Pizzorno, A. (1996) 'The Business Politicians: Reflections from a Study of Political Corruption', *Journal of Law and Society*, 23, 73–94.

della Porta, D. and Vannucci, A. (1999) *Corrupt Exchanges: Actors, Resources and Mechanisms of Political Corruption*, New York: Aldine de Gruyter.

Dellapenna, J. W. (2003) 'The Iraqi Campaign Against the Marsh Arabs' <http://jurist. law.pitt.edu/forum/forumnew92.php>

Denham, D. (2002) 'Marketization as a Context for Crime: The Scandlas in Further Education Colleges in England and Wales', *Crime, Law and Social Change*, 38, 373–88.

de Saussure, H. and Glasser, R. (1975) 'Air Warfare Christmas 1972', in Trooboff, P. (ed.) *Law and Responsibility in War: The Vietnam Experience*, Chapel Hill, NC: University of North Carolina Press.

de Souza Martins, J. (1996) 'Clientelism and Corruption in Contemporary Brazil', in Little, W. and Posada-Carbó, E. (eds) *Political Corruption in Europe and Latin America*, Basingstoke: Macmillan.

de Waal, A. (1997) *Famine Crimes: Politics and the Disaster Relief Industry in Africa*, Oxford: James Currey.

—— (1998) 'US War Crimes in Somalia', *New Left Review*, 230, 131–44.

—— (ed.) (2000) *Who Fights? Who Cares? War and Humanitarian Action in Africa*, Trenton, NJ and Asmara: Africa World Press.

des Forges, A. (1999) *Leave None to Tell the Story*, Washington DC: Human Rights Watch.

Destexhe, A. (1995) *Rwanda and Genocide in the Twentieth Century*, London: Pluto.

Dewalt, B. R., Vergne, P. and Hardin, M. (1996) 'Shrimp Aquaculture Development and the Environment: People, Mangroves and Fisheries on the Gulf of Fonseca, Honduras', *World Development*, 24(7), 1193–208.

Dezalay, Y. and Garth, B. (2001) *The Internationalization of Palace Wars. Lawyers, Economists, and the Contest to Transform Latin American States*, Chicago: University of Chicago Press.

Dillon, M. (1990) *The Dirty War*, London: Hutchinson.

Dixon, D. (1999) 'Issues in the Legal Regulation of Policing', in Dixon, D. (ed.) *A Culture of Corruption: Changing an Australian Police Service*, Sydney: Hawkins Press.

Doig, A. (1984) *Corruption and Misconduct*, Harmondsworth: Penguin.

Doig, A. and Theobald, R. (2000) 'Introduction: Why Corruption?', in Doig, A. and Theobald, R. (eds) *Corruption and Democratisation*, London: Frank Cass.

Dolan, C. (2002) 'Which Children Count? The Politics of Children's Rights in Northern Uganda', *Accord*, 11 <www.c-r.org/accord/index.htm?uganda/accord11/index.htm>

Doyal, K. and Gough, I. (1991) *A Theory of Human Needs*, Macmillan: Basingstoke.

Drescher, S. (1996) 'The Atlantic Slave Trade and the Holocaust: A Comparative Analysis', in Rosenbaum, A. S. (ed.) *Is the Holocaust Unique? Perspectives on Comparative Genocide*, Boulder, CO: Westview.

Drèze, J. (1990) 'Famine Prevention in India', in Drèze, J. and Sen, A. (eds) *The Political Economy of Hunger, Vol. II: Famine Prevention*, Oxford: Clarendon Press

Dufkor, C. (1999) 'Children as Killers', in Gutman, R. and Rieff, D. (eds) *Crimes of War: What the Public Should Know*, New York: W.W. Norton.

Dunèr, B. (1998) 'Atrocities by Non-state Actors', in Dunèr, B. (ed.) *An End to Torture*, London: Zed Books.

Dunnighan, C. and Norris, C. (1999) 'The Detective, the Snout and the Audit Commission: the Real Costs of Using Informers', *Howard Journal*, 38, 67–86.

Dunphy, R. (1995) *The Making of Fianna Fáil Power in Ireland, 1923–1948*, Oxford: Oxford University Press.

Duvall, R. D. and Stohl, M. (1986) 'Governance by Terror', in Stohl, M. (ed.) *The Politics of Terrorism* (3rd edn), New York: Marcel Dekker.

Dyer, G. (1986) *War*, London: Guild.

Earth Summit Watch, (1997) 'Shrimp Tribunal Online: Ecuador' <www.dec.ctu.edu.vn/cdrom/cd6/projects/shrimp_tribunal/ecuabp.html>

EEFIT (1999) *Report on Kocaeli Earthquake of August 1999*, London: Author.

EERI (Earthquake Engineering Research Institute) (1999) *The Izmit (Kocaeli) Turkey Earthquake* <www.eeri.org/earthquakes/Reconn/Turkey0899>

Ellis, S. (1999) *The Mask of Anarchy: The Destruction of Liberia and the Religious Dimension of an African Civil War*, New York: New York University Press.

Ellison, G. and Smyth, J. (2000) *The Crowned Harp: Policing Northern Ireland*, London: Pluto.

Ellwood, W. (2001) *The No-Nonsense Guide To Globalization*, London: Verso/New Internationalist.

Elster, J. (1989) *The Cement of Society*, Cambridge: Cambridge University Press.

Engels, F. (1968) 'Origins of the Family, Private Property and the State', in Marx, K. and Engels, F. (eds) *Selected Works*, London: Lawrence & Wishart (first published 1884).

Environmental Justice Foundation (2003) *Smash and Grab: Conflict, Corruption and Human Rights Abuses in the Shrimp Farming Industry* London: Author.

Erikson, K. T. (1979) *In the Wake of the Flood*, London: George Allen and Unwin.

Etzioni-Halevy, E. (2002) 'Exchanging Material Benefits for Political Support: A Comparative Analysis', in Heidenheimer, A. J. and Johnston, M. (eds) *Political Corruption: Contexts and Consequences* (4th edn), New Brunswick: Transaction.

Falk, R. A. (1975) 'Chapter 1', in Trooboff, P. D., ed. (1975) *Law and Responsibility in Warfare: The Vietnam Experience*. Chapel Hill, NC: University of N. Carolina Press.

Falla, R. (1994) *Massacres in the Jungle: Ixcan, Guatemala, 1975–82*, Oxford: Westview.

Farer, T. (ed.) (1999) *Transnational Crime in the Americas*, London: Routledge.

Farouk-Sluglett, M. and Sluglett, P. (2001) *Iraq Since 1958* (3rd edn), London: I.B. Tauris.

Fattah, E. (1997) *Criminology: Past, Present and Future*, London: Palgrave.

Fedorovich, K. (2000) 'Understanding the Enemy: Military Intelligence, Political Warfare and Japanese Prisoners of War in Australia, 1942–45', in Towle, P., Kosuge, M. and Kibata, Y. (eds) *Japanese Prisoners of War*, London: Hambledon.

Fein, H. (1977) *Imperial Crime and Punishment*, Honolulu: University Press of Hawaii.

—— (1979) *Accounting for Genocide*, New York: Free Press.

—— (1990) 'Genocide: A Sociological Perspective', *Current Sociology*, 38, 1–111.

—— (2000) 'Testing Theories Brutally', in Smith, R. (ed.) *Genocide: Essays Toward Understanding, Early Warning, and Prevention*, Williamsburg, VA: Association of Genocide Scholars.

Feitlowitz, M. (1998) *A Lexicon of Terror: Argentina and the Legacies of Terror*, Oxford: Oxford University Press.

Feldman, A. (1991) *Formations of Violence: The Narrative of the Body and Political Terror in Northern Ireland*, Chicago: University of Chicago Press.

Femia, J. V. (1981) *Gramsci's Political Thought*, Oxford: Clarendon.

Ferguson, N. (2000) 'Why the World Wars were Won' <www.boxmind.com/lecture>

Fine, B. and Millar, R. (eds) (1985) *Policing the Miners' Strike*, London: Lawrence & Wishart/Cobden Trust.

Finkelstein, N. G. and Birn, R. B. (1998) *A Nation on Trial: The Goldhagen Thesis and Historical Truth*, New York: Henry Holt & Co.

Fiorentini, G. and Peltzman S. (1995) (eds) *The Economics of Organized Crime*, Cambridge: Cambridge University Press.

Fisk, R. (2001) '"Smoking Them Out" Is Not New in the Middle East'. *Independent*, 19 September.

—— (2003a) 'America Defends Two Untouchable Ministries from the Hordes of Looters', *Independent*, 14 April.

—— (2003b) 'For the People on the Streets this is not Liberation but a New Colonial Oppression', *Independent*, 17 April.

Flood, Mr Justice (2002) *Second Interim Report of the Tribunal of Inquiry into Certain Planning Matters and Payments* <www.flood-tribunal.ie/images/Report.pdf>

Foot, P. (1996) 'Armed and Dangerous', *Socialist Review*, 195, March.

Foreign and Commonwealth Office (2002) *Saddam Hussein: Crimes and Human Rights Abuses* <www.fco.gov.uk>

Foucault, M. (1977) *Discipline and Punish*, Harmondsworth: Penguin.

Freedom House (1999) *Democracy's Century* <www.freedomhouse.org/reports/century.html>

Friedländer, S. (1998) *Nazi Germany and the Jews. The Years of Persecution, 1933–1939*, London: Phoenix.

Friedrich, R. J. (1980) 'Police Use of Force: Individuals, Situations and Organizations', *Annals of the American Academy of Political and Social Science*, 452, 82–97.

Friedrichs, D. O. (1995) 'State Crime or Governmental Crime: Making Sense of the Conceptual Confusion', in Ross, J. I. (ed.) *Controlling State Crime: An Introduction*, New York: Garland.

Friman, H. R. (1996) *NarcoDiplomacy: Exporting the U.S. War on Drugs*, Ithaca, NY and London: Cornell University Press.

—— (1999) 'Obstructing Markets: Organized Crime Networks and Drug Control in Japan', in Friman, H. R. and Andreas, P. (eds) (1999) *The Illicit Global Economy and State Power*, Lanham: Rowman & Littlefield.

Friman, H. R. and Andreas, P. (ed.) (1999) *The Illicit Global Economy and State Power*, Lanham: Rowman & Littlefield.

Frühling, H. (2000) *Police Reform and Democratic Consolidation: Chile* <www.kas.org.za/Publications/SeminarReports/Crimeandpolicingintransitionalsocieties/fruhling.pdf>

Fyfe, J. J. (1986) 'The Split-second Syndrome and other Determinants of Police Violence', in Campbell, A. and Gibbs, J. J. (eds) *Violent Transactions*, Oxford: Blackwell, 207–23.

Gabelnick, T. and Rich, A. (2000) 'Globalized Weaponry', *Social Justice*, 27(4), 37–44.

Gallagher, M. and Komito, L. (1999) 'The Constituency Role of TDs', in Coakley, J. and Gallagher, M. (eds) *Politics in the Republic of Ireland* (3rd edn), London: Routledge.

Gallant, T. (1999) 'Brigandage, Piracy, Capitalism, and State-Formation: Transnational Crime from a Historical World-Systems Perspective', in Heyman, J. McC. (ed.) *States and Illegal Practices*, Oxford: Berg.

Gambetta, D. (1993) *The Sicilian Mafia: The Business of Private Protection*, Cambridge, MA: Harvard University Press.

GAO (General Accounting Office, U.S.) (1994) *Iraq: U.S. Military Items Exported or Transferred to Iraq in the 1980's*, Report to the Chairman, Committee on Foreign Affairs, House of Representatives, February.

Gardiner, J. A. (1970) *The Politics of Corruption: Organized Crime in an American City*, New York: Russell Sage.

Gardiner, J. A. and Lyman, T. R. (1978) *Decisions for Sale. Corruption and Reform in Land Use and Building Regulations*, New York: Praeger.

Garfield, R. (2000) 'Changes in Health and Well-being in Iraq During the 1990s: What do we Know and How do we Know it?', in Campaign Against Sanctions on Iraq (ed.) *Sanctions on Iraq: Background, Consequences, Strategies*, Cambridge: Editor.

Garland, D. (1990) *Punishment and Modern Society*, Oxford: Clarendon.

Gatrell, V. A. C. (1990) 'Crime, Authority and the Policeman State' in Thompson, F. M. L. (ed.) *The Cambridge Social History of Britain 1750–1950*, Vol. 3, Cambridge: Cambridge University Press.

Gaylord, M. S. and Levine, P. (1987) 'The Criminalization of Official Profiteering: Law-making in the People's Republic of China', *International Journal of the Sociology of Law*, 25, 117–34.

Geller, W. A. (1996) 'Understanding and Controlling Police Abuse of Force', in Geller, W. A. and Toch, H. (eds) *Police Violence: Understanding and Controlling Police Abuse of Force*, New Haven, CT: Yale University Press.

Geller, W. A. and Toch, H. (eds) (1996) *Police Violence: Understanding and Controlling Police Abuse of Force*, New Haven, CT: Yale University Press.

George, A. (ed.) (1991) *Western State Terrorism*, Cambridge: Polity Press.

George, S. (1992) *The Debt Boomerang: How Third World Debt Harms Us All*, London: Pluto Press.

Geraghty, T. (1998) *The Irish War*, London: HarperCollins.

Gerlach, C. (2000) 'German Economic Interests: Policy of Occupation and the Killing of the Jews in White Russia, 1941–1943', in Herbert, U. (ed.) *National Socialist Extermination Policies*, Oxford: Berghahn.

Getty, J. A. and Naumov, O. V. (2000) *The Road to Terror: Stalin and the Self-Destruction of the Bolsheviks, 1932–1939*, New Haven: Yale University Press.

Gewirth, A. (1978) *Reason and Morality*, Chicago: University of Chicago Press.

—— (1982) *Human Rights: Essays on Justification and Applications*, Chicago: University of Chicago Press.

Gibson, J. T. (1990) 'Factors Contributing to the Creation of a Torturer', in Suedfeld, P. (ed.) *Psychology and Torture*, New York: Hemisphere.

Gibson, J. T. and Haritos-Fatouros, M. (1986) 'The Education of a Torturer', *Torture*, Denmark: Torture Rehabilitation Centre, RCT, 16 (Nov.), 50–58.

Gibson, J. W. (2000) *The Perfect War: Technowar in Vietnam*, New York: Atlantic Monthly Press.

Giddens, A. (1985) *A Contemporary Critique of Historical Materialism. Vol. 2: The Nation-State and Violence*, Cambridge: Polity.

Gilroy, P. (1987) *There Ain't No Black in the Union Jack*, London: Hutchinson.

Giraldo, J. (1996) *Colombia: The Genocidal Democracy*, Monroe, ME: Common Courage Press.

Gjorgjevic, Z. (2003) 'Macedonia: New Arrests on Corruption Front', *Balkan Crisis Report*, 398 (16 Jan.) <www.iwpr.net>

Global Witness (2003a) *For a Few Dollars More: How al Qaeda Moved into the Diamond Trade* <www.globalwitness.org/reports/show.php/en.00041.html>

—— (2003b) *The Usual Suspects: Liberia's Weapons and Mercenaries in Côte d'Ivoire and Sierra Leone* <www.globalwitness.org/reports/show.php/en.00026.html>

Goldhagen, D. J. (1997) *Hitler's Willing Executioners: Ordinary Germans and the Holocaust*, London: Abacus.

Gong, T. (1994) *The Politics of Corruption in Contemporary China*, Westport, CT: Praeger.

Gonzalez, D. (2001) 'Guatemala – Conflict Sparked by Shrimp Farming', *New York Times*, 21 July <www.greencrossinternational.net/DigitalForum/digiforum/articles/article2001/guatemala.html>

Gordon, N. and Marton, R. (eds) (1995) *Torture: Human Rights, Medical Ethics and the Case of Israel*, London: Zed Books.

Gourevitch, P. (1999) *We Wish to Inform You That Tomorrow We Will be Killed With Our Families*, London: Picador.

Graham-Brown, S. 1999, *Sanctioning Saddam: The Politics of Intervention in Iraq*, London: I. B. Tauris.

Gramsci, A. (1971) *Selections from the Prison Notebooks*, London: Lawrence & Wishart.

Graziano, F. (1992) *Divine Violence. Spectacle, Psychosexuality and Radical Christianity in the Argentine 'Dirty War'*, Boulder, CO: Westview.

Green, L. (1999) *Fear as a Way of Life: Mayan Widows in Central Guatemala*, New York: Columbia University Press.

Green, P. (1990) *The Enemy Without: Policing and Class Consciousness in the Miners' Strike*, Milton Keynes: Open University Press.

—— (1998) *Drugs, Trafficking and Penal Policy*, Winchester: Waterside Press.

—— (2000) 'Criminal Justice and Democratisation in Turkey: the Paradox of Transition', in Green, P. and Rutherford, A., *Criminal Policy in Transition: Into the New Millenium*, Oxford: Hart Publishing.

Green, P. and Grewcock, M. (2002) 'The War Against Illegal Immigration: State Crime and the Construction of a European Identity', *Current Issues in Criminal Justice*, 13(1) (July).

Green, P. and Ward, T. (2000) 'State Crime, Human Rights and the Limits of Criminology', *Social Justice*, 27, 101–15.

Green, P., Al Hussaini, A. and Curry, C. (2002) 'Disaster Prevention and the 1999 Turkish Earthquake' (ESRC Award reference R000223401).

Grossman, D. (1995) *On Killing*, Boston: Little, Brown & Co.

Grossman, H. I. (1995) 'Rival Kleptocrats: the Mafia Versus the State', in Fiorentini, G. and Peltzman S. (eds) *The Economics of Organized Crime*, Cambridge: Cambridge University Press.

Grossman, P. (2000) 'India's Secret Armies', in Campbell, B. B. and Brenner, A. D. (eds) *Death Squads in Global Perspective*, Basingstoke: Macmillan.

Guidoni, O. V. (2000) 'How Not to Become Deviant: Denial Strategies of Mani Pullite (Clean Hands) defendants', paper presented at the American Society of Criminology conference, San Francisco.

Gurr, T. R. (1986) 'The Political origins of State Violence and Terror: A Theoretical Analysis', in Stohl, M. and Lopez, G. A. (eds) *Government Violence and Repression: An Agenda for Research*, Westport, CT: Greenwood Press.

—— (1998) 'War, Revolution and the Coercive State', in Friedrichs, D. O. (ed.), *State Crime*, Aldershot: Ashgate.

Haberer, E. (2001) 'The German Police and Genocide in Belorussia, 1941–1944' (3 parts), *Journal of Genocide Research*, 3, 13–30, 207–18, 391–403.

Hague, E. (1997) 'Rape, Power and Masculinity: the Construction of Gender and National Identities in the War in Bosnia-Herzegovina', in Lentin, R. (ed.) *Gender and Catastrophe*, London: Zed Books.

Hall, S., Critcher, C., Jefferson, T., Clarke, J. and Roberts, B. (1978) *Policing the Crisis: Mugging, the State and Law and Order*, London: Macmillan.

Halliday, F. (2002) *Two Hours That Shook the World. September 11, 2001: Causes and Consequences*, London: Saqi.

Handelman, S. (1995) *Comrade Criminal: The Theft of the Second Russian Revolution*, London: Michael Joseph.

Haney, C., Banks, C. and Zimbardo, P. (1973) 'Interpersonal Dynamics in a Simulated Prison', *International Journal of Criminology and Penology*, 1, 69–97.

Harff, B. and Gurr, T. R. (1988) 'Toward Empirical Theory of Genocides and Politicides: Identification and Measurement of Cases Since 1945', *International Studies Quarterly*, 32, 359–71.

—— (1998) 'Victims of the State: Genocides, Politicides and Group Repression from 1945 to 1995', in Friedrichs, D. O. (ed.) *State Crime*, Vol. 1, Aldershot: Ashgate.

Haritos-Fatouros, M. (1988) 'The Official Torturer: A Learning Model for Obedience to an Authority of Violence', *Torture* (Denmark: RCT) 26(1), 69–97.

Harman, C. (1996) 'Globalisation: A Critique of a New Orthodoxy', *International Socialism Journal*, 73.

—— (1999) *A People's History of the World*, London: Bookmarks.

Harriott, A. (2000) *Police and Crime Control in Jamaica: Problems of Reforming Ex-Colonial Constabularies*, Kingston: University of the West Indies Press.

Harris, P. (2003) 'Secrets of a Tyranny', *Observer*, 13 April.

Harrison, G. (1999) 'Corruption as "Boundary Politics": the State, Democratisation, and Mozambique's Unstable Liberalisation', *Third World Quarterly*, 20, 537–50.

Hawk, D. (1986) 'Tuol Sleng Extermination Center (Cambodia)', *Index on Censorship*, 15(1) (January), 25–31.

Hayden, R. M. (2002) 'Imagined Communities and Real Victims: Self-Determination and Ethnic Cleansing', in Hinton, A. L. (ed.) *Genocide: An Anthropological Reader*, Oxford: Blackwell, 231–53.

Hayner, P. (2001) *Unspeakable Truths: Confronting State Terror and Atrocity*, London: Routledge.

Hazani, M. (1991) 'The Universal Appplicability of the Theory of Neutralization: German Youth Coming to Terms with the Holocaust', *Crime, Law and Social Change*, 15, 135–49.

Heidenheimer, A. J. (2002) 'Parties, Campaign Finance and Political Corruption' in Heidenheimer, A. J. and Johnston, M. (eds) *Political Corruption: Concepts and Contexts* (3rd edn) New Brunswick: Transaction.

Held, D. (2000) (ed.) *A Globalizing World? Culture, Economics, Politics*, Routledge: London.

Held, D. and McGrew, A. (2002) *Globalization / Anti-Globalization*, Cambridge: Polity.

—— (eds) (2002) *Global Transformations Reader*, Cambridge: Polity.

Held, D., McGrew, A., Goldblatt, D. and Perraton, J., (1999) *Global Transformations*, Polity: Oxford.

Hellman, J. S., Jones, G. and Kaufman, D. (2000) *'Seize the State, Seize the Day': State Capture, Corruption and Influence in Transition*, Washington DC: World Bank Institute.

Henkin, L. (1995) *International Law: Politics and Values*, Dordrecht: Martinus Nijhoff.

Herbert, U. (2000) 'Extermination Policy: New Answers and Questions about the History of the "Holocaust" in German Historiography', in Herbert, U. (ed.) *National Socialist Extermination Policies: Contemporary German Perspectives and Controversies*, New York and Oxford: Berghahn, 1–52.

Herman, E. (1982) *The Real Terror Network*, Boston: South End Press.

—— (2002) Preface to Chandler, D., *From Kosovo to Kabul: Human Rights and International Intervention*, London: Pluto.

Hewitt, K. (1983) *Interpretations of Calamity from the Viewpoint of Human Ecology*, London. Allen & Unwin.

Hewitt, K. and Burton, I. (1971) *The Hazardousness of a Place; a Regional Ecology of Damaging Events*, Toronto: University of Toronto Press.

Hey, H. (1995) *Gross Human Rights Violations: A Search for Causes. A Study of Guatemala and Costa Rica*, The Hague: Nijhoff.

Heywood, P. (1997) 'Political Corruption: Problems and Perspectives', *Political Studies*, 45, 417–35.

Higgins, M. D. (1982) 'The Limits of Clientelism: Towards an Assessment of Irish Politics', in Clapham, C. (ed.) *Private Patronage and Public Power: Political Clientelism in the Modern State*, London: Frances Pinter, 114–41.

Hilberg, R. (1985) *The Destruction of the European Jews*, 3 vols London: Holmes & Meier.

—— (1993) *Perpetrators Victims Bystanders: The Jewish Catastrophe, 1933–1945*, London: Lime Tree.

Hill, P. (1990) *Stolen Years: Before and After Guildford*, London: Doubleday.

Hills, A. (1995) 'Militant Tendencies: Paramilitarism and UK Policing', *British Journal of Criminology*, 35(3).

—— (2000) *Policing Africa*, Boulder, CO: Lynne Rienner.

Hillyard, P. (1987) 'The Normalisation of Special Powers', in Scraton, P. (ed.) *Law, Order and the Authoritarian State*, Milton Keynes: Open University Press.

Hintjens, H. M. (1999) 'Explaining the 1994 Genocide in Rwanda', *Journal of Modern African Studies*, 37, 241–86.

Hinton, A. L. (1996) 'Agents of Death: Explaining the Cambodian Genocide in Terms of Psychosocial Dissonance', *American Anthropologist*, 98, 818–31.

—— (2002) 'A Head for an Eye: Revenge in the Cambodian Genocide', in Hinton, A. L. (ed.) *Genocide: An Anthropological Reader*, Oxford: Blackwell.

Hiro, D. (1990) *The Longest War: The Iran–Iraq Conflict*, London: Paladin.

—— (1992) *Desert Shield to Desert Storm: The Second Gulf War*, New York: Routledge.

—— (2003) *Iraq: A Report from the Inside*, London: Granta.

Hirst, P. (1997) *From Statism to Pluralism*, London: UCL Press.

—— (2001) *War and Power in the 21st Century. The State, Military Conflict and the International System*, Oxford: Polity.

Hirst, P. and Thompson, G. (1996) *Globalisation In Question: The International Economy and the Possibilities of Governance*, Oxford: Polity.

Hobbs, D. (1988) *Doing the Business: Entrepreneurship, the Working Class and Detectives in the East End of London*, Oxford: Clarendon.

—— (2001) 'The Firm: Organizational Logic and Criminal Culture on a Shifting Terrain', *British Journal of Criminology*, 31(4), 549–60.

Holdaway, S. (1983) *Inside the British Police*, Oxford: Blackwell.

—— (1996) *The Racialization of British Policing*, London: Macmillan.

—— (1999) 'Understanding the Police Investigation of the Murder of Stephen Lawrence: A "Mundane Sociological Analysis"', *Sociological Research Online*, 4(1) <www.socreson line.org.uk/socresonline/4/lawrence/holdaway.html>

Holmes, R. (1987) *Firing Line*, Harmondsworth: Penguin.

Holsti, K. (1996) *The State, War and the State of War*, Oxford: Oxford University Press.

Hooper, J. (2003) 'Germans "Sold Iraq Parts for Supergun"', *Guardian*, 15 Jan.

Hovannisian, R. (1994) 'Aetiology and Sequelae of the Armmenian Genocide', in Andreopoulos, G. (ed.) *Genocide: Conceptual and Historical Dimensions*, Philadelphia: University of Pennsylvania Press.

Huggins, M. K. (1998) *Political Policing: The United States and Latin America*, Durham, NC: Duke University Press.

—— (2000) 'Modernity and Devolution: The Making of Death Squads in Modern Brazil', in Campbell, B. B. and Brenner, A. D. (eds) *Death Squads in Global Perspective*, Basingstoke: Macmillan.

Huggins, M. K. and Haritos-Fatouros, M. (1998) 'Bureaucratic Masculinities among Brazilian Torturers and Murderers', in Bowker, L. H. (ed.) *Masculinities and Violence*, London: Sage.

Human Development Report (1999) *Globalization with a Human Face* <www.hdr.undp.org/reports/global/1999/en/>

—— (2001) *Globalization with a Human Face* <hdr.undp.org/reports/global/2001/en/>

Human Rights Foundation of Turkey (1997) *1995 Turkey: Human Rights Report*, Ankara: Author.

—— (1998) *Treatment and Rehabilitation Centers Report 1997*, Ankara: Author.

Human Rights Watch (1993) *Genocide in Iraq: the Anfal campaign against the Kurds* <www.hrw.org/reports/1993/iraqanfal>

—— (1994a) *Generation under Fire: Children and Violence in Columbia* <www.hrw.org/reports/1994/columbia/genertoc.htm>

—— (1994b) 'U.S. Cluster Bombs for Turkey?' Volume 6, Number 19, December <www.hrw.org/reports/1994/turkey2/>

—— (1995a) *Slaughter Among Neighbours: The Political Origins of Communal Violence*, New Haven: Yale University Press.

—— (1995b) *Weapons Transfers and Violations of the Laws of War in Turkey*, New York: Author.

—— (1996) *Colombia's Killer Networks*, Washington DC: Author.

—— (1997a) *Police Brutality in Urban Brazil* <www.hrw.org/reports/1997/brazil>

—— (1997b) *The Scars of Death: Children Abducted by the Lord's Resistance Army in Uganda* <www.hrw.org/reports97/uganda>

—— (1999a) 'Arms Transfers to Abusive End-users,' *World Report* <www.hrw.org/hrw/worldreport99/arms/arms4.html>

—— (1999b) *Behind the Kashmir Conflict* <www.hrw.org/reports/1999/kashmir}

—— (1999c) *Nigeria: Crackdown in the Niger Delta* <www.hrw.org/reports/199/nigeria2/Ngria993.htm>

—— (1999d) *The Price of Oil: Corporate Responsibility and Human Rights Violations in Nigeria's Oil Producing Communities* <www.hrw.org/reports/1999/nigeria/nigeria991-01.htm>

—— (1999e) *Promises Broken: Police Abuse and Arbitrary Detention of Street Children* <www.hrw.org/campaigns/crp/promises/police.html>

—— (2000a) *Burundi: Neglecting Justice in Making Peace* <www.hrw.org/reports/2000/burundi>

—— (2000b) *Civilian Deaths in the NATO Air Campaign* <www.hrw.org/reports/2000/nato>

—— (2000c) *Kosovo: Rape as a Weapon of 'Ethnic Cleansing'* <www.hrw.org/reports/2000/fry>

—— (2000d) *The Ties that Bind: Military-Paramilitary Links in Columbia* <www.hrw.org/reports/2000/colombia>

—— (2000e) *Welcome to Hell: Arbitrary Detention, Torture, and Extortion in Chechnya* <www.hrw.org/reports/2000/russia_chechnya4>

—— (2001a) *Human Rights Watch World Report 2001: events of 2000* <www.hrw.org/wr2k1>

—— (2001b) *'Israel, The Occupied West Bank, Gaza Strip, and Palestininian Authority Territories'*, in *World Report 2001* <www.hrw.org/wr2k1/midwest/israel.html>

—— (2001c) *The 'Sixth Division': Military-Paramilitary Ties and U.S. Policy in Colombia* <www.hrw.org/reports/2001/colombia>

—— (2002a) *The Bakassi Boys: The Legitimization of Murder and Torture*, Vol. 14, No. 5A <www.hrw.org/reports/2002/nigeria2/nigeria0502.pdf>

—— (2002b) *Fast Track Land Reform in Zimbabwe*. Vol. 14, No. 1A <www.hrw.org/reports/2002/zimbabwe/>

—— (2002c). *In a Dark Hour: The Use of Civilians During IDF Arrest Operations* <www.hrw.org/reports/2002/israel2>

—— (2003a) *Briefing to the 59th Session of the UN Commission on Human Rights Israel/Occupied Territories* <www.hrw.org/un/chr59/israelot.htm>

—— (2003b) *Charged With Being Children: Egyptian Police Abuse of Children in Need of Protection* <www.hrw.org/reports/2003/egypt0203/>

—— (2003c)*In the Name of Counter-Terrorism: Human Rights Abuses Worldwide* <www.hrw.org/un/chr59/counter-terrorism-bck.htm>

—— (2003d) *The Iraqi Government Assault on the Marsh Arabs* <www.hrw.org/mideast/iraq.php>

—— (2003e) *The O'Odua People's Congress: Fighting Violence with Violence*. Vol. 15, No. 4A <www.hrw.org/reports/2003/nigeria0203/>

—— (2003f). *Stolen Children: Abduction and Recruitment in Uganda*. New York: Author.

Hunt, J. (1985) 'Police Accounts of Normal Force', *Urban Life*, 13, 315–42.

Icaza, N. C. (1997) *Presentation to UN Commission on Sustainable Development*, New York, NY, 11 April <www.earthsummitwatch.org/shrimp/national_reports/ecuaceli.html>

ICG (International Crisis Group) (2001a) *Aceh: Why Military Intervention Won't Bring Lasting Peace*, Brussels: Author.

—— (2001b) *Indonesia: Natural Resources and Law Enforcement. Asia Report*, 29. Jakarta/Brussels: Author.

—— (2001c) *Myanmar: The Military Regime's View of the World. Asia Reports*, 28. Bangkok/Brussels: Author.

—— (2002a) 'Iraq Backgrounder: What Lies Beneath', *ICG Middle East Report*, 6, Brussels: Author.

—— (2002b) *Macedonia's Public Secret: How Corruption Drags the Country Down*, Skopje/Brussels: Author.

Ignatieff, M. (1994) *Blood and Belonging: Journeys into the New Nationalism*, London: Vintage.

INQUEST (1996) Submission to the UN Committee on the Elimination of Racial Discrimination, London: Author.

—— (1997) Report on the Death in Police Custody of Ibrahima Sey <www.inquest.org.uk>

—— (2000a) Report on the Death in Police Custody of Glenn Howard <www.inquest.org.uk>

—— (2000b) Report on the Shooting of Harry Stanley <www.inquest.org.uk>

International Federation of Red Cross and Red Crescent Societies (1999) *World Disasters Report 1998*, Geneva: Author.

International Panel of Eminent Personalities (2000) *Rwanda: The Preventable Genocide*, Addis Ababa: OAU.

IRCT (International Rehabilitation Council for Torture Victims) (2000), *Annual Report* <www.irct.org>

Ismail, O. (2002) 'Liberia's Child Soldiers: Paying the Price of Neglect', *Conflict, Security & Development*, 2(2), 125–33.

IWPR (Institute for War and Peace Reporting) (2002, Aug 27) 'Chain-Smokers and Official Smugglers', *Balkan Crisis Report*, 362, <www.iwpr.net>

Jackson, M. G. (2001) 'Something Must be Done? Genocidal Chaos and World Responses to Mass Murder in East Timor Between 1975 and 1999', *International Journal of Politics and Ethics*, 1(1).

Jacobs, D. and Britt, D. W. (1979) 'Inequality and the Police Use of Deadly Force: An Empirical Assessment of a Conflict Hypothesis', *Social Problems*, 26, 403–12.

Jacobs, S., Jacobson, R. and Marchbank, J. (eds) (2000) *States of Conflict: Gender, Violence and Resistance*, London: Zed Books.

Jamieson, R. (1998) 'Towards a Criminology of War in Europe', in Ruggiero, V., South, N. and Taylor, I. (eds) *The New European Criminology*, London: Routledge.

—— (1999) 'Genocide and the Social Production of Immorality', *Theoretical Criminology*, 3(2), 131–46.

Jardine, M., (1995) *East Timor: Genocide in Paradise*, Tucson, AZ: Odonian Press.

Jefferson, T. (1990) *The Case Against Paramilitary Policing*, Milton Keynes: Open University Press.

Jessop, B. (1982) *The Capitalist State*, Oxford: Martin Robertson.

Johnson, D. (1998) Paper given at the conference 'Human Rights: The Way Forward', Istanbul: Amnesty International/Istanbul Association.

Johnston, M. (2002) 'Measuring the New Corruption Rankings: Implications for Analysis and Reform', in Heidenheimer, A. J. and Johnston, M. (eds) *Political Corruption: Contexts and Consequences* (4th edn), New Brunswick: Transaction.

Jonas, S. (1991) *The Battle for Guatemala: Rebels, Death Squads and US Power*, Boulder, CO: Westview.

Jones, A. (2002) 'Gender and Genocide in Rwanda', *Journal of Genocide Research*, 4(1), 65–94.

Jordan, D. C. (1999) *Drug politics: dirty money and democracies*, Norman, OK: University of Oklahoma Press.

Jordan, R. E. III (1975) 'Chapter 2', in Trooboff, P. D. (ed.) (1975) *Law and Responsibility in Warfare: The Vietnam Experience*, Chapel Hill, NC: University of North Carolina Press.

Kaldor, M. (1999) *New and Old Wars: Organized Violence in a Global Era*, Stanford, CA: Stanford University Press.

—— (2003) *Global Civil Society: An Answer to Wars*, Cambridge: Polity.

Kamber, R. (2000) 'The Logic of the Goldhagen Debate', *Res Publica*, 6, 155–77.

Kang, D. C. (2002) *Crony Capitalism: Corruption and Development in South Korea and the Philippines*, Cambridge: Cambridge University Press.

Kannyo, E. (2000) 'State Terrorism and Death Squads in Uganda (1971–79)', in Campbell, B. B. and Brenner, A. D. (eds) *Death Squads in Global Perspective*, Basingstoke: Macmillan.

Kappeler, V. E., Sluder, R. D. and Alpert, G. P. (1998) *Forces of Deviance*, 2nd edn, Prospect Heights, IL: Waveland.

Karp, A. (1996) *Ballistic Missile Proliferation, the Politics and Technics*, Stockholm and Oxford: Stockholm International Peace Research Institute and Oxford University Press.

Katz, F. E. (1993) *Ordinary People and Extraordinary Evil: A Report on the Beguilings of Evil*, Albany, NY: SUNY Press.

Katz, J. (1988). *Seductions of Crime: Moral and Sensual Attractions in Doing Evil*, New York: Basic Books.

Katz, S. J. (1994) *The Holocaust in Historical Context, Volume I: The Holocaust and Mass Death Before the Modern Age*, Oxford: Oxford University Press.

Kaufmann, D., Kraay, A. and Zoido-Lobatón, P. (2000) 'Governance Matters: From Measurement to Action', *Finance & Development*, 37(2).

Kaufmann, D. and Wei, S.-J. (1999) 'Does "Grease Money" Speed Up the Wheels of Commerce?', National Bureau of Economic Research Working Paper 7093.

Kauzlarich, D. and Kramer, R.C. (1998) *Crimes of the American Nuclear State: At Home and Abroad*, Boston: Northeastern University Press.

Kauzlarich, D., Matthews, R. A. and Miller, W. J. (2001) 'Toward a Victimology of State Crime', *Critical Criminology*, 10, 173–94.

Keane, J. (1998) *Civil Society and the State: European Perspectives*, London: University of Westminster Press.

Keena, C. (2003) *The Ansbacher Conspiracy*, Dublin: Gill & Macmillan.

Keith, M. (1993) *Race, Riots and Policing: Lore and Disorder in a Multi-Racist Society*, London: UCL Press.

Kelly, L. (2000) 'Wars Against Women: Sexual Violence, Sexual Politics and the Militarized State', in Jacobs, S., Jacobson, R. and Marchbank, K. (eds) *States of Conflict*, London: Zed.

Kelman, H. C. and Hamilton, V. L. (1989) *Crimes of Obedience*, New Haven: Yale University Press.

Keneally, T. (1982) *Schindler's Ark*, London: Hodder & Stoughton.

Kepner, T. (2001) 'Torture 101: The Case Against the United States for Atrocities Committed by School of the Americas Alumni', *Dickinson International Law Journal*, 475 (Spring).

Kershaw, I. (1998) *Hitler 1889–1936. Hubris*, London: Allen Lane.

—— (2000a) *Hitler 1939–1945. Nemesis*, London: Allen Lane.

—— (2000b) *The Nazi Dictatorship: Problems and Perspectives of Interpretation* (4th edn), London: Arnold.

—— (2002) *Popular Opinion and Political Dissent in the Third Reich* (2nd edn), Oxford: Clarendon.

Khadduri, M. and Ghareeb, E. (1997) *War in the Gulf, 1990–91. The Iraq-Kuwaiti Conflict and Its Implications*, Oxford: Oxford University Press.

Khan, M. H. (1999) 'Patron-Client Networks and the Economic Effects of Corruption in Asia', in Robinson, M. (ed.) *Corruption and Development*, London: Frank Cass, 15–39.

Kiernan, B. (1994) 'The Cambodian Genocide – 1975–79', in Totten, S., Parsons, W. S. and Charny, I. (eds) *Genocide in the Twentieth Century: Critical Essays and Eyewitness Accounts*, New York: Garland.

—— (1996) *The Pol Pot Regime*, New Haven, CT: Yale University Press.

Kinzer, S. (1999) 'Smart Bombs, Dumb Sanctions', *New York Times*, 3 January.

Kirchheimer, O. (1969) *Politics, Law and Social Change*, New York: Columbia University Press.

Klitgaard, R. (1988) *Controlling Corruption*, Berkeley: University of California Press.

Klockars, K. (1996) 'A Theory of Excessive Force and Its Control', in Gellner, W. A. and Toch, H. (eds) *Police Violence*, New Haven, CT: Yale University Press, 1–22.

Knight, D. (2000) 'Oil Giants Once Again Accused of Abuses', InterPress Service, Washington, 27 January <www.seen.org/pages/humanrights/nigeria/nignews.shtml>

Kolko, G. (1971) 'War Crimes and the Nature of the Vietnam War', in Falk, R. A., Kolko, G. and Lifton, R. J. (eds) *Crimes of War*, New York: Vintage.

—— (1994a) *Anatomy of a War*, New York: New Press.

—— (1994b) *Century of War*, New York: New Press.

—— (2002) *Another Century of War?*, New York: New Press.

Kramer, R. C. (1992) 'The Space Shuttle Challenger Explosion', in Schlegel, K. and Weisburd, D (eds) *White-Collar Crime Reconsidered,* Boston: Northeastern University Press.

Kramer, R. C. and Michalowski, R. (1990) 'State-Corporate Crime', unpublished paper quoted in Aulette, J. R. and Michalowski, R. (1993) 'Fire in Hamlet: A Case Study of State-Corporate Crime', in Tunnell, K. D. (ed.) *Political Crime in Contemporary America: A Critical Approach*, New York: Garland.

Kraska, P. and Kappeler, V. (1997) 'Militarizing American Police: The Rise and Normalization of Paramilitary Units', *Social Problems*, 44, 1–18.

Kren, G. and Rappoport, L. (1994) *The Holocaust and the Crisis of Human Behavior* (rev. edn), New York: Holmes & Meir.

Kuper, L. (1981) *Genocide: Its Political Use in the 20th Century*, New Haven, CT: Yale University Press.

Kushnick, L. (1999) '"Over Policed and Under Protected": Stephen Lawrence, Institutional and Police Practices' *Sociological Research Online*, 4(1) <www.socresonline.org.uk/socresonline/4/1/kushnick.html>

Kwong, J. (1997) *The Political Economy of Corruption in China*, Armonk, NY and London: M. E. Sharpe.

Lambsdorff, J. G. (1999) *TI Working Paper: Corruption in Empirical Research – A Review*, Berlin: Transparency International.

Layton, L. (2003) 'US Pilots Insulated from the Reality of their Targets', *Washington Post*, 2 April.

LCHR (Lawyers Committee on Human Rights) (2002) *Beyond Collusion: The UK Security Forces and the Murder of Patrick Finucane*. Washington DC: Author.

Ledeneva, A. V. (1998) *Russia's Economy of Favours*, Cambridge: Cambridge University Press.

Lemarchand, R. (1990) 'Burundi: Ethnicity and the Genocidal State,' in van den Berghe, P. L. (ed.) *State Violence and Ethnicity*, Niwot: University Press of Colorado.

—— (1998) 'Genocide in the Great Lakes: Which Genocide? Whose Genocide', *African Studies Review*, 41, 3–16.

Levene, M. (1994) 'Is the Holocaust Simply Another Example of Genocide?', *Patterns of Prejudice*, 28(2).

—— (1998) 'Creating a Modern "Zone of Genocide" in Eastern Anatolia', *Holocaust & Genocide Studies*, 12, 393–433.

—— (1999a) 'A Moving Target, the Usual Suspects and (Maybe) a Smoking Gun: the Problem of Pinning Blame in Modern Genocide', *Patterns of Prejudice*, 33(4), 3–24.

—— (1999b) 'Connecting Threads: Rwanda, the Holocaust and Patterns of Contemporary Genocide', in Smith, R. W. (ed.) *Genocide: Essays Towards Understanding, Early Warning and Prevention*, Williamsburg, VA: College of William and Mary Press, 27–64.

Levi, M. (2002) 'The Organization of Serious Crimes', in Maguire, M., Morgan, R., Reiner, R. and Vagg, J. (eds) *The Oxford Handbook of Criminology* (3rd edn). Oxford: Oxford University Press.

Levin, M. (1982) in *Newsweek*, 7 June.

—— (1990) 'Torture and other extreme measures taken for the general good: Further reflections on a philosophical problem', in Suedfeld, P. (ed.) *Psychology and Torture*, New York: Hemisphere.

Lewis, J. (2001) 'Hell in the Pacific (Part 1)', Channel 4, 14 June.

Lewy, G. (1978) *America in Vietnam*, New York: Oxford University Press.

Lifton, R. J. (1973) *Home From the War. Vietnam Veterans: Neither Victims nor Executioners*, New York: Simon & Schuster.

—— (1986) *The Nazi Doctors: Medical Killing and the Psychology of Genocide*, London: Macmillan.

Lilly, J. R. and Marshall, P. (2001) 'Rape-Wartime', in Bryant, C. D. (ed.) *Encyclopedia of Criminology and Deviant Behavior*, Vol. 3, Philadelphia: Brunner-Routledge.

Locke, H. G. (1996) 'The Color of Law and the Issue of Color: Race and the Abuse of Police Power', in Gellner, W. A. and Toch, H. (eds) *Police Violence*, New Haven, CT: Yale University Press.

Lü, X. (2000) *Cadres and Corruption: The Organizational Involution of the Chinese Communist Party*, Stanford, CA: Stanford University Press.

Lupsha, P. (1996) 'Transnational Organized Crime Versus the Nation State', *Transnational Organized Crime*, 2(1).

Luttwak, E. N. (2001) *Strategy* (2nd edn), Cambridge, MA: Belknap Press.

Lyons, J. (1996) 'Car Crash Scandal Shakes Turkish State', Reuters, 10 November, <www.ozgurluk.org/contrind/reu1110.html>

MacAskill, E. (2000) 'Britain's Ethical Foreign Policy: Keeping the Hawk Jets in Action', *The Guardian*, 20 January.

MacNair, R. (2001) 'Psychological Reverberations for the Killers: Preliminary Historical Evidence for Perpetration-Induced Traumatic Stress', *Journal of Genocide Research*, 3(2), 257–73.

Macpherson, Sir W. (1999) *The Stephen Lawrence Inquiry*. Cm 4262-I, London: The Stationery Office.

Maguire, M. and Corbett, C. (1991) *A Study of the Police Complaints System*, London: HMSO.

Maguire, P. (2001) *Law and War: An American Story*, New York: Columbia University Press.

Mahmood, C. K. (2000) 'Trials by Fire: Dynamics of Terror in Punjab and Kashmir', in Sluka, J. A. (ed.) *Death Squad*, Philadephia: University of Pennsylvania Press.

Makiya, K. (1998) *Republic of Fear* (updated edn), Berkeley: University of Calfornia Press.

Malamud Goti, J. (1998) 'State Terror and the Memory of What', *University of Arkansas at Little Rock Law Review*, 21, 207.

Mamdani, M. (2001) *When Victims Become Killers: Colonialism, Nativism and the Genocide in Rwanda*, Oxford: James Currey

Manne, R. (2001) 'In Denial: The Stolen Generations and the Right', *Australian Quarterly Essay* 1, 1–113.

Manning, P. K. (1997) 'Structure and Control: "Deviance" in Police Organizations', *Research in the Sociology of Work*, 8, 117–38.

Manning, P. K. and Redlinger, L. L. (1977) 'Invitational Edges of Police Corruption', in Manning, P. K. and van Maanen, J. (eds) *Policing: A View from the Street*, New York: Random House.

Maran, R. (1989) *Torture: The Role of Ideology in the French-Algerian War*, New York: Praeger.

Marchak, P. (1999) *God's Assassins: State Terrorism in Argentina in the 1970s*, Montreal: McGill-Queen's University Press.

Marenin, O. (ed.) (1996) *Policing Change, Changing Police*, New York: Garland.

Marshall, S. L. A. (1947) *Men against Fire*, New York: W. Morrow.

Martinez-Alier, J. (2003) 'Ecological Conflicts and Valuation – Mangroves vs. Shrimp in the Late 1990s', *Environment and Planning: Government and Policy* 19(5), 713–28.

Marton, R. (1995) 'Introduction', in Gordon, N. and Marton, R., *Torture: Human Rights, Medical Ethics and the Case of Israel*, London: Zed Books.

Marx, K. (1968) 'Marginal Notes to the Progamme of the German Workers' Party', in Marx, K. and Engels, W. *Selected Works*, London: Lawrence & Wishart.

Matthäus, J. (1996) 'What about the "Ordinary men"? The Order Police and the Holocaust in the Occupied Soviet Union', *Holocaust and Genocide Studies*, 10, 134–50.

Matthews, R. A. and Kauzlarich, D. (2000) 'The Crash of Valujet Flight 592: A Case Study in State-Corporate Crime', *Sociological Focus*, 3, 281–98.

Matza, D. (1964) *Delinquency and Drift*, New York: Free Press.

Mayer, A. J. (2000) *The Furies: Violence and Terror in the French and Russian Revolutions*, Princeton, NJ: Princeton University Press.

McCann and Others v. *United Kingdom* (1995) Judgment of the European Court of Human Rights, reported (1996) 21 EHRR 97.

McCarthy, M. (1974) *The Seventeenth Degree*, New York: Harcourt Brace Jovanovich.

McClintock, M. (1985) *The American Connection*, Vol. II: *State Terror and Popular Resistance in Guatemala*, London: Zed.

—— (1992) *Instruments of Statecraft. U.S. Guerrilla Warfare, Counterinsurgency, and Counter-terrorism, 1940–1990*, New York: Pantheon.

McCoy, A. W. (1999) 'Requiem for a Drug Lord: State and Commodity in the Career of Khun Sa', in Heyman, J. McC. (ed.) *States and Illegal Practices*, Oxford: Berg.

McCracken, Mr Justice (1997) *Report of the Tribunal of Inquiry (Dunnes Payments)* Pn. 4199, Dublin: The Stationery Office.

McCuen, J. J. (1966) *The Art of Counter-Revolutionary War*, London: Faber & Faber.

McCulloch, J. (2001) *Blue Army: Paramilitary Policing in Australia*, Melbourne: Melbourne University Press.

—— (2003) 'Counter-Terrorism, Human Security and Globalisation: From Welfare to Warfare State', *Current Issues in Criminal Justice*, 14 (3).

McDonald, F. (2000) *The Construction of Dublin*, Kinsale: Gandon Editions.

McDowall, D. (1996) *A Modern History of the Kurds*, London: I.B. Tauris

MCEER (1999) *The Marmara, Turkey Earthquake of August 17, 1999: Reconnaissance Report* <http://mceer.buffalo.edu/publications/reports/docs/00–0001/turkeyLessons.asp>

McFadyean, M. (2003) 'A Cold Shoulder for Saddam's Victims', *Guardian Weekend*, 20 March.

Médard, J.-F. (2002) 'Corruption in the Neo-Patrimonial States of Sub-Saharan Africa', in Heidenheimer, A. J. and Johnston, M. (eds) *Political Corruption: Contexts and Consequences* (4th edn), New Brunswick: Transaction.

Meltzoff, S. J. and LiPuma, E. (1996) 'The Social and Political Economy of Coastal Zone Management: Shrimp Mariculture in Ecuador', *Coastal Zone Management Journal*, 14(4), 349–80.

Melvern, L. (2000) *A People Betrayed: The Role of the West in Rwanda's Genocide*, London: Zed.

Melville, N. (1999) *The Taming of the Blue: Regulating Police Misconduct in South Africa*, Pretoria: Human Sciences Research Council.

Mény, Y. (1996) '"*Fin de siècle*" Corruption: Change, Crisis and Shifting Values', *International Social Science Journal*, 149, 309–20.

Michalowski, R. J. and Kramer, R. C. (1987) 'The Space Between Laws: The Problem of Corporate Crime in Transnational Context', *Social Problems*, 34, 34–53.

Milgram, S. (1963), 'Behavioural study of obedience to authority', *Journal of abnormal social psychology*, 67(4) (February), 277–85.

—— (1974) *Obedience to Authority*, New York: Harper & Row.

Miller, J. (2003) *Police Corruption in England and Wales; An Assessment of Current Evidence. Home Office On-Line Report*, 12/03 <www.homeoffice.gov.uk/rds/pdfs2/rdsolr1103.pdf>

Miller, W. L. Grødeland, Å. B. and Koshechkina, T. Y. (2001) *A Culture of Corruption?: Coping With Government in Post-Communist Europe*, Budapest: Central European University Press.

Miller, W. R. (1999) *Cops and Bobbies. Police Authority in New York and London, 1830–1870* (2nd edn), Columbus: Ohio State University Press.

Ministry for Public Works and Housing (1997) 'Turkish Standards (TS) ENV 19998', 1.1–1.4.

Minow, M. (1998) *Between Vengeance and Forgiveness*, Boston: Beacon Press.

Mockaitis, T. R. (1995) *British Counterinsurgency in the Post-Imperial Era*, Manchester: Manchester University Press.

Mokhiber, R. and Weissman, R. (1999) *Corporate Predators: the Hunt for Mega-profits and the Attack on Democracy*, Monroe, ME: Common Courage Press.

Moloney, E. (1999) 'Frightened Informer Claimed RUC Forced his Silence', *Sunday Tribune*, 6 June.

Monbiot, G. (2003) 'One Rule for Them', *Guardian*, 25 March.

Moran, J. (1998) 'Corruption and NIC Development: A Case Study of South Korea', *Crime, Law and Social Change*, 29, 161–77.

Morgan, R. and Evans, M. D. (2001) *Combating Torture in Europe – The Work and Standards of the European Committee for the Prevention of Torture*, Strasbourg: Council of Europe.

Morris, M. (1996) 'By Force of Arms: Rape, War and Military Culture', *Duke Law Journal*, 45, 651–781.

Morton, James (1993) *Bent Coppers*, London: Warner.

Mott, L. R. (1996) *Epidemic of Hate: Violations of the Human Rights of Gay Men, Lesbians and Transvestites in Brazil*, Bahia and San Francisco: Grupo Gay de Bahia and International Gay and Lesbian Human Rights Commission.

Mueller, J. (2002) 'The Remnants of War: Thugs as Political Combatants', paper delivered at the Annual Meeting of the American Political Science Association <psweb.sbs.ohio-state.edu/faculty/jmueller/apsa2002.pdf>

Muir, W. K., Jr (1977) *Police: Streetcorner Politicians*, Chicago: University of Chicago Press.

Munich Re (2001) *Annual Review: Natural Catastrophes 2000*, Munich: Author.

Nadelman, E. A. (1993) *Cops Across Borders. The Internationalization of U.S. Criminal Law Enforcement*, University Park: Pennsylvania State University Press.

National Audit Office (2001) *Inappropriate Adjustments to NHS Waiting Lists*, HC452, London: The Stationery Office.

National Commission on Disappeared People (1986) *Nunca Más*, London: Faber.

National Commissioner (1994) *The Facts Speak for Themselves: The Preliminary Report on Disappearances of the National Commissioner for the Protection of Human Rights in Honduras*, New York: Human Rights Watch.

Naylor, R. T. (1995) 'From Cold War to Crime War: The Search for a New Security Threat', *Transnational Organized Crime*, 1(4) (Winter).

—— (1999) 'Mafias, Myths and Markets: On the Theory and Practice of Enterprise Crime', *Transnational Organized Crime*, Issue 3.3.

Neild, R. (2000) 'Confronting a Culture of Impunity: The Promises and Pitfalls of Civilian Review of Police in Latin America', in Goldsmith, A. J. and Lewis, C. (eds) *Civilian Oversight of Policing*, Oxford: Hart.

Nelken, D. (1996) 'Stopping the Judges', in Caciagli, M. and Kertzer, D. I. (eds) *Italian Politics: The Stalled Transition*, Boulder, CO: Westview.

Newburn, T. (1999) *Understanding and Preventing Police Corruption: Lessons from the Literature*. Police Research Series, 110, London: Home Office.

Newbury, C. and Newbury, D. (2003) 'The Genocide in Rwanda and the Holocaust in Germany: Parallels and Pitfalls', *Journal of Genocide Research*, 5(1) 135–45.

Newbury, D. (1998) 'Understanding Genocide', *African Studies Review*, 41, 79–97.

Ngor, H. (1987) *A Cambodian Odyssey*, New York: Warner.

Ní Aolain, F. (2000) *The Politics of Force: Conflict Management and State Violence in Northern Ireland*, Belfast: Blackstaff Press.

Nickson, R. A. (1996) 'Democratisation and Institutionalised Corruption in Paraguay', in Little, W. and Posada-Carbó, E. (eds) *Political Corruption in Europe and Latin America*, Basingstoke: Macmillan.

Nixon, W. (1996) 'Rainforest Shrimp', *Mother Jones* <bsd.mojones.com/mother_jones/MA96/nixon.html>

Nordlinger, E. A. (1977) *Soldiers in Politics: Military Coups and Governments*, Englewood Cliffs, NJ: Prentice-Hall.

Normand, R. and af Jochnick, C. (1994) 'The Legitimation of Violence: A Critical History of the Laws of War', *Harvard International Law Journal*, 35, 49–95.

Norton-Taylor, R. (1995) *Truth is a Difficult Concept: Inside the Scott Inquiry*, London: Fourth Estate.

Norton-Taylor, R. and Gow, D. (2000) 'The 5bn Pound Conflict of Interest', *Guardian*, 20 January.

Norton-Taylor, R., Lloyd, M. and Cook, S. (1996) *Knee Deep in Dishonour: The Scott Report and its Aftermath*, London: Gollancz.

Norton-Taylor, R. and Pallister, D. (1999) 'Millions in Secret Commissions Paid Out for Saudi Arms Deal', *Guardian,* 4 March.

Nugent, P. (1995) *Big Men, Small Boys and Politics in Ghana*, London: Pinter.

Nuila, R. W., (1998) 'Disrespectful Shrimp Farmers?', *La Tribuna*, 2 June <csf.colorado.edu/mail/elan/jun98/0075.html>

O'Brien, W. V. (1981) *The Conduct of Just and Limited War*, New York: Praeger.

Ofosu-Amaah, W., Soopramanien, R. and Uprety, K. (1999) *Combating Corruption*, Washington DC: World Bank.

O'Hanlon, M. (2000) *Technological Change and the Future of Warfare*, Washington, DC: Broookings Institution Press.

O'Kane, R. T. (1996) *Terror, Force and States*, Cheltenham: Edward Elgar.

OMCT (World Organisation Against Torture) (2001) Press Release: 'One Year After the Beginning of the Al-Aqsa Intifada, OMCT Expresses its Deep Concern Regarding the Deteriorating Human Rights Situation in Israel and the Occupied Territories', 29 December.

—— (2002) Appeals, Israel: 'Palestine children ill-treated and tortured while in detention', 31 April <www.omct.org/displaydocument.asp?DocType=Appeal&Index=1985&Languag=EN>

Osiel, M. (1997) *Mass Atrocity, Collective Memory and the Law*, New Brunswick: Transaction.

—— (1999) 'Obeying Orders: Atrocity, Military Discipline and the Law of War', *California Law Review*, 86, 939.

O'Toole, F. (1995) *Meanwhile, Back at the Ranch: The Politics of Irish Beef*, London: Vintage.

—— (2000) 'Time to Ban all Forms of Political Contribution', *Irish Times*, 25 April.

Paes-Machado, E. and Vilar Noronha, C. (2002) 'Policing the Brazilian Poor: Resistance to and Acceptance of Police Brutality in Urban Popular Classes (Salvador, Brazil)', *International Criminal Justice Review*, 12.

Palmer, A. (1998) 'Colonial and Modern Genocide: Explanations and Categories', *Ethnic and Racial Studies*, 21, 89–115.

Panorama (2000), 'Bent Cop', BBC1, tx 3 December.

—— (2002) 'A Licence to Murder' (2 Parts) BBC1, tx 19 and 26 June <http://news.bbc.co.uk/hi/english/static/audio_video/programmes/panorama/transcripts/transcript_19_06_02.txt>

Parsons, T., Toda, S., Stein, R.S., Barka, A. and Dieterich, J.H. (2000) 'Heightened Odds of Large Earthquakes near Istanbul: An Interaction-based Probability Calculation', *Science*, 288, 661–5.

Passas, N. (1990) 'Anomie and Corporate Deviance', *Contemporary Crises*, 14, 157–78.

—— (ed.) (1995) *Organized Crime*, Aldershot: Dartmouth.

Peffer, R. G. (1990) *Marxism, Morality and Social Justice*, Princeton, NJ: Princeton University Press.

Pellet, A. (2000) 'Brief Remarks on the Unilateral Use of Force', *European Journal of International Law*, 11(2), 385–92.

Perlmutter, A. (1977) *The Military and Politics in Modern Times*, New Haven, CT: Yale University Press.

Peters, E. (1996). *Torture* (expanded edn), Philadelphia: University of Pennsylvania Press.

Phillips, D. (1985) '"A Just Measure of Crime, Authority, Hunters and Blue Locusts": The "Revisionist" History of Crime and the Law in Britain, 1780–1850', in Cohen, S. and Scull, A. (eds) *Social Control and the State*, Oxford: Blackwell.

Philp, M. (1997) 'Defining Political Corruption', *Political Studies*, 45, 436–62.

Phythian, M. (1999) 'Blood on our Hands', *The Guardian*, 25 January.

—— (2000a) 'The Illicit Arms Trade: Cold War and Post-Cold War', *Crime, Law and Social Change*, 33, 1–52.

—— (2000b) *The Politics of British Arms Sales Since 1964: 'To Secure Our Rightful Share'*, Manchester: Manchester University Press.

—— (ed.) (2000c) *Under The Counter and Over The Border: Aspects of the Contemporary Trade in Illicit Arms*, Dordrecht: Kluwer.

Pilger, J. (1999) *Death of a Nation: the East Timor Conspiracy* (video) <http:// pilger. carlton.com/timor>

—— (2002) *The New Rulers of the World*, London: Verso.

Pion-Berlin, D. (1989) *The Ideology of State Terror. Economic Doctrine and Political Repression in Argentina and Peru*, London: Lynne Rienner.

—— (1997) *Through Corridors of Power. Institutions and Civil–Military Relations in Argentina*, University Park: Pennsylvania State University Press.

Police Complaints Authority (2002) *Policing Acute Behavioural Disturbance*, London: Author.

—— (2003) *Review of Shootings by Police in England and Wales 1998 to 2001*, London: Author.

Polk, K. (1994) 'Masculinity, Honour and Confrontational Homicide', in Newburn, T. (ed.) *Just Boys Doing Business? Men, Masculinities and Crime*, London: Routledge.

Porter v. *Magill* [2002] AC 357.

Poulantzas, N. (1980) *State, Power, Socialism* (tr. P. Cammiller), London: Verso.

Poulton, H. (1997) *Top Hat, Grey Wolf and Crescent: Turkish Nationalism and the Turkish Republic*, London: Hurst & Co.

Prosecutor v. *Akayesu* (1998) Case No. ICTR-96-4-T <www.ictr.org/ENGLISH/cases/Akayesu/judgement/akay001.htm>

Prosecutor v. *Kunarac, Kovac and Vukovic* (2001) IT-96-23 and IT-96-23/1 <www.un.org/icty/judgement.htm>

Prunier, G. (1995) *The Rwanda Crisis 1959-94: History of a Genocide*, London: Hurst & Co.

Public Committee Against Torture v. *State of Israel and General Security Service* (1999) HC 5100/94 <www.court.gov.il/mishpat/html/en/system/index.html>

Pujas, V. and Rhodes, M. (2002) 'Party Finance and Political Scandal: Comparing Italy, Spain and France', in Heidenheimer, A. and Johnston, M. (eds) *Political Corruption: Contexts and Consequences* (4th edn), New Brunswick: Transaction.

Punch, M. (1979) *Policing the Inner City*, London: Macmillan.

—— (1985) *Conduct Unbecoming: The Social Construction of Police Deviance and Control*, London: Tavistock.

—— (2003) 'Rotten Orchards: "Pestilence", Police Misconduct and System Failure', *Policing and Society*, 13(2), 171-96.

Putnam, R. (1993) *Making Democracy Work: Civic Traditions in Modern Italy*, Princeton, NJ: Princeton University Press.

Quinney, Richard (1979) *Criminology*, 2nd edn Boston: Little, Brown.

Rai, M. (2002) *War Plan Iraq: Ten Reasons Against War on Iraq*, London: Verso.

Rappert, B. (2002) 'Constructions of Legitimate Force: The Use of CS Spray', *British Journal of Criminology* 42, 689-708.

Rawlinson, P. (1997) 'Russian Organized Crime: A Brief History', in Williams, P. (ed.) (1997) *Russian Organized Crime: a New Threat?*, London: Frank Cass.

Rawls, J. (1971) *A Theory of Justice*, Cambridge, MA: Harvard University Press.

Red Cross, International Committee of (1999), *World Disaster Report* <www.icrc.org/Web/eng/siteeng0.nsf/html/all/5LVHGF?OpenDocument>

Rees, L. (2000) 'Horror in the East', Documentary, BBC2, 4-5 December.

Reiner, R. (2000) *The Politics of the Police* (3rd edn), Oxford: Oxford University Press.

Rejali, D. (1994) *Torture and Modernity*, Boulder, CO: Westview.

Relatives for Justice (1995) *Collusion 1990-94*, Belfast: Author.

REMHI (Recovery of Historical Memory Project) (1999) *Guatemala: Never Again!*, Maryknoll, NY: Orbis.

Reno, W. (1995) *Corruption and State Politics in Sierra Leone*, Cambridge: Cambridge University Press.

—— (1998) *Warlord Politics and African States*, London and Boulder, CO: Lynne Rienner.

Rensselaer, W. L. (1999) 'Transitional Organized Crime: An Overview', in Farer, T. (ed.) *Transitional Crime in the Americas*, London: Routledge.

Richards, P. (1996) *Fighting for the Rain Forest: War, Youth and Resources in Sierra Leone*, Oxford: James Currey.

Riley, S. (1998) 'The Political Economy of Anti-corruption Strategies in Africa', in Robinson, M. (ed.) *Corruption and Development*, London: Frank Cass.

Risse, T., Ropp, S. C. and Sikkink, K. (eds) (1999) *The Power of Human Rights: International Norms and Domestic Change*, Cambridge: Cambridge University Press.

Ritter, S. (2000) 'Redefining Iraq's obligation: the Case for Qualitative Disarmament of Iraq', *Arms Control Today*, June.

Ritter, S. and Pitt, W. R. (2002) *War on Iraq: What Team Bush Doesn't Want You to Know*, London: Profile.

Robertson, G. (2002) *Crimes Against Humanity* (2nd edn), London: Penguin.

Robins, P. (2002) 'From Small-Time Smuggling to Big-Time Racketeering: Turkey and the Middle East', in Berdal, M. and Serrano, M. (eds) *Transnational Organized Crime and International Security: Business as Usual?*, Boulder, CO and London: Lynne Rienner.

Rodriguez, E. L. (2001) 'Mangroves are Life, Long Live Mangroves', *World Rainforest Movement Bulletin*, 51, October <www.wrm.org.uy/bulletin/51/life.html>

Rolston, B. (1991) 'Containment and its Failure: The British State and the Control of Conflict in Northern Ireland', in George, A. (ed.) *Western State Terrorism*, New York: Routledge.

—— (2001) *Unfinished Business: State Killings and the Search for Truth*, Belfast: Beyond the Pale.

Roniger, L. (1994) 'The Comparative Study of Clientelism and the Changing Nature of Civil Society in the Contemporary World', in Roniger, L. and Günes-Ayata, A. (eds) *Democracy, Clientelism and Civil Society*, Boulder, CO: Lynne Rienner.

Roniger, L. and Sznajder, M. (1999) *The Legacy of Human-Rights Violations in the Southern Cone. Argentina, Chile, and Uruguay*, Oxford: Oxford University Press.

Ropp, S. C. and Sikkink, K. (1999) 'International Norms and Domestic Politics in Chile and Guatemala', in Risse, T. Ropp, S. C. and Sikkink, K. (eds) *The Power of Human Rights*, Cambridge: Cambridge University Press.

Rose-Ackerman, S. (1999) *Corruption and Government: Causes, Consequences and Reform*, Cambridge: Cambridge University Press.

Rosenbaum A. S. (ed.) (1996) *Is the Holocaust Unique? Perspectives on Comparative Genocide*, Boulder, CO: Westview.

Ruane, J. and Todd, J. (1996) *The Dynamics of Conflict in Northern Ireland*, Cambridge: Cambridge University Press.

Ruggiero, V. (1994) 'Corruption in Italy: an Attempt to identify the Victims', *Howard Journal*, 33, 319–37.

—— (1996a) 'France: Corruption as Resentment', *Journal of Law and Society*, 23, 113–31.

—— (1996b) *Organised and Corporate Crime in Europe: Offers That Can't Be Refused*, Aldershot: Dartmouth.

—— (2001) *Crime and Markets: Essays in Anti-Criminology*, Oxford: Oxford University Press.

Rummel, R. J. (1994) 'Democide in Totalitarian States: Mortocracies and Megamurders', in Charny, I. W. (ed.) *Genocide: A Critical Bibliographic Review*, Vol. 3, New Brunswick and London: Transaction.

Rutherford, A. and Hodgkinson, P. (eds) (1996) *Capital Punishment: Global Issues and Prospects*, Winchester: Waterside.

Ryan, M. (1998) *Lobbying From Below*, London: UCL Press.

Sabini, J. P. and Silver, M. (1980) 'Destroying the Innocent with a Clear Conscience: a Sociopsychology of the Holocaust', in Dimsdale, J. E. (ed.) *Survivors, Victims and Perpetrators: Essays on the Nazi Holocaust*, Washington, DC: Hemisphere.

Said, E. W. (2002) *The End of the Peace Process* (rev. edn), London: Granta.

Salzman, T. (2000) '"Rape Camps", Forced Impregnation and Ethnic Cleansing: Religious, Cultural and Ethical Responses to Rape Victims in Former Yugoslavia', in Barstow, A. L. (ed.) *War's Dirty Secret: Rape, Prostitution and Other Crimes Against Women*, Cleveland, OH: Pilgrim Press, 63–92.

Scaperdas, S. and Syropoulos, C. (1995) 'Gangs as Primitive States', in Fiorentini, G. and Peltzman, S. (eds) *The Economics of Organized Crime*, Cambridge: Cambridge University Press

Scarry, E. (1985) *The Body in Pain: the Making and Unmaking of the World*, Oxford: Oxford University Press.

Schatzberg, M. G. (1988) *The Dialectics of Oppression in Zaire*, Bloomington: Indiana University Press.

Scheff, T. J. (1994) *Bloody Revenge: Emotions, Nationalism and War*, Boulder, CO: Westview Press.

Schelling, T. (1984) 'What Is the Business of Organized Crime?', in Schelling, T. (ed.) *Choice and Consequence*, Cambridge: Harvard University Press.

Scheper Hughes, N. (1992) *Death Without Weeping*, Berkeley: University of California Press.

Schirmer, J. (1997) 'Universal and Sustainable Rights? Special Tribunals in Guatemala', in Wilson, R. A. (ed.) *Human Rights, Culture and Context*, London: Pluto.

—— (1998) *The Guatemalan Military Project*, Philadelphia: University of Pennsylvania Press.

Schrager, L. S. and Short, J. S. (1977) 'Toward a Sociology of Organizational Crime', *Social Problems*, 25.

Schwendinger, H. and Schwendinger, J. (1975) 'Defenders of Order or Guardians of Human Rights?', in Taylor, I., Walton, P. and Young, J. (eds) *Critical Criminology*, London: Routledge & Kegan Paul.

Scott, J. C. (1972) *Comparative Political Corruption*, Englewood Cliffs, NJ: Prentice-Hall.

Scott, P. D. and Marshall, J. (1991) *Cocaine Politics: Drugs, Armies, and the CIA in Central America*, Berkeley: University of California Press.

Scraton, P. (ed.) (1987) *Law, Order and the Authoritarian State*, Milton Keynes: Open University Press.

—— (1999) 'Policing with Contempt: The Degrading of Truth and the Denial of Justice in the Aftermath of the Hillsborough Disaster', *Journal of Law and Society*, 26, 273–97.

Scully, D. (1990) *Understanding Sexual Violence*, Boston: Unwin Hyman.

Seifert, R. (1994) 'War and Rape: A Preliminary Analysis', in Stiglmayer, A. (ed.) *Mass Rape: The War Against Women in Former Yugoslavia*, Lincoln: University of Nebraska Press.

Sen, A. (1981) *Poverty and Famines: An Essay on Entitlement and Deprivation*, Oxford: Clarendon.

Sereny, G. (1995) *Into That Darkness*, London: Pimlico (orig. edn 1974).

Sharlach, L. (2002) 'State Rape: Sexual Violence as Genocide', in Worcester, K. Bermanzohn, S. A. and Ungar, M. (eds) *Violence and Politics: Globalization's Paradox*, London: Routledge.

Shaw, M. (2002) *Crime and Policing in Post-Apartheid South Africa*, London: Hurst.

Shay, J. (1995) *Achilles in Vietnam: Combat Trauma and the Undoing of Character*, New York: Touchstone.

Shelley, L. I. (1999a) 'Post-Socialist Policing: Limitations on Institutional Change', in Mawby, R. I. (ed.) *Policing Across the World: Issues for the Twenty-first Century*, London: UCL Press.

—— (1999b) 'Transnational Organized Crime: the New Authoritarianism' in Friman, H. R. and Andreas, P. (eds) *The Illicit Global Economy and State Power*, Lanham: Rowman & Littlefield.

Sherman, L. W. (1978) *Scandal and Reform: Controlling Police Corruption*, Berkeley: University of California Press.

—— (1983) 'Reducing Police Gun Use: Critical Events, Administrative Policy and Organizational Change' in Punch, M. (ed.) *The Management and Control of Police Organizations*, Cambridge, MA: MIT Press.

Sierra Club (n.d.) 'Human Rights and the Environment: Nigeria', Survival Africa Background Sheet <http://www.sierraclub.org/human-rights/nigeria/background/survival.asp>

Silove, D. (1999). 'The Psychosocial Effects of Torture, Mass Human Rights Violations and Refugee Trauma: Towards an Integrated Conceptual Framework', *Journal of Nervous and Mental Disease*, 187(4), 200–207.

Silverstein, K. (2002) 'Comrades in Arms – Meet the Former Soviet Mobsters who Sell Terrorists their Guns', *Global Witness, Washington Monthly*, January/February.

Simma, B. (1999) 'NATO, the UN and the Use of Force: Legal Aspects', *European Journal of International Law*, 10(1), 1–22.

Simons, G. (2002) *Targetting Iraq: Sanctions and Bombing in US Policy*, London: Saqi.

—— (2003) *The Scourging of Iraq: Sanctions, Law and Natural Justice* (2nd edn), London: Palgrave.

Sinn Fein (1997) 'An Appalling Vista' <cain.ulster.ac.uk>.

Skolnick, J. and Fyfe, J. (1993) *Above the Law*, New York: Free Press.

Sluka, J. B. (ed.) (2000) *Death Squad: The Anthropology of State Terror*, Philadelphia: University of Pennsylvania Press.

Smart, A., (1999) 'Predatory Rule and Illegal Economic Practices,' in Heyman, J. McC. (ed.) *States and Illegal Practices*, Oxford: Berg.

Smith, D. J. and Gray, J. (1985) *Police and People in London: The PSI Report*, Aldershot: Gower.

Smith, G. (1996) 'Playing Politics with the Law', *Legal Action*, November, 8–9.

Smith, H. (2000) 'Revealed: the cruel fate of war's rape babies', *Observer*, 16 April, 1, 8–9.

Smyth, F. (1999) 'Gulf War', in Gutman, R. and Rieff, D. (eds) *Crimes of War*, New York: W.W. Norton, 162–9.

Sofsky, W. (1997) *The Order of Terror: The Concentration Camps*, Princeton, NJ: Princeton University Press.

Solis, G. D. (1998) *Son Thang: An American War Crime*, New York: Bantam.

Solnick, S. L. (1998) *Stealing the State: Control and Collapse in Soviet Institutions*, Cambridge, MA: Harvard University Press.

Sottas, E. (1998) 'Perpetrators of Torture', in Dunèr, B. (ed.) *An End to Torture: Strategies for its Eradication*, London: Zed Books.

Stanley, E. (2001) 'Evaluating the Truth and Reconciliation Commission', *Journal of Modern Afrian Studies*, 39(3), 525–45.

Staub, E. (1989) *The Roots of Evil: The Origins of Genocide and Other Group Violence*, Cambridge: Cambridge University Press.

Steinberg, J. (1992) *All or Nothing*, London: Routledge.

Steiner, H. and Alston, P. (2000) *International Human Rights in Context*, Oxford: Oxford University Press.

Steiner, J. M. (1980) 'The SS Yesterday and Today: A Sociopsychological View', in Dimsdale, J. E. (ed.) *Survivors, Victims and Perpetrators: Essays on the Nazi Holocaust*, Washington, DC: Hemisphere.

Stevens, J. (2003) *Stevens Enquiry: Overview and Recommendations* <http://cain.ulst.ac.uk/issues/violence/docs/stevens3/stevens3summary.htm>

Stiglmayer, A. (ed.) (1994) *Mass Rape: The War Against Women in Bosnia-Herzegovina*, Lincoln: University of Nebraska Press.

Stonich, S. C., (1991) 'The Promotion of Non-traditional Agricultural Exports in Honduras: Issues of Equity, Environment and Natural Resource Management', *Development and Change*, 22, 725–55.

Stonich, S. C. and Bailey, C. (2000) 'Resisting the Blue Revolution: Contending Coalitions Surrounding Industrial Shrimp Farming', *Human Organization*, Spring (Washington), 23–36.

Stover, E. and Nightingale, E. O. (1985) *The Breaking of Bodies and Minds: Torture, Psychiatric Abuse and the Health Professions*, New York: Freeman.

Straus, S. (2001) 'Contested Meanings and Conflicting Imperatives: A Conceptual Analysis of Genocide', *Journal of Genocide Research*, 3(3) 349–75.

Suárez-Orozco, M. (1992) 'A Grammar of Terror: Psychocultural Responses to State Terrorism in Dirty-War and Post Dirty-War Argentina', in Nordstrom, C. and Martin, J. (eds) *The Paths to Domination, Resistance and Terror*, Berkeley: University of California Press, 219–39.

Suedfeld, P. (ed.) (1990) *Psychology and Torture*, New York: Hemisphere.

Sumner, C. (1982) *Crime, Justice and Underdevelopment*, London: Heinemann.

Sung, H.-E. (2002) 'A Convergence Approach to the Analysis of Political Corruption: A Cross-National Study', *Crime, Law & Social Change*, 38, 137–60.

Susman, P., O'Keefe, P. and Susman, B. (1983) 'Global Disasters: a Radical Interpretation', in K. Hewitt (ed.) *Interpretations of Calamity*, London: Allen & Unwin.

Sustainable Energy and Economy Network (2001) 'IFC Ignores Nigerian Community Concerns, Approves Loan With Shell', Press Release, 21 June <www.seen.org/pages/humanrights/nigeria/ifcapprovepr.shtml>

Sutherland, E. H. (1949) *White Collar Crime*, New York: Dryden.

Sweeney, J. (2000) 'Boys Taught to Torture and Maim', *Observer*, 21 May.

Sykes, G. and Matza, D. (1957) 'Techniques of Neutralization: a Theory of Delinquency', *American Sociological Review*, 22, 664–70.

Szeftel, M. (1998) 'Misunderstanding African Politics: Corruption and the Governance Agenda', *Review of African Political Economy*, 76, 221–40.

Tanaka, Y. (1996) *Hidden Horrors: Japanese War Crimes in World War II*, Boulder, CO and London: Westview.

Tanzi, V. (1998) 'Corruption Around the World: Causes, Consequences, Scope and Cures', *IMF Staff Papers*, 45(4), 560–94.

Taussig, M. (2002) 'Culture of Terror – Space of Death: Roger Casement's Putumayo Report and the Explanation of Torture', in Hinton, A. L. (ed.) *Genocide: An Anthropological Reader*, Oxford: Blackwell.

Taylor, C. C. (1999) *Sacrifice as Terror: The Rwandan Genocide of 1994*, Oxford: Berg.

Taylor, D. (1997) *Disappearing Acts*, Durham, NC: Duke University Press.

Taylor, I. (2002) 'Liberal Markets and the Republic of Europe: Contextualizing the growth of Transnational Organized Crime', in Berdal, M. and Serrano, M. (eds) *Transnational Organized Crime and International Security: Business as Usual?*, Boulder, CO and London: Lynne Rienner.

Taylor, J. (1991) *Indonesia's Forgotten War: The Hidden History of East Timor*, London: Zed Books.

Taylor, P. (1987) *Stalker: The Search for Truth*, London: Faber.

—— (1999) *Loyalists*, London: Bloomsbury.

—— (2001) *Brits*, London: Bloomsbury.

Teicher, H. (1995) 'The Teicher Affidavit: Iraqgate' (sworn court declaration of former National Security Council official Howard Teicher, US District Court, Southern District of California 31 January).

Theobald, R. (1990) *Corruption, Development and Underdevelopment*, Basingstoke: Macmillan.

—— (1999) 'So What Really is the Problem about Corruption?', *Third World Quarterly*, 20, 491–502.

Thompson, D. F. (1995) *Ethics in Congress: From Individual to Institutional Corruption*, Washington DC: Brookings.

Thoumi, F. E. (1999) 'The Impact of the Illegal Drug Industry on Colombia', in Farer, T. (ed.) *Transnational Crime in the Americas*, London: Routledge.

Tilly, C. (1985) 'War Making and State Making as Organized Crime', in Evans, P. B., Rueschmeyer, D. and Skocpol, T. (eds) *Bringing the State Back In*, Cambridge: Cambridge University Press.

—— (1992) *Coercion, Capital and European States 990–1990* (rev. edn), Oxford: Blackwell.

Tomasevski, K. (1998) 'Foreign Policy and Torture', in Dunèr, B. (ed.) *An End to Torture: Strategies for its Eradication*, London: Zed Books.

Tomlinson, M. (1998) 'Walking Backwards into the Sunset: British Policy and the Insecurity of Northern Ireland', in Miller, D. (ed.) *Rethinking Northern Ireland*, Harlow: Longman.

Toussaint, E. (1999) *Your Money or Your Life: The Tyranny of Global Finance*, London and Dar es Salaam: Pluto Press and Mkuki na Nyota Publishers.

Transparencia Mexicana (2001) *Encuesta Nacional de Corrupción y Buen Gobierno 2001* <www.transparenciamexicana.org.mx/encuesta_nacional.html>

Transparency International (2002) *Corruption Perceptions Index 2002* <www.transparency.org/cpi/2002/cpi2002.en.html>

Traverso, E. (1999) *Understanding the Nazi Genocide*, London: Pluto.

Tripp, C. (2000) *A History of Iraq*, Cambridge: Cambridge University Press.

Trooboff, P. D. (ed.) (1975) *Law and Responsibility in Warfare: The Vietnam Experience*, Chapel Hill, NC: University of North Carolina Press.

Trucco, L. (2002) 'Summary Notes on the First Meeting of the International Inquiry Committee for the Protection of Basic Human Rights in the Face of Globalisation' <www.statewatch.org/news/2002/jul/08agenoa1.htm>

Tyler, L. and King, L. (2000) 'Arming a Traditionally Disarmed Police: An Examination of the Police Use of CS Gas in the UK', *Policing: An International Journal of Strategies and Management*, 23, 390–400.

Uildriks, N. and van Mastrigt, H. (1991) *Policing Police Violence*, Dordrecht: Kluwer.

UN (1948) *Convention on the Prevention and Punishment of the Crime of Genocide*, New York: United Nations.

—— (1999) Annex Iis/1991/35b: *Report on Humanitarian Situation in Iraq*, 30 March.

—— (2000a) *Convention Against Transnational Organized Crime* <www.odccp.org/crime_cicp_convention.html>

—— (2000b) ODCCP Uganda Project <www.unodc.org/unodc/en/corruption_projects_uganda.html>

—— (2002) 'United Nations International Strategy for Disaster Reduction. Natural Disasters and Sustainable Development: Understanding the Links Between Development, Environment and Natural Disasters': Background Paper No. 5 DESA/DSD/PC2/BP5.

UNDP Emergency Relief Division (2001) *ERD Disaster Profiles of the Least Developed Countries* <www.undp.org/erd>

Ung, L. (2001) *First They Killed My Father*, Edinburgh: Mainstream.

Ungar, M. (2002) 'State Violence and LGBT Rights', in Worcester, K., Bermanzohn, S. A. and Ungar, M. (eds) *Violence and Politics: Globalization's Paradox*. London: Routledge.

UNHCR (United Nations High Commission for Refugees) (1997) 'Refugees and others of Concern to UNHCR: 1997 statistical overview', Geneva: Author.

UNICEF (1997) 'Situation Analysis of Children and Women in Iraq', Baghdad: Unicef.

Urban, M. (1992) *Big Boys' Rules*, London: Faber.

—— (1996) *UK Eyes Alpha*, London: Faber.

US Geological Survey (2000) 'Implications for earthquake risk reduction in the United States from the Kocaeli, Turkey earthquake of August 17 1999', USGS Circular 1193.

US Senate, Committee on Banking, Housing and Urban Affairs (1994), *U.S. Chemical and Biological Warfare-Related Dual Use Exports to Iraq and Their Possible Impact on the Health Consequences of the Persian Gulf War*, 25 May.

Uvin, P. (2000) 'Rwanda: The Social Roots of Genocide', in Nafziger, W., Stewart, F. and Väyrynen, R. (eds) *War, Hunger and Displacement: The Origins of Humanitarian Emergencies*, Vol. 2, Oxford: Oxford University Press.

Uyangoda, J. (1996) 'Militarization, Violent State, Violent Society: Sri Lanka', in Rupesinghe, K. and Mumtaz, K. (eds) *Internal Conflicts in South Asia*, London: Sage.

van Creveld, M. (1991) *The Transformation of War*, New York: Free Press.

—— (2001) *Men, Women and War*, London: Cassel.

van Maanen, J. (1985) 'The Asshole', in Blumberg, A. S. and Niederhoffer, E. (eds) *The Ambivalent Force: Perspectives on the Police* (3rd edn), New York: Holt, Rinehart & Winston.

Varela, J. M. (2001) 'The Human Rights Consequences of Inequitable Trade and Development Expansion: The Abuse of Law and Community Rights in the Gulf of Fonseca, Honduras', in Barnhizer, D. (ed.) *Effective Strategies for Protecting Human Rights: Prevention and Intervention, Trade and Education*, Aldershot: Ashgate Dartmouth, 155–62.

Varela, J. M., Cissna, K. and Stonich, S. (2001) 'Artisanal Fisherfolk of the Gulf of Fonseca' <http://www.redmanglar.org/noticia5.html>

Vásquez-Léon, M. (1999) 'Neoliberalism, Environmentalism and Scientific Knowledge: Redefining Use Rights in the Gulf of California Fisheries', in Heyman, J. McC. (ed.) *States and Illegal Practices*, Oxford: Berg.

Vaughan, D. (1997) *The Challenger Launch Decision: Risky Technology, Culture, and Deviance at NASA*, Chicago: University of Chicago Press.

Verbitsky, H. (1996) *The Flight: Confessions of an Argentine Dirty Warrior*, New York: New Press.

Voronin, Y. A. (1997) 'The Emerging Criminal State: Economic and Political Aspects of Organized Crime in Russia', in Williams, P. (ed.) *Russian Organized Crime: a New Threat?*, London: Frank Cass.

Waddington, P. A. J. (1999a) 'Armed and Unarmed Policing', in Mawby, R. I. (ed.) *Policing Across the World*, London: UCL Press, 204–25.

—— (1999b) 'Police (Canteen) Sub-Culture: An Appreciation', *British Journal of Criminology*, 39, 287–309.

—— (1999c) *Policing Citizens*, London: UCL Press.

Walker, S. (1993) *Taming the System: The Control of Discretion in Criminal Justice 1950–1990*, New York: Oxford University Press.

Walter, E. V. (1969) *Terror and Resistance*, New York: Oxford University Press.

Ward, T. (forthcoming, 2004) 'State Harms', in Hillyard, P., Pantazis, C., Gordon, C. and Tombs, S. (eds) *Beyond Criminology; Taking Harm Seriously*, London: Pluto.

Ward, T. and Green, P. (2000) 'Legitimacy, Civil Society and State Crime', *Social Justice*, 27, 76–93.

Ware, J. and Seed, G. (1998) 'Assassination by Proxy', *Electronic Telegraph*, 1038, 29 March.

Warren, I. and James, S. (2000) 'The Police Use of Force: Contexts and Constraints', in Coady, T., James, S., Miller, S. and O'Keefe, M. (eds) *Violence and Police Culture*, Carlton South, Victoria: Melbourne University Press.

Warren, K. B.. (2000) 'Conclusion: Death Squads and Wider Complicities: Dilemmas for the Anthropologizing of Violence' in Sluka, J. A. (ed.) *Death Squad*, Philadephia: University of Pennsylvania Press.

Watts, M. (2001) 'Black Acts', *New Left Review*, 9, 125–39.

Weber, M. (1968) *Economy and Society*, Vol. 3, New York: Bedminster Press.

Welsh, B. (2002) 'Globalization, Weak States and the Death Toll in East Asia', in Worcester, K., Bermanzohn, S. A. and Ungar, M. (eds) *Violence and Politics: Globalization's Paradox*, London: Routledge, 67–89.

Westmarland, L. (2002) *Gender and Policing*, Cullompton: Willan.

White, M. D. (2002) 'Identifying Situational Predictors of Police Shootings Using Multivariate Analysis', *Policing: An International Journal Strategy and Management*, 25(4), 726–51.

Wolfreys, J. (2000) 'Controlling State Crime in France', in Ross, J. I. (ed.) *Varieties of State Crime and Its Control*, Monsey, NY: Criminal Justice Press.

Wolpin, M. (1986) 'State Terrorism and Repression in the Third World: Parameters and Prospects', in Stohl, M. and Lopez, G. A. (eds) *Government Violence and Repression: An Agenda for Research*, Westport, CT: Greenwood Press.

Wood, Hon. Justice J. R. T. (1997) *Royal Commission into the New South Wales Police Service. Final Report*, Vol. 1, Sydney: Government of New South Wales.

Woodiwiss, M. (2001) *Organized Crime and American Power*, Toronto: University of Toronto Press.

Woodworth, P. (2001) *Dirty War, Clean Hands*, Cork: Cork University Press.

Worden, R. E. (1996) 'The Causes of Police Brutality: Theory and Evidence on Police Use of Force', in Geller, W. A. and Toch, H. (eds) *Police Violence*, New Haven, CT: Yale University Press.

World Bank (2000) *Selected World Development Indicators*, Washington DC: Author.

—— (2000–01) *World Development Report, 2000–1*, Washington DC: Author.

World Rainforest Movement (2001a) 'Colombia: Local Communities Affected by Shrimp Companies', *World Rainforest Movement Bulletin*, 51, October <www.wrm.org.uy/bulletin/51/Colombia.html>

—— (2001b) 'Ecuador: Action to save Mangroves in Guayas', *World Rainforest Movement Bulletin*, 43, February <www.wrm.org.uy/bulletin/43/Ecuador.html>

—— (2001c) 'Ecuador: Mangroves and Shrimp Farming Companies', *World Rainforest Movement Bulletin*, 51, October <www.wrm.org.uy/bulletin/51/Ecuador.html>

—— (2001d) 'Environmental, Social and Economic Impacts of Shrimp Farming', *World Rainforest Movement Bulletin*, 51, October <www.wrm.org.uy/bulletin/51/impacts.html>

—— (2001e) 'Guatemala: Security for Shrimps: Insecurity for the Local Population', *World Rainforest Movement Bulletin*, 51, October <www.wrm.org.uy/bulletin/51/Guatemala.html>

—— (2001f) 'Guatemala: Shrimp-farm Generates Violence and Death', *World Rainforest Movement Bulletin*, 46, April <www.wrm.org.uy/bulletin/46/Guatemala.html>

—— (2001g) 'Honduras: Shrimp Farming Destruction', *World Rainforest Movement Bulletin*, 51, October <www.wrm.org.uy/bulletin/51/Honduras.html>

—— (2001h) 'Honduras: World Bank Involvement in Mangrove Destruction', *World Rainforest Movement Bulletin*,46, April <www.wrm.org.uy/bulletin/46/Honduras.html>

—— (2001i) 'Mexico: Growing Opposition to Industrial Shrimp Farming', *World Rainforest Movement Bulletin*, 51, October <www.wrm.org.uy/bulletin/51/Mexico.html>

Young, J. (1999) *The Exclusive Society*, London: Sage

—— (2002) 'Crime and Social Exclusion', in Morgan, R. Maguire, M. and Reiner, R. (eds) *The Oxford Handbook of Criminology* (3rd edn), Oxford: Oxford University Press.

Young, M. (1991) *An Inside Job: Policing and Police Culture in Britain*, Oxford: Oxford University Press.

Zulaika, J. and Douglass, W. A. (1996) *Terror and Taboo*, London: Routledge.

Zvekic, U. (1998) *Criminal Victimisation in Countries in Transition*, Rome: UNICRI.

Index